Facility Management
for
Physical Activity and Sport

Second Edition

D1258534

Thomas H. Sawyer
Lawrence W. Judge
Tonya L. Gimbert

SAGAMORE
P U B L I S H I N G

Publishers: Joseph J. Bannon and Peter L. Bannon
Sales Manager: Misti Gilles
Marketing Manager: Emily Wakefield
Director of Development and Production: Susan M. Davis
Technology Manager: Keith Hardyman
Production Coordinator: Amy S. Dagit
Graphic Designer: Marissa Willison

Library of Congress Control Number: 2015940136
 ISBN print edition: 978-1-57167-755-6
ISBN ebook: 978-1-57167-756-3

Printed in the United States.

SAGAMORE
P U B L I S H I N G

1807 N Federal Dr.
Urbana, IL 61801
www.sagamorepublishing.com

This book is dedicated to my new wife, Tonya Lynn Sawyer, who has been instrumental in the completion of this second edition, and to my five grandchildren, who give me extra reasons to continue writing and enjoying life— Alexandra, Grayson, Findley, Aubree, and Kollyn.

Contents

Part IV
Facility Design, Event Management, and
Facility Operations and Maintenance

Acknowledgments

Appreciation is expressed to the Editorial Committee members of the Council on Facilities and Equipment (CFE) for assuming initial responsibility for outlining the content and chapters for the text and selection of the chapter authors. While some served as authors/editors for specific chapters in the text, all served as reviewers for assigned chapter drafts. The Editorial Committee members include:

Dr. Thomas H. Sawyer, Chair and Editor-in-Chief, 1999-2008 (first and second editions)
    Emeritus, Indiana State University
    Chair CFE, 1995-97
Dr. Michael G. Hypes, Indiana State University,
    Chair CFE, 2001-03, 2008-09, 2009-11
Dr. Julia Ann Hypes, Indiana State University,
    Chair CFE, 2007-08
Dr. Lawrence W. Judge, Ball State University
    Chair CFE, 2011-12
Dr. Richard LaRue, University of New England
    Chair CFE, 1994-96
Dr. Tonya L. Gimbert, Indiana State University

We are indebted to a number of authoritative sources for permission to reproduce material used in this text:

- Special recognition is due those professionals who served as chapter authors or editors, including Kimberly L. Bodey, Tonya L. Gimbert, Julia Ann Hypes, Michael G. Hypes, Darrell L. Johnson, Thomas J. Rosandich, Gary Rushing, and Bryan Rosma. These individuals worked diligently to present chapter material in an informative and useful manner.
- Without the great assistance from a number of very special and important folks, this book would not have been possible. Thanks to Sagamore Publishing for invaluable advice, counsel, patience, and encouragement during the final edit of the manuscript.

About the Editors/Authors

Editors

Thomas H. Sawyer
Editor-in-Chief
Contributing Author

Thomas H. Sawyer, EdD, NAS Fellow, professor of physical education, and professor of recreation and sport management, is a 44-year veteran of higher education. He began as an instructor of health and physical education, has been a director of recreational sports, department head, department chair, associate athletic director, director of articulation and transfer, director of a college prison education program, executive director of regional education centers, and an interim dean of continuing education and is ending his career, by choice, as a full professor teaching sport management theory to undergraduate and graduate students.

He has written over 175 peer-reviewed articles for notable professional journals, made over 250 state, regional, national, and international presentations, and written 10 professional books and 20 chapters in other publications.

Further, he has served as a state AHPERD president (Indiana), district vice president (Midwest), association president (AAALF), chaired numerous district and national committees, editor of the Indiana *AHPERD Journal* and newsletter, chaired the *JOPERD* editorial and policy boards, is a member of the AAHPERD Board of Governors, and the editor-in-chief for *ICHPER·SD Journal of Research* and vice president for ICHPER·SD North American Region (which includes the United States and Canada). He is presently a member of the Indiana AHPERD, AAHPERD, Midwest AHPERD, NASPE, AAPAR, NASSM, NRPA, and SRLA.

Dr. Sawyer has received numerous awards for his leadership and service to the American Red Cross, YMCA, a regional alcohol and drug consortium, Council on Facilities and Equipment, Indiana AHPERD, American Association for Active Lifestyles and Fitness, American Alliance for Health, Physical Education, Recreation and Dance, and Indiana State University. Further, he has received the Caleb Mills Outstanding Teaching Award, the Outstanding Service Award from Indiana State University, and the Howard Richardson Outstanding Teacher/Scholar Award from the School of Health and Human Performance at Indiana State University. Finally, NASPE recognized him as the Outstanding Sport Management Professional for 2008 as did the Indiana AHPERD.

Lawrence W. Judge
Associate Editor

Associate professor Lawrence Judge is in his sixth year at Ball State University. He serves as the coordinator of the Athletic Coaching Education program and has also served as the undergraduate advisor for the Sport Administration program. As both an associate head coach and head coach, Larry has a total of 18 years work experience coaching Division I track and field/cross country. In addition to field experience (training eight Olympians, 10 NCAA Champions and coaching over 100 All-Americans), Judge has firsthand knowledge of NCAA rules and current issues in amateur, intercollegiate, and professional athletics.

Widely recognized as the premiere track and field throws coach in the USA, Larry Judge completed his collegiate coaching career with the University of Florida in 2005. In 2005, Judge capped off a stellar career at the University of Florida with four former Gator athletes competing in the world championships in Helsinki. Judge served as an assistant coach for Trinidad and Tobago. Judge has guided eight athletes in the last three Olympic Games.

As a scholar, Dr. Judge has co-authored 41 peer-reviewed publications, including 21 first-author publications in prestigious journals such the *International Review for the Sociology of Sport, Journal of Strength and Conditioning Research*, and the *International Journal of Sports Science and Coaching*. Dr. Judge has also been active in the area of textbook publishing, contributing 12 textbook chapters. In 2008, Dr. Judge coauthored the text book, *Sport Governance and Policy Development: An Ethical Approach to Managing Sport in the 21st Century* and authored the books *The Complete Track and Field Coaches' Guide to Conditioning for the Throwing Events* and *The Shot Put Handbook*. He is currently a contributing author for a resource book in the design and planning of Sport and Recreational Facilities (twelfth edition). He has also given 84 peer-reviewed academic presentations at a wide variety of state, national, and international conferences, while also acquiring $118,425 in grant funding that have primarily focused on cultivating healthy lifestyle habits for children through physical activity and the study of fair play as a social construct in sport. Dr. Judge currently holds the following positions: (1) Vice President of the Indiana Association for Health, Physical Education, Recreation, and Dance Sport Council; (2) Past President for the National Council for the Accreditation of Coaching Education; (3) Chair for the American Alliance for Health, Physical Education, Recreation, and Dance Council on Facilities and Equipment; and (4) National Chairman of the United States Track and Field Coaches Education for the Throwing Events. Dr. Judge serves as a level II and level III instructor in the IAAF coach's education program and also lectures in the Professional Figure Skaters Association nationwide coach's education program. Dr. Judge serves on the editorial board of *The Physical Educator* and *Techniques Magazine*.

Tonya L. Gimbert
Associate Editor
Contributing Author

Tonya Gimbert received her bachelor of science degree (2003) in elementary education from Saint Mary-of-the-Woods College, a master of science degree (2005) in recreation and sport management (2009) with a concentration in sport management, and a PhD in curriculum and instruction with an emphasis in sport management teaching (2013) from Indiana State University. She currently works in the Department of Intercollegiate Athletics as the NCAA Compliance Coordinator. Dr. Gimbert has served as an adjunct faculty member in the Department of Kinesiology, Recreation, and Sport, as well as Athletic Academics. Dr. Gimbert has given numerous presentations at professional conferences and authored numerous articles found in professional journals concentrating on sport management and numerous textbook chapters.

Authors

Kimberly J. Bodey

Kimberly J. Bodey is an associate professor and sport management concentration coordinator in the Department of Recreation and Sport Management at Indiana State University. She earned an EdD in recreation management from the University of Arkansas. She holds a BS in kinesiology from the University of Illinois. While on faculty at Indiana State, Dr. Bodey has taught graduate and undergraduate courses in administrative theory and management practice, organizational leadership and ethics, governance and policy development, research and evaluation, and sport law. Dr. Bodey has given more than 20 presentations in the United States and abroad.

Julia Ann Hypes

Dr. Hypes is an associate professor in the Department of Health, Physical Education and Sport Sciences at Morehead State University in Morehead, Kentucky, where she teaches undergraduate and graduate courses in sport management. Dr. Hypes has been a sports information director, administrative assistant for athletic facilities, game operations, and budgeting. She serves as the coordinator for the undergraduate internships and as the Department of HPESS technology coordinator. She has presented at the state, regional, national and international levels. She earned a bachelor of science in mass communications from Middle Tennessee State University, a master of sport science from the U.S. Sports Academy, and a PhD in Curriculum and Instruction from Indiana State University. Currently, Dr. Hypes is serving as president-elect of the American Association for Physical Activity and Recreation (AAPAR).

Michael G. Hypes

Dr. Hypes is an associate professor of sport management at Morehead State University in Morehead, Kentucky, where he teaches graduate and undergraduate courses. He has served as chair for the Council for Facilities and Equipment, vice-president for the Indiana Center for Sport Education, Inc., assistant editor of the Indiana *AHPERD Journal,* assistant editor of the *Journal of Legal Aspects of Sport*, Director of Higher Education for Indiana AHPERD, chair of the *JOPERD* editorial board, Management Division Representative for AAPAR, cabinet member for AAPAR, and various other leadership positions in professional organizations. He has completed numerous presentations and articles for publication at the state, national, and international levels. Dr. Hypes received his bachelor of science and master of arts degrees in physical education from Appalachian State University and a doctor of arts from Middle Tennessee State University.

Darrell L. Johnson

He earned his EdD in physical education at The University of Alabama. Dr. Johnson completed his BS at Grace College and his MA at Kent State University. He has taught at Grace College for 28 years and currently serves as chair of the Sport Management Department. He previously taught, coached, and was athletic director on the high school and collegiate level. He also has experience in event management and merchandizing in the golf industry.

Dr. Johnson has published in the *Sport Behavior Journal, Journal of Sport Administration,* and the *Journal of Physical Education, Recreation, and Dance.* He has served on state and national committees. He was president of the Indiana Association for Health, Physical Education, Recreation, and Dance in 1994.

Dr. Johnson has been very active in volunteering at major sporting events having worked at Super Bowl XLVI, NCAA Men's and Women's Final Fours, The Memorial Golf Tourney and The President's Cup.

Gary Rushing

Dr. Gary Rushing is chair of the Human Performance Department at Minnesota State University, Mankato. He teaches both undergraduate and graduate courses in sport law and has taught Facility Design/Management, Principles of Sport Management, and Leadership/Management of Sport courses. He is a member of the American Alliance for Health, Physical Education, Recreation and Dance (AAHPERD), Minnesota Alliance of Health Physical Education Recreation and Dance MAHPERD, and the Sport and Recreation Law Association (SRLA) since 1995. Dr. Rushing has taught at the high school (eight years) and college levels (28 years). He has also served as an athletic director (H.S.) and coach at the high school (eight years) and college (13 years) levels.

Bryan Romsa

Dr. Bryan Romsa is an assistant professor of sport management at Minnesota State University, Mankato. A native of Wyoming, Dr. Romsa received his EdD and MS from Minnesota State University, Mankato. Prior to Minnesota State and Mankato, he received his BA from Concordia College, Moorhead. Dr. Romsa teaches courses in Sport Facility Management, Sport Ethics, Sport Management, and Sport Marketing. His research interests include leadership in sport management, service learning in sport management education, and facility and event risk management. Dr. Romsa resides in North Mankato, MN, with his wife and their two children.

Thomas J. Rosandich

Dr. T. J. Rosandich serves as vice president and chief operating officer for the United States Sports Academy, where he earned both his master's and doctoral degrees. In addition to having oversight responsibility for the Academy's administrative and financial functions, he also chairs the Institutional Effectiveness Committee and is responsible for international programs. Dr. Rosandich rejoined the staff at the Academy's main campus in 1994 after spending nine years in Saudi Arabia, where he was general manager of Saudi American Sports. In addition to running the company, based in Riyadh, Dr. Rosandich also served in other roles during his stay in the Middle East, such as the development of sports programs in the Arabian Gulf region and as the advisor to the President of the General Organization for Youth and Sports in Bahrain. A published author, Dr. Rosandich has served as a member of the Academy faculty, teaching in both the graduate degree and international certification programs.

Preface

In an era of unprecedented expansion, sport has become even more significant and pervasive in American society. As sport has continued to grow, so have the facilities that support sporting events. As the number of facilities has grown, so has the number of people who management the various sport facilities on college and university campuses as well as large public assembly facilities found in every large metropolitan area worldwide.

This growing global industry places unique demands on its personnel and increasingly requires specialized education. The job requirements in the sport industry involve many skills applicable to the sport setting and specific to the increasingly complex and multifaceted areas it represents. This text provides the student and practitioner with enough information on a variety of subjects to know where to proceed without assistance and when it would be wise to seek additional professional assistance.

Since the early 1970s, a new breed of specialists has emerged—the public assembly facility manager. Public assembly facility managers receive similar training as sport managers. These two professionals generally complete degrees in sport management with minors in business administration. Sport management has been considered a legitimate field of study for the past 20 years in higher education. Sport management is an umbrella term that includes such areas as fitness, physical activity, recreation, and sport.

A major concern for sport management, its students and practitioners, is the continued need for a variety of textbooks and related resources in this expanding field of study. Some texts are generalized and others more focused. Facility Management for Physical Activity and Sport is a comprehensive compilation of concepts and practical subject matter published for the sport management student and future facility manager as well as practitioners.

Audience

An increasing number of students with a wide variety of backgrounds are selecting sport management as a course of study both at the undergraduate and graduate levels. The intention of this book is to cater to this changing and rapidly growing audience nationwide. Further, this book has been written for the upper-division or graduate-level course. Students using this text will have a fundamental understanding of financial accounting, managerial accounting, finance, marketing, management, and management information systems. This book will also be a valuable resource for practitioners.

Features

Content

The text has 22 chapters and numerous appendices (the appendices can be found at www.sagamorepub.com). The chapters are designed to focus on the management of health, fitness, physical activity, recreation, and sport facilities. These facilities could be in settings such as interscholastic, intercollegiate, professional sport, public recreation, health and fitness, and more.

Instructor's Guide

There will be an instructor's guide including chapter learning objectives, chapter summaries, self-testing exercises, additional references, the appendices and suggested readings.

PowerPoint™ Slides

There will PowerPoint™ slides for each chapter. They will have a neutral background and no graphics so that the instructor can add a specific background and graphics as he/she sees appropriate.

Introduction

The second edition of *Facility Management for Physical Activity and Sport* is a combination of the best content and chapters from four other texts authored/coauthored/edited by Dr. Sawyer that relate to the facility management field. The chapters have been revised and expanded to make this new edition of *Facility Management for Physical Activity and Sport* the best publication available. This process ensures added value added for both students and instructors. Combining the best chapters from each book eliminates the need for multiple books to be purchased by students and provides all the best materials in one publication. The authors recognize the need for content to change as the digital revolution continues. This practice will become more prevalent in the future and will help to keep textbooks current and reasonably priced for students.

Dr. Sawyer and his coauthors have selected the best chapters from his works and applied them to specific areas such as facility planning, facility management, financial management, and governance. The chapters were then revised and expanded upon before being used to develop the second edition of *Facility Management for Physical Activity and Sport*.

In 2005, the Council on Facility and Equipment (CFE) and Thomas H. Sawyer, editor-in-chief, decided to expand the 11th edition of *Facility Planning and Design for Health, Physical Activity, Recreation, and Sport* to include 10 chapters related to management (Chapter 1, Facility and Event Leadership and Management; Chapter 2, Human Resource Management; Chapter 3, The Planning Process; Chapter 5, Financial Management Process; Chapter 8, Retail Operations: Concessions, Merchandising, and Ticket Operations; Chapter 9, Promotions and Customer Relations; Chapter 10, Public Relations; Chapter 11, Facility and Event Risk Management; and Chapter 13, Volunteers: The Soldiers in Fund-Raising and Event Management). These new chapters that were added came from a book published in 1998 by Sawyer and Smith entitled *Management of Clubs, Recreation, and Sport*. Those 10 chapters were revised and expanded and then added to four additional chapters (Policy Development; Marketing, Advertising, Promotions, Personal Selling, and Sponsorship; Programming and Scheduling; and Special Event Management). However, based on user concerns due to the size of the book, the 12th edition of the facility planning book eliminated these chapters and inserted them into a new book, *Facility Management for Physical Activity and Sport*, edited by Sawyer, which was published in 2009.

All the chapters used in both of the manuscripts outlined above, except Policy Development and Special Event Management were the content of a book published in 1998 entitled *Management of Clubs, Recreation, and Sport* by Sawyer and Smith. Once that book went out of print, its chapters were revised and expanded then inserted into the 11th edition of the facility planning text as well as the first edition of *Facility Management for Physical Activity and Sport*.

In 2010 it was decided to rework the 1998 manuscript entitled *Management of Clubs, Recreation, and Sport* by Sawyer and Judge. The original book included 15 chapters that have been used in the books outlined above that were revised and expanded. The new text, *Management of Fitness, Physical Activity, Recreation, and Sport*, by Sawyer and Judge published in 2012, coupled those 15 chapters after revising and expanding them, then added them to an additional 18 chapters for a total of 33 chapters.

In 2013, it was decided to use many of the chapters (18) in the second edition of the *Facility Management for Physical Activity and Sport*, specifically Chapter 2, Management Principles; Chapter 3, Organizational Principles and Leadership; Chapter 5, Planning for Success; Chapter 6 Programming for Success; Chapter 8, Managing Human Resources; Chapter 20, Financial Principles; Chapter 21 Purchasing and Inventory Control Principles; Chapter 22, Revenue Generation; Chapter 23, Marketing Principles; Chapter 24, Retail Principles; Chapter 25, Sales, Sponsorships, and Licensing Principles; Chapter 26, Fund-Raising Principles; Chapter 27, Customer Retention Principles; Chapter 28, Facility Design Principles; Chapter 29, Event Planning Principles; Chapter 30, Volunteers the key to successful event management; Chapter 31, Communication Principles; Chapter 32, Media Relation Principles; and Chapter 33, Public Relations.

Further, there are five chapters used from *Financing the Sport Enterprise* by Sawyer, Hypes, and Hypes (2004) that have been revised and expanded: Chapter 7, Purchasing and Inventory Management; Chapter 9, Understanding the Revenue Streams; Chapter 15, Retail and Sales Operations; Chapter 16, Customer Retention: A Key to Financial Stability; Chapter 23, Volunteers: The Soldiers in Fund-Raising.

Finally, this second edition of the *Facility Management for Physical Activity and Sport* is edited and coauthored by Thomas H. Sawyer, Lawrence W. Judge, and Tonya L. Gimbert.

Note: All the books listed above are published by Sagamore Publishing, LLC.

PART I
Fundamentals of Management

CHAPTER 1

Management Principles

Thomas H. Sawyer
Professor Emeritus, Indiana State University

Introduction

Sport, in its broadest sense, refers to all recreational and competitive sports, physical activity, fitness, and dance. Sport has become a dominant influence in many societies. No single aspect of any culture receives more media attention than sport. Sport is big business and continues to grow at a phenomenal rate globally. It provides the visibility for its star participants to enter the political arena or become broadcasters or movie stars or entrepreneurs.

Further, recreational participation in sport continues to grow in popularity each year driven by increased time for leisure activities and discretionary income to spend on exercise and fitness pursuits. This increase in growth has required development of new undergraduate programs to prepare a new type of sport and fitness managers. This new sport/fitness manager needs to understand the management process in order for the demands of the fitness and sport businesses to be successful.

Finally, management is critical in keeping any organization operating smoothly and efficiently. A facility that is well maintained and managed is one of the best public and consumer relations tools in an organization's arsenal. An organization's facility manager must become involved in many tasks, including, but not limited to, leadership, facility and event management, crowd control, security, emergency operations, facility maintenance, operational policies and procedures, and human resources to name a few.

What is Management?

Management is an organizational function, like sales, marketing, or finance. It does not necessarily mean managing people. We can manage ourselves or the material assigned to us at work. If you managed a project very well on your own, it would mean that you did the job in a well-organized, efficient manner, making good use of all resources at your disposal.

Further, management in all business and organizational activities is also the act of getting people together to accomplish desired goals and objectives efficiently and effectively. Management comprises planning, organizing, staffing, leading or directing, and controlling an organization (a group of one or more people or entities) or effort for the purpose of accomplishing a goal. Resourcing encompasses the deployment and manipulation of human, financial, technological, and natural resources.

Finally, management in sport management is an investment. The sport manager has resources to invest—money, time, talent, and human resources. The function of sport management is to get the best return by getting things done efficiently. The sport manager's management style is a personal and situational matter and evolves over time. Skilled sport managers know how to flex their style, coach, and motivate a diverse body of employees.

Management—Why Is It Needed by Organizations?

There are three key reasons why organizations need management—to establish objectives, to maintain balance among stakeholders, and to achieve efficiency and effectiveness. The initial task for management is to develop objectives for the organization. The objectives become the organizational energy currency. Once the objectives are established, the organization's human, financial, and physical resources attempt to accomplish them. Generally, top management establishes overall objectives for such areas as profitability, market share, growth, or new product development. Lower level objectives are commonly determined by all of the employees.

In working to achieve objectives, managers need to maintain balance among the conflicting objectives of the stakeholders. The stakeholders are all those having a stake in the organization's success, including employees, owners, customers, government authorities, and creditors. Management holds in trust and must balance the interest of many different groups including community leaders, creditors, customers, employees, government needs and demands, public (consumer groups, environmentalists, and civil rights advocates) stockholders, suppliers, trade associations, and union leaders.

Further, management performs the function of stewardship on behalf of the owners who are seeking a satisfactory return on investment (ROI). The ROI may be profits (as in a business) or service (as in local, state, or federal governments). Finally, management must also consider the interests of its employees who seek good pay, safe and comfortable working conditions, fair and equitable treatment, the greatest possible job security, and more time off.

The last reason for management is achieving effectiveness and efficiency. The concept of effectiveness relates to the ability of management to set and achieve proper objectives. The other side of the management performance coin is efficiency. Efficiency is management's ability to get things done, achieving higher outputs relative to inputs. In the case of managing a sport retail store, this would include such resources as employees, food, and time. The store manager who achieves the same sales volume with another store, while having only 15% of the payroll and inventory costs would be considered more efficient in using resources.

Definitions of Management

There are two common definitions of management:

- Management is the practice of organization and coordination of the activities of an enterprise in accordance with certain policies and the achievement of clearly defined objectives. Management is often included as a factor of production along with machines, materials, and money According to management guru Peter Drucker (1909–2005), the basic task of a management is twofold: marketing and innovation (Drucker, 2006).

- Directors and managers have the power and responsibility to make decisions to manage an enterprise. As a discipline, management comprises the interlocking functions of formulating corporate policy and organizing, planning, staffing, controlling, and directing (leading) the firm's resources to achieve the policy's objectives. The size of management can range from one person in a small firm to hundreds or thousands of managers in multinational companies. In large firms, the board of directors formulates the policy that is implemented by the chief executive officer (*Business Dictionary*, 2013).

Theoretical Scope

At the beginning, sport managers think management is functionally the actions of

- measuring a quantity on a regular basis,
- adjusting an initial plan, and
- taking steps to reach an intended goal.

This applies even in situations where planning does not take place. From this perspective, Kreitner and Cassidy (2012) and Daft (2013) indicate that Frenchman Henri Fayol (1841–1925) considered management to consist of six functions: forecasting, planning, organizing, commanding, coordinating, and controlling. They also suggested that another way of thinking would be like Mary Parker Follett (1868–1933), who wrote on the topic in the early 20th century, defined management as "the art of getting things done through people." She described management as a philosophy.

This definition is considered useful but far too narrow. The phrase "management is what managers do" occurs widely, suggesting the difficulty of defining management, the shifting nature of definitions, and the connection of managerial practices with the existence of a managerial class (Daft, 2013).

Another train of thought regards management as equivalent to "business administration." However, more realistically every organization, whether it is for-profit or nonprofit, must manage its financial resources, people, processes, technology, and so forth, in order to maximize its effectiveness.

This becomes more confusing when people refer to university departments that teach management as "business schools." Some institutions (such as the Indiana University's Kelly School of Business) use that name, while others (such as Purdue's Krannert School of Management) employ the more inclusive term "management." So what is it—business or management?

Kreitner and Cassidy (2012) suggest in for-profit work, management has as its primary function the satisfaction of a range of stakeholders. This typically involves

- making a profit (for the shareholders),
- creating valued products at a reasonable cost (for customers), and
- providing rewarding employment opportunities (for employees).

In nonprofit management, keeping the faith of donors is of utmost importance. In most models of management, shareholders vote for the board of directors, and the board then hires senior management; however, this is not always true in the nonprofit world (e.g., American Red Cross). A number of organizations have experimented with other methods (e.g., employee-voting or board and employee-voting models) of selecting and/or reviewing managers.

Contemporary Theories of Management

The following are contemporary theories of management:

- Psychological aspects of management
- Sociological aspects of management
- Applied management

- Statistical aspects of management
- Operations research (management science) a combination of microeconomic theory and statistical theories
- Theory of constraints
- Management-by-objectives
- Six Sigma—information-technology-driven theory,
- Group management theories

Daft (2013) suggests that business management has come to consist of separate branches, such as
- financial,
- human resource,
- information technology,
- marketing,
- nonprofit,
- public administration,
- public management,
- operations management or production,
- social entrepreneurship, and
- strategic.

The Management Process

At one time in America, Europe, and Japan, the world of work was largely composed of individuals working alone, rather than groups of people working together. Farmers produced food for themselves and their families and, if they were lucky, had a surplus to sell. Potters, silversmiths, and other craft workers produced their goods independently. Families who needed homes built them alone or with help from their neighbors. Even government was individualized, consisting of a lord or knight or governor who reigned over a relatively small territory.

This individualized work pattern no longer exists in developed countries in the 21st century. Goods such as appliances, airplanes, automobiles, train engines, television sets, and many other usable items could not be replaced efficiently by a single individual. Seldom does one person possess the necessary capital, knowledge, abilities, or resources to "go it alone."

Functions of Management

Management operates through various functions, often classified as planning, organizing, staffing, directing/leading, and controlling/monitoring (see Figure 1.1) (Drucker, 1934; Follet, 1918; & Fayolo & Irwin, 1984).

Planning

Planning, according to Drucker (1973) and Gomez-Mejia & Balkin (2012), is the ongoing process of developing the business's mission and objectives and determining how they will be accomplished. It includes the broadest view of the organization (e.g., its mission) and the narrowest (e.g., a tactic for accomplishing a specific goal).

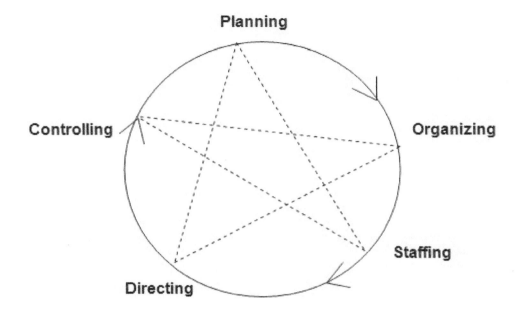

Figure 1.1. Management Tasks. Source: Drucker, Peter F. (1973). Management: Tasks, responsibilities, practices. New York: Harper & Row.

It is concerned with the impact of decisions. Planning is the fundamental function of management from which the other four (controlling, directing, organizing, and staffing) stem. The need for planning is often apparent after the fact. However, planning is easy to postpone in the short run (Daft, 2013).

The key planning terms are vision, mission, goals, objectives, and action strategies. They are defined below.

Vision. Vision is a directional and motivational guidance for the entire organization. Top managers normally provide a vision for the business (*Business Dictionary*, 2013).

Mission. Mission is the organization's reason for existing. It is concerned with scope of the business and reflects the culture and values of top management (*Business Dictionary*, 2013).

Goals. Goals are specific statements of anticipated results that further define the organization's objectives. They are expected to be **SMART: S**pecific, **M**easurable, **A**ttainable, **R**ewarding, and **T**imed ((Smart, 2013).

Objectives. Objectives refine the mission within the organization including market standing, innovation, productivity, physical and financial resources, profitability, and management and worker performance and efficiency. They are expected to be general, observable, challenging, and untimed (Kreitner & Cassidy, 2012).

Action strategies. Development of action strategies is a fifth level of planning. Strategies describe who, what, when, where, and how activities will take place to accomplish a goal (Daft, 2013).

Organizing

Organizing, according to Daft (2013), is establishing the internal organizational structure of the organization. The focus is on division, coordination, and control of tasks and the flow of information within the organization. This function allows managers to distribute authority to job holders. Each organization has a unique organizational structure. By action and/or inaction, the sport manager structures the business. Ideally, in developing an organizational structure and distributing authority, the sport manager's decisions reflect the vision, mission, goals, objectives, and action strategies that grew out of the planning function. Specifically, the sport manager will decide and define the following:

- Coordination
- Delegation of authority
- Departmentalization
- Division of labor
- Span of control

Staffing

When a sport manager fills and keeps filling with qualified people all positions in the business, it is called staffing. The following are the functions of staffing—recruiting, hiring, training, evaluating, and compensating.

Directing/Leading

Northouse (2012) suggests directing/leading is influencing people's behavior through motivation, communication, group dynamics, leadership, and discipline. Further, he states the purpose of directing is to channel the behavior of all personnel to accomplish the organization's mission and objectives while simultaneously helping them accomplish their own career objectives.

The directing function gives the manager an active rather than a passive role in employee performance, conduct, and accomplishments and a helping role assisting people in the organization accomplish their individual career goals. Daft (2013) and Northouse (2012) note that organizations do not succeed while their people are failing and assisting people in the organization with career planning and professional development is an integral part of the directing function.

Controlling

Controlling is a four-step process of establishing performance standards based on the organization's objectives, measuring and reporting actual performance, comparing the two, and taking corrective or preventive action as necessary.

Performance standards come from the planning function. Standards should be established for every key task. The sport manager needs to understand that lowering standards to what has been attained is not a solution to performance problems. However, a sport manager does need to lower standards when they are found to be unattainable due to resource limitations and factors external to the business. Kreitner and Cassidy (2012) indicate that corrective action is necessary when performance is below standards. If performance is anticipated to be below standards then preventive action must be taken to ensure that the problem does not recur. If performance is greater than or equal to standards, it is useful to reinforce behaviors that led to the acceptable performance.

Designing Effective Control Systems

Daft (2013) suggests that effective control systems have the following characteristics:
- "Acceptability to those who will enforce decisions
- Accuracy
- Balance between objectivity and subjectivity
- Control at all levels in the business
- Coordinated with planning, organizing, and leading

- Cost effectiveness
- Flexibility
- Timeliness
- Understandability (p. 213)"

Management vs. Leadership
(See Chapter 3 for Greater Detail regarding Leadership)

Gomez-Mejia and Balkin (2012) indicate that people are always needed who can efficiently coordinate the human and material resources required to accomplish desired goals. These people are often called managers, or are they leaders? Management can be defined as the process of achieving desired results through efficient utilization of human and material resources. Leadership can be defined as the art of influencing individual or group activities toward achievement of an organization's goals and objectives. Can a person be both a manager and a leader?

Another burning question is how management differs from leadership. For some, there is no difference. But increasing complexity drives ever greater specialization, so we really need to recognize that leadership and management are two different functions. This is the same as saying they serve two different purposes. A clear way of differentiating the two is to say that leadership promotes new directions, while management executes existing directions as efficiently as possible. But the work of the manager is not just the mundane monitoring of daily operations. It includes getting the most complex projects done, like putting the first man on the moon.

Management is different from leadership and just as important. It is the function that organizes the execution of today's business. Leadership is the evolutionary mechanism that changes organizations to prosper in the future. Whenever a species or individual animal runs into obstacles, adaptations occur and new directions are selected from those adaptations. Leadership is a risk-taking type of action that explores new frontiers and promotes new ways of behaving. It follows that in a stable environment, good management is all that is needed to prosper, but leadership in this context is not required.

The goal of management is to deliver results in a cost-effective way in line with customer expectations and profitably. It is not only leaders who can be inspiring. Inspiring leaders move us to change direction while inspiring managers motivate people to work harder. Management is a vital function that coordinates the input of many diverse stakeholders, experts, and customers. It requires a manager with enormous patience and highly developed facilitative skills. Excellent managers know how to bring the right people together and, by asking the right questions, draw the best solutions out of them (Daft, 2013; Drucker, 2006; Humphrey, 2013; Kreitner & Cassidy, 2012). To facilitate well, a sport manager must work very closely with all relevant stakeholders.

Sport managers manage facilities and people. Leadership is only required to sell the tickets for the game or to resell it periodically if resistance develops, but management drives the organization to success. The best managers are very strategic about themselves. They recognize that time and other resources are scarce and that competitive pressures demand efficient use of everything. Being strategic is the same thing as being proactive. Smart investors regularly monitor their investments in order to shift them around to get a better return on their money. Managers also have to be strategic about the business. It is not enough to do the work right and efficiently. It is essential to do the right things. Both of these imperatives can be thought of in terms of wise investment. Management is primarily a decision-making role. Managers are charged with the responsibility to make a profit and this requires them to make sound decisions.

By contrast, Bennis (1989, 1994) suggests leadership is strictly informal influence. Leaders persuade people to change direction. Leaders are masterful change agents. It is important to recast leadership in this way. Leadership is an occasional act. Management is an ongoing role.

Management Skills

Blanchard (2013), Daft (2013), and Humphrey (2013) suggest that becoming a successful manager will require the development of a variety of broad categories of skills including the following:

- Analytic thinking—interpreting and explaining patterns in information
- Behavioral flexibility—modifying personal behavior to react objectively rather than subjectively to accomplish organizational goals
- Conceptual skills—seeing the big picture
- Human relations—being a good communicator and coach
- Leadership—being able to influence others to perform tasks
- Oral communication—expressing ideas clearly in words
- Personal impact—creating a good impression and instill confidence
- Resistance to stress—performing under stressful conditions
- Roles performed by managers—being a planner, organizer, cheerleader, coach, problem solver, and decision maker, all rolled into one
- Self-objectivity—evaluating yourself realistically
- Technical skills—knowing technology and technical skills
- Tolerance for uncertainty—performing in ambiguous situations
- Written communication—expressing ideas clearly in writing

Finally, managers' schedules are usually jam-packed. Whether they're busy with employee meetings, unexpected problems, or strategy sessions, managers often find little spare time on their calendars.

In his classic book, *Managing,* Henry Mintzberg (2011) describes a set of 10 roles that a manager fills. These roles fall into three categories:

- **Interpersonal:** This role involves human interaction.
- **Informational:** This role involves the sharing and analyzing of information.
- **Decisional:** This role involves decision making.

Table 1.1 contains a more in-depth look at each category of roles that helps managers carry out all five functions described in the preceding "Functions of Managers" section.

Management Theories: A Historical Review

Scientific Management Theory (1890–1940)

Frederick Taylor developed the "scientific management theory," which espoused this careful specification and measurement of all organizational tasks. Tasks were standardized as much as possible. Workers were rewarded and punished (*Encyclopedia of Business*, 2014).

Bureaucratic Management Theory (1930–1950)

Max Weber (2003) focused on dividing organizations into hierarchies, establishing strong lines of authority and control. He suggested organizations develop comprehensive and detailed standard operating procedures for all routine tasks (*Encyclopedia of Business*, 2014).

Table 1.1
Mintzberg's Set of Ten Roles

Category	Role	Activity
Informational	Monitor	Seek and reveive information; scan periodicals and reports; maintain personal contact with stakeholders.
	Disseminator	Forward information to organization members via memos, reports, and phone calls.
	Spokesperson	Transmit information to outsiders via reports, memos, and speeches.
Interpersonal	Figurehead	Perform ceremonial and symbolic duties, such as greeting visitors and signing legal documents.
	Leader	Direct and motivate subordinates; counsel and communicate with subordinates.
	Liaison	Maintain information links both inside and outside organization via mail, phone calls, and meetings.
Decisional	Entrepreneur	Initiate improvement projects; identify new ideas and delegate idea responsibility to others.
	Disturbance handler	Take corrective action during disputes or crises; resolve conflicts among subordinates; adapt to environments.
	Resource allocator	Decide who gets resources; prepare budgets; set schedules and determine priorities.
	Negotiator	Represent department during negotiations of union contracts, sales, purchases, and budgets.

Human Relations Movement (1930–Today)

Eventually, unions and government regulations reacted to the rather dehumanizing effects of the above theories. Human resource departments were added to organizations. The behavioral sciences played a strong role in helping to understand the needs of workers and how the needs of the organization and its workers could be better aligned (*Encyclopedia of Business*, 2014).

Contingency Theory

The contingency theory asserts that when managers make a decision, they must take into account all aspects of the current situation and act on those aspects that are key to the situation at hand (*Encyclopedia of Business*, 2014).

Systems Theory

The systems theory has had a significant effect on management science and understanding organizations.

What is a system? A system is a collection of parts unified to accomplish an overall goal. If one part of the system is removed, the nature of the system is changed as well (*Encyclopedia of Business*, 2014).

Systems share feedback among each of these four aspects within an organization:
- Inputs
- Outputs (i.e., services, products, and programs)

- Outcomes
- Feedback from employees and customers/clients

The effect of systems theory in management is that writers, educators, consultants, and so forth are helping managers to look at the organization from a broader perspective. Systems theory has brought a new perspective for managers to interpret patterns and events in the workplace. They recognize the various parts of the organization and, in particular, the interrelations of the parts.

Decision Making

Decision making is a key activity at all levels of management. It may be defined as the act of choosing between two or more alternatives. It involves identifying alternatives and selecting the one judged best. This identification and selection can occur under conditions that vary dramatically. In a free-enterprise system, managers make decisions under conditions of certainty, risk, and uncertainty.

According to Humphrey (2013) and Bennis (1989, 1994), a good leader makes a good decision under conditions of (1) certainty when a manager knows the available alternatives and the benefits or costs associated with each; (2) risk when a manager knows the alternatives, the likelihood of their occurrence, and the potential benefits (or costs) associated with each but their outcomes are in doubt; and (3) uncertainty when a manager does not know the available alternatives, the likelihood of their occurrence, or their potential outcomes. The latter of these three is the most difficult.

Humphrey (2013) and Bennis (1989, 1994) indicate there are three steps in decision making: (1) available alternatives must be identified, (2) each alternative must be evaluated in light of premises about the future, and (3) based on the preceding evaluation and the alternative with the highest estimated probability of success should be selected. It is in this final step that a plan of action is adopted and the climax of the decision-making process occurs.

What is the Most Appropriate Leadership Theory for Sport Managers to Concentrate On?

The most appropriate leadership theory for sport managers to become acquainted with is situational leadership. The theory that best lends itself to sport managers is the Path-Goal Theory of Leadership (Humphrey, 2013). However, sport managers need to pay close attention to their leadership styles as well as their decision-making methods. Sport managers who are as concerned about people as they are about results will be the most successful in the long run.

Management Approaches

The most successful management process is characterized by two major elements—strong leadership and a participative management approach. Leadership has been discussed. Now it is time to shift gears and discuss a variety of management approaches that will be best suited for sport managers who are concerned equally about people and results.

Management By Objectives

Management by Objectives (MBO) is a management approach designed to integrate individual and organization objectives. MBO encourages the meshing of individual and organization objectives. It is a form of participatory management that engages the individual in the assisting management in attaining organizational goals. It is based on the belief that joint subordinate-superior participation in translating overall objectives into individual objectives will have a positive influence on employee performance and organizational goal attainment. The central idea behind MBO is that the mutual establishment and acceptance of objectives will elicit a stronger employee commitment than if a superior unilaterally establishes objectives and imposes them on subordinates. The enhanced commitment by employees who have helped to set personal objectives should, in turn, lead to improved performance. The MBO process is composed of five steps: (1) discuss job requirements with employee; (2) develop performance objectives for the employee that are (a) clear and concise, (b) achievable, (c) challenging, (d) measurable, (e) consistent with overall organization objectives, and (f) accompanied by an anticipated completion date; (3) discuss objectives with employee; (4) determine mutually agreed upon checkpoints; and (5) evaluate results together (Odiorne, 1965; Drucker, 2008).

Baldrige Management Model/System

The Baldrige management model/system serves two main purposes: (1) to help organizations assess their improvement efforts, diagnose their overall performance management system, and identify their strengths and opportunities for improvement; and (2) to identify Baldrige Award recipients that will serve as role models for other organizations (*Encyclopedia of Business*, 2014).

In addition, the system assists in strengthening U.S. competitiveness by

- improving organizational performance practices, capabilities, and results;
- facilitating communication and sharing of information on best practices among U.S. organizations of all types;
- serving as a tool for understanding and managing performance and for guiding planning and opportunities for learning

Total Quality Management

Total Quality Management (TQM) is a collection of roles and practices that are oriented and strive to always meet or exceed the needs and expectations of the consumer in an ongoing, planned system. What TQM attempts to achieve is a workplace where employees perceive that they have a personal stake in the output. Workers seek to measure against expectations that are achievable and that they have had a hand in setting. Performance is reviewed by their peers and by managers who are active participants in the daily operation of the workplace (Besterfield, Besterfield-Michna, Besterfield, & Besterfield-Sacre, 2002).

PDSA Cycle

Dr. W. Edwards Deming stressed the importance of management's role, both at the individual and company level, in the delivery of quality. According to Deming, 80%-90% of quality problems were under management's control, emphasizing organization-wide cultural change and worker/management cooperation as the path to achieving high quality (Deming Institute, 2013).

Shewart's Learning and Improvement Cycle became popularized through Deming as the PDSA Cycle, as a methodology for pretesting and perfecting before implementation and for continual improvement (PP&S, 2010b; Deming, Orsini, & Chaill, 2012; *Encyclopedia of Business,* 2014). With the goal of reducing the difference between the customer requirement and process performance, Deming developed a number of theories, including his "System of Profound Knowledge" (theories of optimization, variation, knowledge, and psychology), Deming's Seven Deadly Diseases of management that contribute to quality crises, and his 14 points to eliminate these mistakes and help organizations flourish (Deming, 2013; Deming, Orsini, & Cahill, 2012). Deming's 14 points for management (listed below) serve as his complete philosophy of management, a plan that he believed applied to any size or type organization:

- Create constancy of purpose toward improvement of product and service.
- Adopt the new philosophy. We can no longer live with commonly accepted levels of delay, mistakes and defective workmanship.
- Cease dependence on mass inspection. Instead, require statistical evidence that quality is built in.
- End the practice of awarding business on the basis of price.
- Find problems. It is management's job to work continually on the system.
- Institute modern methods of training on the job.
- Institute modern methods of supervision of production workers. The responsibility of foremen must be changed from numbers to quality.
- Drive out fear, so that everyone may work effectively for the company.
- Break down barriers between departments.
- Eliminate numerical goals, posters and slogans for the workforce asking for new levels of productivity without providing methods.
- Eliminate work standards that prescribe numerical quotas.
- Remove barriers that stand between the hourly worker and their right to pride of workmanship.
- Institute a vigorous program of education and retraining.
- Create a structure in top management that will push on the above points every day" (p. 110).

In addition to Toyota, Deming's principles have contributed to the global success of Proctor & Gamble, Ritz Carlton, Harley-Davidson and other well-known organizations.

Quality Trilogy

Dr. Joseph Juran was an important contributor to the Japanese quality movement and a seminal figure in the evolution of quality management in the U.S. In addition to creating the "Pareto principle" for identifying vital processes (80% of the return comes from 20% of the effort), he wrote the first reference work on quality management, the *Quality Control Handbook* (Juran, 2010). Outlining the sequential steps to achieve breakthrough improvement, Juran's book, *Managerial Breakthrough* (1995) serves as the basis for Lean, Six Sigma, and other important quality initiatives.

Juran (2010) describes quality from a customer viewpoint, where the degree of quality achieved is proportional to the number of features that meet customers' needs, especially in design, availability, safety, conformance and use. Rather than just focusing on the end customer, Juran believed that each person along the chain, from internal "customers" to the final user is both a supplier and a customer. While Juran developed numerous quality theories, two concepts in particular serve as the basis for establishing a traditional quality system and to support strategic quality management: Juran's "Quality Trilogy" for managing quality (quality planning, quality control and quality improvement), and his "Quality Planning Roadmap" (Juran 1995, 2010). Juran (2010) identified eight milestones as integral to a quality planning roadmap:

- Determine who are the customers.
- Determine the needs of those customers.
- Develop a product that responds to those needs
- Optimize the product features to meet your needs as well as customer needs.

- Develop a process that is able to produce the product.
- Optimize the process
- Prove that the process can produce the product under operating conditions.
- Transfer the process to operations. (p. 127).

Kaizen

Maurer (2014) notes throughout the 1950s and 60s, the Japanese not only embraced the teachings of these Western quality "gurus" but also expounded on what became enduring concepts. Originally developed and applied by Japanese industry, "Kaizen" is a core principle of quality management in general, and specifically within the methods of TQM and "lean manufacturing" (PP&S, 2010a).

While Kaizen teams analyze systems to find opportunities for continuous improvement, most importantly, Kaizen is a philosophy embedded in the organization's values. As such, Kaizen is lived rather than imposed, employing the following key concepts (Miller, Wroblewski, & Villafuerte, 2013):

- *Every* is a key word in Kaizen: improving everything that everyone does in every aspect of the organization in every department, every minute of every day.
- Evolution rather than revolution: making 1% improvements to 100 things is more effective, less disruptive and more sustainable than improving one thing by 100% when need becomes critical.
- Everyone involved in a process or activity, however apparently insignificant, has valuable knowledge and participates in a working team or Kaizen group.
- Everyone is expected to participate, analyzing, providing feedback and suggesting improvements to their area of work. Management facilitates this empowerment" (p. 176).

International Organization for Standardization (ISO)

Since 1947, the International Organization for Standardization has developed management and leadership standards for business, government, and community, ranging from environmental management to business applications of risk and quality management. The ISO 9000 series, standards that focus specifically on quality management and quality assurance, were developed to help companies achieve customer satisfaction, continuous improvement and regulatory requirements, as well as effectively document the elements needed to maintain an efficient quality system (PP&S, 2010b). The series now includes ISO 9000:2005 (definitions), ISO 9001:2008 (requirements) and ISO 9004:2009 (continuous improvement) (ISO, 2011). It is based on eight quality management principles that can be applied by management for organizational improvement (ISO, 2011):

- Customer focus
- Leadership
- Involvement of people
- Process approach
- System approach to management
- Continual improvement
- Factual approach to decision making
- Mutually beneficial supplier relationships" (p. 17).

After a major update in 2000, the new standards are built around business processes, emphasizing improvement and meeting the needs of customers. Adaptable to all types of organizations, ISO 9001 is unique in that it not only specifies the requirements for a QMS, but also provides tools and a philosophical basis (PP&S, 2010b). While some approaches are based on attitudinal factors, ISO 9001 provides the framework to institutionalize the right attitude by supporting it with policies, procedures, documentation, resources and structure. The benefits of building an ISO 9001-based QMS include the following (ISO, 2011):

- Documenting processes forces an organization to focus on how they do business
- Documented processes create repetition, eliminate variation, improve efficiency and reduce costs
- Corrective and preventative measures are developed and become permanent company-wide solutions
- Employee morale is increased as they're empowered to take control of their work
- Customer satisfaction/loyalty grows as the company delivers proactive rather than reactive solutions
- Better products and services arise from continuous improvement process
- Improved profit levels as productivity improves and rework costs are reduced
- Improved internal/external communications— employees, customers and suppliers are assured a voice
- Verification by third party auditor builds credibility with customer, supplier and competitive organizations (p. 31).

On the downside, ISO 9001-based quality management systems have been criticized for the amount of money, time and paperwork required for registration and maintenance. Further, ISO 9001 certification does not guarantee product or service quality, especially in cases where receiving certification is prioritized over achieving quality.

Six Sigma

Six Sigma is a methodology developed by Motorola in 1986 to improve business process by minimizing defects (iSixSigma, 2011). Six Sigma has since evolved into a broadly used organizational approach that focuses on reducing variations and achieving output improvements through problem solving. Six Sigma practitioners utilize the DMAIC method (define [the problem], measure, analyze, improve, control). Features that distinguish Six Sigma from earlier quality initiatives include the following:

- Achieving measurable financial returns from the project.
- Increased emphasis on passionate management leadership and support.
- A hierarchy of "Champions," "Black Belts," "Green Belts," etc. to implement the Six Sigma process.
- Making decisions on the basis of verifiable data, rather than assumptions" (iSixSigma, 2011).

Six Sigma employs many widely used quality management tools, such as Design of Experiments, Pareto charts, Chi-square test, Cost-benefit analysis, root cause and regression analyses, and more. While the approach has achieved significant bottom-line results for many organizations, it has also been criticized for potential negative effects such as ignoring the customer, stifling creativity (especially in research) and being oversold or inappropriately applied by consultants.

References

Bennis, W. (1989). *Why leaders can't lead: The unconscious conspiracy continues*. San Francisco: Jossey-Bass Publishers.

Bennis, W. (1994). *On becoming a leader*. Cambridge, MA: Perseus Books.

Besterfield, D. H., Besterfield-Michna, C., Besterfield, G., & Besterfield-Sacre, M. (2002). *Total quality management* (3rd ed.). Saddlebrook, NJ: Pearson/Prentice-Hall.

Blanchard, K. (2013). Critical management skills. Retrieved from http://www.kenblanchard.com/img/pub/pdf_critical_leadership_skills.pdf

Business Dictionary. (2014). Retrieved from http://www.businessdictionary.com

Juran/About Juran/Dr. Juran Life and Times. (2011). *Juran/The Source for Quality/Superior Quality, Sustainable Results. N.p.* Retrived from http://www.juran.com/about_juran_institute_drjuran_life_and_times.html

Juran, J. M., & Defeo, J. (2010). *Juran's quality handbook: The complete guide to performance excellence* (6th ed.). New York: McGraw-Hill.

Juran, J. M., & Godfrey, D. A. B. (1995). *Managerial breakthrough.* New York: McGraw-Hill.

Deming Institute. (2013). Retrieved from https://www.deming.org

Deming, W. E., Orsini, J., & Cahill, D. D. (2012). *The essential Deming: Leadership principles for the father of quality.* New York: McGraw-Hill.

Deming, W. E. (1982). *Quality, productivity, and competitive position.* Cambridge, MA: MIT Center for Advanced Engineering Study.

Daft, R. L. (2013). *Management* (11th ed.). Mason, OH: South-Western Cengage Learning.

Daft, R. L. (2007). *Organizational theory and design* (7th ed.). Cincinnati: South Western Publishers.

Daft, R. L. (2001). *Essentials of organizational theory ad design* (2nd ed.). Cincinnati: South Western Publishers.

Drucker, P. F. (*1973). Management: Tasks, responsibilities, practices.* New York: Harper & Row.

Drucker, P. F. (2006). *The Practice of management.* New York: Harper Collins.

Drucker, P. F. (2008). *Management* (rev ed.). New York: Harper Collins.

Encyclopedia of Business (2nd ed). (2014). Retrieved from http://www.referenceforbusiness.com/encyclopedia

Fayol, H., & Gray, I. (1984). *General and industrial management.* New York: Harper Collins.

Follett, M. P. (2009). *The new state: Group organization, the solution of popular government (1918).* Whitefish, MT: Kessinger Publishing, Inc.

Gomez-Mejia, L. R., & Balkin, D. B. (2012). *Management.* Upper Saddle River, NJ: Prentice-Hall.

Humphrey, R. H. (2013). *Effective leadership: Theory, cases, and applications.* Los Angeles: Sage.

SMART. (2013). Retrieved from http://topachievement.com/smart.html

iSixSigma. (2011) http://www.isixsigma.com

ISO. The ISO Story. ISO – International Organization for Standardization. (2011). Retrieved from http://www.iso.org/iso/about/the_iso_story.htm

Kreitner, R., & Cassidy, C. (2012). *Management* (12th ed.). Mason, OH: South Western Cengage Learning.

Maurer, R. (2014). *One small step can change: The Kaizen Way.* New York: Workman Publishing Co., Inc.

Miller, J. Wroblewski, M. , & Villafuerte, J. (2013). *Creating a Kaizen culture: Align organization, achieve breakthrough results, and sustain the gains.* New York: McGraw-Hill.

Mintzberg, H. (2011). *Managing.* San Francisco, CA: Berrett-Koehler Publications.

Northouse, P. G. (2012). *Leadership: Theory and practice* (6th ed.). Los Angeles: Sage.

Odiorne, G. S. (1965). *Management by objectives: A system of managerial leadership.* New York: Pitman Publishing Company.

PP&S White Paper. (2010a). "What are the benefits of Kaizen?: Introduction to Kaizen." *Graphic Products: The Leader in Industrial Sign and Label Printers for creating Pipe Markers, Arc Flash labels, Safety Signs and more!.* Retrieved from http://www.graphicproducts.com/tutorials/kaizen/index.php

PP&S White Paper. (2011b) *Quality management: Then, now, and toward the future.* Retrieved from http://www.pp-s.com

Taylor, F. W. (2011). *The principles of scientific management.* New York: Harper Collins.

Weber, M. (2003). *General economic history.* Dover, RI: Dover Publications.

CHAPTER 2

Organizational Principles and Leadership

Thomas H. Sawyer
Professor Emeritus, Indiana State University

James H. Conn
Professor Emeritus, Central Missouri State University

Kimberly J. Bodey
Professor, Indiana State University

Introduction

Managers who oversee sport and recreation facilities face many decisions each day. They are charged with being responsive to changes in the marketplace while maintaining a degree of consistency and stability over time within the organization. Policies and procedures play an important role in the operation of sport and recreation facilities because they are the means by which the agency's mission is put into motion. They reflect the manner in which the agency's strategic goals are integrated into day-to-day management decisions. Policies and procedures provide a common understanding of workplace operations, clarify managerial instructions, and serve as a resource to quickly resolve problems.

The successful operation of a sport and recreation facility also depends on an effective system of internal controls. A valid control system can assure that baseline operations are being implemented as required and can warn facility managers of changes in the environment that requires a new set of commands. A system of policies and procedures allows for the efficient use of all human and financial resources because it reduces intentional and unintentional errors and permits the agency to meet its strategic objectives (Odiorne, 1965; Rodenz, 2006; Slack, 1997).

What Is an Organization?

An organization is when two or more people interact to achieve a common objective. This includes families and clubs, small businesses and larger ones, public and private organizations, profit-oriented and not-for-profit organizations, manufacturing firms, service organizations, consulting firms, professional sport teams, global organizations, and multinational firms. Every organization has an organizational environment composed of external and internal factors or elements that influence the way it functions. These factors or elements include the general environment, task environment, and internal environment (Bedeian, 1986; Draft, 2001, 2007; Drucker, 1974).

The **general environment** includes external factors such as legal/political, international, technological, economic, and social factors that affect all organizations.

The **task environment** includes other external factors such as customers, competitors, suppliers, and so on that interact directly with the organization as it seeks to operate.

The **internal environment** includes internal factors such as organizational structure, personnel, policies, and so on, over which the organization has a large degree of control.

What is Organizational Behavior?

Organizational behavior is defined as the study of individuals and small groups within the organization and the characteristics of the environment in which the people work (Draft, 2001, 2007; Hersey & Blanchard, 1972). It is a microperspective of an organization. Many of the concepts used in organizational behavior research are drawn from social psychology. Researchers in organizational behavior are concerned with individually based issues such as job satisfaction, leadership style, communication, team building, and motivation. The sport management students should understand that the dominant trend of the empirical work in our field has been concerned with organizational behavior topics – level of job satisfaction, leadership traits, and motivations of sport managers (Draft, 2001, 2007; Slack, 1997).

What is Organization Theory?

Organization theory is the study of the design and structure of organizations. Scholars in this field seek to identify patterns and regularities in organizations. They attempt to understand the causes patterns and regularities and their consequences. The study of organizational theory assists managers in their daily challenges of managing an organization. It is a macro perspective of the organization. The various theories draw heavily from sociology (Draft 2001, 2007).

Further, organizational theory can assist sport managers by providing a better understanding of the way sport organizations are structured and designed, how they operate, and why some are more effective than others. This knowledge can assist sport managers in analyzing and diagnosing more effectively the problems they face and enable them to respond with appropriate solutions (Slack, 1997; Draft 2001, 2007).

Classical Organization Theories

Classical organization theories (Fayol, 1949; Taylor, 1947; Weber, 1947) deal with the formal organization and concepts to increase management efficiency. Taylor presented scientific management concepts, Weber gave the bureaucratic approach, and Fayol developed the administrative theory of the organization. They all contributed significantly to the development of classical organization theory.

Taylor's Scientific Management Approach

The scientific management approach developed by Taylor is based on the concept of planning work to achieve efficiency, standardization, specialization, and simplification. Acknowledging that the approach to increased productivity was through mutual trust between management and workers, Taylor suggested that, to increase this level of trust

- the advantages of productivity improvement should go to workers,

- physical stress and anxiety should be eliminated as much as possible,

- capabilities of workers should be developed through training, and

- the traditional "boss" concept should be eliminated.

Taylor developed the following four principles of scientific management for improving productivity:

- **Science, not rule-of-thumb.** Old rules-of-thumb should be supplanted by a scientific approach to each element of a person's work.

- **Scientific selection of the worker.** Organizational members should be selected based on some analysis, and then trained, taught, and developed.

- **Management and labor cooperation rather than conflict**. Management should collaborate with all organizational members so that all work can be done in conformity with the scientific principles developed.

- **Scientific training of the worker.** Workers should be trained by experts, using scientific methods.

Weber's Bureaucratic Approach

Considering the organization as a segment of broader society, Weber (1947) based the concept of the formal organization on the following principles:

- **Structure.** In the organization, positions should be arranged in a hierarchy, each with a particular, established amount of responsibility and authority.

- **Specialization.** Tasks should be distinguished on a functional basis and then separated according to specialization, each having a separate chain of command.

- **Predictability and stability.** The organization should operate according to a system of procedures consisting of formal rules and regulations.

- **Rationality.** Recruitment and selection of personnel should be impartial.

- **Democracy**. Responsibility and authority should be recognized by designations and not by persons.

Weber's theory is invalid on account of dysfunctions (Hicks & Gullett, 1975) such as rigidity, impersonality, displacement of objectives, limitation of categorization, self-perpetuation, and empire building, cost of controls, and anxiety to improve status.

Administrative Theory

The elements of administrative theory (Fayol, 1949) relate to accomplishment of tasks and include principles of management, the concept of line and staff, committees, and functions of management:

- **"Division of work or specialization**. This increases productivity in both technical and managerial work.

- **Authority and responsibility.** These are imperative for an organizational member to accomplish the organizational objectives.

- **Discipline.** Members of the organization should honor the objectives of the organization. They should also comply with the rules and regulations of the organization.

- **Unity of command**. This means taking orders from and being responsible to only one superior.

- **Unity of direction.** Members of the organization should jointly work toward the same goals.

- **Subordination of individual interest to general interest**. The interest of the organization should not become subservient to individual interests or the interest of a group of employees.

- **Remuneration of personnel**. This can be based on diverse factors such as time, job, piece rates, bonuses, profit-sharing or non-financial rewards.

- **Centralization**. Management should use an appropriate blend of both centralization and decentralization of authority and decision making.

- **Scalar chain**. If two members who are on the same level of hierarchy have to work together to accomplish a project, they need not follow the hierarchy level but can interact with each other on a "gang plank" if acceptable to the higher officials.

- **Order.** The organization has a place for everything and everyone who ought to be so engaged.

- **Equity.** Fairness, justice, and equity should prevail in the organization.

- **Stability of tenure of personnel.** Job security improves performance. An employee requires some time to get used to new work and do it well.

- **Initiative.** This should be encouraged and stimulated.

- **Esprit de corps.** Pride, allegiance, and a sense of belonging are essential for good performance. Union is strength.

- **The concept of line and staff.** The concept of line and staff is relevant in organizations that are large and require specialization of skill to achieve organizational goals. Line personnel are those who work directly to achieve organizational goals. Staff personnel include those whose basic function is to support and help line personnel.

- **Committees.** Committees are part of the organization. Members from the same or different hierarchical levels from different departments can form committees around a common goal. They can be given different functions, such as managerial, decision making, recommending, or policy formulation. Committees can take diverse forms, such as boards, commissions, task groups, or ad hoc committees. Committees can be further divided according to their functions. In agricultural research organizations, committees are formed for research, staff evaluation, or even allocation of land for experiments.

- **Functions of management.** Fayol (1949) considered management as a set of planning, organizing, training, commanding, and coordinating functions. Gulick and Urwick (1937) also considered organization in terms of management functions such as planning, organizing, staffing, directing, coordinating, reporting, and budgeting (p. 126)."

Neoclassical Organization Theory

Neoclassical theorists recognized the importance of individual or group behaviour and emphasized human relations. Based on the Hawthorne experiments, the neoclassical approach emphasized social or human relationships among the operators, researchers and supervisors (Roethlisberger & Dickson, 1943). It was argued that these considerations were more consequential in determining productivity than mere changes in working conditions. Productivity increases were achieved as a result of high morale, which was influenced by the amount of individual, personal, and intimate attention workers received.

Principles of the Neoclassical Approach

The classical approach stressed the formal organization. It was mechanistic and ignored major aspects of human nature. In contrast, the neoclassical approach, according to Mayo (2003), introduced an informal organization structure and emphasized the following principles:

- **"The individual.** An individual is not a mechanical tool but a distinct social being, with aspirations beyond mere fulfillment of a few economic and security works. Individuals differ from each other in pursuing these desires. Thus, an individual should be recognized as interacting with social and economic factors.

- **The work group.** The neoclassical approach highlighted the social facets of work groups or informal organizations that operate within a formal organization. The concept of "group" and its synergistic benefits were considered important.

- **Participative management**. Participative management or decision making permits workers to participate in the decision making process. This was a new form of management to ensure increases in productivity (p. 172)."

Note: The difference between Taylor's "scientific management," which focuses on work, and the neoclassical approach, is that the latter focuses on workers and not work.

What is Organizational Culture?

Organizational culture can be best defined as the shared philosophies, values, beliefs, and behavior patterns that form the organization's core identity. As people come into contact with organizations, they become familiar with the organization's formal rules and practices, the dress norms, the stories of coworkers, and the informal codes of behavior, rituals, reward and promotion system, tasks, pay systems, jargon, and jokes understood only by insiders (Bremer, 2012; Deming, 1982; 2012). These elements are some of the manifestations of organizational culture.

Leaders or managers, by their actions, send signals about what they value, and regardless of what may be written in organizations value statements, it is the actions of leaders or managers that send the clear message. However, when employees see a key leader contradict the written values, development of the culture is undermined.

Governance = Organization Design, Authority, and Power

Governance is the combination of organizational structure or design, authority, and locus of power. Every organization has a specific form of governance. The governance system, although unique to each organization, is responsible for the development of policies and implementation procedures.

Organizations, which are groups of individuals with a common goal bound together by a set of authority-responsibility relationships, are required wherever groups of people work together to reach common goals. One of management's functions is to organize and coordinate all organization resources into an effective and efficient operation.

The term *organize* refers to a management task of determining resources and activities required to achieve organizational objectives, combining the resources into a formal structure, assigning responsibilities for achieving the objectives to capable individuals, and delegating to them the authority needed to implement their assignments.

Organizing can be (a) developing a formal structure to use the financial, physical, material, and human resources of an organization; (b) grouping various activities and assigning managers to supervise each group; (c) establishing connections among functions, jobs, tasks, and employees; or (d) subdividing the tasks to be accomplished in various departments and delegating authority to complete the tasks (Alvesson, 2012; Bremer, 2012; Deming, 1982).

Organizational Structure

All organizations have a formal organizational structure that is depicted in an organization chart. Such a chart depicts key aspects of organization including division of labor or specialization, chain of command, unity of command, management levels, and bureaucracy. The chart represents the type of game plan the management has developed to reach the organization's objectives. However, formal organization charts often only remotely describe the important relationships that exist. Frequently, the pecking order of the informal organization is completely out of line with the formal organizational chart. In such cases, the informal organization carries greater weight since it describes the way things actually get accomplished.

Division of Labor

Division of labor is captured in an organization chart, a pictorial representation of an organization's formal structure (Mosley, Megginson, & Pietri, 2005; Rodenz, 2006; Williams, 2007). An organization chart is concerned with relationships among tasks and the authority to do the tasks. Eight kinds of relationships can be captured in an organization chart (Williams, 2007):

- "The division/specialization of labor
- Relative authority
- Departmentalization
- Span of control
- The levels of management
- Coordination centers
- Formal communication channels
- Decision responsibility (p. 186)"

Organization charts have important weaknesses that should be of concern to managers developing and using them (Williams, 2007):

- "They may imply a formality that does not exist.
- They may be inconsistent with reality.
- Their usual top-down perspective often minimizes the role of customers, front-line managers,and employees without management responsibilities.
- They fail to capture the informal structure and informal communication.
- They often imply that a pyramidal structure is the best or only way to organize.

- They fail to address the potential power and authority of staff positions compared with line positions (p. 112)."

Delegation of Authority

Authority is legitimized power. Power is the ability to influence others. Delegation is distribution of authority. Delegation frees the manager from the tyranny of urgency. Delegation frees the manager to use his or her time on high-priority activities. Note that delegation of authority does not free the manager from accountability for the actions and decisions of subordinates.

Delegation of authority is guided by several key principles and concepts (Bible & Bivins, 2010; Mosley, Pietri, & Megginson, 1996; Rodenz, 2006):

- **Exception principle.** Someone must be in charge. A person higher in the organization handles exceptions to the usual. The most exceptional, rare, or unusual decisions end up at the top management level because no one lower in the organization has the authority to handle them.

- **Scalar chain of command.** The exception principle functions in concert with the concept of scalar chain of command; formal distribution of organizational authority is in a hierarchical fashion. The higher one is in an organization, the more authority one has.

- **Decentralization.** Decisions are to be pushed down to the lowest feasible level in the organization. The organizational structure goal is to have working managers rather than managed workers.

- **Parity principle.** Delegated authority must equal responsibility. With responsibility for a job must go the authority to accomplish the job.

- **Span of control.** The span of control is the number of people a manager supervises. The organizational structure decision to be made is the number of subordinates a manager can effectively lead. The typical guideline is a span of control of no more than five or six people. However, a larger span of control is possible depending on the complexity, variety, and proximity of jobs.

- **Unity principle.** Ideally, no one in an organization reports to more than one supervisor. Employees should not have to decide which of their supervisors to make unhappy because of the impossibility of following all the instructions given them.

- **Line and staff authority.** Line authority is authority within an organization's or unit's chain of command. Staff authority is advisory to line authority. Assume a crew leader reports to the garden store manager who in turn reports to the president. Further assume that the crew leader and store manager can hire and fire and give raises to the people they supervise. Both the crew leader and store manager have line authority. To contrast, assume that the president has an accountant who prepares monthly financial summaries with recommendations for corrective action. The accountant has staff authority but not line authority.

- **Departmentalization.** This is the grouping of jobs under the authority of a single manager, according to some rational basis, for the purposes of planning, coordination and control. The number of departments in an organization depends on the number of different jobs (i.e., the size and complexity of the business).

- **Informal structure.** The formal structure in each organization that has been put in place by management has an accompanying informal structure. Management does not and cannot control the informal structure.

The informal structure has no written rules, is fluid in form and scope, is not easy to identify, and has vague or unknown membership guidelines.

For management, the informal structure may be positive or negative. Positive qualities include the ability to quickly spread information and provide feedback to the information. The informal structure gives people a sense of being in the know. Management can feed information into the informal structure at very low cost. The informal structure can also help satisfy employees' social needs.

The negative qualities of the informal structure mirror the positive qualities in several ways. The juicier a rumor, the more likely is the informal structure to repeat it, expand it and make it into the "truth." Management may not know what information is flowing through the informal structure. Employees can waste a great deal of time nurturing and participating in the informal structure. Finally, the informal structure can fence out new employees, "rate breakers," and change agents no matter the extent to which the formal structure makes them a part of the organization.

Chain of Command

Organizational charts depict the authority-responsibility relationship within a sport organization that link superiors and subordinates together through the entire organization. This depiction is a chain of command (COC). The COC flows from the chief executive down to the lowest worker in the organization. The COC will fail if there is not a unity of command. Unit of command is the principle that each employee in an organization reports to and is accountable to only one immediate superior. This simplifies communication and placement of responsibility.

Types of Organizations

Any understanding of organizational design requires an explanation of the most common types of organizations. There are two popular types—line and line-and-staff.

Line organization. This refers to those departments of an organization that perform the activities most closely associated with its mission or purpose. A good example is the military, where the line organization consists of the combat units: infantry, artillery, MASH, and so on.

Line-and staff organization. This is an organization structure in which staff positions are added to serve the basic line departments and help them accomplish the organization's objectives more effectively. For example, ordinarily, maintenance is considered a staff function in a sport goods manufacturing facility. The organization is not in the business of providing maintenance. However, with a sport venue (i.e., arena or stadium), facility maintenance is critical to the spectators; it is considered a line activity. Remember, line activities are the organization's fundamental reason for existence—the bread-and-butter activities, so to speak.

Policy-Based Management

Policy-based management is an administrative approach to simplify business operations by establishing a way to deal with situations that are likely to occur. Policies are the operating rules that maintain consistency, order, and security in the workplace. For example, a sport and recreation agency may have a refund policy in place. Then, each time a patron requested a refund, staff members could refer to the policy rather than discovering the best way this business transaction should be completed. Essentially, policies provide decision-makers with guidelines, alternatives, and limits in order to channel decisions and actions to efficiently accomplish the goal.

A policy is a predetermined course of action established to guide staff members toward accepted business practices. A procedure is the step-by-step instructions by which a policy is to be achieved. Simply put, policies create expectations and guide action while a procedure provides details about how a policy is carried out.

The facility manager, working through the agency's board of directors, develops the policies and procedures needed for the facility to operate efficiently. Strategic goals and objectives cannot be achieved without consistent and congruent decision-making by facility managers as well as the coordination of all staff and work processes. Thus, the policies and procedures manual is the means by which business operations are documented and published. Through the manual, facility managers delegate specific responsibility and authority to staff members in order to carry out the necessary business functions. Policies and procedures allow staff members to freely execute their duties within defined boundaries and minimize over-control by managers.

Policies and Procedures Manual

There are any number of reasons why it is important to have written policies and procedures for governing facility/event management. According to Conn and Malloy (1989), Peabody (2006), and Page (2009), the primary reasons are to (1) provide a formal policy that guides administrative decisions, (2) reduce the organization's vulnerability to litigation, and (3) clearly communicate to staff and customers/clients a set of uniform and standard practices to guide decisions and behaviors.

Conn and Malloy (1989), Peabody (2006), and Page (2009) suggest a well-designed policy and procedure manual for facility/event management can assist in answering questions, such as these:

- What type of reports, records, or documentation are staff required to file and keep?

- What are the due process procedures?

- What are the staff's legal responsibilities and procedures for implementing them?

- What is the policy regarding requisitioning, purchasing, inventorying, servicing, maintaining, and inspecting equipment?

- What is the recruiting, hiring, and evaluating process?

- What are the emergency procedures?

- What are the crowd control procedures?

- What process is utilized for inspecting and maintaining the facilities?

- What procedures are employed for program evaluation?

- What process is implemented to control admission?

- How is the facility scheduled?

- What are the procedures for evaluating whether or not a person can return to activity after injury or illness?

Suggested Contents

A facility's/event's policies and procedures manual should delineate general as well as specific program guidelines. According to Conn and Malloy (1989), Conn (1991), Peabody (2006), and Page (2009), the kind of information that should be contained in the policies and procedures manual will vary from one organization to another. In general, the policies should reflect (1) the rights of all participants, (2) the philosophy of the organization and the rationale for the existence of the program, (3) such legislative dictates as Title VII (sexual harassment), Title IX (gender equity), and the Americans with Disabilities Act (equal access for disabilities participants).

Steps for Developing a Policy and Procedure Manual

Conn and Malloy (1989) recommended the steps for the development of a policy and procedure manual that are described below. This manual should be a flexible, dynamic document that guides employees. Further, the document should be reviewed and revised annually after implementation. Finally, Peabody (2006) and Page (2009) indicate the primary reasons for a policies and procedures manual for facility/event management are to (1) provide a formal policy that guides decisions, (2) reduce the organization's vulnerability to litigation, and (3) clearly communicate to staff and customer/clients a set of uniform and standard practices to guide decisions and behaviors.

Step 1. Developing a policy and procedure manual is a long arduous, task that requires management's complete involvement and support. It is important that all personnel (management as well as staff) are involved in the development of the policies and procedures for the organization. The typical approach is to appoint a committee to carefully research and ultimately recommend policies and procedures. Management must be prepared to allocate resources (i.e. time and funds) and encourage the involvement of all staff members. Policies and procedures must be carefully researched and synthesized before being written. Therefore, it is extremely important to involve people who look at policies and procedures from many different angles. The more widespread the involvement, the greater the chances are that the manual will be used and maintained after completion.

Several factors, suggested by Conn (1991) and Page (2009), should be considered when deciding who will be appointed to the committee:

- **Size of the staff.** Every member of a small staff will have intimate involvement on the committee; however, larger staffs should be divided into sub-committees that will prepare specific sets of policies and procedures.

- **Administration and board.** The manual must be approved by management and the board (if one exists); therefore, it is important that management and the board is represented on the committee.

- **Customer/client/student-athlete.** It is important to involve those most affected by the policies and procedures on the committee who develops them.

- **Community interest.** Most organizations have links with the community and community representation could be very useful in future activities; therefore, it is important to involve community members on the committee.

- **Diversity or inclusiveness.** The committee should be a mirror image of the organization and the community as a whole.

Step 2. The format of the manual must be flexible. It is suggested that (1) a three-ring binder be used to store the information, (2) the information be divided into logical sections and subsections with appropriate paginations (i.e., section one: 1.1, 1.2, 1.3; section two: 2.1, 2.2, 2.3), (3) a table of contents, definition section for acronyms and terms, and index be included, and (4) the various sections be color-coded.

Step 3. The committee should assign one person to write the manual after collecting the appropriate data from the various task groups. The committee needs to adopt an outline and structure for the manual as well as a timeline for completion of the various sections. The writer should be using a computer and appropriate word processing software.

Step 4. The completed manual is dynamic in nature and must be reviewed periodically. A procedure for reviewing the manual must be established. All staff members should be encouraged to periodically review the policies and procedures within their domain and then recommend any changes to the appropriate authorities. Making policy and procedure changes a regular agenda item at staff meetings sensitizes the staff to the importance of the manual and maintains its currency.

Strategic Role of Policies and Procedures

Organizing involves analyzing, identifying, and defining the tasks to
place. If this process is done properly, it will result in some logical order.
for individuals to cooperate efficiently and effectively to achieve identified ఓ
duties is outlined in the organizational structure. The structure then serves as ⅂
ing policies that assign responsibilities to functional areas within the sport and r.
ultimately, to specific staff positions. For example, policies may dictate hiring lifegu
pool operations and therefore is the responsibility of the aquatics director while hirin₂
the responsibility of the sports programming and leagues supervisor.

Each job within the sport and recreation facility has corresponding constraints. Wi௹
policies and procedures, staff members would be left to discover these constraints by triఒ
causing the agency to be highly disorganized. Policies give managers a means to direct and h
staff activities as well as control events in advance. Before work begins, staff members know ৳
cess and are more likely to produce the correct outcome on the first attempt. For instance, coౖ
the refund policy. Two different employees are involved in this process: customer service staff menಽ
and business manager. The staff member asks the patron to fill out a refund requisition form and checಽ
to make sure the form is properly completed before submitting the form to the business manager. The
business manager confirms the refund is appropriate and then authorizes and records the release of
funds. Policies coordinate these activities and increase the likelihood the business transaction is completed correctly.

The usefulness of policies and procedures is largely dependent on how well they are aligned with
the sport and recreation facility's mission, strategic plan, and core processes. The mission captures an
agency's purpose and values and controls the destiny of the organization. The strategic plan is the road
map that establishes specific, measurable goals to achieve the mission while the core processes are the
primary functions and activities utilized in an agency. Policies and procedures support core processes
by channeling managerial decision-making and staff behavior.

Maintaining alignment is a continuous and iterative process. As one component is revised, each of
the remaining components must be reviewed to determine if modifications are necessary. For instance,
consider a facility which plans to renovate its outdoor pool area to include a splash play space. Here a
core process will be changed. Thus, the policies and procedures must be revised to guide manager and
staff behaviors to support this change. Similarly, the strategic plan must also be updated to reflect the
change in the design and operation of the facility.

Content and Structure of the Policies and Procedures Manual

The environment in which the sport and recreation facility operates is always changing. There are
external forces and internal forces that impact how the facility functions on a daily basis. Problems that
result from these environmental factors must be managed appropriately. The policies and procedure
manual, as suggested by Conn and Malloy (1989), Conn (1991), and Peabody (2006), contributes to
proactive management so long as it is perceived by staff members as accurate, comprehensive, and user
friendly. Facility managers should think of the policies and procedures manual as a constantly evolving
document. The content and structure changes to meet the demands placed on the facility.

Manual content. It is best to think of policy making as a method of applied problem solving.
Therefore, the process of preparing a new manual or revising the current policies and procedures manual begins with problem identification. Identified problems may result from a breakdown of current
operations (e.g., double scheduling the gymnasium) or from new or unusual situations that are likely
to reoccur (e.g., vandalism). Problems may also result from an incongruity between current practices
and professional standards or regulations (e.g., storage of chemicals).

Any problems may exist in a sport and recreation facility at any given time. Therefore, the facility [manag]er must prioritize problem areas based on the degree of risk to business operations. Risks may [includ]e increased operating costs, diminished customer satisfaction, loss of revenue, loss of competi- [tive a]dvantage, and noncompliance with regulations. The facility manager must take care to determine [the] underlying cause when constructing the problem statement. Policies can only resolve the problem [if th]ey address causes rather than symptoms. Sometimes, the cause is obvious. At other times, the fa- [cil]ity manager must critically think about the nature of business operations to discover the underlying [ca]use. When analyzing operations, it may be useful to create a flowchart to visually represent all activi- ties and behaviors associated with a particular problem. The flowchart allows for a comparison of what is happening and what should be happening in the workplace. Central issues and potential solutions are likely to emerge from this comparison.

If no policy exists to address the cause of a problem, then one must be created. If a policy exists, the facility manager must decide whether to revise the current policy or construct a new policy. Some- times tweaking the current policy will result in the desired outcome. At other times, a clear change in direction is needed. The advantage of "re-engineering the process" (e.g., to set aside the current policy and start over from scratch) is that it permits the manager to take a fresh look at the steps required to achieve the desired outcome. The aim is to increase efficiency by determining a different, better way to solve the problem.

Regardless of whether the current policy is revised or a new policy is created, the facility manager must check its alignment. First, is the policy aligned with the agency's mission, strategic plan, and core processes? Second, is the policy aligned with the remaining policies? In other words, what is the ripple effect of implementing this new or revised policy? The goal is to develop consistent, repeatable processes and avoid causing an incongruity with the current policies, core processes, strategic plan, and mission.

When looking for ways to solve identified problems, the facility manager should seek out best or acceptable practices in the industry. This may be done by researching online resources, networking, and benchmarking. Frequently, state and federal agencies as well as professional organizations provide online resources that list current standards and practices. The Internet may also be used to search for manuals from other sport and recreation facilities. Caution is warranted. Policies and procedures do not come in a one-size-fits-all package. Rather, policies and procedures must be adapted to meet the sport and recreation facility's specific needs.

Networking involves interacting with others who have relevant knowledge and information. The more people the facility manager talks with inside and outside the agency, the better the chance of finding someone with needed answers. External networking contacts may be made at conferences and symposiums, workshops and seminars, and business meetings. These professional colleagues may share their agencies' manuals, provide names of other contacts within their facility or others, or bring forth information that has been published in journals, magazines, newsletters, blogs, and the like. Internal networking involves talking with front-line staff and supervisors as well as facility users. These indi- viduals will have insights on how the system works. They may provide information to shed light on the problem or offer suggestions for change.

Benchmarking is an ongoing process where information and knowledge is exchanged between similar agencies. The purpose is to identify and evaluate best or innovative practices and explore how these may be integrated into the facility. The facility manager must have a thorough understanding of current operations when utilizing this investigative tool. Otherwise, it is unlikely the manager will have the appropriate perspective by which to ask or respond to questions thereby diminishing the value of this approach.

Manual structure. The method and sequencing of information within the policies and pro- cedures manual should be similar to other manuals in the sport and recreation facility. According to

Conn (1991), Peabody (2006), and Page (2009), the policies and procedures manual should include the following:

- **Cover and title.** Specifies introductory information, approvals, and dates.

- **Revision history.** Records additions, modifications, and deletions to policies and procedures.

- **Table of contents.** Lists approved polices and procedures and corresponding documents. It is best to organize by topic area (e.g., compensation and benefits, hiring and evaluating personnel, concessions operations and maintenance, etc.) then to alphabetize within the groupings.

- **Policies and procedures.** Contains published policies and procedures and related documents. Pages should be clearly labeled and correspond to the title and pages listed in the table of contents.

The policies and procedures manual must be thought of as an accessible document that contributes to the sport and recreation facility's day-to-day operation. To be accessible, the manual must be up to date, focus on relevant policies and procedures, and represent efforts to continually improve the facility. Moreover, the manual must contain a user-friendly table of contents, complete set of approved policies and procedures written in a standardized format, and easy-to-find forms, templates, diagrams, and other documents referenced in the policies and procedures.

Writing Policies and Procedures

A system of policies and procedures serves many functions within a sport and recreation facility. It provides a common understanding of workplace operations, clarifies managerial instructions, serves as a resource to solve problems, and acts as a control system. Policies and procedures are the means by which the facility's mission is integrated into day-to-day tasks. Policies and procedures reduce the range of individual decision making; that is, they set parameters on what can and cannot be done within the facility in order to enhance consistency. Policies and procedures also encourage management by exception. The facility manager can focus time and effort on unusual problems rather than routine or reoccurring situations (Conn, 1991; Peabody, 2006).

Standardized Writing Format

The standardized writing format is the plan for organizing and presenting information in a consistent way. A logical, structured format is a basic requirement for a system of policies and procedures. It provides a framework for converting the ideas and concepts collected during the research phase into paragraphs, sentences, and words. Without a standardized writing format, the policies and procedures would lack the formality needed for the efficient operation of sport and recreation facilities.

The standardized writing format allows the manual to be straightforward and to the point. The consistent presentation of policies and procedures reduces frustration and saves time. The staff member's ability to find information quickly is inhibited when headings are ambiguous or uninformative, major ideas or important details are hard to locate, and instructions are either nonexistent or difficult to understand. A standardized writing format reduces frustration because the necessary information can be found in the expected place. A standardized writing format saves time by allowing the staff member to focus on policy and procedure content rather than overcome distractions in format. The end result is the reader believes the manual is a quality document that deserves attention.

The standardized writing format is presented in outline style with seven principle headings. The headings are arranged in a logical, unchanging sequence so staff members can quickly skim pages to find the relevant section. The writing format is structured so that the first six headings provide a foundation while the seventh heading provides the details necessary to accomplish the identified purpose. According to Conn and Malloy (1989), Conn (1991), and Peabody (2006) suggest the seven principle headings of the writing format are outlined below:

- **Purpose.** Explains the primary objective(s) for writing the policy or procedure. It should be comprehensive yet concise, typically one to three sentences in length. Abbreviations or acronyms should not be used.

- **Revision history.** Shows all revisions to a policy or procedure. Revisions may include minor improvements, major changes, or typographical corrections. The date of change, revision number, and specific modification are included in the revision history.

- **Persons affected**. Identifies the users of the policy or procedure. The title may be changed to reflect categories of users (e.g., locations affected, departments affected, patrons affected, etc.).

- **Policy statement.** Is a predetermined course of action established to guide decision making in the facility. It reflects the agency's strategic direction as well as its culture. The aim is to support the core processes by channeling manager and staff behavior.

- **Definitions**. Explain abbreviations, acronyms, technical terms, or anything else that may not be understood through casual reading. Clearly describing forms is as important as defining technical terms. Any pertinent information should be included in the definition as well as the location of a current sample form.

- **Responsibilities.** Provides a summary of the personnel who have a duty to perform actions outlined in the policy or procedure. Responsibilities are listed in the same sequence as the activities listed in the policy or procedure section. Therefore, this section is typically written after the policy or procedure sections are completed.

- **Procedures.** Specifies the step-by-step instructions necessary to implement the policy from start to finish. The personnel, method, timing, and place for accomplishing specific tasks are outlined in detail.

It may seem as if the procedure section and the responsibilities section are repetitive, but each serves a distinct purpose. The procedures section tells which staff member should take action in a particular way at a given time. The responsibilities section focuses on where the policy or procedure fits within the agency's chain of command. Consider the refund policy example described in Figure 2.1.

It is important to include each of the seven principle headings when prescribing the facility's system of policies and procedures. It is not acceptable to eliminate a heading. If there is no content to be included in the section, then the words "not applicable" are inserted under the appropriate heading. The instructions for completing forms should be incorporated into the form itself. Instructions should not be contained in the body of the procedure unless the main point of the procedure is completion of the form.

Writing Style and Numbering System

Writing well is not an easy process. It requires tremendous effort to combine creativity with attention to detail to produce a thorough, meaningful policies and procedures manual which is easy to navigate and comprehend. Good writing expresses ideas in a way that is clear, concise, tactful, courteous, and reader specific. Sentences are typically 20 words or less. It is best to use short, familiar words that are easy to retain for later application. The same verb tense should be maintained throughout the manual. Typically, simple present tense is used; although, there may be occasions when past or future tense is appropriate (Conn, 1991).

Policy Title: Refund Policy

1.0 Purpose
This policy establishes guidelines for the business process by which patrons may request a refund.

2.0 Revision History

Date	Revision #	Change	Reference Section
10/20/2009	1.0	New procedure	Forms – Refund Requisition

3.0 Persons Affected
All employees authorized to complete financial transactions.

4.0 Policy Statement
The Sport and Recreation Facility permits refunds in the event that programs and services are changed to an alternative time or place not listed in the programming brochure. Further, patrons may withdraw from any program and request a refund within seven (7) days of the first session.

5.0 Definitions
Not applicable

6.0 Responsibilities
6.1 Staff members will use the current Refund Requisition form and adhere to established guidelines   for completion.

6.2 Business manager will ensure compliance with policy and authorize release of agency funds.

7.0 Procedures
7.1   Staff member asks the patron to complete and sign a current Refund Requisition form.

7.1.1 The staff member reviews the form to confirm all entries are complete and the patron has signed the form.

7.1.2 The staff member submits the form to the business manager for approval and processing.

7.2   Business manager confirms the rationale for refund complies with policy.

7.2.1 If approved, the business manager enters the refund amount into the financial tracking system software and authorizes the release of funds. Refund check is processed within 5 business days.

7.2.2 If not approved, the business manager authorizes the release of customer service letter indicating why refund is not approved.

Figure 2.1. Example of a Policy Using the Seven Principle Headings

Policies and procedures should be written using gender neutral terms and preferred styles in spelling, capitalization, and punctuation. Stereotypical or biased terms should not be used. Abbreviations and acronyms should be avoided unless the facility manager is certain the casual reader will understand. When abbreviations are used, spell out the word first and then place the abbreviation in parentheses immediately following the spelled out word. Generally speaking, the policies and procedures manual should be prepared at a reading level appropriate to the intended user. Examples may be incorporated into the manual to illustrate key points and processes.

The numbering system used in the policies and procedures manual should be straightforward and easy to comprehend. The numbers may be assigned sequentially, beginning with an even number such as 100 or 1,000. If necessary, provisions could be made to assign a predetermined range of numbers to specific topic area (e.g., 2,000–2,999 may refer to hiring, training, evaluating, and terminating employees). There are three common numbering systems: Roman numerals, Arabic numbers, or decimal numbers. Any method is acceptable so long a each entry in the policies and procedures manual is numbered.

Drafting and Revising Documents

Once the facility manager identifies the problem and researches potential solutions, the next step is to draft and revise the propose policy and procedure. The goal of the drafting process is to quickly fill in each of the seven section headings. Somewhat like free style writing, the principle is to capture and sort as much information as possible.

Initial and subsequent drafts are then revised to improve the organization and presentation of information. Ideally, more than one person is reviewing draft documents. Efficient editing does not come from a single, all purpose review. Rather, quality editing happens in stages, each with a different focus. The first reading checks the content of the document to confirm the material is complete, accurate, and appropriate for the intended audience. The second reading reviews language including vocabulary, grammar, punctuation, and spelling. The final reading checks content and language simultaneously. The writing style must be consistent throughout the document. Once complete, the professional tone and error free writing promotes confidence among users.

Forms Management

Forms are management tools that help in the writing, transmission, and reporting of business transactions in sport and recreation facilities. Simply put, forms are critical to an agency, because without them important information may be overlooked or processes done incorrectly. When creating or revising policies and procedures, the facility manager must determine whether a form must be created, changed, or eliminated. The essence of forms management is to create useful tools that meet the needs of the intended user. Potential barriers must be identified and removed if the form is to be completed correctly.

Distribution, Implementation, and Compliance

Once the policies and procedures manual is published, the writing process stops, and the distribution, implementation, and compliance processes begin. The goal is to ensure staff members read, understand, and comply with established guidelines. Regardless of whether the facility manager is producing a printed or online manual, the methods for writing the policies and procedures are the same. It is important to remember that establishing a system of policies and procedures is an ongoing, cyclical process. The cycle consists of writing, publishing, training, measuring, and revising policies and procedures. This process continues for the entire lifespan of the policy and procedure.

Distribution

A policies and procedures manual can be prepared using several different media. Printed text can be placed in a binder or stored on a CD-ROM. Electronic text may be posted on the sport and recreation facility's network or website. The decision as to whether the policies and procedures manual should be produced as a print or electronic document, or both, is typically made by the facility manager with input from staff members.

There are several advantages to having an online manual. Electronic manuals can be resized for easy reading and may include animation, voice, music, and video files. Keywords can be searched and clickable hypertext can be used to jump to corresponding forms. Online manuals are less likely to be lost in the workplace or carried off and not returned by a single user. Electronic manuals may also be updated and distributed instantly. However, should the computer system be inoperable for any length of time, the policies and procedures manual would not be accessible. It is recommended that at least a few hard copies of the manual be produced and stored in a central location.

Hard copy policies and procedures manuals are typically assembled in three-ring binders. Hard shell binders are preferred because this allows for the manual to be stored upright on the desk or shelf. Soft shell binders lie flat on the surface and may be covered with other documents. Slanted ring binders are recommended because it is easier to move between sheets. All documents should be organized with clearly labeled section dividers to facilitate quick and easy reference.

Implementation

Policies and procedures are considered implemented when they are distributed. However, distributing the policies and procedure manual does not guarantee staff members have read, understand, and apply the guidelines. There are two methods to ensure policies and procedures are understood and implemented as prescribed: control points and training.

A control point is a person within the agency who is a watchdog to ensure policies and procedures are being followed. When a violation occurs, the control point either explains the policies and procedures or refers the staff member to the manual. A control point should use a mentoring or coaching approach to help the staff member incorporate the proper methods into daily work.

Policies and procedures training seeks to increase the staff member's expertise and level of mastery in order to perform at the desired level. The repetition and reinforcement will enable the staff member to assimilate information more quickly than by trial and error. Training may be presented as staff meetings, workshops, or seminars; written text or online learning modules; and informal conversations between facility managers and staff members or between staff members. The best environment for training is when there is an organizational culture that encourages open sharing of knowledge and ideas, continuous learning, and practicing new skills.

Compliance

Compliance measures begin as soon as the policies and procedures have been implemented. The facility manager does not really know if policies and procedures are accepted, understood, and applied unless steps are taken to verify conformity. The compliance plan is developed to determine the extent to which policies and procedures are implemented as prescribed, strengths and weaknesses of the policies and procedures infrastructure, and areas in need of refinement or change.

There are many techniques available to access compliance. Two common techniques used in sport and recreation facilities are system audits and self assessment checklists. A system audit involves a thorough review of the daily processes within the facility to determine if policies and procedures are being put into action and whether they are working to manage problems as intended. As part of this process, the facility manager conducts interviews with staff members as well as creates Fishbone diagrams (i.e., graphic display of cause and effect relationships with increasing detail at lower levels) and matrix diagrams (i.e., graphic display of the presence and strength of relationship).

Self-assessment checklists are a feedback tool in which the staff member responds to a series of yes/no type questions. Checklists of 5 to 15 questions are used periodically to focus on specific areas of interest or concern. All policies and procedures are assessed over a period of time, although the facility manager should take care to avoid inundating staff members with checklists. Too many assessments at any one time will decrease the likelihood that the information received reflects the true state of affairs in the workplace.

Overcoming resistance to change is another important component of the compliance plan. Committed and insightful leadership is needed to develop an organizational culture that embraces change. Staff members must be able to talk openly and express opinions about problem causes and cures. The facility manager must work with staff members to ensure changes in policies and procedures are a smooth, nonthreatening process. Ultimately, it is the facility manager's responsibility to communicate the importance of change and its impact on achieving strategic goals. Moreover, changes in policies and procedures may have a significant impact on the staff member's quality of life.

Leadership

Facility management is critical in keeping any organization operating smoothly and efficiently. A facility that is well maintained and managed is one of the best public and consumer relations tool in an organization's arsenal. Further, event management is intimately related to facility management. They go hand in hand with each other and cannot be easily separated. An organization's facility and event manager must become involved in many tasks including, but not limited to, leadership, facility and event admission access control, crowd control and security, emergency operations, facility maintenance, operational policies and procedures, and human resources.

Leadership by Example

Attila the Hun, Napoleon, Marshall, Eisenhower, Patton, and Rommel believed that, under the right circumstances, every soldier in his army had the potential to be a general and lead the army in his absence (Beerel, 2009). Whether you hold that belief or not, the plain fact is that "natural" leaders do not just happen, nor does anyone have a divine right to lead or rule.

You do indeed have a marshal's baton in your own knapsack. Recognizing your leadership potential is the first step toward leading others. The second is being able to manage yourself before trying to manage others (Bennis, 1989). Finally, a third is self-expression, and the key to self-expression is understanding one's self and the world and the key to understanding is learning from one's own life and experience.

Leaders are people who are able to express themselves fully. They know who they are, what their strengths and weaknesses are, and how to fully deploy their strengths and compensate for their weaknesses. "Further, they know what they want, why they want it, and how to communicate what they want to others in order to gain their cooperation and support" (Bennis, 1994, p. 37).

Finally, success of leaders often is based on four steps: (1) becoming self-expressive, (2) listening to the inner voice, (3) learning from the right mentors, and (4) giving oneself over to a guiding vision. (Bennis, 1994; Miller, 2012; Night, 2014)

Leadership and the Facility and Event Manager

Leadership has been defined by many and it continues to be redefined. For the purposes of this chapter, leadership will be defined as a set of qualities that causes people to follow. Leadership requires at least two parties, a leader and a follower. Many experts have argued over what exactly causes a group to follow one person and not another, but the decision to follow a leader seems to come down to few common traits (See Table 2.1).

Table 2.1
Ten Characteristics of a True Leader

The following are the 10 characteristics of a true leader:

- Eager
- Cheerful
- Honest
- Resourceful
- Persuasive

- Cooperative
- Altruistic
- Courageous
- Supportive
- Assertive

(Bennis, 1994)

Leaders have the ability to inspire people to go beyond what they think they are capable of doing making it possible for a group to attain a goal that was previously thought unattainable. According to Miller (2012), leaders carry their followers along by (1) inspiring their trust, (2) acting consistently, and (3) motivating them by words and deeds.

Leadership boils down to a willingness to accept responsibility and the ability to develop three skills that can be acquired through practice—elicit the cooperation of others, listen well, and place the needs of others above your own needs. When you properly put these skills together, people begin to turn to you when they need direction.

Responsibility and Accountability

Leadership begins with the willingness to embrace responsibility. You cannot be a leader if you are afraid of responsibility and accountability. With responsibility comes the concept of accountability. If you cannot answer yes to the following question, you are not ready to become a leader. Do you have enough confidence in yourself to accept responsibility for failure?

One of the realities about placing the needs of others above your own is that you cannot blame other people. If you are the type of person who looks outward for an excuse instead of inward for a reason, you will have a hard time earning the trust of others. An absence of trust makes eliciting their cooperation more difficult which, in turn, makes it more difficult for you to lead, even if you have been given the title of leader.

On the other hand, the leader receives most of the accolades and rewards when things go well. No matter how hard your followers worked, no matter how modest you are, no matter how much you attempt to deflect credit to your entire team, yours is the name that people will remember. That is the great benefit of being the leader. Can you handle the limelight of success?

The Basic Ingredients of Leadership

Leaders come in every size, shape, and disposition. Yet they share some of the following ingredients (Bennis, 1994; Night, 2014):

- guiding vision;

- passion;

- integrity (i.e., self-knowledge, candor, and maturity);

- trust (i.e., constancy, congruity, reliability, and integrity);

- curiosity; and

- daring.

Table 2.2
Ten Ways to Master Leadership Skills

The following are the 10 ways to master leadership skills:

- Prepare
- Volunteer
- Keep an open mind
- Give speeches
- Develop discipline

- Meet deadlines
- Stay in touch
- Listen
- Cooperate
- Do things for others

Key Leadership Abilities

The trick to becoming a leader is to be able to elicit cooperation, to listen to the needs of others, and to put other people's needs ahead of your own with great consistency. After you decide that you can and want to embrace responsibility, leadership requires that you be able to do three things very well (Bennis, 1994; Miller, 2012; and Night, 2014) (See Table 2.2):

- Elicit the cooperation of others. You must be able to get others to buy into your vision of the future and the right way to get there.

- Listen well. You have to be able to gather many kinds of information from others in order to lead; doing so requires that you hone your listening skills. The old adage, "listen and HEAR before you speak," is very important when dealing with people.

- Place the needs of others above your own needs. Leadership requires that you be willing to sacrifice for a greater good.

Characteristics of Leaders Coping with Change

There are 10 characteristics for coping with change and creating learning organizations (Beerel, 2009; Bennis, 1994), including the following:

- leaders manage the dream;

- leaders embrace error;

- leaders encourage reflective backtalk;

- leaders encourage dissent;

- leaders possess the Nobel Factor (optimism, faith, and hope);

- leaders understand the Pygmalion effect in management (if you expect great things, your colleagues will give them to you — stretch, don't strain, and be realistic about expectations);

- leaders have what I think of as the Gretzky Factor (a certain "touch");

- leaders see the long view;

- leaders understand stakeholder symmetry; and

- leaders create strategic alliances and partnerships.

Building Leadership Tools

John F. Kennedy once said, "Leadership and learning are indispensable to each other." Learning about the job, the employees, and yourself is very important to a leader and his/her leadership ability. There are a number of leadership traits that need to be developed by the leader. The remainder of this section will discuss these traits (Bennis, 1994; Miller, 2012; Night, 2014).

- **Learning to use what you have**. Intelligence is critical to leadership because synthesizing information is often necessary in order to create a vision.

- **Responding to situations flexibly.** Gathering new information and adjusting a response to a particular situation requires intelligence. Instead of responding in a knee-jerk way, an intelligent person responds flexibly based on circumstances and needs.

- **Taking advantage of fortuitous circumstances.** You not only have to be smart enough to adapt to new information with flexibility, but you also have to have the courage to seize opportunities when they present themselves.

- **Making sense of ambiguous or contradictory messages.** A good leader listens to all the information and then sorts through it. You test contradictory messages by asking for more information in order to find the truth.

- **Ranking the importance of different elements.**

- **Finding similarities in apparently different situations.** One of the normal characteristics of intelligence is a talent for analogies. Analogous intelligence in leaders is the ability to draw on prior experience, no matter how tenuous the connection is, to find a similarity that you can use to solve a problem.

- **Drawing distinctions between seemingly similar situations.** You can find differences among situations just as often as you can find similarities and a good leader learns to recognize when A is not like B and emphasize the differences over what the two have in common.

- **Putting concepts together in new ways.** Along with analogies, one of the components of intelligence is the ability to synthesize new knowledge by putting together time-tested concepts in new ways.

- **Coming up with novel ideas.**

Communicating Effectively

First and foremost, a leader has to keep the vision in the minds of his or her followers in every conversation, whether in a spoken or unspoken manner. When a leader is speaking as a leader and not as a friend or confidante, he or she needs to remind people in a simple and straightforward manner and without a lot of additional explanation why they are being asked to turn the vision into reality. The responsibility of leadership is to communicate the vision so clearly that no room is left for doubt among those who must execute it. Finally, leaders must not only explain. They must also motivate their followers.

Assessing the Situation

One of the central components of leadership is listening. Your first challenge is to listen carefully to what you are being told about the position and situation. You need to gather information about the responsibilities your superiors are asking you to assume. Long before you meet your team, you need to make a quick but detailed examination of the group you are expected to lead and the current situation. Beerel (2009) suggests the questions to ask are these:

- What has the group's past performance been?

- Does management care about the group?

- Has the group's success or failure been short term or long term?

- Have there been many personnel changes in the team or is it stable?

- What are the group's goals?

- How does the group compare to similar groups in its ability to command resources?

- What is the commitment of the larger organization to the group?

Leaders are calculated risk takers. They get ahead by knowing when to say yes and they stay ahead by knowing when to say no.

Leaders Are Not Managers

A leader is not a manager and a manager is not a leader. There are enormous differences between leaders and managers (see below).

Manager ↓	Leader ↓
Administrators	Innovates
Copy	Original
Maintains	Develops
Focuses on systems and structure	Focuses on people
Short-range view	Long-range perspective
Relies on control	Inspires trust
Asks how and when	Asks what and why
Eye always on the bottom line	Eye on the horizon
Imitates	Originates
Accepts status quo	Challenges status quo
Classic good soldier	His own person
Does things right	Does the right thing
Wear square hats	Wear sombreros
Learn through training	Learn through education
Deductive	Inductive
Firm	Tentative
Static	Dynamic
Memorizing	Understanding
Facts	Ideas
Narrow	Broad
Surface	Deep
Direction	Initiative
Left brain	Whole brain
Common sense	Imagination
Rules	Risk
Rigid	Flexible
Reactive	Active

Leadership Theories

Over the past 50 years, a number of leadership theories have been developed; however, only a few have gained any popularity. The leadership theories that follow have remained popular in one form or another. Before discussing the leadership theories, it is important to understand that a manager's assumptions about people will influence how he or she behaves as a leader. Therefore, it is appropriate to review Douglas McGregor's Theories X and Y assumptions about people.

McGregor's Theory X and Theory Y

McGregor (1957) hypothesized that managers generally hold one of two contrasting sets of assumptions about people. He asserted that a manager's behavior as a leader would be influenced by the particular set of assumptions he or she held. Managers with Theory X assumptions (see Table 2.3) are autocratic leaders and rely on coercion, discipline, and penalties to accomplish organization objectives. However, managers with Theory Y assumptions (see Table 2.3) are democratic leaders, emphasize self-management and openly encourage subordinates to seek responsibility and share in the decision making necessary to accomplish organizational objectives.

Table 2.3
Assumptions about People

Theory X

1. The average person has an inherent dislike of work and will avoid it if possible.
2. Most people must be coerced, controlled, directed, and threatened with punishment to get them to put forth adequate effort toward achievement of organization objectives because of their intrinsic dislike of work.
3. The average person prefers to be directed, wishes to avoid responsibility, has relatively little ambition, and wants security above all.

Theory Y

1. The expenditure of physical and mental effort in work is as natural as play or rest.
2. External control and threat of punishment are not the only means for bringing about effort toward organization objectives.
3. People will exercise self-direction and self-control in the service of objectives to which they are committed.
4. Human beings learn, under proper conditions, not only to accept but also to seek responsibility.
5. The capacity to exercise a relatively high degree of imagination, ingenuity, and creativity in the solution of organization problems widely, not narrowly, distributed among the population.
6. The intellectual potentialities of the average person are only partially utilized under the conditions of modern industrial life.

Source: Adapted from *The Human Side of Enterprise* by Douglas McGregor, pp. 33–34, 47–48.

Trait Phase

The first leadership theory to be discussed will be the trait phase. The earliest attempts to understand leadership centered on determining what specific traits make a person an effective leader. A trait is generally defined as a distinctive physical or psychological characteristic that accounts for a person's behavior. This was later called the "great man" theory. After a number of years of study, researchers found little evidence for distinguishing leaders from followers. As a consequence, in the 1940s, researchers began to question the existence of unique leader traits.

Behavioral Phase

Researchers then shifted their attention to the study of leader behavior. This shift marked the beginning of the behavioral phase of leadership research. This phase of research held that leaders may be best characterized by how they behave, rather than by their personal traits. Underlying this phase was the assumption that effective leaders utilize a particular behavioral style that causes others to follow them.

A third phase in leadership research is known as the situational phase. Contemporary leadership theories are almost entirely situational in nature. In contrast to earlier theories, which focused on leader behavior, the newer theories attempt to explain effective leadership within the context of the larger situation in which it occurs. The most prominent of these situational theories are Fielder's contingency theory (1967, 1981; Fielder & Potter, 1983), House's path-goal theory (1971, 1974), and Vroom and Yetton's normative theory (1973; Vroom, 1984). The Contingency Theory defines leader effectiveness in terms of work group performance. It holds that work group performance is contingent upon the match between (1) a person's leadership style and (2) the favorableness of the leadership situation (Fielder, 1967, 1981; Fielder & Potter, 1983). Leadership style refers to a leader's manner of acting in a work situation. Situational favorableness refers to the degree a situation enables a person to exert influence over a work group.

The second situational leadership theory is called Path-Goal Theory of Leadership. This theory describes how leader behavior affects motivation, which depends on a person's belief that effort will lead to performance. The leader's task, in this model, contains two elements: (1) goal element, which is linked to the increased number and kinds of rewards subordinates receive for work-goal attainment, and (2) path-element, which makes the paths to these rewards easier to travel by removing obstacles that inhibit goal accomplishment. House (1974) and Beerel (2009) described four types of leader behavior:

- **Directive leadership** is characterized by a leader who informs subordinates what is expected of them and provides specific guidance on how to do it.

- **Supportive leadership** is epitomized by a leader who is friendly and approachable and shows concern for the status, well-being, and personal needs of subordinates,

- **Achievement-oriented leadership** is illustrated by a leader who sets challenging goals, expects subordinates to perform at their best, and shows confidence that subordinates will perform well.

- **Participative leadership** is portrayed by a leader who consults with subordinates and asks for their suggestions before making a decision.

The third leadership theory is the Normative Theory of Leadership. It offers normative guidelines for how decisions should be made in a specific situation. In doing so, it focuses on the extent a leader should allow subordinates to share in decision making. The following distinct decision-making methods have been identified (Vroom & Yetton, 1973):

- **Autocratic I** is characterized by managers solving the problem alone, using whatever is available at the time.

- **Autocratic II** is portrayed by managers who obtain necessary information from subordinates before making the decision alone.

- **Consultative I** is illustrated by managers sharing problems with subordinates individually, getting their ideas and suggestions before making the decision.

- **Consultative II** is epitomized by managers sharing problems with subordinates as a group, getting their ideas and suggestions before making the decision.

- **Group participation** is characterized by managers sharing problems with subordinates as a group, and together they make the decision.

The Leadership Grid Theory

Blake and Mouton (1985) developed the managerial grid (See Figure 2.1), which was later refined by Blake and McCanse (1991) as the Leadership Grid. The x-axis of the grid is labeled "concern for production" and the y-axis "concern for people." Each axis is divided into nine sections, numbered one through nine. Values are expressed as a pair of interdependent numbers. The first representing the x-axis (production) and the second representing the y-axis (people). There are five possible combinations, including 1,9 country club management (i.e., thoughtful attention to the needs of people for satisfying relationships leads to a comfortable, friendly organization atmosphere and work tempo), 9,9 team management (i.e., work accomplishment is from committed people, interdependence through a "common stake" in organization purpose leads to relationships of trust and respect), 5,5 middle-of-the-road management (i.e., adequate organizational performance is possible through balancing the necessity to get out the work while maintaining morale of people at a satisfactory level), 1,1 impoverished management (i.e., exertion of minimum effort to get required work done is appropriate to sustain organization membership), and 9,1 authority-compliance (i.e., efficiency in operations results from arranging conditions of work on such a way that human elements interfere to a minimum degree).

The Five Styles

Here is a snapshot of the five different leadership styles resulting from the grid (Blake & McCanse, 1991):

(1,1) Impoverished. The leader exerts (and expects) minimal effort and has little concern for either staff satisfaction or work targets. This is a leader who is going through the motions is indifferent, noncommittal, resigned, and apathetic. S/he is doing just enough to keep the job.

(1,9) Country Club. The leader is attentive to his/her people's needs and has developed satisfying relationships and work culture but at the expense of achieving results. The leader is defined as agreeable, eager to help, nonconfrontational, comforting, and uncontroversial.

(5,5) Middle of the Road (Politician). This leader is a compromiser who wants to maintain the status quo and avoid any problems. Is aware of and wants a focus on productivity but not at the expense of the morale of his/her team.

(9,1) Authoritarian. The leader concentrates almost exclusively on achieving results. People are viewed as a commodity to be used to get the job done. Communication is de-emphasized and conflict is resolved by suppressing it. Leadership is controlling, demanding, and overpowering.

(9,9) Team Leader. The leader achieves high work performance through "leading his/her people to become dedicated to the organizational goals. There is a high degree of participation and teamwork, which satisfies the basic need of people to be involved and committed to their work. The leader may be characterized as open-minded, flexible and one who inspires involvement" (p. 76).

Cautionary note: This model could lead you to think there is one best style. Please avoid that mistake. Certain styles work extremely well in different circumstances. If your plane is crashing, you would want the captain to use a 9, 1 style of leadership in that moment. At another time, a different style of leadership may be more appropriate (Blake & McCanse, 1991).

Leadership grid explains how leaders help organizations to achieve to achieve their objectives through the factors of concern for production or results (task behavior) and concern for people (relationship behavior). The grid consists of two axes: Y-axis represents concern for production while X-axis represents concern for people on a scale 9 points. 1 represents minimum concern and 9 the maximum.

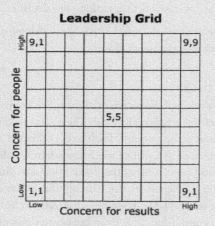

Authority–compliance management or task management (9,1)

Leaders who fall in this category heavily emphasize results with minimum concern for people. They consider people merely as a means to achieve desired results. The leader is often characterized as controlling, overpowering, overdriving, and coercive.

Country club management (1,9)

Leaders falling in this category are those who are concerned more welfare and personal needs of people and lack the focus on task accomplishment. The leader is often characterized as democratic but is also seen as ineffective in driving the people toward achievement of goals.

Impoverished management (1,1)

Leaders in this category are generally those who arrived here merely by means of their position, and are simply viewed as going through the motions of being a leader. They are characterized as indifferent, noncommittal, uninvolved, and withdrawn.

Middle of the road management (5,5)

Leaders in this category seem to achieve a "balance" between people relationships and results but are basically compromisers in nature. They compromise on conviction to make some progress and as a result miss out on push for results and also on drive for creating a true team culture. Such leader is characterized as avoiding conflicts.

Team management (9,9)

Leaders in this category consider people relationships, commitment, and empowerment as a means of achieving goals. They are open to learning, view conflicts as opportunity for innovative thinking, clarify goals, and set high expectations and provide learning opportunity for people in the course of completion of the task. Such a leader is characterized as driving trust and learning in the teams.

Figure 2.1. Blake and Mouton's Leadership Grid

Ethical Decision Making in the Workplace

Introduction

It is an often repeated statement that leaders do the right thing while managers do things right. In recent years, there has been more discussion about what is "right" than ever before. But, who sets the criteria for judging what the right things are? And right for whom?

In the workplace, recreation managers routinely face ethical issues that require making choices between a competing set of priorities and values. Principled decision makers make these choices while balancing a commitment to the individuals directly impacted by the decisions as well as the community they serve. Moreover, managers must have a clear understanding of their personal and professional standards (see an example of a code of ethics in Appendices available in the student and faculty resource center at www.sagamorepub.com) which set the parameters for decision making and allow the manager to model ethical behavior in the recreation setting. Of course, doing what is "right" sounds deceptively simple. Doing the right thing is grounded in an understanding of the sources of ethical standards, how ethical issues are created, and how to apply guidelines for ethical decision making.

Professionals in the recreation and sport industry routinely confront ethical issues when solving problems in the workplace. Managers and staff members are committed to doing what is right; although, the right decision may be difficult to discern at any given point in time. This is because co-workers bring with them differing beliefs and values that affect their ability to act as moral agents. This section begins by defining key terms and explains why moral reasoning is not always a rational process.

Beliefs, Values, and Morals

Any idea held to be true is called a belief. A manager's reasoning process involves using several types of beliefs. Descriptive beliefs can be empirically measured and determined to be true or false. For instance, the practice of consuming a sports drink immediately after a workout has been positively correlated with rehydration. After physical activity, many people now prefer to consume a sports drink rather than another type of liquid, such as water. Evaluative beliefs involve some positive or negative judgment about a characteristic or object of the belief. For example, it is widely accepted that completing 30 minutes of moderate cardiovascular exercise every day is associated with a healthy lifestyle. Prescriptive beliefs reflect a decision about the desirability of some action or means to an end. For instance, many people think it is a good idea to swim in a warm pool in order to increase joint mobility. Proscriptive beliefs reflect a judgment about the undesirability of some action or means to an end. For example, some managers think mowing sport fields following several weeks of arid weather will permanently damage the grass infrastructure. Therefore, they recommend the staff members to avoid mowing the lawns given certain conditions.

A person's belief system, developed over time through interaction with parents, peers, mentors, educational material, and social institutions may have a profound impact on how the manager makes decisions. Interestingly, Green (1971) explains humans have the innate capacity to maintain a system of beliefs that are inconsistent with one another. This is largely because humans have the ability to compartmentalize their thinking and are seemingly able to make judgments based on a system of hidden or unconscious beliefs. Consider the individual who says, "I don't know why, but I think people who do workouts at midnight are wrong." This belief may be related to several issues, such as a perception that nighttime workouts are shorter or less intense than daytime workouts and therefore less beneficial. The position may be based on a safety concern, such as participants are at more risk of assault in a relatively empty fitness center or walking to and from the parking lot. What is important to understand is that in the workplace, the manager's belief system can impact decision making in many ways, including his commitment to the employer or position, relationships with coworkers, or decisions about leaving the organization.

A manager's values are grounded in his belief system. A value is a construct that reflects a preference for specific behavior or achieved outcome. For example, the manager may value truthfulness, so he speaks honestly and avoids lies by omission. Similarly, the manager may prefer to be evaluated on work performance rather than years of service in the organization as the primary criterion for promotion. Keep in mind that while society through its various educational, religious, and political institutions attempts to sway the individual to appreciate certain ways of behaving or desired outcomes, the individual does not passively internalize these values. Rather, the manager is an active participant, merging social norms with his unique history and experience to transform and adopt particular values (Bodey, 2008). Individuals in a work group–division, department, committee, team, or partnership –can have considerably different value systems. Sometimes, it is difficult to discern what their values are because values cannot be directly observed rather they are inferred from the individual's behavior (Hughes et al., 2012).

Various researchers have suggested that values are largely influenced by broad social forces, such as significant historical events (e.g., 9/11 attack of the World Trade Center), technological changes (e.g., evolution of mobile phone), and economic conditions (e.g., worldwide banking crisis). Groups of people of a particular time seem to have a common value system that distinguishes them from people who mature at a different time. Misunderstandings that may persist between older leaders and younger followers are often attributed to differing value systems. However, researchers have found little evidence to suggest a generation gap in basic values exists. Rather, the tension generated through interactions between some leaders and followers may be related to differing tastes among older and younger coworkers rather than a different set of fundamental values (Hughes, Ginnett, & Curphy, 2012).

A person may hold many types of values. For instance, there are aesthetic, cultural, economic, educational, political, and religious values. Moral values, or morals, are the fundamental baseline values that dictate appropriate behavior in a society (Solomon, 1992). To put this in a slightly different way, moral values are the guideposts a society needs to function properly. For example, honesty, justice, fairness, responsibility, and respect are moral values. A non-moral value is happiness. While a manager may prefer to be happy and desire to associate with others who have a happy disposition, society would not break down if people did not value happiness.

Moral Agents and Moral Reasoning

A moral agent organizes his values into a value system. These sets of values then form prescriptions (i.e., statements of what to do) and proscriptions (i.e., statements about what not to do) that guide daily life (Lennick & Keil, 2004). Moral reasoning refers to the cognitive process managers use to make decisions about ethical and unethical behaviors in order to solve problems (Hughes et al., 2012). Values play an essential role in the moral reasoning process because value differences among individuals can result in different judgments about the "right" course of action. However, determining the "right" thing to do is not an entirely rational process. The nature of information processing in the human brain is a complex blend of neurological and cognitive activities and inherently involves non-conscious processes of association and judgment. One line of ethical decision-making research suggested that humans make moral judgments based on inner scripts that are triggered by the situation rather than formal or rational ethical reasoning. These scripts may be derived from religious training or vicariously learned from significant others. Advocates of this point of view suggested that promoting ethical decision making comes from a combination of training people to be better at ethical reasoning as well as increasing people's awareness of their ways of constructing the moral dimensions of a given situation (Hughes et al., 2012).

While most people believe they make ethical decisions, there is evidence to suggest their actions are not entirely consistent with their self-perceptions. Researchers have found four relatively pervasive unconscious biases which interfere with moral reasoning in the workplace.

Implicit prejudice. This involves unconscious beliefs or feelings toward certain people or groups that distorts the manager's expectations and judgments about the person or group. For instance, suppose the aquatics director has had previous experiences in which college-aged lifeguards contracted to work through pool closing at the end of the summer only to quit unexpectedly and with little notice several weeks early. During future hiring sessions, the aquatics director may select to hire high school-aged lifeguards rather than college-aged lifeguards not based on merit but on a disposition that all college-age workers are not trustworthy and likely to resign unexpectedly. Even when managers do build positive relationships with individuals from such groups, unconscious negativity may persist.

In-group favoritism. This involves showing preference for individuals who are similar to perceived personal characteristics (e.g., "like me"). Preference may take overt forms, such as hiring someone with the same educational background or experiences. Or preference may be more subtle, such as asking all assistant managers for project feedback but only considering the comments from those managers who have the same philosophical leanings. Overclaiming credit is a bias that exists when the manager overrates the quality of his work or contribution to the group. For instance, the individual may claim credit for an innovative program idea when, in fact, the program plan was a result of an iterative discussion among the manager and several staff members. A conflict of interest exists when competing professional or personal interests does not allow the manager to perform his duties impartially. A conflict of interest can create an appearance of impropriety that will undermine staff and patron confidence in the manager (Hughes et al., 2012). The manager should be aware these types of biases exist and routinely check for these biases either through self reflection or by sharing decision-making processes with a trusted colleague who may be able to point out flawed thinking.

Foundations of Ethical Decision Making

Many managers think that ethics is a question of individual scruples, a confidential matter between the individual and his conscience (Paine, 1994). If a recreation agency hires good people with strong values, then it will be an ethical organization. However, the ethical issues that arise in the recreation setting are complex. Beliefs and values are only a part of the discussion. This section will discuss sources of ethical standards, how to recognize ethical issues, and why good people sometimes do bad things.

Sources of Ethical Standards

In general, ethics is a branch of philosophy that delineates principles of right (versus wrong) action. Historically, ethics scholars have emphasized the importance of reasoning to determine rules or standards for proper conduct. Morality scholars consider how the rules and standards are applied in a given context to determine specific behavior. Business ethics, a subfield of ethics, focuses on the application of moral standards to the production, distribution, and sale of goods and services and other business activities.

Ethicality is a term used to describe the extent to which behavior is consistent with social standards. Sauser (2005) explains in the business context, ethics in assessed by comparing the manager's behavior to five types of standards. Statutory, administrative, and case law is a legitimate source of ethical guidance. While violating the law is almost always considered unethical, compliance with the letter of the law does not necessarily make a behavior ethical. Organizational policies are standards of behavior by specifying the right way to do the job task within the agency. Professional and trade association codes are similar to agency policies but tend to be more aspirational in nature in order to uphold the reputation of the profession or trade. Community (social) expectations are unwritten guidelines and change overtime. These social mores pertain to fairness or rightness and can be powerful determinants of a person's reputation. Finally, the individual's conscience reflects a moral standard based on personal, religious, or philosophical understandings of morality. None of these types of standards should be consider more important than the others. Rather, each standard provides a set of parameters which serve as a means to judge ethical behavior in the business setting.

Recognizing Ethical Issues

An ethical issue is a problem, situation, or opportunity that requires the individual to select among several actions that may be evaluated as right or wrong, good or bad, benefit or harm, propriety or impropriety, and ethical or unethical (Foster, 2005). Some examples may be padding expenses, violating confidentiality, misleading someone through false statements or omissions, or misusing company equipment. However, ethical decision making is not necessarily a matter of selecting a "right" action over a "wrong" action. A far more likely event is the choice between two or more "right" actions (Hughes et al., 2012). Suppose a manager has limited gymnasium space and must decide whether the space will be reserved on Saturday mornings for seniors' co-ed pickle ball matches, men's basketball games, or girls' volleyball practices. Alternatively, the manager may find that there is $2,000 remaining in the summer program budget. Should the money be given as bonuses to hard-working, underpaid staff members or rolled into the winter program budget? On the surface, each of these actions could be considered a "right" or "ethical" action. What is the manager to do?

Kidder (1995) has identified four common dilemmas that serve as models for framing ethical issues. Truth versus loyalty may be the manager's conflict between giving a negative performance evaluation (truth) to a long-term co-worker who has been a committed member of the organization (loyalty). Individual versus community may take the form of paying a new employee with much needed expertise a greater than market value salary (individual) which would result in no wage increases for the rest of the staff members (community). Short term versus long term may be the manager's decision to close the facility for several weeks to upgrade activity spaces that would reduce the revenue generated in the quarter (short term); however, the renovated spaces will allow for innovative programs to stimulate community use of the facility (long term). Suppose a staff member was 30 minutes late to work. Justice versus mercy would have the manager decide whether to dock the worker's pay (justice) or ask the worker to remain 30 minutes after hours to complete the work that must be done (mercy). While recognizing or categorizing issues does little to resolve ethical dilemmas, it is the first step in ethical decision making. Further, an integrity-based approach to ethical decision making combines a concern for the sources of ethical standards with an emphasis on managerial responsibility to respond in an ethical manner (Paine, 1994).

Why Good People Do Bad Things

What would motivate a manager to risk his career – often based on years of educational preparation, experience, and professional networking – when he has so much to lose from making an unethical decision? While each individual has a differing set of motives, the common dominator seems to be the manager took advantage of an opportunity when it was presented. The decision to act ethically or unethically is largely associated with the unique set of circumstance found in the situational context. In other words, research suggests it is less about faulty character or not possessing an ethical understanding and more about being in the wrong place at the wrong time (Gellerman, 2003).

There are many reasons why good managers do bad things in recreation settings. In some cases, there is no intention to reach an unethical decision. The manager may not be aware or does not have the relevant information and time to make an appropriate decision. In other cases, the manager lacks sufficient capacity to reconcile multiple and diverse pressures. However, there is evidence to suggest individuals knowingly engage in "mental maneuvers" when faced with difficult decisions. The outcome of these decisions, in some cases, may result in unethical behavior (Bodey, 2008).

Several barriers which undermine ethical decision making in the workplace are described in the literature. Managers sometimes oversimplify the problem and then select the familiar and easily formulated alternative when making a decision. Euphemistic labeling involves using terms to reduce the anxiety associated with unethical behaviors. For example, a manager may not feel compelled to report a coworker for "inappropriately completing a time card" when, in fact, the employee is "falsifying payroll documents." Advantageous comparison occurs when the manager compares his behavior to more odious behavior. Unethical behavior is made to appear ethical when it is compared to worse behavior. For example, reducing the participant slots in an after-school program for children with autism is compared to local agencies that completely eliminated programs designed for children with disabilities.

Displacement of responsibility is a mechanism by which the manager attributes responsibility to another for violating personal moral standards. For instance, the manager could justify a decision because "the board said I must make these staff changes" to achieve a cost-savings outcome. While the board may have requested cost-savings measures be implemented, it may not have specified the manner to achieve the outcome (i.e., cut staff). A related mental maneuver is to attribute blame elsewhere by justifying immoral behavior by claiming it was caused by someone else. For example, consider a staff member who overcharges for admission but blames the customer for not checking the receipt. Diffusion of responsibility exists when inappropriate behavior is easier to do when it is justified by an "Everybody is doing it" rationalization. For instance, a significant reduction in membership services without telling patrons about the changes is justified because other local agencies have cut services and we need to remain competitive in the marketplace. Disregard for consequences minimizes the harm caused by the specific behavior.

In general, people want to be liked; but, when the need to be liked interferes with impartiality or objectivity, it then becomes a problem because the manager may ignore ethical transgressions. The overconfident manager discounts the perceptions of other people, preferring to consider only his preference about alternatives. As a result, the individual may be blind to the most appropriate ethical choice (Hughes et al., 2012; Kerns, 2005).

Guidelines to Ethical Decision Making

A regular decision involves a choice between two or more alternatives. An ethical decision has an additional connotation of what "should" be done in a particular situation. "Should" statements come from individual values and ethical principles as well as organizational values and mission statement. Most people consider what is "right" to be the action that betters the community, organization, and fellow human beings and complies with existing ethical standards. Once an ethical issue has been identified, the manager must decide how to resolve it. In many cases, the "right" course of action is not entirely clear. The manager should remember that ethical decision-making is less about finding the one and only "right" thing to do than it is about finding the "better" thing to do (Bodey, 2008). This section outlines some specific strategies for ethical decision making and provides suggestions for building a strong ethical culture in the workplace.

Three Principles

Kidder (1995) suggested three underlying principles for resolving ethical issues. Ends-based thinking considers the consequences of a decision and selecting the option that is best for the greatest number of people. Rules-based thinking defends standards for behavior outlined in laws, regulations, and policies. Finally, case-based thinking considers the Golden Rule: Do to others as you want others to do to you. Kidder recommended applying all three principles to the specific circumstance in order to reach an ethical decision among competing options.

Stakeholder approach. Using this approach, the manager attempts to create a win-win situation so that all the relevant constituents benefit to some degree from a decision. Essentially, this involves an analysis of benefits and burdens. For each possible decision, consider who will receive the benefit and to what degree from the action and who will carry the burden and to what degree from the action. Consider the following request from long time club members, "We would like the fitness center to remain open until 10 p.m. each night" when the club usually closes at 8 pm. There are two assistant managers and 10 full-time staff members employed by the agency. What is the ethical thing to do in this situation?

Result approach. This strategy suggests the manager consider a series of assessments. In end-result ethics, the action or decision outcome is evaluated against the expected consequences. Rules ethics consider relevant policies and procedures. Organizational values ethics requires the manager to consider the acknowledged written and unwritten agency rules. Personal conviction ethics is an assessment of how a decision corresponds with personal beliefs and principles. For example, consider a proposal where the local parent-operated soccer club wishes to rent all the outdoor playing fields all day on Saturdays and Sundays from May through December. Using end-results ethics, the manager judges whether the consequences (revenue generated from rental fees) justify the decision (reduction in participation opportunities for other participants). Rules ethics determine the appropriate course of action based on governing or authorizing body policies (e.g., park board, city council). When assessing organizational values, the manager determines whether renting to a private community organization fits the agency's mission and goals. Finally, the manager must ascertain whether he believes it is right to provide exclusive use of public facilities (for a fee) for private entities.

FILOP. Much like the previous guidelines, using the FILOP method requires the manager to consider a series of questions in order to develop a well-rounded perspective on an ethical problem. Using FILOP, the manager determines: What are the Facts shaping the dilemma?, How can the ethical Issue be framed?, What Laws (or regulations) are relevant in the situation?, What are the potential Options for consideration?, and How do Principles shape behavior?

For instance, consider the concessions manager at the community softball complex. It has become apparent the concessions inventory does not match the purchase orders. The concession stand staff is primarily high school-aged workers. First, the manager must determine the facts. What is the extent of the problem? Who may be involved? How long has the problem existed? Second, the issue must be identified. This assessment may be difficult because most problems are complex with overlapping causes and effects. For instance, was all the ordered merchandise received from the distributor? Are the concessions being stored in the wrong place? Are staff members stealing or giving concessions away for free? Is the food not fit for consumption so the workers are disposing of the merchandise but not properly recording the information?

In terms of laws and regulations, clearly, if staff members are stealing merchandise there is a legal concern; but the manager must also consider how operating policies and staff training may have contributed to the situation. Next, the manager must generate options. Should the involved staff members be fired, reprimanded, or moved to another position? Should the operating manual or staff training be revised? Should additional supervisory personnel be assigned to games? Should the facility stop selling concessions? Finally, the manager must consider his personal values and principles. Perhaps, the manager believes mistakes are part of human nature and ought to be overlooked; but preparation and supervision are important. Training and accessible resources should be provided for staff members, and a supervisor will check inventory once the concession stand is closed at the end of the day. Using the FILOP process, the manager has a better understanding of the ethical issue and potential courses of action. Alternative decisions emerge which may be judged as "right" or "wrong." The manager proceeds to select the "best" or "most ethical" decision based on the circumstances.

Building a Strong Ethical Culture

A climate of integrity requires managers to build an ethical infrastructure that includes multiple strategies (Hatcher, 2003; Paine, 1994; Sauser, 2005). Recreation managers who wish to take measures to build a strong ethical culture in the workplace are advised to take the following steps:

1. Communicate mission and values statements to reflect important organizational obligations and aspirations. The guiding values and commitments must be integrated into the day-to-day business operations and routine decision making. Staff members will take them seriously if they see their practical importance and integration into strategic plans, allocation of resources, performance evaluations, and the like.

2. Adopt a code a conduct to extend the mission and value statements. These should be written in a language staff members understand. The code reflects an expectation for proper behavior and provides some guidance when ethical issues arise.

3. Conduct a core process analysis on an annual basis to spot ethical bottlenecks and leverage points. Specifically, look for conditions that create barriers or obstacles to desired outcomes or times when staff members may be highly stressed to meet deadlines or quotas. Next, empower staff members to demonstrate a commitment to ethical decision making in their relationships with suppliers, patrons, and so forth.

4. Implement a needs assessment to garner information from stakeholders about the organization's ethical strength and weaknesses. The manager must then take steps to any existing ethical disconnects.

5. Hire ethical people by investigating the applicant's character and checking references carefully. Approximately 90% of an interview is related to job capabilities with little time on character-based questions. The manager can interview for character by asking questions such as (a) What are your three core values?, (b) When was a time when you were challenged to compromise your integrity?, and (c) What would you do if your best friend did something illegal?

6. Provide ethics training as part of new employee orientation as well as during in-service professional development activities. Highly respected, ethical members of the organization may tell stories about how staff members are rewarded for ethical behavior. Keep the sessions informal and use "real-world" examples to facilitate discussions about ethical solutions.

7. Correct unethical behavior with specific, constructive feedback. Remember to ask the employee probing questions in order to uncover unknown bottlenecks, stresses, or other infrastructure mechanism that may contribute to unethical decision making. Use of a progressive discipline system signals to all staff members that unethical behavior will not be tolerated.

8. Leading by example is an essential component of a strong ethical culture. Managers must be credible, committed, and able to scrutinize their own decision making. Further, the manager must have the competencies needed to make tough calls when ethical obligations conflict.

9. Be proactive by adopting best practices from other agencies or national recreation organizations.

Collectively these strategies will facilitate a climate for responsible and ethical behavior. However, strong ethical culture relies on an ongoing commitment of attention, time, and resources in order to thrive.

Building an Ethical Workplace

An ethical climate in the workplace exists when the standards and norms are clearly and pervasively communicated throughout the agency. The manager embraces and enforces these standards through words and actions. An unethical climate exists when questionable (or obvious) unethical behaviors are condoned or little action is taken to address such misbehavior. Fostering an ethical climate begins by empowering staff members to address perceived ethical problems in a civil and constructive manner as well as creating a sense of shared leadership. Nonetheless, creating an ethical climate is not as easy as it sounds. Even when the agency has clear mission and value statements, conflict may exist when managers or staff members have divergent perceptions of whether each other's decision making or actions embody the agency's values. Moreover, conflict may exist if the agency's formal and informal operating policies and procedures appear inconsistent with its stated values.

Managers play a vital role in establishing the ethical climate in a workplace. First, a manager can reinforce organizational values by having a clear understanding of his or her philosophy—consisting of personal and professional values and ethical principles—and formally and informally communicating this point of view to all staff members in the agency. Next, the manager must strive to be an ethical role model. Not all ethical role models are the same, but there are categories of attitudes and behaviors that seem to exemplify ethical leadership (Hughes et al., 2012; Northouse, 2004):

1. **Respect others.** Show care, concern, and compassion for others. Seek input from staff members and truly listen to what they say in the conversation. Demonstrate value for the person, not just the worker, by focusing on positive contributions and forgiving honest mistakes. Value individual differences and exhibit appreciation for divergent viewpoints amid disagreements.

2. **Be honest and fair.** Be open with others and represent reality in a full and complete way. Being honest is more than telling the truth. It means not promising more than can be delivered, avoiding obligations, and evading accountability for decisions. Being fair means treating all staff members in an equitable way. There is a just distribution of work and equal opportunity for rewards. Any grounds for differential treatment are clear, reasonable, and based on sound moral values.

3. **Establish and enforce high ethical standards.** Articulate an ethical vision and do not compromise the high standards for behavior that it implies. Mentor all staff members to accept responsibility for their actions and to hold one another accountable for behavior. Prioritize ethical behavior above personal or short-term agency interests.

4. **Serve others.** Nurture staff members' needs, values, and purposes. Prioritize workers' welfare and act in ways to benefit staff members through mentoring, team building, and empowered self-direction. Help workers to be competent and to feel competent.

Finally, the manager can build an ethical workplace by implementing multiple strategies, including the following:

1. **Communicate a core ideology reflected in the agency's mission statement.** It represents the agency's purpose, guiding principles, and fundamental values. The ideology must be integrated into the day-to-day business operations and routine decision making. Staff members will view the core ideology as legitimate if they see it integrated into strategic plans, allocation of resources, performance evaluations, and the like.

2. **Adopt formal ethics policies and procedures to complement the mission and value statements.** This code reflects an expectation for proper behavior and provides some guidance when ethical issues arise as well as reporting mechanisms, disciplinary procedures, and penalties for suspected violations. The policies and procedures should be written using language staff members understand and be as unambiguous as possible.

3. **Perform a core process analysis such that the agency's structure and standard operating procedures are designed to encourage higher ethical performance.** Look for conditions that create barriers to desired outcomes. Focus attention on *how* goals are achieved rather than simply on *if* the goal was achieved.

4. **Hire ethical people by interviewing for character and checking references carefully.** Ask questions to discern personal and professional core values and experience handling ethical issues in the workplace. Select individuals whose values and behaviors are congruent and transparent.

5. **Provide ongoing ethics training as part of new employee orientation as well as during in-service professional development activities.** Use storytelling to convey key concepts and keep the sessions informal. Ground the discussions in "real-world" examples to facilitate conversations about ethical problems and solutions.

6. **Correct unethical behavior with specific, constructive feedback.** Performance evaluation systems that allow opportunities for staff members to give anonymous feedback increases the likelihood that unacceptable behaviors will be reported. Implement reward systems that emphasize repeated desired behaviors in the workplace.

7. **Be proactive by communicating with colleagues in similar agencies and adopting best practices from other sport and recreation facilities** (Paine, 1994; Sauser, 2005).

Implemented well, these strategies will collectively facilitate a climate for responsible and ethical behavior among staff members. However, strong ethical culture relies on the manager's and staff members' ongoing commitment for it to be a living part of the agency.

References

Alvesson, M. (2012). *Understanding organizational culture* (2nd ed). Los Angeles: Sage Publications Ltd.

Beerel, A. (2009). *Leadership change management.* Los Angeles: Sage Publications Ltd.

Bennis, W. (1989). *Why leaders can't lead: The unconscious conspiracy continues.* San Francisco: Jossey-Bass Publishers.

Bennis, W. (1994). *On becoming a leader.* Cambridge, MA: Perseus Books.

Bedeian, A. G. (1986). *Management.* New York: The Dryden Press.

Bible, M., & Bivins, S. (2010). *Managing project portfolio management.* Fort Lauderdale, FL: J. Ross Publishing

Blake, R. R. & Mouton, J. S. (1981). *Grid approaches for managerial leadership in nursing.* St. Louis, MO: CV Mosby.

Blake, R. R., & McCanse, A. A. (1991). *Leadership dilemmas-grid solutions.* Houston, TX: Gulf Publishing Co.

Bodey, K. J. (2008). Foundations of ethical decision making. In T. H. Sawyer, K. J. Bodey, & L. W. Judge (Eds.), *Sport governance and policy development: An ethical approach to managing sport in the 21st century* (pp. 63–76). Urbana, IL: Sagamore.

Bremer, M. (2012). *Organizational culture change.* Zwollw, Netherlands: Kikker Groep.

Conn, J. H., & Malloy, B. P. (1989). *Organizing policy for interscholastic athletic programs.* Carmel, IN: Benchmark Publishing.

Conn, J. H. (1991). An open-book policy. *Athletic Business, 15*(2), 57–60.

Deming, W. E. (1982). *Quality, productivity, and competitive position.* Cambridge, MA: MIT Center for Advanced Engineering Study.

Draft, R. L. (2001). *Essentials of organizational theory and design* (2nd ed). Cincinnati: South Western Publishers.

Draft, R. L. (2007). *Organizational theory and design* (9th ed.). Cincinnati: South Western Publishers.

Drucker, P. F. (1974). *Management: Tasks, responsibilities, practices.* New York: Harper & Row.

Fayol, H. (1949). General and industrial management, (translated by Constance Storrs). London: Pitman.

Fielder, F. E. (1967). *A theory of leadership effectiveness.* New York: McGraw-Hill.

Fielder, F. E. (1981). Leadership effectiveness. *American Behavorial Scientist, 24*, 619–632.

Fielder, F. E., & Potter III, E. H. (1983). In H. Glumberg, P. Hare, V. Kent, & F. Martin (Eds.), *Dynamics of leadership effectiveness. Small Groups and Social Interaction,* (1) 407–412. Chester, U,K,: Wiley.

Foster, G. D. (2005). Ethics: Time to revisit the basics. In J. E. Richardson (Ed.), *Business ethics* (17th ed.) (pp. 5–10). Dubuque, IA: McGraw-Hill.

Gellerman, S. W. (2003). Why corporations can't control chicanery. *Business Horizons, 3*, 17–24.

Green, T. (1971). *The activities of teaching.* New York: McGraw-Hill.

Gulick, L., & Urwick, L. (Eds.). (1937). *Papers on the science of administration*. New York, NY: Institute of Public Administration.

Hersey, P., & Blanchard, H. (1972). *Management of organizational behavior: Utilization of human resources* (2nd ed.). Englewood Cliffs, NJ: Prentice Hall.

Hicks, G. H., & Gullet, C. R. (1975). *Organizations: Theory and behaviour*. New York, NY: McGraw-Hill.

House, R. J. (1971). A path-goal theory of leader effectiveness. *Administrative Science Quarterly, 16,* 138–139.

House, R. J. & Mitchell, T. R. (1974). Path-goal theory leadership. *Journal of Contemporary Business,* (2) 81–87.

Hughes, R. L., Ginnett, R. C., & Curphy, G. J. (2012). *Leadership: Enhancing the lessons of experience* (7th ed.). New York: McGraw Hill/Irvin Publishers.

Kerns, C. D. (2005). Why good leaders do bad things. In J. E. Richardson (Ed.), *Business ethics* (17th ed.) (pp. 13–15). Dubuque, IA: McGraw-Hill.

Kidder, R. (1995). *How good people make tough choices: Resolving the dilemmas of ethical living*. New York: Harper Collins.

Lennick, D., & Keil, F. (2004). *Moral intelligence*. Upper Saddle River, NJ: Pearson Education.

Mayo, G. E. (2003). *The human problem of industrial civilization* (Reprint). NY: Routledge, Taylor & Francis Group.

McGregor, D. M. (1957). *The human side of enterprise*. New York: McGraw-Hill.

Miller, M. (2012). *The 30-day leadership management course*. New York: Kindle.

Mosley, D. C., Pietri, P. H., & Megginson, L. C. (1996). *Management: Leadership in action*. New York: HarperCollins College Publishers.

Mosley, D. M., Megginson, L. C., & Pietri, P. H. (2005). *Supervisory management: The art of inspiring, empowering, and developing* (6th ed). Cincinnati: South Western Publishing.

Night, B. (2014). *Management and leadership skills*. New York: Kindle.

Northouse, P. G. (2004). *Leadership theory and practice*. Thousand Oaks, CA: Sage Publications.

Odiorne, G. S. (1965). *Management by objectives: A system of managerial leadership*. New York: Pitman Publishing Company.

Page, S. (2009). *Best practices in policies and procedures*. Los Angeles: Company Manuals, Inc.

Paine, L. S. (1994). Managing for organizational integrity. *Harvard Business Review, 2,* 106–117.

Peabody, L. (2006). *How to write policies, procedures, and task outlines* (3rd ed.). New York: Writing Services, Inc.

Rodenz, E. (2006). *Management fundamentals*. Cincinnati: South Western Publishing.

Roethlisberger, F. J., & Dickson, J. W. (1943). *Management and the worker*. Cambridge, MA: Harvard University Press.

Sauser, Jr., W. I. (2005). Business ethics: Back to basics. Society for the Advancement of Management, 2, 1-4.

Slack, T. (1997). *Understanding sport organizations: The application of organization theory*. Champaign, IL: Human Kinetics.

Solomon, R. C. (1992). *Above the bottom line: An introduction to business ethics*. Fort Worth, TX: Harcourt Brace.

Taylor, F. W. (1947). *Principles of scientific management*. New York, NY: Harper.

Vroom, V. H., & Yetton, P. W. (1973). *Leadership and decision making*. Pittsburgh, PA: University of Pittsburgh Press.

Vroom, V. H. (1984). Reflections on leadership and decision making. *Journal of General Management,* (9) 18-36.

Weber, M. (1947). The theory of social and economic organization (translated by Talcott Parsons). New York, NY: Free Press.

Williams, C. (2007). *Management* (4th ed). Cincinnati: South Western Publishing

Yukl, G. (2010). *Leadership in organizations* (7th ed.). Upper Saddle River, NJ: Prentice Hall.

CHAPTER 3

Planning for Success

Thomas H. Sawyer

Professor Emeritus, Indiana State University

Introduction

Planning is the process of determining the organization's goals and objectives and selecting a course of action to accomplish them within the environment and within and outside the organization. Its primary purpose is to offset future uncertainties by reducing the risk surrounding the organization's operations. It requires the organization to review its internal accomplishments (strengths) and challenges (weaknesses) and external opportunities and threats.

SWOT Analysis
A Key Tool in Situational Analysis

It requires the organization to review its internal accomplishments (strengths) and challenges (weaknesses) and external opportunities and threats. During this process the organization will develop a SWOT chart (i.e., the depiction of internal strengths and weakness and external opportunities and threats) and identify internal and external connections that will allow the organization to become strategically competitive in the future (see Figure 3.1). Planning is essential for facility managers. The planning process is best facilitated by the use of brainstorming.

The SWOT analysis is a valuable step in situational analysis. Assessing your firm's strengths, weaknesses, market opportunities, and threats through a SWOT analysis is a very simple process that can offer powerful insight into the potential and critical issues affecting a venture.

The SWOT analysis begins by conducting an inventory of internal strengths and weaknesses in the organization. Next are the external opportunities and threats that may affect the organization, based on the market and the overall environment. Do not be concerned about elaborating on these topics at this stage. Bullet points may be the best way to begin. Capture the factors that are relevant in each of the four areas.

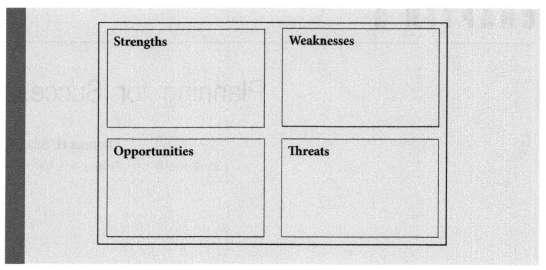

Figure 3.1. SWOT Analysis Chart

The primary purpose of the SWOT analysis is to identify and assign each significant factor, positive and negative, to one of the four categories. The SWOT analysis will be a useful tool in developing and confirming goals and a marketing strategy.

Strengths

Strengths describe the positive attributes, tangible and intangible, that are internal to the organization. They are within the organization's control. What does the organization do well? What resources does the organization have? What advantages does the organization have over the competition?

An organization may want to evaluate its strengths by area, such as marketing, finance, manufacturing, and organizational structure. Strengths include the positive attributes of the people involved in the organization, including their knowledge, backgrounds, education, credentials, contacts, reputations, or the skills they bring. Strengths also include tangible assets such as available capital, equipment, credit, established customers, existing channels of distribution, copyrighted materials, patents, information and processing systems, and other valuable resources within the organization.

Strengths capture the positive aspects internal to the organization that add value or offer a competitive advantage. This is the organization's opportunity to remind itself of the value existing within the organization.

Weaknesses

Note the weaknesses within the organization. Weaknesses are factors that are within the organization's control that detracts from the ability to obtain or maintain a competitive edge. Which areas might the organization improve?

Weaknesses might include lack of expertise, limited resources, lack of access to skills or technology, inferior service offerings, or the poor location of your business. These are factors that are under the organization's control, but for a variety of reasons they are in need of improvement to effectively accomplish the organization's objectives.

Weaknesses capture the negative aspects internal to the organization that detract from the value of the organization or place the organization at a competitive disadvantage. These are areas the organization needs to enhance in order to compete with its best competitor. The more accurately the organization identifies its weaknesses, the more valuable the SWOT will be for the organization assessment.

Opportunities

Opportunities assess the external attractive factors that represent the reason for the organization to exist and prosper. These are external to organization. What opportunities exist in the market or in the environment from which the organization hopes to benefit?

These opportunities reflect the potential you can realize through implementing your marketing strategies. Opportunities may be the result of market growth, lifestyle changes, resolution of problems associated with current situations, positive market perceptions about your business, or the ability to offer greater value that will create a demand for your services. If it is relevant, the organization should place timeframes around the opportunities. Does it represent an ongoing opportunity, or is it a window of opportunity? How critical is the timing?

Some experts suggest that you first consider outlining the external opportunities and threats before the strengths and weaknesses. Either Business Plan Pro or Marketing Plan Pro software (http://www.businessplanpro.com) will allow you to complete your SWOT analysis in whatever order works best for you. In either situation, you will want to review all four areas in detail.

Threats

What factors are potential threats to the organization? Threats include factors beyond the organization's control that could place the marketing strategy or the organization at risk. These are also external; the organization has no control over them, but you may benefit by having contingency plans to address them if they should occur.

A threat is a challenge created by an unfavorable trend or development that may lead to deteriorating revenues or profits. Competition—existing or potential—is always a threat. Other threats may include intolerable price increases by suppliers, governmental regulation, economic downturns, devastating media or press coverage, a shift in consumer behavior that reduces sales, or the introduction of a "leap-frog" technology that may make the organization's products, programs, or services obsolete. What situations might threaten the organization's marketing efforts? Get the organization's worst fears on the table. Part of this list may be speculative in nature and still add value to the SWOT analysis.

It may be valuable to classify your threats according to their "seriousness" and "probability of occurrence." The better the organization is at identifying potential threats, the more likely it can position itself to proactively plan for and respond to them. The organization will be looking back at these threats when it considers contingency plans.

The Implications

The internal strengths and weaknesses compared to the external opportunities and threats can offer additional insight into the condition and potential of the organization. How can the organization use the strengths to better take advantage of the opportunities ahead and minimize the harm that threats may introduce if they become a reality? How can weaknesses be minimized or eliminated? The true value of the SWOT analysis is in bringing this information together to assess the most promising opportunities and the most crucial issues.

An Example *(modified from Wright, Pringle, Kroll, & Parnell, 1998)*

Sawyer Sports is a sport retail store in a medium-sized market in the United States. Lately, it has suffered through a steady business decline caused mainly by increasing competition from larger sporting goods stores with national brand names. The following is the SWOT analysis.

Strengths

- ***Knowledge.*** Sawyer's competitors are retailers selling sporting goods products. Sawyer's is locally owned, provides local service and programs for the youth, and competitively prices its retail merchandise.

- *Relationship selling.* Sawyer's knows its customers on a one-on-one basis. Sawyer's direct sales force maintains a strong relationship with customers.

- *History.* Sawyer's is a fourth-generation business in this community. It has loyal customers and vendors. It is a local business.

Weaknesses

- *Costs.* The chain stores have better economics. Their per-unit costs of selling are quite low. They are not offering what Sawyer's offers in terms of knowledgeable selling, but their cost per square foot and per dollar of sales is much lower.

- *Price and volume.* The major sport retailers can afford to sell for less. Their component costs are less and they benefit from volume buying with the main vendors.

- *Brand power.* Take a look at their full-page color advertisement in the Sunday paper. Sawyer's cannot match that. They do not have the national name that allows national advertising.

Opportunities

- *Local area networks.* The franchise stores do not have local connections with students, parents, coaches, officials, and athletics directors.

- *Training.* The major stores do not provide training, but Sawyer's offers youth coaching seminars and other types of training.

- *Service.* As Sawyer's target market needs more service, its competitors are less likely than ever to provide it. Their business model does not include service, just selling the sporting goods.

Threats

- *Sporting goods.* Volume buying and selling of sporting goods as products in boxes, supposedly not needing support, training, services, etc. As people think of sporting goods in those terms, they think they need Sawyer's service orientation less.

- *The larger price-oriented store.* When they have huge advertisements of low prices in the newspaper, Sawyer's customers think they are not getting good value.

Brainstorming

Brainstorming, developed by Alexander F. Osborn (1888–1966), involves forming a group of six to eight members who are presented a problem and asked to identify as many potential solutions as possible. The session usually lasts from 30 minutes to an hour. According to Hussey (2012), at least two days before a session, group members are given a one-page summary of the problem they are to consider. There are four rules of brainstorming: (1) Criticism is prohibited; judgment of ideas must be withheld until all ideas have been generated. (2) "Freewheeling" is welcome; the wilder and further out the idea, the better. It is easier to "tame down" than to "think up" ideas. (3) Quantity is wanted; the greater the number of ideas, the greater the likelihood of an outstanding solution. (4) Combination and improvement are sought; in addition to contributing ideas of their own, members are encouraged to suggest how the ideas of others can be improved or how two or more ideas can be combined into still another idea.

Business leaders all over the world have used brainstorming techniques to solve problems for many years. Brainstorming is time consuming. If you only have a short period of time to loosen up a group and get everyone talking about solutions to a problem or inventing new initiatives, the answer is "fun and games" brainstorming.

Ensman's humorous, slightly offbeat techniques can be used to stimulate out-of-the-box thinking and discussion. They can be used to overcome marketing obstacles and productivity problems. They can help identify ways to enhance customer service, lower costs, improve an organization's image, and position an organization's operations for the future. Here are a few examples of "fun and games" brainstorming activities (Hussey, 2002):

- **"Castles in the sand.** The participants physically build a solution to the problem using blocks, putty, sand, or other materials.

- **Communication gaps**. Seat the participants in a circle. Whisper some variation of your current business problem into the ear of the first person sitting on the right in the circle. Ask that individual to repeat what was heard to the next person and so on until the message comes back around full circle. By that time, it will have changed—and the group may have a new perspective on the situation.

- **Detective work.** Appoint members of the group as detectives and charge them with solving the crime at hand. Group members must conduct an investigation, seek clues bearing on the problem, identify suspect causes of the problem, and eventually, pose a resolution of the case.

- **Make it worse.** Invite members of the group to imagine all the possible ways they could make the solution worse. In stark contrast to this humorous exercise, prospective solutions will probably abound.

- **Playmates.** Invite participants to bring a partner not connected to the group along to the brainstorming session and become part of the proceedings. Or, invite members of the group to select imaginary playmates such as historical figures, celebrities, or competitors and conduct imaginary discussions about the issues at hand with these individuals.

- **Pretend**. Invite the members of the group to portray the customers, employees, or vendors involved with the issue at hand. Then, let these characters address the issue in their own words (p. 96)."

The best way to identify items under each category is through the use of brainstorming with the organization's employees and others outside the organization. The category "external opportunities" relates to those unique favorable circumstances that the organization might be able to take advantage of in the future; whereas, the external threat category refers to those circumstances that might be harmful to the organization if not carefully understood.

Conducting a Needs Assessment Survey

Busser (2010), Fogg (2010), Hussey (2002), and others indicate the success of a facility or event thrives on its ability to fulfill the needs of its employees. Many facility and event managers administer needs assessment surveys to gauge client or community needs. Needs assessment surveys can help pinpoint the factors that determine everything from if employees plan to use employee services programs to whether or not the programs fit their needs. Use needs assessment surveys to evaluate current services or to predict if patrons will use new programs. The most difficult aspect of coordinating a needs assessment survey is determining which information is needed to plan for the future of your facility or event.

Categories of Needs Assessment Information

Busser (2010), Fogg (2010), and Hussey (2002) indicate there are eight major categories of information that can be collected through a needs assessment. Consider these categories of data collection to determine the information that will be needed: demographic data, user participation patterns or current levels of use, attitudes of employees, barriers to participation, predictions of future participation, appraisal of existing facilities and programs, health hazard appraisal, and areas of improvement.

Demographic data. This includes all relevant information regarding the demographics of employees. Demographic data includes age, gender, marital status, residential location, number of family members living at home, number and ages of children, work shift, and job classification. Demographic data is useful in constructing a profile of the needs for particular groups of users or participants. For example, single users or participants may be interested in fitness activities, while others with children may desire family programs. Use this information to focus your program development on the needs of that particular audience.

User participation patterns or current levels of use. This category assesses the frequency of participation in existing programs and services. These data are useful in determining participation trends (i.e., examining if existing programs and services are under- or overutilized given the allocated resources and tracking changes in participation from year to year). This information is also valuable when you are faced with the need to purchase additional equipment or to justify requests for new facilities. Registration data is often used to construct participation trends. However, the patterns of facility and equipment use usually are not contained in registration date.

Attitudes of the consumer. Busser (2010), Fogg (2010), and Hussey (1991) indicate it is essential to identify the attitudes and beliefs of consumers regarding the prominent aspects of program plans. Attitudes are the consumers' feelings related to the importance of various issues or services. Consider addressing consumers' attitudes such as the value they place on family programs, child care, elder care, and the opportunity to socialize with fellow users. The determination of these attitudes may be beneficial in setting objectives and establishing priorities for the facility or event.

Barriers to participation. Busser (2010), Fogg (2010), and Hussey (1991) suggest the barriers to participation are the constraints that consumers perceive as preventing their participation in programs or services. One significant barrier to participation revolves around consumers' lack of awareness or knowledge that a program or service exists. Other potential barriers include work schedules, family responsibilities, lack of interest, and lack of convenience. If these and similar perceived barriers to participation are explored in a needs assessment, the programmer can resolve those issues that may prevent consumers from participating in programs and services and thereby increase the effectiveness of the facility or event.

Predictions of future participation. If the provider is more concerned with long-term planning, ask the respondents to project their future needs. This is a very useful category of needs identification when considering equipment purchases, constructing new facilities, or deliberating contractual arrangements to supplement the existing services and programs.

Appraisal of existing facilities and programs. Give the consumers the opportunity to rate the quality of existing facilities, services, and programs. Use the feedback and evaluation data to prove the need for appropriate changes. In addition, this information provides insight into the current level of consumer satisfaction with the association.

Health hazard appraisal. Health hazard appraisals are standardized instruments used to evaluate the current health status of consumers and to estimate the presence of potential risk factors that are predictors for disease. Risk factors include smoking, stress, family history of disease, high blood pressure, high cholesterol, and poor nutrition. The health hazard appraisal evaluates a respondent's risks compared to national statistics on the causes of death, the consumer's medical history and lifestyle. Comparisons are then made with others in the same age and gender group. Use the results of the appraisal to explain specific recommendations to an employee. Results can also indicate potential areas for the development of services and programs.

Areas for improvement. This component of a needs assessment provides employees with the opportunity to share suggestions or issues related to the association and its programs, services, facilities, policies, and procedures. This willingness to go to the employees for their opinions fosters a dialogue, which indicates a commitment on the part of the association to resolve problems and to provide quality programs.

Collecting Data on Needs

Busser (2010) suggests once the facility or event manager has determined the kind of information he or she would like to uncover from the needs assessment, the next step is to collect the data. There are many research methods available to collect data on needs. Using research methods to conduct a needs assessment requires specific knowledge and skills in order to ensure that the data collected is valid and reliable. The validity of a need assessment refers to the degree to which the information collected accurately portrays the needs of employees. For example, a needs assessment that focuses only on satisfaction with special events is not a valid assessment of overall satisfaction with the facility or event and should not be used as such.

Reliability is concerned with the consistency of the data. Consistency indicates that the information obtained through the assessment truly represents the employees' perspective and is not influenced by outside factors. For example, a needs assessment that asks for overall program satisfaction may obtain different responses if conducted in the summer versus the winter, especially if a strong summer activities program is offered and no activities are provided in the winter. If the planner wants to determine comprehensive levels of satisfaction, the reliability of this assessment is doubtful. While several methods of data collection are appropriate for needs assessment, we will focus on the survey.

Surveys

Busser (2010) and Fogg (2002) suggest surveys provide the greatest opportunity to solicit consumer input and to generalize the findings from a smaller group of consumers to the community as a whole. Surveys require expertise from knowledgeable individuals to implement them successfully. Consider consulting the local and state chamber of commerce or a market research firm. Busser (2010), Fogg (2002), and Hussey (1991) suggest there are five steps in the survey process: (1) an operational definition of the purpose of the survey, (2) the design and pretesting of data collection instruments (e.g., the questionnaire or the interview guide), (3) the selection of a community sample, (4) the data collection, and (5) an analysis of the data.

The design of the questionnaire includes the development of the specific questions to be answered by consumers and decisions concerning the form of the questions (e.g., multiple choice, fill in the blank). At this stage, determine the directions for completing the survey, the procedures for carrying out the survey, and the method of returning completed questionnaires. Pretesting the data collection instrument is essential to uncovering and eliminating any difficulties that may exist in the data collection procedure. Pretests are mini-surveys you can conduct with a small group of employees by administering them the questionnaire and asking them to identify any difficulties in understanding directions, questions, or the type of information solicited.

Sampling is the use of particular procedures that allow you to generalize the findings of a representative small group of consumers to the whole corporate workforce. By selecting employees through a random process (e.g., selecting every 10th person from a random listing of employees), the results of the assessment are likely to be representative of the needs of all employees, even though all consumers were not surveyed (Busser, 2010).

In collecting the data from consumers, it is important that the cover letter of the questionnaire explains the purpose of the survey and indicates that the contributed information will be kept confidential. It is the ethical responsibility of those individuals conducting the survey to ensure anonymity for respondents. After sending the questionnaire to consumers, follow up with phone calls, memos, or other methods to continue to solicit the return of surveys. To be considered sufficiently representative, at least 35% of the surveys must be completed and returned. Try offering incentives to increase the return rate. For example, the organization could offer consumers a discount on programs or purchases in the pro shop for completing and returning the survey.

Once the provider has collected and tabulated the data, it can be analyzed. The frequencies and percentages of responses to particular questions may reveal significantly desirable information. The data should be carefully analyzed to answer the questions and purpose of the survey. These results, then, become the basis for decision-making regarding the needs of employees and the provided programs and services.

Developing a Needs Assessment Report

Compile a needs assessment report and present it to management. The most appropriate method of sharing this report is to compile tables, graphs, and statistics in a manner that is easily understood. Provide a comprehensive report to management and an executive summary to interested consumers. According to Busser (2010), the report should consist of the following components:

- "Title page

- Executive summary (i.e., a short introductory summary of the entire report to allow the reader a quick overview of the report prior to reading the entire report)

- Introduction to the needs assessment study purpose

- Overview of methods and procedures

- Results

- Conclusions and recommendations (p. 127)."

The Steps in the Planning Process

Busser (2010) and Fogg (2010) have suggested there are six steps involved in the planning process: identifying internal and external connections and relationships, establishing objectives, developing premises, decision making, implementing a course of action, and evaluating the results.

Step 1: Identifying Internal and External Connections and Relationships

The initial step in the planning process is identifying internal strengths (accomplishments) and weaknesses (challenges) and external opportunities and threats (concerns). This information is placed into a SWOT analysis chart that will assist in the identification of connections and relationships relating to the internal organizational environment and external environment.

Step 2: Establishing Objectives

The next step in the planning process is the establishment of the organization's objectives. Objectives are an essential starting point as they provide direction for all other managerial activities. Objectives are generally based on perceived opportunities that exist in an organization's surrounding environment.

Step 3: Developing Premises

Once organizational objectives have been established, developing premises about the future environment in which they are to be accomplished is essential. This basically involves forecasting events or conditions likely to influence objective attainment.

Step 4: Decision Making

After establishing objectives and developing premises, the next step is selecting the best course of action for accomplishing stated objectives from the possible alternatives. There are three phases of decision making: (1) available alternatives must be identified, (2) each alternative must be evaluated in light of the premises about the future and the external environment, and (3) the alternative with the highest estimated probability of success should be selected.

Step 5: Implementing a Course of Action

Once a plan of action has been adopted, it must be implemented. Plans alone are no guarantee of success. Managers must initiate activities that will translate these plans into action.

Step 6: Evaluating the Results

Plans and their implementation must be constantly monitored and evaluated. All managers are responsible for the evaluation of planning outcomes. Comparing actual results with those projected and refining plans are both necessary.

Classification of Plans

Plans can be viewed from a number of different perspectives. From the viewpoint of application, plans can be classified in terms of functional areas (e.g., marketing plans, production plans, human resource management plans, financial plans, etc.). Plans may also be classified according to the period of time over which they are projected (e.g., short or long range) or with respect to their frequency of use (standing versus single use). The nature of functional plans is evident. However, further explanation is needed for period of time and frequency of use plans.

Short- and Long-Range Plans

Short- and long-range plans are the most popular classification of plans. In practice, however, the terms short range and long range have no precise meaning, but rather express relative periods of time. These plans are interrelated in at least two respects. First, they compete for the allocation of resources. Consequently, there can be a dangerous tendency to sacrifice long-term results for short-term gains. Second, short-range plans should be compatible with long-range plans. It is usually difficult, if not impossible, for long-range plans to succeed unless short-range plans are accomplished. Thus, both are important in achieving an organization's objectives.

The term *short range* is often titled "operational" in many organizations, and *long term* has been changed to "applied strategic." These terms will be used interchangeably throughout the remainder of the chapter.

Paley (2005) and others suggest there are three criteria most often used in determining the length of a plan: (1) how far into the future an organization's commitments extend, (2) how much uncertainty is associated with the future, and (3) how much lead time is required to ready a good or service for sale.

Planning by most effective organizations is often done on a "rolling" basis. This simply means that those organizations that develop applied strategic plans for a five-year period and two-year operational plans are updating both plans on an annual basis. As the current year of a five-year plan closes, it is extended or rolled forward to include a new fifth year. This procedure allows an organization to revise its plans on the basis of new information and to maintain a degree of flexibility in its commitments. A general guideline outlined by Fogg (2010) is to refrain from formalizing plans until a final commitment is absolutely necessary.

Standing Plans

Standing plans are used again and again. The focus is on managerial situations that recur repeatedly. Standing plans include policies, procedures, and rules. Policies are general statements that serve to guide decision making. They are plans in that they prescribe parameters within which certain decisions are to be made. Policies set limits, but they are subject to interpretation because they are broad guidelines. Table 3.1 provides examples of policies. Notice that each example is purposefully broad and only provides a general guideline subject to managerial discretion. However, each statement does prescribe parameters for decision making and, thus, sets limits to the actions of organization members.

Table 3.1
Examples of Policies

Customer service	It is the policy of this organization to provide customers with the finest service possible within the limits of sound financial principles. [Interpretation = What are the limits of sound finance?]
Employee benefits	It is the policy of this organization to provide its employees with acceptable working conditions and an adequate living wage. [Interpretation = What is acceptable and adequate?]
Promotion from within	It is the policy of this organization to promote qualified employees from within organization ranks whenever possible. [Interpretation = What is meant by qualified or possible?]
Gifts from suppliers or vendors	It is the policy of this organization that no employee shall accept any gift from any supplier or vendor unless it is of nominal value. [Interpretation = What is nominal?]

Procedures

A procedure is a series of related steps that are to be followed in an established order to achieve a given purpose. Procedures prescribe exactly what actions are to be taken in a specific situation. Procedures are similar to policies in that both are intended to influence certain decisions. They are different in that policies address themselves to single decisions while procedures address themselves to a sequence of related decisions. Table 3.2 shows how an organization might write procedures for processing a bill of sale.

Table 3.2
Procedure for Processing a Bill of Sale

Step 1	Prior to recording, all noncash sales will be forwarded to the credit department for approval.
Step 2	Following necessary credit approval, all bills of sale will be presented to production scheduling for an estimated product completion date.
Step 3	Subsequent to production scheduling, all bills of sale will be delivered to the accounting department where they will be recorded.
Step 4	Pursuant to their processing in the accounting department, all bills of sale will be filed with the shipping department within 24 hours.

Rules

Rules are different from policies and procedures in that they specify what personal conduct is required of an individual. Stated differently, rules are standing plans that either prescribe or prohibit action by specifying what an individual may or may not do in a given situation. Therefore, the statements "Eye goggles must be worn," "No swimming alone," "No smoking," and "No drinking on premises," are all examples of rules. Rules are usually accompanied by specifically stated penalties that vary according to the seriousness of the offense and number of previous violations. Unlike policies that guide but do not eliminate discretion, rules leave little room for interpretation. The only element of choice associated with a rule is whether it applies in a given situation. Of the three forms of standing plans discussed, rules are the simplest and most straightforward. They are without question the narrowest in scope and application.

Single-Use Plans

Single-use plans are specifically developed to implement courses of action that are relatively unique and are unlikely to be repeated. Three principle forms of single-use plans are budgets, programs, and projects. A budget is a plan that deals with the future allocation and utilization of various resources to different activities over a given time period. Budgets are perhaps most frequently thought of in financial terms. However, they also are used to plan allocation and utilization of labor, raw materials, floor space, machine hours, and so on. A budget simply is a tool that managers use to translate future plans into numerical terms. Further, they are a method for controlling an organization's operations.

Programs are typically intended to accomplish a specific objective within a fixed time. Table 3.3 offers six guidelines for effective program development.

Table 3.3
Guidelines for Effective Program Development

1. Divide the overall program into parts, each with a clearly defined purpose.
2. Study the necessary sequence and relationships between the resulting parts.
3. Assign appropriate responsibility for each part to carefully selected individuals or groups.
4. Determine and allocate the resources necessary for the completion of each part.
5. Estimate the completion time required for each part.
6. Establish target dates for the completion of each part.

Projects are usually a subset or component part of a specific program. Accordingly, projects often share some of the same characteristics with the overall programs of which they are a part. Projects are less complex than their supporting programs and are, by definition, narrower in scope. Table 3.4 summarizes the various standing and single-use plans.

Strategic Planning

Strategic planning, unlike operational planning which focuses on more direct aspects of operating an organization, focuses on an organization's long-term relationship to its environment. The strategic plan should be developed through the participatory involvement by all members of the organization and its clients. By focusing on an organization as a total system, strategic planning recognizes that all organizations face many uncontrollable elements within the environment.

Table 3.4
Summary of Standing and Single-Use Plans

Type	Definition	Example
Standing Plans		
Policy	A general statement that guides decision making	"Preference will be given to hiring persons with disabilities."
Procedure	A series of related steps that are to be followed in an established order to achieve a given purpose.	Filing for travel expenses reimbursements
Rule	A statement that either prescribes or prohibits action by specifying what an individual may or may not do in a specific situation	"No eating at work stations."
Single-Use Plans		
Budget	A plan that deals with the future allocation and utilization of various resources to different enterprise activities over a given time	The allocation and utilization of machine hours
Program	A plan typically intended to accomplish a specific objective within a fixed time	A membership recruitment program
Project	A subset or component part of a specific program	A telemarketing project

Competitors' actions, economic conditions, regulatory groups, labor unions, and changing customer preferences represent factors over which an organization achieves its objectives. Therefore, strategic planning concerns itself with shaping an organization so it can accomplish its goals. Ansoff and Antoniou (2006), Park and Antoniou (2007), and others suggest that a strategic plan attempts to answer such questions as the following:

- What is the organization's business and what should it be?

- What business should the organization be in five years from now? Ten years?

- Who are the organization's customers and who should they be?

- Should the organization try to grow in this business or grow primarily in other businesses?

Ansoff and Antoniou (2006) and Park and Antoniou (2007) suggest that there are 10 steps in most strategic planning processes. These steps are as follows:

- Establishing a purpose, mission, and vision for the plan

- Evaluating the environment in which the organization operates through a needs assessment couples with a SWOT analysis

- Making assumptions based on the implications drawn from step 2

- Establishing goals and objectives

- Development of action strategies to reach the goals and objectives

- Preparing operational plans
- Developing an evaluation process for reviewing the overall plan
- Preparing a controlling process to maintain the movement of the plan
- Developing a plan for performance appraisal and reward

Goals and Objectives

Goals are those ends that an organization seeks to achieve by its existence and operation. Objectives are the key steps that must be taken to complete the goal. There are two essential characteristics of an objective: (1) objectives are predetermined, and (2) objectives describe future desired results toward which present efforts are directed. There are eight key result areas in which all organizations should establish objectives: market share, innovation, productivity, physical and financial resources, profitability, manager performance and development, worker performance and attitude, and social responsibilities.

There are two ways to establish objectives. The first is the entrepreneurial method. Entrepreneurs establish objectives in the entrepreneurial method (top management or stockholders). An organization's objectives are defined as the entrepreneur's objectives. The entrepreneur ensures that employees' actions are consistent with these objectives by paying them salaries, bonuses, or pensions to support the goals.

The second method is the consensual method. In this method, the objectives of an organization are established by the general consent of those concerned. Organization members share in setting the objectives and, thus, eliminate conflict by identifying common or consensual goals.

The Planning Premise

Once the enterprise objectives have been established, developing planning premises about the future environment in which they are to be accomplished is essential. Unfolding environmental conditions almost invariably influence enterprise objectives, forcing modifications in both current and anticipated activities. Premises, which attempt to describe what the future will be like, provide a framework for identifying, evaluating, and selecting a course of action for accomplishing enterprise objectives (Ansoff & Antoniou, 2006; Park & Antoniou, 2007).

The applied strategic plan is composed of a situational analysis, highlights, introduction, vision statement(s), value(s), mission statement, internal environment, external environment, connections, major action plans, major action priorities, monitoring and evaluating, and review, approval, and commitment (Ansoff & Antoniou, 2006; Park & Antoniou, 2007). The situational analysis has five sections, including a description of the geographical location and pertinent demographics (e.g., population, economic indicators, industry, average income, etc.), a description of the organization, a SWOT summary, an overview of major strategies and plans, and an organization progress since last review.

The highlights section describes major challenges, customer/client needs, and major accomplishments. The introduction provides the reader with a brief description of the planning process and the people involved in the process. The vision statement describes the dream of the future for the organization. The values section describes that which is desirable or worthy of esteem by the organization (e.g., fostering a "we care" image with our clients). The mission statement is a statement outlining the purpose and mission of the organization. The internal environment is composed of a description of the organization's strengths (accomplishments) and weaknesses (challenges) and the external environment consists of a description of the organization's external opportunities and threats (concerns). After the internal and external environments have been analyzed, a series of connections are established based on the relationships found in the analysis. From the connections, a series of major action plans are established. The actions plans are then translated into major action priorities. These major action priorities are the foundation for the one- or two-year operational plan. The applied strategic plan must have established monitoring and evaluating procedures in place to assure the proper implementation of the plan. Finally, there must be review, approval, and commitment steps established for the final acceptance of the plan (See Sample Applied Strategic Plan in Appendices available in the student and faculty resource center at www.sagamorepub.com).

The operational plan includes the following components: major action priorities, problems, project summary, priority issue(s), background, vision of success, goals and objectives of the plan, and action plans (strategies, objectives, baseline data, and action steps).

Each major action priority will have a specific problem(s) that will be resolved at the completion of the project. The project summary describes briefly the project that will be undertaken by the organization. Each project will have one or more priority issues to be tackled during the project. Each major action priority will have a section that outlines the historical significance of the issue(s) relating to the action priority. This section is called background. The authors of the operational plan will describe a vision of success for each major action priority. Each major action priority will have one or more goals and a series of objectives for each goal.

Each major action priority has an action plan. The action plan can have one or more strategies which can have one or more objectives. Each action plan has baseline data to be used to compare what was with what is. This comparison over the years will establish progress. For each action plan, there will be a series of action steps. Each action step will outline the resources to be used to complete the step, who's responsible for the completion of each step, and when the project will start and end (see Sample Business Plan in Appendices available in the student and faculty resource center at www.saga-morepub.com).

Pitfalls of Planning

Strategic planning is a process requiring great skill (see Table 3.5 for tips for writing plans). It can be frustrating and require a great deal of time. An inability to predict the future can create anxiety and feelings of inadequacy.

According to Ansoff and Antoniou (2006) and Park and Antoniou (2007), the 10 biggest pitfalls to successful planning include the following:

- Top management assuming that it can delegate its planning function and, thus, not become directly involved.

- Top management becoming so involved in current problems that it spends insufficient time on planning. As a consequence, planning becomes discredited at lower levels.

- Failing to clearly define and develop enterprise goals as a basis for formulating long-range goals.

- Failing to adequately involve major line managers in the planning process.

- Failing to actually use plans as a standard for assessing managerial performance.

- Failing to create a congenial and supportive climate for planning.

- Assuming that comprehensive planning is something separate from other aspects of the management process.

- Creating a planning program that lacks flexibility and simplicity and fails to encourage creativity.

- Top management failing to review and evaluate long-range plans that have been developed by department and division heads.

- Top management making intuitive decisions that conflict with formal plans.

Table 3.5
Tips for Writing Plans

The following are a few tips that may assist the organization planner in preparing the applied strategic or operational plans:

- Include a table of contents describing the overall content and organization of the plan, including page numbers.

- Format the plan consistently using the same style for sections, subsections, headings, and subheadings, etc., with a consistent use of numbers or letters for headings.

- Number all pages consecutively.

- Spell out and define all acronyms so that readers unfamiliar with the organizations, programs, and operations will understand the plan.

- Write clearly and concisely, with short declarative sentences and active verbs.

- Order the plan elements, provide cross-references when necessary, and develop a topic or subject index so that a reader can follow major ideas and themes throughout the document.

- Make all references to other documents, plans, or reports clear and specific enough to allow a reader to easily find the item or section referenced.

- Include in an appendix any information that is not critical to understanding the plan, but which provides useful background or context.

- Structure the plan in a way that will permit sections to be excerpted and distributed to specific audiences, and that will permit changes, edits, or updates without revising the whole plan.

- Test the understandability of the document by having it reviewed by individuals who were not directly involved in its development.

- On each section, type its computer file name (to speed retrieval in the future). In addition, during the draft process, include date/time code (to keep track of the most up-to-date revision). During the draft process, it helps to also hand-write the draft (revision) number in the corner as each revision is printed or to establish a water-

The Steps in Benchmarking

Benchmarking is generally considered a measurement of the quality of an organization's policies, products, programs, strategies, and so forth, and their comparison with standard measurements, or similar measurements of its peers. The objectives of benchmarking are (1) to determine what and where improvements are called for, (2) to analyze how other organizations achieve their high performance levels, and (3) to use this information to improve performance.

There are six common steps in benchmarking and they are determining what to benchmark; preparing to benchmark; conducting research; selecting with whom to benchmark; collecting and sharing information; and analyzing, adapting, and improving (Stapenhurst, 2009). The first step, determining what to benchmark, is critical to the entire process. The manager must review carefully all products and services provided to ascertain which ones need to be compared to benchmarks for purposes of improvement. The manager answers seven basic questions in this process (Stapenhurst, 2009): "(1) Which aspects of the service are excellent?, (2) Which aspects are above average?, (3) Which aspects are average?, (4) Which aspects are below average?, (5) Which aspects are poor?, (6) Which aspects are very important?, and (7) Which aspects are not important? (p. 153)."

The second step is to prepare to benchmark. It is important to baseline current services for two reasons: (1) to identify weaknesses or gaps that can be concentrated upon, and (2) to identify strengths. Next, the manager or team conducts research to select the organizations that are comparable in size and function and that have outstanding services in this specific area and to gather information about each of these companies and their services.

In step four, the benchmark companies and programs will be chosen from the list prepared in step three. In this step, a short questionnaire (pilot study) is prepared to ascertain which companies have excelled in this particular service. After reviewing the returns, the benchmark group will be selected from the results.

The next step is to collate all information about the benchmarked companies and programs, visit the companies and programs (on site) to gather additional information, and share all the information gathered with the team, management, and the other companies.

Finally, the data is analyzed and discussed among the team members and recommendations for modification are prepared and communicated. Do any of these statements sound familiar? "If you want something done right, do it yourself!" "It will take me more time to explain it to you than if I do it myself!" "It is easier and faster for me to do it, so I will do it!" One of the traps a manager falls into is perfectionism (i.e., feeling as though he or she is the only person who can work with a special supplier, handle a ticklish situation, or create the promotional materials for a program). A manager is much more effective if he or she teaches others how to do various tasks and then supervises their efforts. It is impossible to do everything equally well when one is spread too thin.

Effective delegation requires that the delegator (1) state a clear objective, (2) determine guidelines for the project, (3) set any limitations or constraints, (4) grant the person the authority to carry out the assignment, (5) set the deadline for its completion, and (6) decide the best means for the person to provide regular progress reports (e.g., oral or written, weekly, monthly, semiannually, or annually.

Further, the manager can employ any one of seven levels of delegation: (1) Decide and take action; you need not check back with me; (2) Decide and take action, but let me know what you did; (3) Decide and let me know your decision. Then take action unless I say not to; (4) Decide and then let me know your decision, but wait for my go-ahead; (5) Decide what you would do, but tell me your alternatives with the pros and cons of each; (6) Look into this problem and give me the facts. I will decide; or (7) Wait to be told.

Finally, there are five common reasons why managers fail to delegate. They are (1) nobody does it better, (2) guilt, (3) insecurity, (4) lack of trust, and (5) takes time.

Planning Teams ... Friend or Foe?

If a planning team is formed the right way, it can accelerate the planning process, reduce the time to complete a plan, and reduce operating costs. But if it is done incorrectly, just the opposite can happen. Schmidt (2009) and others suggest there are number of wrong reasons for initiating a team approach to planning, including (1) a belief that teams will produce better results automatically, (2) it is the popular thing to do, (3) we have downsized and have fewer managers, and (4) we have downsized and have fewer employees. However, there are a number of right reasons to consider utilizing teams, including (1) an organizational belief in creating an environment where people can give their best, (2) an increase in the flexibility of the organization, and (3) an organization's structure is already suited to a team approach.

There are two categories of teams: performance and problem solving. Performance teams are structured around work processes. The members are employees who have been hired to do the work. It is a permanent structure of the organization and operates on a daily basis. Participation on the team is mandatory. The team establishes its mission, identifies key performance indicators, measures and monitors performance, solves problems, removes barriers to performance, and holds itself account-able for high levels of performance. Further, the team is empowered to change work processes and has decision-making authority within boundaries. Finally, the team requires training in identifying customers, performance measurement, work process evaluation, team leadership, problem solving, group dynamics, and coaching.

While the problem-solving team is structured around expertise in the problem area, its members are hand selected for their expertise in the problem area. It has a temporary structure that is disband-ed after the problem is solved. It represents extra work for those assigned. Participation is voluntary. The team is provided a mandate outlining the problem to be solved. It uses a systematic approach to problem solving. Further, the team makes recommendations for change and has no decision-making authority. Finally, the team requires training in complex problem solving.

Transforming a group of people into a team requires the following (Schmidt, 2009):

- "Management values individual initiative and high levels of employee participation versus maintaining the status quo.

- Employees are eager to learn and welcome the opportunity for training.

- Employees have a "We-can-solve-anything" attitude.

- Accountability is based on process and results.

- Performance management systems are aligned with and support teams.

- Management is willing to walk the talk.

- Strong team values are established (p. 37)."

Sample team values include perform with enthusiasm, share time, resources, and ideas with each other, consult together to achieve unity of thought and action, listen to each other, encourage, clarify points of view, ask questions, and support other coworkers' opinions, continuous improvement in work and in learning, do things right the first time, will not initiate or receive gossip, use appropriate channels to express disagreement/concern, work through problems and look for win-win solutions; and be tough on problems, easy on people.

In Table 3.6, Schmidt (2009) and others have delineated common team problems and how to solve them.

Table 3.6
Common Team Problems and How to Solve Them

Problem	Solution
Too much time spent in meetings	One hour a week set aside for a meeting
Lots of responsibility, no authority	Clarify boundaries and level of authority
Lack of direction	Management sets clear direction
Over-/underempowerment	Empowerment tied to competency level
Unclear purpose	Clarify mission and performance objectives
Lack of training	Provide necessary training
Withdrawal of management support	Build team structure to sustain itself

Policies and Procedures Manual Development

There are any number of reasons why it is important to have written policies and procedures for governing facility/event management. The primary reasons are to (1) provide a formal policy that guides administrative decisions, (2) reduce the organization's vulnerability to litigation, and (3) clearly communicate to staff and customers/clients a set of uniform and standard practices to guide decisions and behaviors (Conn, 1991; Conn & Malloy, 1989; Page, 2009; Peabody, 2006).

A well-designed policy and procedure manual for facility/event management can assist in answering questions such as the following:

- What types of reports, records, or documentation are staff required to file and keep?

- What are the due process procedures?

- What are the staff's legal responsibilities and procedures for implementing them?

- What is the policy regarding requisitioning, purchasing, inventorying, servicing, maintaining, and inspecting equipment?

- What is the recruiting, hiring, and evaluating process?

- What are the emergency procedures?

- What are the crowd control procedures?

- What process is utilized for inspecting and maintaining the facilities?

- What procedures are employed for program evaluation?

- What process is implemented to control admission?

- How is the facility scheduled?

- What are the procedures for evaluating whether or not a person can return to activity after injury or illness?

Suggested Contents

A facility/event, policies, and procedures manual should delineate general as well as specific program guidelines. The kind of information that should be contained in the policies and procedures manual will vary from one organization to another. In general, according to Conn and Malloy (1989), the policies should reflect (1) the rights of all participants, (2) the philosophy of the organization and the rationale for the existence of the program, and (3) such legislative dictates as Title VII (sexual harassment), Title IX (gender equity), and the Americans with Disabilities Act (equal access for disabled participants). Figure 3.2 outlines a suggested table of contents for the policies and procedure manual.

Steps for Developing a Policies and Procedures Manual

The steps for the development of a policies and procedures manual are described below. This manual should be a flexible, dynamic document that guides employees. Further, the document should be reviewed and revised annually after implementation. Finally, the primary reasons for a policies and procedures manual for facility/event management are to (1) provide a formal policy that guides decisions, (2) reduce the organization's vulnerability to litigation, and (3) clearly communicate to staff and customer/clients a set of uniform and standard practices to guide decisions and behaviors (Conn 1991; Conn & Maloy, 1989; Page, 2009; Peabody, 2006).

The following are the 10 ways to master leadership skills:

- **Accountability.** Annual financial audits, facility and equipment maintenance audits, facility and equipment inspection audits, inventory control, personnel evaluation, program evaluation, risk assessment survey, and ticket inventory control and sales audits

- **Sports/athletics council.** Purpose, function, structure, and operating rules

- **Governance structures/authorities**

- **Equipment.** Acceptable supplier or vendor list, requisition process, purchasing process, bidding procedures, inventory process, inspection audits, and maintenance procedures

- **Budgeting.** Formulation, accountability, and control

- **Events.** Staging, concessions, entertainment, scheduling, traffic, and parking

- **Computer operations**

- **Conduct and ethics.** Staff and participants

- **Courtesy car program**

- **Disbursements.** Goods and services, payroll, and travel expenses

- **Employment conditions.** Educational benefits, hiring, holidays and vacations, leaves of absence, parking, and performance evaluation

- **Expansion and curtailment of programs**

- **Expansion/renovation of facilities**

- **Facilities.** Maintenance, inspection, risk assessment, usage, and key distribution

- **Film office.** Equipment and operations

- **Fund raising and booster organizations**

- **Advertising, marketing, and promotion**

- **Media relations.** Events, news releases, publicity materials, television and radio programs, and printed media

- **Philosophy, mission, goals, and objectives**

Figure 3.2. Suggested Table of Contents for a Policies and Procedures Manual

Step 1

Developing a policies and procedures manual is a long, arduous task that requires management's complete involvement and support. It is important that all personnel (management as well as staff) are involved in the development of the policies and procedures for the organization. The typical approach is to appoint a committee to carefully research and ultimately recommend policies and procedures. Management must be prepared to allocate resources (e.g., time and funds) and encourage the involvement of all staff members. Policies and procedures must be carefully researched and synthesized before being written. Therefore, it is extremely important to involve people who look at policies and procedures from many different angles. The more widespread the involvement, the greater the chances are that the manual will be used and maintained after completion.

Several factors should be considered when deciding who will be appointed to the committee:

- Size of the staff—every member of a small staff will have intimate involvement on the committee; however, larger staffs should be divided into subcommittees that will prepare specific sets of policies and procedures.

- Administration and board—the manual must be approved by management and the board (if one exists); therefore, it is important that management and the board are represented on the committee.

- Customer/client/student-athlete—it is important to involve those most affected by the policies and procedures on the committee that develops them.

- Community interest—most organizations have links with the community and community representation could be very useful in future activities; therefore, it is important to involve community members on the committee.

- Diversity or inclusiveness—the committee should be a mirror image of the organization and the community as a whole.

Step 2

The format of the manual must be flexible. It is suggested that (1) a three-ring binder be used to store the information; (2) the information be divided into logical sections and subsections with appropriate paginations (e.g., section 1—1.1, 1.2, 1.3, section 2—2.1, 2.2, 2.3), (3) a table of contents, definition section for acronyms and terms, an index be included, and (4) the various sections be color coded.

Step 3

The committee should assign one person to write the manual after collecting the appropriate data from the various task groups. The committee needs to adopt an outline and structure for the manual as well as a timeline for completion of the various sections. The writer should be using a computer and appropriate word processing software.

Step 4

The completed manual is dynamic in nature and must be reviewed periodically. A procedure for reviewing the manual must be established. All staff members should be encouraged to periodically review the policies and procedures within their domain and then recommend any changes to the appropriate authorities. Making policy and procedure changes a regular agenda item at staff meetings sensitizes the staff to the importance of the manual and maintains its currency.

When One Manual Will Not Do

Depending on the size of the organization, one thick manual may not be the most efficient way to operate. This is particularly true if there are a large number of specialists working within the program who do not need to know everything. What may be more efficient is a series of special manuals. One or more manuals may be given to employees as needed. Here is a listing of possible policy manuals to be used by an organization (Conn 1991; Conn & Malloy, 1989; Page, 2009; Peabody, 2006):

- scheduling manual,

- fitness manual,

- operations manual,

- emergency manual,

- in-service training manual,

- risk management manual,

- sales and marketing manual,

- repair and maintenance manual,

- human resources manual,

- fund-raising manual,

- employee benefits manual,

- special event manual,

- membership retention manual, and

- recruitment/motivation manual for volunteers.

References

Ansoff, I. H., & Antoniou, P. H. (2006). *The secrets of strategic management: The Ansoffian approach.* North Charleston, NC: Booksurge Publishing.

Busser, J. A. (2010). Human resource management. In M. Moiseichic (Ed.), *Managing park and recreation organizations* (3rd ed., pp. 433–460). Ashburn, VA: National Recreation and Park Association.

Conn, J. H., & Malloy, B. P. (1989). *Organizing policy for interscholastic athletic programs.* Carmel, IN: Benchmark Publishing.

Conn, J. H. (1991). An open-book policy. *Athletic Business, 15*(2), 57–60.

Drucker, P. F. (1994). *Managing the future: The 1990s and beyond.* New York: Dutton

Fogg, D.C. (2010). *Team-based strategic planning: A complete guide to restructuring, facilitating, and implementing the process.* New York: American Management Association.

Hussey, D. E. (2002). *Business-driven HRM: A best practice blueprint.* New York: John Wiley & Sons LTD.

Page, S. (2009). *Best practices in policies and procedures.* Los Angeles: Company Manuals Inc.

Paley, N. (2005). *Manage to win: Revitalize your business.* London: Drift Design.

Park, D. J., & Antoniou, P. H. (2007). *Management, zen, and I: 100 questions for management thinking.* North Charleston, SC: Booksurge Publishing.

Peabody, L. (2006). *How to write policies, procedures, and task outlines.* New York: Writing Services.

Schmidt, T. (2009). *Strategic project management made simple: Practical tools for leaders and teams.* Hoboken, NJ: John Wiley & Sons.

Stapenhurst, T. (2009). *The benchmarking book.* Florence, KY: Routledge.

Tobey, D. D. (2005). *Needs assessment basics.* Danvers, MA: ASTD Press.

Wright, P. L., Pringle, C. D., Kroll, M. & Parnell, J. A. (1998). *Strategic management: Text and cases.* Boston: Allyn & Bacon.

CHAPTER 4

Managing Human Resources

Thomas H. Sawyer
Professor Emeritus, Indiana State University

Introduction

The most important asset in any organization is its human resources. People are the key to a business's success or failure. The goal is to obtain competent employees and provide the means for them to function optimally. Sport organizations are service-oriented operations. Therefore, the management of human resources, whether it be a manager of the human resource department in a large organization or the owner or manager of a small organization, plays a primary role in the organization. Further, the human problems of management are often the most complex because of the variability of human nature and behavior. This makes the management of human resources of the organization a key to its success.

Managing Human Resources

Management of human resources involves all the policies and procedures developed for employees to interact with the organization both formally and informally. Reece, Brandt, and Howie (2010) indicate the common components of human resource management include

- "hiring competent and qualified employees,

- assigning and classifying employees effectively,

- motivating employees to perform optimally,

- stimulating employees' professional growth and development,

- evaluating and compensating employees fairly,

- rewarding employees for their efforts, and

- providing in-service education opportunities (p. 216)."

Types of Employees

There are basically two types of employees: professional (salary) and hourly. These employees can be paid, volunteer, or independent contractors. The professional employees are paid a salary, have a college degree, hold higher-level positions, do not have fixed work schedules, do not punch time clocks, and perform specific duties that do not fit into fixed day/hour schedules (e.g., club manager, program director, marketing director, and instructors). The hourly employees usually have specific day/hour schedules, punch time clocks, may have specified lunch and rest breaks, receive specified vacation time and sick leave, and are not expected to work after hours without additional compensation (e.g., custodians, secretaries, maintenance personnel, equipment managers, security officers, and other office personnel). Some special types of employees include part-time and seasonal employees, volunteers, and independent contractors.

Every organization at one time or another has the need for part-time personnel. In determining personnel needs, the manager should decide which work tasks can be clustered into jobs that can be accomplished by part-time employees. Part-time positions may include aerobic dance instructors, fitness instructors, professional trainers, instructors, day care personnel, janitors, secretaries, accountants, lifeguards, ticket sellers, ticket takers, concessions personnel, and post-event cleanup, to name a few. These positions need to have job descriptions developed the same as full-time positions.

Some organizations employ seasonal employees to meet the demands of their clientele. The need for seasonal employees depends on the time of year (e.g., summer, June or/to August, and winter, November or/to March), activities (e.g., water sports, winter sports), and region of the United States (e.g., Southeast, South, Southwest, Northeast, Upper Midwest, or Northwest). The summer increases the need for personnel in organizations that cater to school-aged children. Many fitness centers need to employ more personnel for day care centers during the summer months because the younger children are out of school and during the first quarter of the new year to meet the demands of the increased number of clients after the holiday eating binges.

Many tasks and services can be accomplished by volunteers. Managers have to determine the specific work tasks (e.g., answering the phone, working the registration desk, working in the day care center, assisting in raising funds). All volunteer positions should have job descriptions. A volunteer service program should be considered and initiated.

Finally, many organizations use independent contractors to provide services. An independent contractor is someone from another organization who contracts with the primary organization to provide a specific service for a specific amount of time and for an agreed upon amount of money. Traditionally, these contracts are for services including aerobic dance, clerical, custodial, trash collection, laundry, lawn, professional trainers, snow plowing, marketing, advertising, concessions, and so forth. The organization pays for the service and the individual or other organization is responsible for paying employment taxes, fringe benefits, and liability insurance. It is imperative that the independent contractor carry liability insurance to cover errors of commission and omission. Another caution is to be certain that the aerobic dance instructor has gained copyright permissions on all the music used in the performance of the contracted service. The organization should not be responsible for the independent contractor's infringement upon the artist's copyright on the music.

All organizations should have a chart that provides a graphic view of the organization's basic structure and illustrates the lines of authority and responsibility of its various members. All employees should be familiar with this chart and understand how their positions and duties contribute to the overall structure. Lussier (2009), Reece and Brandt (2006), and others indicate the limitations of an organizational chart are that (1) it is easily outdated, (2) it fails to show precise functions and amounts of authority and responsibility, and (3) it does not portray the informal relationships that exist.

Hiring Process

Every organization needs to have a manual outlining policies and procedures for recruitment and appointment of personnel. The manager of human resources must have appropriate hiring procedures in place. Denhardt, Denhardt, and Aristigueta (2012), Dresang (2012), Lussier (2009), and Reece et al. (2010), have determined the components of a hiring process should be (1) gaining approval for the position, (2) establishing a search and screen committee (i.e., appointing/selecting a committee chair and outlining the responsibilities of the chair and the committee), (3) informing the search and screen committee of the appropriate Affirmative Action and Equal Opportunity Employment statutes, (4) developing a job description, (5) preparing a position announcement, (6) establishing a plan for advertising the position, (7) screening the pool of candidates, (8) verifying the candidates' credentials, (9) interviewing the candidates, (10) selecting the final candidate, and (11) negotiating the appointment with the selected candidate.

Developing the Job Description

The job description could be the responsibility of the search and screen committee. Dresang (2012) indicates the job description should include, but not be limited to "(1) a position title (i.e., the position title should describe generally the responsibilities of the position), (2) the qualifications for the position (i.e., experience, education, certifications), and (3) the responsibilities and duties for the position (p. 146)."

When developing the qualifications for the position, do not be too prescriptive. An example of an overly prescriptive set of qualifications would be: The candidate must have earned a MA/MS degree in exercise physiology, have five years experience in a club setting, current certification in CPR, and currently hold a director's certification from the ACSM. This set of qualifications may narrow the pool of qualified candidates. A set of qualifications such as the following, however, is less restrictive and allows for a larger candidate pool: The candidate will have a BS in physical education, adult fitness, sport sciences, recreation and sport management, prefer an MA/MS in physical education, adult fitness or cardiac rehabilitation, have three to five years experience in a clinic, club, college/university, corporate, or hospital setting, have completed a class in CPR from either the American Red Cross or the American Heart Association, prefer current certification; and a fitness instructor or exercise technician certification from the ACSM, prefer director certification. If you are truly searching for a strong candidate, the larger the candidate pool, the better.

The duties of any position have four basic components: duty period, tasks to be accomplished, ethical practices, and expectations. Policies concerning responsibilities and expectations common to specific employee groups should be found in a human resources handbook. All organizations should have a human resources handbook.

The job description will not be used only for the search process. Every position, whether it is full time, part time, or volunteer, should have a job description. It will become the basis of the performance appraisal document. Therefore, it is imperative that the job responsibilities and duties be very detailed and can be evaluated objectively after the candidate is employed. Further, include a statement toward the end or at the end of the responsibilities section that allows the employer some flexibility, such as "and any other responsibilities or duties assigned in writing by the immediate supervisor."

After the job description is completed, the committee will design an appropriate position announcement. Denhardt et al. (2012) and Dresang (2012) say a position announcement should include (1) the position title, (2) a short description of the organization, (3) a summary of the job description, (4) qualifications, (5) the application procedure, (6) the deadline, and (7) an AA/EEO employer designation. It is important to be flexible in establishing the deadline. A statement such as "The review of applications will begin September 1 and continue until the position is filled" allows the committee to review later applicants who qualify.

Communicating a Position Announcement

Reece et al. (2010) suggest the following are a few common ways of communicating a position announcement: "(1) referral and employment agencies, public and private; (2) college and university placement services and bulletin boards in departments of exercise science, kinesiology, physical education, recreation, and sports management; (3) professional journals and newsletters; (4) job marts at professional conventions (e.g., American College of Sports Medicine [ACSM]; American Alliance for Health, Physical Education, Recreation, and Dance [AAHPERD]; International Dance Exercise Association [IDEA]; National Strength and Conditioning Association [NSCA]; National Recreation and Park Association [NRPA]; and the annual Athletic Business Convention); (5) local newspapers; (6) national/ regional newspapers; (7) employee referrals; (8) cooperative fieldwork, internship, or work study programs with colleges and universities; and (9) job listings on the Internet or Listservs (p. 227)."

Recruitment

Recruiting strong, effective employees is the key to the success of any organization. The efforts in the area of recruitment are critical to the future of the organization. One mistake can spell doom for an organization. An important question to be answered when filling positions is whether it is desirable to fill the positions from within the existing staff through promotion or transfer or to seek outside applicants. It is the philosophy of many organizations always to look first within to promote loyal and competent employees as a preference to bringing in new, outside personnel. This practice has the advantage of building staff morale and a conscious effort by employees to achieve and thus earn their way to more desirable positions. It rewards loyalty and provides a strong base for tradition and standardization of operation.

However, outsiders may have qualifications superior to any current members of the organization. They will be more likely to provide new ideas and approaches to their assigned duties. In most cases, it is best to solicit applicants from both within and outside the organization. Careful judgment will then produce the best selection from the potential candidates. If the internal candidate is selected, in the end, he or she will be stronger because of the process.

In-Service Training

Training personnel is not a luxury. It is a necessity. Personnel can never be too well trained to perform their responsibilities. The training program should be for all personnel. No employee should be exempted from training.

Providing regular, planned, and systematically implemented in-service education programs for the staff can only benefit the organization staff members. The education program(s) should be based on the needs of the individual(s) in relation to the demands of the job. The employee and employer should see the process as career development designed to make the employee a more effective member of the organization.

The human resources manager should develop an ongoing staff development program. Lussier (2009) says the development program should be composed of the following elements: (1) new staff orientation, (2) safety training (e.g., CPR and first aid), (3) career development, and (4) technology upgrades. A few examples of staff development seminars or workshops are time management, communication skills, risk assessment and management, or computer skills. These are only a few examples of the need for staff development that will continue to increase in a rapidly changing society.

Lussier (2009) and Dresang (2012) suggest the new staff orientation should include a discussion of

- organization history, structure, and services;

- area and clients served by the organization;

- organization policies and regulations;

- relation of managers and human resources department;

- rules and regulations regarding wages and wage payment, hours of work and overtime, safety (accident prevention and contingency procedures), holidays and vacations, methods of reporting tardiness and absences, discipline and grievances, uniforms and clothing, parking, fringe benefits, identification badges, office space, key(s), and recreation services; and

- opportunities for promotion and growth, job stabilization, and suggestions and decision making.

Common Errors Related to In-Service Education Programs

Lussier (2009) says it is important for the human resources manager to avoid the following errors when designing an in-service education program:

- feeding too much information at one time,

- telling without demonstrating,

- lack of patience,

- lack of preparation,

- failure to build in feedback, and

- failure to reduce tension within the audience.

Evaluating Employee Performance

All employees should be evaluated. The evaluation period varies from six weeks for new employees to annual performance reviews for established employees. The evaluation should take the form of a performance appraisal. The performance appraisal is drafted by using the job description for the position as well as the mutually agreed upon annual performance objectives.

A performance appraisal (i.e., work plan, progress review, and annual performance review) is a systematic review of an individual employee's job performance to evaluate the effectiveness or adequacy of his or her work. Performance appraisals are the essence of human resources management. They are the means for evaluating employee effectiveness and a basis for producing change in the work behavior of each employee. Performance appraisals should be used as learning tools.

The task of assessing performance is a difficult and extremely complex undertaking. For this reason, significant planning and supervisory time should be devoted to the appraisal process. All organizations should require annual performance appraisals of all employees. In every case, they provide the opportunity for employee and supervisor to discuss the employee's job performance and to identify any desired redirection efforts. The human and financial resources devoted to conducting performance appraisals pay-off in the long haul. It is valuable for both large and small organizations.

Denhardt et al. (2012) and Dresang (2012) indicate other purposes for performance evaluations are to

- provide employees with an idea of how they are doing;

- identify promotable employees or those who should be demoted;

- administer the salary program;

- provide a basis for supervisor–employee communication;

- assist supervisors in knowing their workers better;

- identify training needs;

- help in proper employee placement within the organization;

- identify employees for layoff or recall;

- validate the selection process and evaluate other personnel activities (e.g., training programs, psychological tests, physical examinations);

- improve department employee effectiveness;

- determine special talent;

- ascertain progress at the end of probationary periods (i.e., new employees or older employees with performance difficulties);

- furnish inputs to other personnel programs; and

- supply information for use in grievance interviews.

Performance Improvement Plans (PIP)

A performance improvement plan or PIP, according to the Society for Human Resource Management (SHRM) (2013), is a formal process used by supervisors to help employees improve performance or modify behavior. The performance improvement plan identifies performance and/or behavioral issues that need to be corrected and creates a written plan of action to guide the improvement and/or corrective action.

Fundamentally, a PIP is a structured communication tool designed to facilitate constructive discussion between the employee and the supervisor. SHRM (2013) suggests an effective PIP will

- specifically identify the performance to be improved or the behavior to be corrected, and

- provide clear expectations and metrics about the work to be performed or behavior that must change.

Further, SHRM (2013) indicates, the PIP should

- identify the support and resources available to help the employee make the required improvements;

- establish a plan for reviewing the employee's progress and providing feedback to the employee for the duration of the PIP, and

- specify possible consequences if performance standards as identified in the PIP are not met.

When an employee is not performing or meeting expectations, supervisors have at their disposal several options to correct the behavior. They can rely on corrective actions such as oral and written warnings. In more serious cases, they can move to suspension without pay, demotion or dismissal. The PIP, in many cases, can be used in place of these disciplinary processes. A PIP can be given at almost any point in performance discussions with the employee. SHRM (2013) suggests some common uses for the PIP include the following:

- To correct workplace behaviors affecting performance, productivity, or staff relationships on the heels of an unsatisfactory annual review.

- To provide employees an opportunity to correct a situation rather than implementing a more serious step in the disciplinary process.

A basic tenet with all performance management efforts is the notion that taking action early is better than waiting. The same holds true for the performance improvement plan. A PIP is more likely to be successful when the supervisor recognizes there is a performance or behavioral issue that needs to be corrected. Early communication and early feedback (both positive and corrective) are good ways to prevent future performance problems. Investing time early is always time well spent, and the performance improvement plan can be an effective tool in preventing problems from getting worse or for intervening when performance and/or workplace behaviors have become counterproductive (See Appendices available in the student and faculty resource center at www.sagamorepub.com for a sample PIP plan template, and sample plan).

Personnel Records

A personnel file should be established as a depository for all pertinent information concerning the employment status and productivity of each employee. These files serve the purpose of recording all aspects of employment status including, but not limited to position title, job description, contract provisions, an accounting of benefits, accumulated sick leave, vacation time, awards received, performance appraisals, disciplinary actions, letters of commendation, salary history, home address and phone number, person(s) to contact in case of emergency, name of spouse and children, social security number, income tax data, life and/or disability insurance, and family physician.

Personnel files are confidential. When an item is placed into a personnel file, the employee must be notified. The employee may have access to his or her personnel file at any time under the guidelines established by the Freedom of Information Act. The employer cannot maintain a secondary personnel file that contains information that the employee is not aware of its existence. It should be general practice that only an employee's supervisor(s) has access to personnel files. Care must be exercised to protect the confidentiality of the employee. There should be policies and procedures established for the handling and accessibility of personnel files. Files should be retained a specific number of years to meet statute of limitations requirements, which differ from state to state. Always check with an attorney before destroying files. Finally, all files should be stored on a computer with appropriate backup.

Reward System

A reward system, whether intrinsic or extrinsic, is essential to maintain employee morale. People need to feel that their efforts are appreciated or they will seek appreciation elsewhere. An intrinsic reward is personal—"I know I am doing a good job." The person feels good about him- or herself; whereas extrinsic rewards are tangible and provided by the organization. Common extrinsic rewards are salary increases above the average provided, promotional opportunities, bonuses not attached to salary, payment for attendance at conferences, special recognition dinners, and newspaper recognition.

The rewards system should be developed by the human resources manager. The system should concentrate on celebrating personnel for jobs well done. There should be a specific line item in the annual budget to cover all costs for the system.

Fringe Benefits

It is essential that a fringe benefit packet be established for all personnel in the organization. Dresang (2012) suggests fringe benefits typically include group health insurance (including prevention coverage, doctor visits, surgical interventions, drug purchases, and eye and dental coverage), group term life insurance, disability insurance (Rehabilitation Act 1973, Veterans Readjustment Assistance Act 1974, Vocational Rehabilitation Act 1973), retirement programs, contributions to social security, leaves of absence for various reasons (e.g., personal emergency, death in the family, and jury duty), vacations, sick leave, holidays, and tuition assistance for advanced education.

The health benefits program should be administered by the human resources manager. The fringe benefits packet needs to be budgeted. The organization should not pay for the entire program but share the costs with the employees (e.g., the organization will pay 80% of the medical plan and the employees will pay 20% or 70%/30%).

Termination

Termination, like appointment, is a two-way street: the person may choose to leave the organization or the organization may decide that the person must leave. Whichever the case, policies and procedures need to be established and placed in the human resources policy and procedure manual. There are two policies that need to be developed. The first relates to when an individual is considering termination (i.e., quitting). This policy might say, "All personnel are expected to give due notice, in writing, of intention to leave the organization whether by resignation or retirement. Due notice is construed as not less than …? for supervisory personnel, and for all other personnel…?."

Denhardt et al. (2012) and Dresang (2012) outline the following procedures for terminations by the employee should include, but not be limited to

- an indication of the persons to whom written notice should be sent;

- a statement regarding turning over such items as reports, records, and equipment; and

- completion of an exit interview.

The second policy, which is the most sensitive of all human resources policies, is when the organization terminates an employee. The policy might read: "Termination of a staff member is based upon consideration of quality of performance in relation to achievement of the goals of the organization. The judgments of peers and supervisors are taken into account by the executive when recommending terminations to the board."

Procedures for terminations by the organization might describe the following:

- How is quality performance considered?

- What are the roles of the peers and supervisor(s)?

- When is notice given?

- How is notice given?

- What, if any, severance pay is offered?

- What about the employee's due process?

- How are the specific reasons for termination communicated?

Either the human resources manager or immediate supervisor will complete the dismissal (See Appendices available in the student and faculty resource center at www.sagamorepub.com for more information on How to Deal with Difficult People).

Grievance Policies and Procedures

All organizations need to establish a grievance policy and appropriate procedures to guarantee the employee's due process rights. The individual who is either terminated or disciplined has the right to due process. This aspect is generally covered by a policy on grievance and provides detailed procedures of implementation. The policies and procedures developed should have the intent to resolve differences at the lowest level of the professional relationship and as informally as possible.

Sexual Harassment Policy Development

Sexual harassment is the imposition of unwanted sexual advancements on a person or persons within the context of an unequal power relationship. There are many forms of sexual harassment in the workplace, including but not limited to unwelcome physical touching, hugs, and kisses, physically cornering someone, sexual jokes, derogatory sexual names, or pornographic pictures, promises of reward or threats of punishment coupled with sexual advances. A man as well as a woman may be the victim of harassment and a woman as well as a man may be the harasser. The victim does not have to be of the opposite sex from the harasser.

Since 1976, the courts and the U.S. Equal Employment Opportunity Commission (EEOC) have defined sexual harassment as one form of sex discrimination. As such, it violates Title VII of the 1964 Civil Rights Act (42 U.S.C. §2000e-5-9) which guarantees that a person shall not be discriminated against in an employment setting because of race, color, religion, sex, or national origin.

In the workplace, sexual harassment occurs when a person who is in a position of authority or influence or can affect another person's job or career uses the position's authority to coerce the other person (male–female, female–male, female–female, male–male) into sexual acts or relations or punishes the person if he or she refuses to comply. It is important that the organization's human resources handbook have policies and procedures to assist employees faced with this type of action. According to the EEOC (1964, 1987), such a policy might read as follows:

> Unwelcome sexual advances, requests for sexual favors, and other verbal or physical conduct of a sexual nature constitute sexual harassment when (1) submission to such conduct is made either explicitly or implicitly a term or condition of an individual's employment, (2) submission or rejection of such conduct by an individual is used as the basis for employment decisions affecting such individuals, or (3) such conduct has the purpose or effect of unreasonably interfering with an individual's performance or creating an intimidating, hostile, or offensive environment.

The policy rests on three conditions established by the EEOC (1964, 1987):
- Submission to the conduct is made as either an explicit or implicit condition of employment.

- Submission to or rejection of the conduct is used as the basis for an employment decision affecting the harassed employee.

- The harassment substantially interferes with an employee's work performance or creates an intimidating, hostile, or offensive work environment.

A sexually hostile work environment can be created by (EEOC, 1964, 1987):
- discussing sexual activities;

- unnecessary touching;

- commenting on physical attributes;

- displaying sexually suggestive pictures;

- using demeaning or inappropriate terms, such as "babe";

- ostracizing workers of one gender by those of the other; or

- using crude and offensive language.

If you are sexually harassed, what should you do? Hoping the problem will go away or accepting it as "the way things are" only perpetuates and encourages such inappropriate behaviors. It is important that the organization outlines a similar procedure as follows: (1) report the incident immediately, (2) know your rights and the organization's policies and procedures, (3) keep a written, dated record of all incidents and any witnesses, (4) consider confronting the harasser in person or writing the harasser a letter (i.e., outlining the facts of what has occurred, how you feel about the events, and what you want to happen next), and (5) evaluate your options and follow through.

False accusations of sexual harassment can be prevented if the following suggestions are taken seriously (EEOC, 1964, 1987):

- Schedule one-on-one meetings in businesslike settings, preferably during the daytime.

- Leave doors open.

- Focus on the purpose of meeting.

- Respect the personal space of others.

- Limit touching to the conventional handshake.

The charge of sexual harassment is not to be taken lightly by a charging party, a respondent, or any member of the organization. Both the charging party and the respondent may anticipate a confidential, impartial review of the facts by the human resources manager. Finally, all staff in positions of authority need to be sensitive to the hazards in personal relationships with subordinate employees. When significant disparities in age or authority are present between two individuals, questions about professional responsibility and the mutuality of consent to a personal relationship may well arise.

Americans with Disabilities Act

The Americans with Disabilities Act (ADA) Public Law 101-336 (July 26, 1990) provides certain protections for those with statutorily defined disabilities in the areas of employment, government services, places of public accommodation, public transportation, and telecommunications. Health clubs, fitness and exercise facilities, health care provider offices, day care or social service establishments, as well as gymnasiums, health spas, and other places of exercise or recreation are all covered under the ADA.

Disability means, with respect to an individual, a physical or mental impairment that substantially limits one or more of the major life activities of such individual, a record of such an impairment, or being regarded as having such an impairment. The phrase physical or mental impairment includes, but is not limited to, such contagious and noncontagious diseases and conditions as orthopedic, visual, speech, and hearing impairments, cerebral palsy, epilepsy, muscular dystrophy, multiple sclerosis, cancer, heart disease, diabetes, mental retardation, emotional illness, specific learning disabilities, HIV disease, tuberculosis, drug addiction, and alcoholism.

The phrase major life activities means functions such as caring for one's self, performing manual tasks, walking, seeing, hearing, speaking, breathing, learning, and working. The phrase has a record of such an impairment means an individual has a history of or has been misclassified as having a mental or physical impairment that substantially limits one or more major life activities.

The ADA is a federal antidiscrimination statute designed to remove barriers that prevent qualified individuals with disabilities from enjoying the same employment opportunities that are available to persons without disabilities. Like the Civil Rights Act of 1964 that prohibits discrimination on the basis of race, color, religion, national origin, and sex, the ADA seeks to ensure access to equal employment opportunities based on merit. It does not guarantee equal results, establish quotas, or require preferences favoring individuals with disabilities over those without disabilities. Rather, it focuses on when an individual's disability creates a barrier to employment opportunities. The ADA requires employers to consider whether reasonable accommodation could remove the barrier. The ADA establishes a process in which the employer must assess a disabled individual's ability to perform the essential functions of the specific job held or desired. However, where that individual's functional limitation impedes such job performance, an employer must take steps to reasonably accommodate and thus overcome the particular impediment, unless to do so would impose an undue hardship. An accommodation must be tailored to match the needs of the disabled individual with the needs of the job's essential functions.

Guidelines for Managing AIDS in the Workplace

HIV/AIDS is a serious health problem. Many people do not understand the disease and make certain inappropriate judgments. It is important for organizations to develop a response to AIDS in the workplace. The following principles are a starting point for the development of a policy relating to AIDS in the workplace (developed by the Citizens Commission on AIDS for New York City and Northern New Jersey):

- People with HIV/AIDS infection are entitled to the same rights and opportunities as people with other serious or life-threatening illnesses.

- Employment policies must, at a minimum, comply with federal, state, and local laws and regulations.

- Employment policies should be based on the scientific and epidemiological evidence that people with HIV/AIDS infection do not pose a risk of transmission of the virus to coworkers through ordinary workplace contact.

- The highest levels of management and union leadership should unequivocally endorse nondiscriminatory employment policies and educational programs about HIV/AIDS.

- Employers and unions should communicate their support of these policies to workers in simple, clear, and unambiguous terms.

- Employers have a duty to protect the confidentiality of an employee's medical information.

- Employers and unions should undertake education for all employees in order to prevent work disruption and rejection by coworkers of an employee with HIV/AIDS.

- Employers should not require HIV/AIDS screening as part of general pre-employment or workplace physical examinations.

- In those special occupational settings where there may be a potential risk of exposure to HIV/AIDS (e.g., health care, exposure to blood or blood products), employers should provide specific, ongoing education and training, as well as the necessary equipment, to reinforce appropriate infection control procedures and ensure that they are implemented.

Sport Agent

According to Hernandez (2012) and Shropshire and Davis (2008), a sport agent is a person who procures and negotiates employment and endorsement deals for an athlete (principal) (See Table 4.1, regarding duties of the principal to the sport agent). In return, the agent receives a commission that is usually between 4% and 10% of the contract, although this figure varies. In addition to finding incoming sources, agents often handle public relations matters for their clients. Sport agents may be relied upon by their clients for guidance in all business aspects of life and sometimes even more broadly (See Table 4.2, Functions of a Sport Agent). Many sport agents have a major in law background, mainly to help understand the large and complicated legal matter in contracts (See Table 4.3, Models for a Sport Representation Business).

Sport Law Firms

Sport law firms provide services for sport agents and the men and women who play professional sports. They generally provide services including drug, steroid, and disciplinary appeals for players, agent disciplinary appeals, agent and player fee disputes, litigation management, mediation and dispute resolution, agent state registrations, players association regulations compliance, and confidentiality, non-compete, and agent/employer fee assignment agreements.

Table 4.1
Duties of the Principal to the Sport Agent

There are three duties the principal owes to the agent under agency law:

- To compensate the agent
- To reimburse the agent
- To indemnify the agent

Further, the principal is liable on contracts negotiated by the agent where the agent possesses the authority to enter into the contract on the principal's behalf.

(Shropshire & Davis, 2008)

Table 4.2
Functions of a Sport Agent

- Negotiating player contracts
- Legal counseling
- Managing the athlete's finances
- Marketing
- Resolving disputes
- Career planning
- Obtaining and negotiating endorsement contracts and other income opportunities

(Hernandez, 2012)

Table 4.3
Models for a Sport Representation Business

- Free-standing sports management firms
  - Representation of athletes only
  - Combined athlete representation, event management, and facility management
- Law practice only
- Sports management firms affiliated with law firms

In large sports agencies, agents deal with all aspects of an athlete's finances, from investment to filing taxes. (See Table 4.4, the top sport agencies).

(Shropshire & Davis, 2008; Hernandez, 2012)

Table 4.4
Top Sport Agencies

ACES	Octagon
Athletes First	Priority Sports and Entertainment
BDA	Rosenhaus Sports
BEST	SFX Baseball Group
Boras Corporation	The Orr Hockey Group
CAA Sports	The Sports Corporation
Excel Sports Management	Wasserman Media Group
Newport Sports Management	

Need for Regulation of Sport Agents

The federal government and states have been developing legislation to safeguard men and women in sport from unethical sport agents. There are six common reasons why there is a need for regulation of sport agents. These six common reasons include

- unethical solicitation,

- charging excessive fees,

- conflicts of interest,

- general incompetence,

- income mismanagement, and

- fraud.

The Uniform Athlete Agent Act (UAAA) was approved by the NCAA and the National Conference of Commissioners for Uniform States Laws (2000). By 2002, 18 jurisdictions had passed the UAAA, and three years later, an additional 12 jurisdiction passed the act. Table 4.5 outlines the components of a UAAA.

Labor Law

Labor law is designed to protect both employees and employers from the sometimes antagonistic relationship that may develop between two parties. Labor law is a set of rules that govern the workplace and affect both employees and employers. Further. Labor law outlines what rights employees have and what rights their employers have. The cornerstone is the right of employees to choose to join or assist a labor union.

Beginning as early as 1950, professional athletes started to organize in to unions. Table 4.6 lists the professional leagues with collective bargaining agreements.

Statutory Labor Laws

The Federal laws governing labor are outlined below:
- Clayton Act (1914)
    - Exempted unions from Sherman Act
- Norris-LaGuardia Act (1932)
    - Limited the power of federal government from issuing injunctions against unions

Table 4.5
Components of a Uniform Athlete Agent Act

- Definitions
- Registration of athlete agents
- Registration requirements
- Certification of registration
- Suspension, revocation, or refusal to renew registration
- Temporary registration
- Registration and renewal fee
- Form of contract
- Warning to student-athlete
- Notice to educational institution

- Student-athlete's right to cancel
- Required records
- Prohibited acts
- Criminal penalties
- Civil remedies
- Administrative penalty
- Application and construction
- Severability
- Repeals
- Effective date
- Sample letter

(The Uniform Athlete Agent Act (UAAA) was approved by the NCAA and the National Conference of Commissioners for Uniform States Laws [2000].)

Table 4.6
Collective Bargaining Agreements (CBA) in Professional Sports

- MLB
- MLS
- NBA
- NFL
- NHL
- WNBA

- Wagner Act (1935)
    - Known as the National Labor Relations Act gave workers the right to organize
- Taft-Hartley Act (1947)
    - Know as the Labor Management Relations Act, which limited the amount of pressure unions could place on employees to join … unfair labor practice

Collective Bargaining

According to Carrell and Heavrin (2012), Gold (2014), and Smith (2011), collective bargaining is a type of negotiation used by employees to work with their employers. During a collective bargaining period, workers' representatives approach the employer and attempt to negotiate a contract that both sides can agree with. Typical issues covered in a labor contract are hours, wages, benefits, working conditions, and the rules of the workplace. Once both sides have reached a contract that they find agreeable, it is signed and kept in place for a set period of time, most commonly three years. Gold (2014) indicates the final contract is called a collective bargaining agreement to reflect the fact that it is the result of a collective bargaining effort.

Smith (2011) indicates the roots of collective bargaining lie in the late 19th century, when workers began to agitate for more rights in their places of employment. Many skilled trades started using their skills as bargaining tools to force their employers to meet their workplace needs. Other workers relied on sheer numbers, creating general strikes to protest poor working conditions. Several labor pioneers started to establish a collective bargaining system so that labor negotiations could run more smoothly.

Typically, the employees are represented by a union. Collective bargaining actually begins with joining a union, agreeing to abide by the rules of the union, and electing union representatives. In general, experienced people from the union will assist the employees with putting together a draft of a contract, and will help them present their desires to the company. Numerous meetings between representatives of employer and employees will be held until the two can agree on a contract (See Table 4.7, Components of Players Agreement).

Table 4.7
Components of Players Agreement

- ACES
- Union/management rights
- Commissioner discipline
- Standard player contract
- Grievance procedure
- College draft
- Salary cap
- Free agency
- Related player/club issues

- Salaries/economies
- Benefits
- Incidentals (expenses)
- Anti-collusion
- Agent certification
- Duration
- Definitions
- League expansion

Modified from Carrell & Heavrin (2012) and Gold (2014)

As the contract is being negotiated, general employees also have input on it through their union officers. Thus, the agreement reflects the combined desires of all the employees, along with limitations that the employer wishes to see put in place. The result is a powerful document that usually reflects co-operative effort. In some cases, however, the union or the employer may resort to antagonistic tactics, such as striking or creating a lockout, in order to push the agreement through.

Bargaining Unit

Associated with the process of collective bargaining between employees and an employer according to Carrell and Heavrin (2012), a bargaining unit is composed of persons who are recognized by both the company and a legally organized labor union to negotiate matters involving employment issues. Some of these issues include safety conditions on the job, salary and benefits, job qualifications, and general working conditions and procedures. The main purpose of a bargaining unit is to create a working situation that is advantageous for both the employer and the employee.

Generally, a bargaining unit must be formed in compliance with standards that are set by the industry and often by agencies that are designed to ensure the proper function of these unions and unionized employees who are associated with the entities. Along with meeting the union requirements to participate in the bargaining unit, individuals must also be acceptable to the employer as well. The result of creating this type of communication between the bank of unionized employees and the employer is a clear means of addressing labor issues before they cause disruption in the work process. In addition, these bargaining units help to prevent the spread of incorrect information about the current status of the working relationship between the workers, the union, and the employer.

Gold (2014) and Smith (2011) note that from the perspective of the employee, the bargaining unit provides a means of seeking benefits that are considered equitable for the type and amount of work that is required by the employer. This may involve a request for an increase in the rate of pay, the addition of overtime benefits, improvements to health insurance or pension plans, and the improvement of safety conditions on the job. The bargaining unit acts to make the needs and the desires of the employees known in a manner that presents a united voice that can work with the employer to explore all options that are relevant to the matter at hand.

An advantage to the employer is that a bargaining unit typically does not present an item for discussion unless two factors are present, according to Gold (2014) and Smith (2011). They say first, there must be a significant amount of support for the item manifested among the unionized workers and secondly, the union will have investigated the claim or proposition thoroughly and approved the item for presentation to the employer. This helps to eliminate a lot of wasted time responding to requests and ideas that may or may not have any real support among the employees. The bargaining unit also provides a focused means of addressing the matter with the employees, making communication back and forth much more effective and concise (See Table 4.8, Subjects of Bargaining).

Table 4.8
Subjects of Bargaining

- Mandatory
    - Rate and method of pay
    - Work rules, discipline, drug testing
    - Safety
    - Grievance and arbitration procedures
    - health, insurance, pensions, and layoff compensation
- Permissive
    - Change in the bargaining unit
    - Identity of the bargaining agent
    - Status of supervisors
    - Settlement of unfair labor practice charges
    - Internal union or company affairs

Modified from Gold (2014)

For workers, collective bargaining is an excellent tool. Many workplaces benefit from unionization, which allows workers to speak together as a body to assert their rights. Employers also benefit from collective bargaining agreements that set out clear expectations for both sides. The experience of collective bargaining can also be a learning experience for both sides of the discussion as it encourages employers and employees alike to consider each other's positions (See Table 4.9, Professional Player Associations).

Unfair Labor Practices

Unfair labor practices lead to strikes and lock outs. The common types of practices include interference with organizing or bargaining collectively, domination and assistance, discrimination, retaliation, duty to bargain in good faith, and protection from union (See Table 4.10, Professional Sport Labor Disputes)

Table 4.9
Professional Player Associations

- NHL Players Association
- NFL Players Association
- NBA Players Association
  - NBA Players
  - WNBA Players
- MLB Players Association
- Canadian Football League Players Association
- Arena Football Leagues Players Association
- Major League Soccer Players Association

Source: SportBusiness Journal Research, 2013

Strike

Strike action, often simply called a strike, is a work stoppage caused by the mass refusal by employees to perform work. A strike usually takes place in response to employee grievances. Strikes became important during the industrial revolution, when mass labor became important in factories and mines.

Table 4.10
Professional Sport Labor Disputes

- Strikes
  - MLB: 1972, 1980, 1981, 1985, 1994–95
  - NHL: 1992
  - NFL: 1970, 1974, 1982, 1987
- Lockouts
  - NBA: 1995, 1996, 1998
  - MLB: 1973, 1976, 1990
  - NHL: 1994–95, 2004–05, 2012–2013
  - NFL: 1968, 2011
- Walkouts
  - NFL: 1968
- Impasse
- Boycotting Free Agent Market (1986, MLB)

Source: SportBusiness Journal Research, 2013

Lock Out

A lockout is a work stoppage in which an employer prevents employees from working. This is different from a strike, during which employees refuse to work. A lockout may happen for several reasons. When only part of a trade union votes to strike, the purpose of a lockout is to put pressure on a union by reducing the number of members who are able to work.

Union v. Agency Shop

In a union shop, a worker must join the union. In an agency shop, a worker is not required to join the union but must pay initiation fees and union dues.

Free Agency

Free agency was first established in baseball in 1976. Unrestricted free agency for players means that after a specific duration of professional service, a player is free to negotiate with any team in the league. At present, the NHL, NBA, NFL, and MLB all have some form of free agency.

Salary Caps

The salary cap is a restriction or limit on the amount of money that may be made available by the leagues to pay player salaries. Salary caps in professional sports have been designed as a percentage of certain league revenues. Salary caps require an agreement between the league and the player association as to what will constitute "defined gross revenue" (DGR). The DGR usually consists of gate receipts, local and national television and radio broadcast revenue, and a percentage of income from luxury suites, licensing income, concessions, and merchandising.

There are two types of salary caps currently in use in professional sports. They are a hard and soft cap. The hard cap used by the NFL means a team cannot exceed the cap established in the agreement. The soft cap used by the NBA has exceptions such as the Larry Bird exemption (hometown player) and the middle-class exemption for middle-class players. Major League Baseball uses a luxury tax system to maintain its softball salary cap. The luxury tax is assessed when a team goes above the soft cap established by the league.

References

Carrell, M. R., & Heavrin, C. (2012). *Labor relations and collective bargaining: Private and public sectors* (10th ed.). Upper Saddle River, NJ: Prentice-Hall.

Denhardt, R. B., Denhardt, J. V., & Aristigueta, M. P. (2012). *Managing human behavior in public and non-profit organizations* (8th ed). Thousand Oaks, CA: SAGE Publications.

Dresang, D. L. (2012). *Personal management in government agencies and nonprofit organizations* (15th ed). New York: Pearson.

Equal Employment Opportunity Commission. (1964, 1987) Sexual Harassment. Washington, DC: Equal Employment Opportunity Commission.

Gold, M. E. (2014). *An introduction to labor law* (3rd ed.). Ithaca, NY: ILR Press, Cornell University Press.

Hernandez, J. (2012). *How to become a sport agent: Step-by-step instructions*. New York: PlayerPress.

Lussier, R. (2009). *Human relations in organizations: Applications and skill building* (8th ed).New York: McGraw-Hill/Irwin.

Reece, B., Brandt, R., & Howie, K.T. (2010). *Effective human relations: Personal and organizational applications*. Cincinnati, OH South Western College Publishing.

Shropshire, K. L., & Davis, T. (2008). *The business of sport agents* (2nd ed). College Station, PA: University of Pennsylvania Press.

Smith, A. (2014). *Unions, labor law, and collective bargaining*. Winter Haven, FL: Ironwood Publications.

Society for Human Resource Management. (2013) Performance Improvement Plan. Retrieved from http://www.shrm.org

CHAPTER 5

Facility and Event Risk Management

Garold M. Rushing
Bryan Romsa

Minnesota State University, Mankato

A well-designed sports or recreation facility can significantly enhance the ability of providers to achieve the goals and benefits of its organization. Unfortunately, even well-designed sports facilities can and do produce adverse outcomes, such as injuries, death, contract disputes, civil rights violations, and so forth. In today's litigious society, these situations frequently produce lawsuits that can lead facility personnel to the courtroom. Loss to the facility arising from these lawsuits can be in the form of time, reputation, and money, and as a result significantly interfere with the achievement of a facility's mission.

Risk Management

The most effective way for sports facility operators to avoid losses is to design and implement a strategy that identifies those situations in which legal or financial difficulties can arise and then take corrective actions that will either eliminate the exposure, significantly reduce the chances of the situation from occurring, or reduce the impact of the happening should it occur. This process is called risk management (Appenzeller, 2008).

Risks are viewed broadly as physical injury or death, potential litigation, and financial loss (Jensen & Overman, 2003) and can be defined as those occurrences that expose a provider to the possibility of loss.

Benefits of a Risk Management Program

Sawyer and Judge (2012) and Sawyer and Smith (1999) stated that a good risk management program increases the safety of the patrons, reduces the losses to the organization, and increases effective use of funds. Additionally, it serves as a deterrent to a lawsuit and demonstrates intent to act in a reasonable and prudent manner. Appenzeller and Lewis (2000) reinforced this notion when they explained, "the law does expect that sport managers develop and implement loss-control and risk management programs to ensure a safe environment for all who participate in the sport activities" (p. 314). The overriding benefit is that a good risk management program significantly enhances the achievement of goals and the mission of a facility.

Risk Management Manager

Safety and risk management are shared responsibilities; all workers in a venue should know their roles and be aware of the need to minimize risk. To clarify each employee's role in risk management and to oversee the development and implementation of the risk management program, someone should be designated as the risk manager. This could be an individual who is a full-time professional risk manager or someone who has additional responsibilities. It should be noted that for a risk manager to be effective, he or she must have the support of the upper management in a facility.

Risk Management Committee

Further, it is unlikely that one person would know all the risk exposures that a venue may encounter, nor can one person effectively manage a risk management program. Therefore, it is extremely beneficial to have a risk management committee to help provide guidance and oversight to a risk management program. The ideal committee should be composed of experts in insurance and law and have representation from the various units in the facility. Unit representation helps ensure support for the program and provides valuable input from those most familiar with risks in their department (Buisman, Thompson, & Cox, 1993). Ammon and Unruh (2010) recommended that at the very least, the committee should be composed of knowledgeable senior members of the organization.

Risk Categories

Although there are many ways that loss can occur within facility operations, most loss exposure can be categorized in one of four general areas. These include 1) public liability caused by negligence, 2) public liability excluding negligence, 3) business operations, and 4) property exposures (Brown, 2003). The extent to which a particular facility needs to be concerned with each area varies depending on the purpose of the facility, the unique situations of the facility, the types of programs and populations served, and specific injuries and incidents that have occurred in the past (Eickhoff-Shemek, 2008). Facility operators should familiarize themselves with safety and welfare concerns in each of these areas.

Public Liability Caused by Negligence

Negligence in a sports or recreation facility is failure on the part of the owner/operator to manage a facility in a reasonably prudent and careful manner and this failure results in damage to the plaintiff. This definition implies that facility management must provide a reasonably safe environment in which to work or participate. This general obligation can be translated into more specific duties such as providing proper warnings and instructions to participants, providing proper supervision/security, providing proper equipment and facilities, providing medical/emergency precautions and care, and providing proper travel and transportation (Appenzeller, 2008). A claim of negligence could result from poor risk management caused by failure on the part of a facility operator to fulfill any of the above duties. Examples of claims in this area include injuries due to poorly maintained facilities (*Woodring v. Board of Education of Manhasset Union Free School District*, 1981) and attacks by third parties (*Bearman v. University of Notre Dame*, 1999).

Public Liability Excluding Negligence

This area is composed of circumstances in which facility personnel cause harm to patrons, fellow employees, or volunteers in ways other than negligence. Tort law provides an avenue for people to be compensated for damages caused by these injurious situations. Examples of these situations include hiring and employment practices, professional malpractice, product liability, intentional torts, sexual harassment, and civil liberty violations. Examples of claims in this area include age, gender, disability and racial discrimination; wrongful termination; sexual harassment; invasion of privacy; and false imprisonment.

Business Operations

Business operations include business interruptions, employee health, theft, embezzlement, and contract disputes. Examples of risks in this area include fraud by workers, such as cheating on hours worked, admitting people into events free of charge, stealing money, and work interruptions such as strikes and sickness of key personnel.

Property Exposures

This category consists of risk exposures to equipment, buildings, and grounds as a result of fire, natural disasters (earthquakes, floods, blizzards, hurricanes, tornadoes), vandalism/terrorism, and theft.

Risk Management Program Development Steps

The foundation of effective risk management is taking logical and proactive steps to handle uncertain financial and other losses that may occur from the activities of a facility (Jensen & Overman, 2003). The following steps enable a risk manager to develop a program that identifies risks, eliminates the unacceptable ones, and manages the remainder:

- Identify applicable areas of concern (public liability excluding negligence, business operations, property exposures, and public liability caused by negligence).

- Identify specific risk exposures in each category.

- Estimate the probable impact of the risk and classify.

- Select the optimum method of treating the risk.

- Implement a plan to carry out the selected method, monitor, and evaluate.

Step One: Identify Applicable Areas of Concern

The first step in developing a risk management program is to determine the areas or categories of risks with which the facility operator should be concerned. A reference outline can be developed from the previously mentioned general categories of risks (public liability caused by negligence, public liability excluding negligence, business operations, and property exposures) or more specific categories can be selected such as accidents, security, contracts, personnel, financial, natural disasters, speculative risks (strikes), terrorist threats, design and construction, and so forth. The purpose of selecting the areas of concern is to provide risk reviewers with a reference for brainstorming and finding more specific risk exposures.

Step Two: Identify Risk Specific Exposures in Each Category

After the general categories have been selected, risk managers can enlist the help of risk management committee members or unit heads in the facility to do a risk inventory and compile a list of specific hazards that they may face in each category. Research must be done. Sawyer and Judge (2012) recommended utilizing interviews with pertinent personnel, loss analysis questionnaires, physical site inspections, or business plan reviews. He further suggested that those responsible for identifying risks should use their imaginations and conduct "what-if" scenarios. Professional literature, knowledgeable professionals, manufacturer's recommendations, historical claims data, and professional standards and practices can also be consulted. Finally, equipment and facility checklists or audits designed to help expose risk situations can be utilized. Not all risks are identifiable; however, if the above suggestions are applied, a fairly comprehensive list of risks can be identified.

Step Three: Estimate the Probable Impact of the Risk

The next step in developing a risk management program is to assess each risk on the risk master list and estimate the level of loss that each risk occurrence may impose on the operation of a facility. Various assessment tools in the form of frequency and severity matrices have been developed to assist risk managers with this task. Frequency is how often the risk could occur and the severity is the degree of loss resulting from the occurrence. The more frequent a risk occurs and the more severe the occurrence, the greater the potential impact on the facility (Ammon & Unruh, 2003; Mulrooney, Farmer, & Ammon, 1995; Sawyer & Judge, 2012; Sawyer & Smith, 1999). Risk managers may wish to devise a matrix that reflects their own facility's specific needs. Table 5.1 provides one means of evaluating a risk. Each risk, should it occur, is rated 1 to 5 on four criteria, with 5 being the highest. The first criterion is the likelihood of occurrence, which is an estimate of the probability that the risk will occur. The second criterion is the potential human impact, which deals with death or injury caused by the particular risk occurrence. The third criterion is the potential property impact and relates to the loss or damage of property and the cost to replace or repair it. The last criterion is an estimate of the impact of the loss to business resulting from business interruptions, employees unable to work, contractual violations, fines and penalties or legal costs, etc. The scores for each risk should be totaled and the risks classified according to estimated impact. For example, a score of 17 to 20 might be considered severe, 13 to 16, high, 9 to 12, medium, and below 9, low. The higher scores result in greater impact (IAVM, 2012).

It is not critical that this process is exact; however, the assessment that is performed should enable the risk manager to classify the impact of the risk on the facility's operation. The example above is one means of classifying the impact (i.e., severe, high, medium, and low). Knowing classifications of impact will provide some guidance in determining a strategy for managing each risk and will help determine planning and resource priorities.

Table 5.1

Typical Sport Organization Risk Management Problems

Property Loss
- Stationary property
- Mobile property
- Leased property

Employee Safety and Health
- Accident prevention
- Industrial hygiene

Personnel
- Workers compensation
- Life insurance
- Disability insurance
- Health insurance
- Pension plans
- Key personnel loss (i.e., turn-over)
- Contractual employees

Liability Control
- General negligence
- Vehicle liability
- Product liability

Environmental Protection
- Storage
- Pollution control
- Waste disposal

Emergency Planning
- Crowd control
- Fire
- Bombing
- Spectator health emergencies

Financial Risk
- Interest-rate risk
- Credit risk
- Currency risk
- Liquidity risk
- Theft of product
- Theft of money
- Market risk

Step Four: Select the Optimum Method of Treating the Risk

After risks have been identified and classified, the next step is to apply a strategy that will appropriately control the loss resulting from the risk occurrence. Controlling the loss of assets is the goal of risk management (Jensen & Overman, 2003; Wong & Masterelexis, 2012) and can be accomplished in one or a combination of four general ways: avoid, retain, transfer, and reduce.

Avoid. The first way is through loss avoidance, which entails avoiding or abandoning activities that have been deemed to have a loss potential that is too great (catastrophic or high loss) and that are nonessential to the mission of the venue. Examples of the application of this strategy are the removal of trampoline competition at a high school gymnastic competition or not booking an unruly rock band that is known to create serious problems. These are situations where the potential loss clearly outweighs the value of the event.

Retain. A second strategy is to retain the risk and prepare for potential loss through budgeting, deductibles, or self-insurance. Some situations or activities are inconsequential, uninsurable, nontransferable, or the cost of insurance is prohibitive. Risks associated with these situations/activities may be assumed by the facility as part of the cost of doing business. An example of the application of this strategy is budgeting for the loss of game balls at sporting events.

Transfer. A third means of controlling loss is transferring or shifting the loss to another person or entity through insurance or contractually by way of waivers of liability, indemnity clauses, and use of an independent contractor. This transfer strategy is applicable in situations where loss potential is substantial and the entity does not want to eliminate the risk (Sawyer & Smith, 1999; Sawyer & Judge, 2012).

Insurance is an excellent way to control for loss; however, it is expensive and therefore should be a last resort and done in conjunction with risk reduction. Reduction of risk lowers the potential for loss, which translates into lower premiums.

Facility operators need to have coverage that protects staff, participants, volunteers, administrators, and visitors. Typically, facilities need to have four major forms of insurance: 1) liability insurance for loss-related claims for damages to persons or to their property; 2) accident insurance, which pays medical expenses for injured patrons; 3) property insurance, which covers facilities against natural disasters, theft, vandalism, and other events; and 4) workers compensation, which covers injury claims of workers.

Additional insurance may be needed for special events. Selection of the appropriate types and amounts of coverage should be prepared in consultation with a reputable insurance specialist.

Use of waivers or releases. Facility operators can use waivers or releases of liability as a means of transferring loss arising from negligent acts of the facility provider or its employees. These documents are contracts that relinquish the right of patrons to sue for ordinary negligence. It must be noted that they only provide relief for mere negligence and not for extreme forms of negligence, such as reckless misconduct or gross negligence. Also, it is unlikely that the courts will enforce waivers signed by or on behalf of minors (Cotten, 2010 a). Waivers can provide a valuable means for transferring loss to the participant; however, the use of these documents must adhere to legal restrictions of the jurisdiction in which the facility is located.

Indemnity clauses. These are agreements that hold owners/landlords harmless for any negligent acts or omissions by rental groups or independent contractors, such as vendors or concessionaires. These agreements have obvious value in that they relieve the facility owners from any negligent loss resulting from the use of their facility.

Independent contractor. An independent contractor is a person or business that agrees to perform a specific job for a facility. They are not considered employees of the venue if they are only hired to perform a specific task, and the venue does not retain control over the method by which the task is performed (Cotten, 2010b). As a result of this arrangement, independent contractors are responsible for their own unemployment and liability insurance and are, typically, solely liable for their negligent actions. As with any contractor, their references and credentials should be carefully checked. Also, make sure the firm is adequately insured. Security guards and some vendors at many facilities are independent contractors.

Reduce. The fourth and final way of controlling loss is managing risk through loss reduction (loss prevention and loss control). This strategy is most effective when performed in conjunction with transfer and retention and is achieved by employing prudent practices that eliminate or reduce the effects of risk occurrences. The following are a few general ways of reducing risk in all risk categories: hiring qualified personnel, educating and training them effectively, selecting appropriate venues, abiding by all laws and codes, and implementing standard operating procedures for all significant risks. Specific strategies should be developed in each risk category (public liability caused by negligence, public liability excluding negligence, business operations, property exposures).

Risk reduction for public liability caused by negligence. There are many ways to increase safety and decrease public liability risk exposures related to negligence. Facility operators must apply the best option for each risk based on their resources and characteristics. Risk managers must consider the characteristics of their users (age, skill level, etc.) and the types of activities in which they engage. They also must know their legal obligations as an owner of property versus a renter or leaser of property. They must meet local, state, regional, and federal code requirements. They must develop regularly scheduled inspections of the facility (floors, ventilation, restrooms, equipment, food preparation areas, toxic materials disposal, and security). They must regularly schedule maintenance with safety concerns given priority; monitor visitors for security; supply emergency/crisis plans for natural disasters and terrorist exposures such as bomb threats; hire or select qualified personnel (lifeguards, aerobics instructors, etc.); supply appropriate signage; provide proper supervision; and insure proper transportation. Additionally, dram shop laws related to alcohol sales and use must be followed.

An example of a method for reducing negligence risk exposures is properly designing and constructing a facility. This strategic measure enhances supervision and security and, as a result, reduces risk exposures. Another application of a reduction strategy is illustrated by a facility that chooses to book a rowdy rock band knowing that it will create a very high-risk situation. They reduce the risk by increasing the quantity of security, limiting festival seating, and/or halting alcohol sales early. Both examples increase the safety of patrons and reduce the likelihood of loss through lawsuits.

Risk reduction for public liability excluding negligence. There are a number of risk situations, exclusive of negligence, in which facility personnel can cause harm and expose the facility to loss. Examples of these risk exposures include illegal searching of patrons, false imprisonment (retaining patrons), improper employment practices, sexual harassment, assault/battery, invasion of privacy, and professional malpractice. Each of these areas should be evaluated for exposure and proper policies and procedures developed to mitigate them.

A major risk area that must be addressed is employment practices. Risk incidents that occur in this area usually allege some form of discrimination in employee recruitment, hiring and firing, evaluation, promotion, transfers, salary, etc. Employers cannot effectively discriminate against applicants or employees in any of the above areas on the basis of gender, race, color, national origin, religion, age, or disabilities unless there is a substantial, demonstrable relationship between the trait and the job. For example, if an employer can prove that a specific gender is essential to performing a specific job, then it is legal to discriminate against the opposite gender. To reduce loss in this area, policies and procedures must be designed based on Equal Opportunity Commission guidelines, Affirmative Action, Equal Pay Act, Title VII of the Civil Rights Act, Americans with Disabilities Act, and other pertinent employment law. Employees must be aware of these policies and be required to abide by them.

Sexual harassment is another area that should be of utmost concern of facility managers. Sexual harassment is a form of sexual discrimination that violates Title VII of the Civil Rights Act of 1964 and Title IX of the Educational Amendments Act of 1972. There are two primary forms: "quid pro quo" and "hostile environment." Quid pro quo sexual harassment occurs when promotions, raises, or any other job benefits are contingent on sexual favors. The second form, hostile environment, occurs when employees or participants are subjected to a sexually offensive atmosphere that is so pervasive that it interferes with their ability to perform. If the facility employer knew, or should have known, about a sexual harassment occurrence and failed to take immediate corrective action, then the facility could be held liable. To prevent such occurrences, risk managers must implement policies and procedures to educate personnel, to investigate complaints, and to provide sanctions for violations.

Sanctions may include, but are not limited to, reprimand, transfer, reassignment, removal from the complainant's area, and/or dismissal of the offending party from the organization (Roberts & Mann, 2012).

Risk reduction in business operations. Strategies in this area primarily involve knowing and adhering to appropriate business practices. Specific strategies may include providing employees with an in-house fitness program to reduce sick days, monitoring the conduct of employees to prevent fraud, and seeking legal advice periodically to insure that contracts are comprehensive and enforceable.

Risk reduction in property exposures. This area involves eliminating or reducing loss related to equipment, facilities, and grounds. Strategies in this category include providing proper fencing, an adequate lock system, keycard access, and closed-circuit television (CCTV) to prevent vandalism and theft; fire prevention strategies including sprinkler system, fire extinguishers, and having the fire department inspect the premises; proper site selection (e.g., avoid flood plain, avoid high seismic areas, close to emergency facilities) and construction planning for natural disasters; and providing checklists and periodic inspections to help identify situations that may lead to property damage.

Step Five: Implement a Plan to Carry Out the Selected Method

The last step in a risk management program is to implement, monitor, and evaluate the strategies that have been selected for each risk. Implementation means integrating the selected strategies into the ongoing facility operations, training employees, and evaluating the program (IAVM, 2012).

Integration. After the strategies for dealing with risks have been identified, the director must then integrate these strategies into the ongoing facility operations. For the risks that have been deemed to be too risky to have, the risk manager must ensure that these situations are either discontinued or never included in the facility operations. He or she also needs to be certain that proper insurance (e.g., type, amount, and deductibles) is purchased from a reputable company and that it is monitored on a regular basis to ensure adequate coverage for the specific identified losses.

If self-insurance or "budgeting for loss" is in the risk management program, the risk manager needs to make sure that these have been addressed at the appropriate time in the budgeting cycle. If waivers, informed consent, incident reports, form contacts or any other written documents have been identified as necessary, then the risk manager should develop them and incorporate them into operational procedures through orientation and training of personnel. These documents should be reviewed on an annual basis.

For the remainder of the risk-control strategies, it is most likely that the risks are addressed through safety audits (inspections) or checklists, regular maintenance schedules or standard operating procedures (SOPs). To effectively integrate these tools into the facility operations, personnel must be assigned responsibility, trained and held accountable. Communication is the key to achieving these objectives.

Assigning risk management responsibilities can be done through a job orientation interview together with a job description that provides specific risk management responsibilities. The job description should include the workers' roles in the risk management program and their responsibilities in specific emergency response procedures.

An additional tool that aids in communication and accountability is an operations manual that outlines policies and procedures for dealing with various risk situations. For this tool to be effective, management must emphasize its importance and require enough training that personnel are proficient in the cited procedures. Preemployment and annual in-service training should be used to keep the risk management procedures current and workers proficient. The International Association of Venue Managers (IAVM) recommends that drilling of emergency procedures such as medical, fire, terrorist threats, and so on be a part of the worker training (IAVM, 2012). Additionally, workers should be educated about pertinent codes, laws, and regulations relative to safety and patron service. These include fire codes, Americans with Disabilities Act, OSHA regulations, and so forth. Workers not only need to know how to perform risk management tasks, they also must know that they have the authority to perform their tasks. An organizational chart that provides clear lines of authority between the risk manager and workers should be developed and published for reference. If this is done properly, communication can be enhanced, conflicts and confusion reduced, and the program elements integrated into an ongoing approach to managing risks. Risk management must become part of the organizational culture, and the risk manager should look for ways to build awareness and to educate and train personnel.

Monitoring and evaluation. Periodic program monitoring and evaluation enable the risk manager to determine how effective the risk management program is and where improvements may be needed. IAVM (2012) recommended a yearly evaluation and an evaluation

- after each training drill,
- after each emergency,
- when personnel or responsibilities change,
- when the layout or design of the facility changes, and
- when policies or procedures change.

The risk management program evaluation should also include individual performance appraisals of employees based on their job descriptions. These individual assessments compel personnel to be accountable for fulfillment of their risk management responsibilities and help insure that the risk management program is successful. Success or failure of a risk management program depends on how well individual workers perform their responsibilities; therefore, it is important that workers be held accountable.

Event Risk Management

Events that are hosted by sports and recreation facilities are frequently the lifeblood of the facility; therefore, it is imperative that participants and spectators be provided a safe, secure, and accommodating environment. Each event, whether it is a sporting event or fitness activity, has unique risk concerns that may require specific attention that cannot be addressed by a generic plan. In order to address these unique risks, a written event risk management plan for each type of event should be developed. The plan should be a part of an overall facility risk management plan.

The plan should be constructed using the risk management steps mentioned previously. Following the steps allows the planner to identify the unique needs of an event and develop a plan comprising the strategies for managing them. The following areas may need the special attention of the risk manager, depending on the size and type of event: pre-event venue preparation and safety audits, a crowd-management plan (if a large crowd is expected), described as part of pre-event venue prep, event insurance, and transportation and parking.

Pre-Event Venue Preparation and Safety Audits

An important element of an event risk management plan is ensuring that the facility and its equipment are prepared for the event. This may include such activities as proper markings of fields, clearing egress and ingress passageways, or placing collapsible fencing around a playing area in addition to doing safety audits of pertinent spaces and equipment. The purpose of these inspections is to ensure a safe environment to participate in and/or observe examples of possible checks.

A thorough review of safety codes, ordinances, and laws is also important to ensure compliance. Permits or special licenses, such as a temporary liquor license, may need to be secured. In addition to the above, event planners should be prepared to accommodate individuals with special needs. If the venue has not been properly designed to accommodate persons with disabilities, then "reasonable accommodation" must be made for viewing or participation.

Event Insurance

After identifying risk exposures associated with an event (step two of the risk management process), consult with an insurance advisor to determine suitable coverages, deductibles, policy terms, and prospective carriers. Auto insurance should not be overlooked; while autos may not be used frequently, there may be increased exposure during certain events. Additional coverage may be necessary, especially if volunteers or employees are using their own vehicles in conjunction with the event.

Transportation and Parking

A comprehensive event risk management plan must include methods for handling vehicles that bring attendees to events. Parking lots should be a source of concern for risk managers in that assaults, vandalism, vehicle collisions, and personal injury accidents can occur. Well-trained and supervised parking aids may be needed to direct and park vehicles. They should have bright clothing and flashlights if it is an evening event. The parking area should be well lit and maintained to avoid trips and falls. If vandalism and theft are a significant risk, then the parking area should be patrolled and possibly monitored by CCTV.

If shuttles or chauffeuring special guests from parking areas is necessary and the facility is using its own employees, then they should be screened for acceptable driving records and appropriate licenses to drive the type of vehicle that they drive.

Event Crowd Management Plan

Another important consideration of an event risk management plan is crowd management. This is especially important if a large crowd is expected; but even in a small group, some crowd control is important. If planned appropriately, it should provide facility management with a tool that will mitigate many of the event risks. Suggested components of a crowd management plan include the following: 1) trained and competent staff; 2) crisis management and emergency action plans to prevent and reduce the consequences of crises such as bomb threats, tornado, or other inclement weather, fire, and medical emergency; 3) procedures for dealing with unruly or intoxicated patrons; 4) communications network; and 5) effective signage (Ammon & Unruh, 2010). The crowd management plan should be formulated based on the characteristics of the crowd (IAVM, 2012). This enables the risk manager to anticipate problems and adjust crowd management procedures accordingly.

The first, and arguably the most important, element of a crowd management plan is trained and competent personnel. Whether the workers are volunteers or paid, close attention to acquiring an adequate number of competent personnel and then training them how to respond appropriately to patron requests, to emergency situations, and to security concerns is essential to an effective crowd management plan. If a facility does not have a sufficient number of trained persons needed for a particular event, the operator may consider outsourcing the work to trained specialists from a reputable company.

The second component of crowd management is crisis management and emergency action plans to prevent and reduce the consequences of crises, such as bomb threats, tornado, or other inclement weather, fire, and medical emergency. These plans should be in writing, and personnel should be trained in how to perform the procedures so that they are done in a proficient and timely manner.

Closely allied with crisis management is crowd security. Security is a significant element of a crowd-management plan and is a term used to describe a facility's strategy for protecting patrons or property from actions of a third party during an event. Typical security risk situations that may arise during an event are riotous behavior of spectators, such as a celebratory rushing of the field, throwing objects, spectators attacking participants, officials, other event attendees, and stadium/arena vandalism and graffiti. Additionally, sporting events may be attractive targets for terrorists' activities. Without effective security, the safety of those in attendance as well as those participating in the event may be compromised.

Quality personnel, appropriate technology, and a good strategy are the keys to effective security. Good security should include a team of trained personnel such as hired police, peer security, ushers, and ticket takers. Each should understand his or her role in securing the event. If a large crowd is expected, it may be best to hire a security firm. These personnel can be very useful if it becomes necessary to escort troublemakers or intoxicated attendees from the premises. In addition to security personnel, security technology such as scanners, CCTV, cell phones or multi-channeled phones, should be incorporated into the crisis management strategy. The security strategy should begin at the time patrons enter the facility (probably a parking lot) and end when all patrons have left the venue.

A third element of a crowd management plan is having written procedures for ejecting disruptive, unruly, or intoxicated patrons. It is very important that these procedures address the rights and the safety of the ejected individual. Ejections should be documented and only trained and authorized staff should take part in an ejection. Using untrained personnel to handle these disturbances could prove disastrous (Ammon & Unruh, 2010).

An effective communications network is another element of a crowd management plan. Many aspects of a crowd management plan require communication between facility staff, the patrons, or possibly outside emergency agencies. Facility personnel should anticipate communications needs related to handling emergencies and crowd supervision and accommodate these needs with communications strategies and technology.

The last crowd management plan component suggested by Ammon and Unruh (2010) is effective signage. Signage that provides information about the facility's rules of behavior, prohibited items, and warnings and "directional" signage such as egress and ingress signage are invaluable in providing safe and enjoyable environment.

References

Ammon, R., & Unruh, A. (2010). Crowd management. In D. J. Cotton & J. Wolahan (Eds.), *Law for recreation and sport managers* (5th ed., pp. 338–350). Dubuque, IA: Kendall/Hunt Publishing Company.

Appenzeller, H. (2008). Risk assessment and reduction. In H. Appenzeller & T. Appenzeller (Eds.), *Successful sport management* (3rd ed., pp. 239–248). Durham, NC: Carolina Academic Press.

Cotton, D. (2010a). Which parties are liable? In D.J. Cotton & J. Wolahan, (Eds.), *Law for recreation and sport managers* (5th ed., pp.53–65). Dubuque, IA: Kendall/Hunt Publishing Company.

Cotton, D. (2010b). Waivers and releases. In D.J. Cotten & J. Wolahan (Eds.), *Law for recreation and sport managers* (5th ed., pp. 96–106). Dubuque, IA: Kendall/Hunt Publishing Company.

Eickhoff-Shemek, J. (2008). *Minimizing legal liability: Risk management for health fitness facilities* (videotape). ACSM, Healthy Learning Videos. Monterey Bay Video Production Co.

International Association of Venue Managers. (2012). Retrieved from www.iavm.org

Jensen, C. R., & Overman, S. J. (2003). *Administration and management of physical education and athletic programs.* Long Grove, IL: Waveland Press, Inc.

Roberts, S., & Mann, B. S. (2012). *Sexual harrassment in the workplace: A primer.* Retrieved from www3.uakron.edu/lawrev/robert1.html

Sawyer, T. H., & Smith, O. R. (1999). *The management of clubs, recreation, and sport.* Urbana, IL: Sagamore Publishing, LLC.

Sawyer, T. H., & Judge, L.W. (2012). *The management of fitness, physical activity, recreation, and sport.* Urbana, IL: Sagamore Publishing, LLC.

Wong, G. M., & Masteralexis, L. P. (2012). Legal principles applied to sport management. In L. P. Masterelexi, C. A. Barr, & M. A. Hums (Eds.), *Principles and practice of sport management* (pp. 85–117). Sudbury, MA: Jones & Barlett Learning.

CHAPTER 6

Security Management

Thomas H. Sawyer

Professor Emeritus, Indiana State University

Since 9/11, security in and around sport facilities has become a flashpoint for managing those facilities. It has had a major financial impact upon facility operations in general. This has been followed by a dramatic increase in multiple shootings that have taken place in public facilities such as schools, colleges, and universities, and in private facilities, including movie theaters and retail complexes. These incidents have made security a major concern for sport facility managers worldwide.

Sport facility managers are responsible for ensuring that a proper security system is in place in and around the building premises, including parking lots and garages. Security includes, but is not limited to alarm systems (e.g., aquatic area alarm, fire alarm, intruder alarms, steam room and sauna alarms, etc.), sprinkler systems, and emergency escape plans in case an evacuation is necessary. In addition to these responsibilities, the sport facility manager needs to have trained emergency/security personnel available at all public assembly events.

What is Security?

Security is the degree of resistance to, or protection from, harm. It applies to any valuable asset, such as a clients, employees, facilities, and equipment. Establishing or maintaining a sufficient degree of security is the aim of a security and/or risk management plan.

What is Security Management?

According to Sennewald (2011), security management is a broad field of management related to asset management, physical security, and human resource safety functions. It encompasses the identification of an organization's information assets and the development, documentation and implementation of policies, standards, procedures and guidelines for client, employee, and facility. Hopkin (2012) suggests that security management utilizes tools such as information classification, risk assessment, and risk analysis are used to identify threats, classify assets, and to rate system vulnerabilities so that effective control can be implemented.

Security Planning

Facility managers need to implement a comprehensive risk management plan that includes sections related to alcohol, crisis, crowd, evacuation, emergency, and security management. Planning for security for facilities and/or special events includes defining financial, human, and physical assets, assessing risks, analyzing threats, and developing appropriate plans, policies, and protective measures. The U.S. Department of Homeland Security (2009) suggests that the following steps should be followed when planning for effective security:

- Clarify the problem(s)
- Canvas resources
- Explore alternatives
- Provide solutions
- Define priorities
- Develop action plans
- Follow up

Once the plan has been established, it is important to practice the plan, evaluate the plan, and modify the plan. The key to successful security strategies is to have a well-documented plan in place and to exercise it regularly. According to Hall, Cooper, Marciani, and McGee (2012), the plan most likely will depend on multiple agencies for safety and security operations and must coordinate planning efforts with those agencies.

The U.S. Department of Homeland Security (2009) indicates that public assembly facilities should have in place in the following key areas, policies, procedures, and protective measures:

- ADA
- Alcohol
- Communications
- Credentialing
- Emergency medical services
- Evacuation
- Fan conduct
- Fire
- Media and communications
- Missing child or person
- Natural disasters common to the area
- Parking
- Prohibited items
- Protecting critical system controls
- Search policy
- Tailgating
- Ticket taking

According to Hall et al. (2012) and the U.S. Department of Homeland Security (2009), sport programs should also consider implementing protective security measures in the following areas:

- Physical security
  - Establish security zones
  - Create perimeters
  - Provide law enforcement presence before, during, and after all events
  - Secure buildings surrounding the public assembly facility

- Protect all HVAC systems
- Make safe all electrical systems
- Technical security
    - Secure utility areas with alarms
    - Use closed-circuit television for monitoring the public assembly facility
    - Ensure adequate lighting in and outside the facility as well as emergency lighting
    - Implement interoperable communication system
    - Consider cyber security
    - Use telephone trap and trace
- Access control
    - Use designated entry checkpoints
    - Conduct searches for prohibited items
    - Search ALL staff
    - Scan tickets electronically
    - Lock down the facility before the event
    - Conduct staff background checks
    - Issue staff photo credentials
- Emergency management
    - Develop an emergency action plan
    - Establish a command post
    - Develop an evacuation plan
    - Establish mutual aid agreements with response agencies
    - Develop a natural disaster plan specific to the geographical location
    - Conduct briefing and debriefing event meetings
    - Perform a risk assessment
- Training and exercise
    - Use ONLY currently licensed and certified security providers
    - Conduct emergency response and evacuation exercises
    - Orient ALL event staff to their specific job responsibilities
    - Educate ALL event staff in security awareness and evacuation procedures
    - Train ALL event staff in CPR

Security Staffing and Training

Security and/or safety staffing is the key component to any security safety, and risk management plan (See Table 6.1 for a listing of Security Staffing). The staff implements and evaluates the plan. Those individuals employed to implement the plan must be properly prepared, certified, and recertified.

Each job description for each position should clearly delineate the minimum types of certifications required. For example, those who are authorized to carry firearms must be certified to carry and use firearms. All personnel should be trained in the use of an AED and to perform CPR.

Table 6.1

Security / Emergency Medical Personnel

The common types of security and emergency medical personnel are as follows:

- Fire personnel
- Law enforcement personnel
  - City/local police
  - Sheriff
  - State police
  - Campus police
  - Federal law enforcement (sometimes)
- Emergency medical personnel (EMTs)

It is a fact that most certifications have a shelf life of one to three years. At the end of the shelf life, a training schedule should be developed to ensure that all certifications will be renewed before expiring. If a certification lapses, then the employee would be immediately suspended.

It would be good to have instructors and/or instructor-trainers on staff to provide the retraining. This will reduce the cost of retraining for the organization. Further, it will make the recertification process more employee friendly, efficient, and convenient. Finally, this in-service training will require resourcing to pay for the necessary equipment (one-time expense), supplies, certifications, and a training area.

Facility Risk Assessment Audit

A key exercise in facility security and safety is the development and regular implementation of a facility risk assessment audit. There should be a facility risk management committee that would develop a comprehensive risk assessment tool to be used in an annual risk management audit implemented by the various area directors/coordinators. The information gathered would be collated, analyzed, and action strategies developed for reducing risk within the facility as well as outside.

What is a Risk Assessment?

A risk assessment is basically a careful examination of what could cause harm to people, equipment or facilities (see sample risk management assessment tool, in the Appendices available in the student and faculty resource center at www.sagamorepub.com. The assessment is completed to assess whether or not enough precautions have been taken or there is a need for further precautions to prevent harm from occurring.

Participants (clients, spectators, or employees) have a right to be protected from harm caused by "hazards" present in an activity. Oftentimes, straightforward measures can control risks, but not always.

What Is a Hazard?

According to Fay (2010) and Hall et al. (2012), a hazard is anything that may cause harm such as tripping; falling; broken bones from trauma, contact, or object impact; flying balls; slipping; exposure to hazardous environments or substances; and injury from contact with machinery or equipment, and so forth. Anything that may cause harm is a hazard. The facility manager or activity director should assign a "risk level" to these hazards and record who might be exposed to them.

What Is Meant by "Risk Level"?

Risk level is the chance—low, medium, or high—that somebody could be harmed by a hazard. It includes an indication of how serious the harm might be. The level of risk is assigned as follows (Fay, 2010):

- Low: Unlikely, although conceivable

- Medium: Could occur sometimes but not often

- High: Could occur quite easily and frequently

What Are the Functions of Risk Assessment?

The functions of a risk assessment audit are threefold (Hall et al., 2012):
- Identify the risks,

- evaluate the severity of the risks, and

- select methods of treatment for the risks.

What Are the Steps in Risk Assessment?

The facility manager and others should walk around the facility periodically, conducting an extensive risk evaluation. This will help to identify potential danger areas and diminish the organizations exposure to liability. The facility manager should establish a system for regular inspection documenting (a) the dates of inspection, (b) any potential problem areas, and (c) all necessary corrective measures. This will also dramatically cut down on a facility's potential liability.

The facility manager needs to ask six key questions before beginning a risk assessment (Hall et al., 2012; Hopkins, 2012; Ortmeier, 2012):
- What is the hazard?

- Who is at risk from these hazards, and what accidents may result?

- Is the risk low, medium, or high?

- What is already being done about this hazard?

- What measures can be taken to prevent accidents and reduce the risk?

- Who is responsible for taking these actions and by what date will this be completed?

There are five steps, according to Sennewald (2011), that can reduce facility liability exposure that a facility manager should follow:
- Periodic maintenance will identify potential problems and replace or repair any equipment that is damaged, reducing the risk of liability.

- Competent employees who are knowledgeable in the activities they supervise will reduce liability.

- Proper supervision of all activities will ensure liability will be reduced.

- Ensure that all appropriate warnings about proper use of equipment and the risk of improper usage must be posted.

- Implement the use of waivers as a means of reducing a facility's liability. According to Cotten and Cotten (2012), in at least 45 states, a well-written waiver, signed by an adult, will protect the facility from any injuries that might arise as a result of the negligence of the facility or its employees.

Risk Assessment (Why Do It?)

Every facility has a responsibility to provide a safe environment for players, coaches, referees, and spectators, not only to reduce the potential of injury, but also to meet or exceed the minimum standard of care. In order for the facility to create a safe environment, the facility manager needs to develop a risk assessment audit and use it regularly (See Appendices available in the student and faculty resource center at www.sagamorepub.com for an example). Sport safety planning and implementation is not hard, it is common sense. Sports should be safe and enjoyable. It will never be risk free, but with good planning and a regular risk assessment, injuries can be prevented. Safety is the key.

Alcohol Management

Alcohol sales are a large piece of revenue generation for sport and entertainment facilities, but they also bring a great deal of liability as well as management headaches. Table 6.2 outlines the top 20 claims most common in lawsuits against facility managers. Many patrons enjoy alcohol while they are being entertained. They sometimes exceed their limits and lose control, causing problems for other patrons and themselves. Every facility that serves alcohol must have an alcohol management plan and certified personnel. This will reduce insurance claims, insurance premiums, and overall liability.

There are many risks related to alcohol to customers, business, and staff. The following are just a few of those risks to be considered (Beer Institute, 2013):

- Drunk customers can be more difficult to deal with

- More mess to clear up (e.g., spillages, breakages, vomit, etc.)

- More disorder, issues may escalate into aggression and violence more quickly

- Staff more at risk of harm

- Increased costs to premises of replacing fixtures and fittings

- Increased staffing costs—need more staff to deal with disorder and cleaning, likely to have a higher staff turnover

- Premises get a reputation that in turn attracts more rowdy people and puts better behaved customers off

- Extra visits from the police, which puts license at risk

- Drunk customers are more at risk than sober individuals when returning home, whether driving, walking, or using public transportation—as they are most vulnerable to attacks or having an accident

Alcohol Management Plan

Sport and entertainment facilities must have an alcohol management plan. The alcohol management plan should include, but not be limited to, the following:

- Planning committee
    - Who is involved in developing and managing the plan?
- Planning process

Table 6.2

The Top 20 Claims Most Common in Lawsuits against Facilities Managers

The following are the top twenty claims most common in lawsuits against facility managers:

1. Failure to supervise.

2. Failure to use proper learning progressions when teaching personnel.

3. Failure to use appropriate equipment.

4. Failure to maintain equipment and facility.

5. Failure to warn the participant about inherent risks in the use of exercise equipment or the activity itself.

6. Failure to owe a duty to the plaintiff to keep the premises safe and without hazard.

7. Failure to inspect facility or equipment and conduct reasonable risk management procedures on such.

8. Failure to research equipment purchases for problems or defects in design or appropriateness for activities that are to be conducted in said facility.

9. Failure to take a medical history of participants prior to doing the activity.

10. Failure to require a physical exam before beginning the activity.

11. Failure to instruct users in exercise classes as to how to take their own vital signs.

12. Failure to use proper warm-ups.

13. Failure to hire properly credentialed professional staff.

14. Failure to teach instructors to properly evaluate the physical risk factors of the participants to determine the correct level of activity they should be involved with.

15. Failure to teach instructors to advise the participant about exercise and the effects of such on the human body.

16. Failure to provide expert professional instruction advertised or expressly warranted to participants.

17. Failure to provide as expressly warranted, an exercise program best suited for the participants.

18. Failure to require continuing education or other methods for these professionals to update their skills.

19. Failure to properly evaluate the professional staff as to their performance as instructors.

20. Failure to act as a reasonable and prudent professional, meeting the standards of care as promulgated by professional societies, publications, or research.

- • Timeline for development
- Oversight of the plan
- The plan
  - • Events
  - • Promoting the event
  - • How the plan will address alcohol-related issues in the facility
  - • Roles and responsibilities of all stakeholders
  - • How the plan will be reviewed

- Serving guidelines
  - Timelines
  - Quantity per customer
  - Age
- Signage
- Safe transportation
- Staff training
- Security
- Incident reporting
- Assessment of the plan

Sample Alcohol Management Plan

Tom Sawyer Stadium Alcohol Management Plan

Introduction

Responsible management of alcohol means (1) providing a safe and enjoyable environment for guests and (2) serving alcoholic beverages responsibly.

The Stadium will obtain and adhere to all applicable local and state permits governing the sale of alcoholic beverages. In addition, the Tom Sawyer Stadium Alcohol Management Plan will incorporate two segments: TEAM training and rigid enforcement of policies and procedures. The Stadium is committed to satisfying all requirements of the applicable permits, to retain the ability to offer alcoholic beverages as an option for customers. Further, the Stadium is also committed to the proper management of sales and consumption to retain a game environment that is conducive to family entertainment.

Techniques for Effectice Alcohol Management Team

Alcohol management strategies have been developed at many arenas and stadiums where professional entertainment and sporting events are held across the United States. Key in developing these strategies in many arenas and stadiums has been a nonprofit organization called Techniques for Effective Alcohol Management (TEAM).

TEAM training represents the most comprehensive thinking about alcohol management. The TEAM program encapsulates a highly effective approach to preparing facility operations managers to train alcohol servers and event-day employees to manage the sale, service and consumption of alcohol at public gatherings.

Stadium will adopt the TEAM approach by either joining TEAM. All Stadium employees and the employees of the security agency and other potential game day partners (concessions, etc.) will be trained to this program to provide the safest environment possible for the fans.

Policies and Procedures

The Stadium will vigorously enforce its policies and procedures with respect to the service of alcoholic beverages at the Stadium:

1. There will be no alcohol sales past the 7th inning or 10 p.m., whichever comes first.

2. No patron may purchase more than two alcoholic beverages at one time.

3. Patrons who return multiple times for alcoholic beverages will be refused further servcie if it appears they are overindulging.

4. Alcoholic beverages, cans, glass bottles, or coolers are prohibited from being brought into the ballpark.

5. Designated driver program: free soda and gift for signing up as a designated driver.

6. No tailgating, picnics, or alcohol consumption in parking lots or ballpark perimeter permitted.

7. Team staff and security personnal will patrol all seating sections in order to detect early any signs of overindulging fans or other unruly behavior.

Modified from the MLB, NBA, NFL, and NHL alcohol management policies, 2014.

Serving Guidelines

According to Service Alcohol, Inc. (2014), selling alcohol requires many skills and involves legal responsibilities. In serving alcohol, there are several different aspects to the position:

- "To be a police officer, ensuring no one breaks any laws (e.g., underage drinking)

- To be a sales person, knowledgeable about the products being sold

- To be a cleaner, making sure premises are clean and tidy

- To be a good host, helping to create a friendly atmosphere

- To be a safety officer, thinking about the well-being of the customers and reducing any risks (Serving Alcohol Inc., 2007)"

It is important for facility managers to set times for the sale of alcohol. Many professional leagues have established specific times when alcohol is restricted, such as the following:

- Major League Baseball: alcohol cannot be served after the seventh inning.

- National Basketball Association: alcohol cannot be served after the 3rd quarter.

- National Football League: alcohol cannot be served after the 3rd quarter.

- National Hockey League: alcohol cannot be served after the 2nd period.

It is also important to limit the amount of alcohol consumed by each patron. Many facilities limit the sale of alcohol to no more than two containers at a time per patron. Further, the container sizes should be controlled as well as the types of alcohol available (e.g., beer and wine only).

Staff Training

All staff working for an entertainment and sport facility must complete alcohol training and become certified. Since 1985, TEAM (Techniques for Effective Alcohol Management) Coalition has succeeded as a unique alliance of professional (MLB, MLS, NASCAR, NBA, NFL, and NHL) and collegiate (NCAA) sports, entertainment facilities (Live Nation, International Association for Venue Managers, Contemporary Services Corporation, and Stadium Managers Association), concessionaires (ARAMARK and DNC Sportservice, Ovations Food Services, Elite, and SMA), the beer industry (Beer Institute, National Beer Wholesalers, Anheuser-Busch Companies, and Miller-Coors), broadcasters (National Association of Broadcasters), and the U.S. Department of Transportation (National Highway Traffic Safety Administration) and others are working together to promote responsible drinking and positive fan behavior at entertainment and sports facilities. The mission of TEAM Coalition is "to enhance the entertainment experience, provide effective alcohol management training in public assembly facilities and promote responsible alcohol consumption through the use of positive messages that reward responsible behavior and help to reduce negative alcohol-related incidents both in facilities and on surrounding roadways, recognizing that the vast majority of the fans are responsible" (http://www.teamcoalition.org/about/about.asp). Table 6.3 below outlines an alcohol information checklist for event organizing.

Table 6.3

Alcohol Information Checklist for Event Organizing

- How many people are expected to attend?
- Free admission?
- Paid admission?
- Space capacity?
- Is the event BYOB?
- Is alcohol being given away?
- Is alcohol being sold?
- What type of alcohol will be available?
- What type of containers will be available?
- Will the staff (all) be TEAM certified?
- Have the proper permits/licenses been secured to sell alcohol?
- Is there an alcohol management plan?
- Will there be signage promoting low-alcohol drinks, food, and water?
- Will the management impose alcohol restrictions—quantity and sale hours?
- Will the management ban alcohol promotions?
- Will the management control drink containers?
- Will the management limit the alcohol to wine and beer?

Modified from Beer Institute (2013) Managing Alcohol.

Crowd Management

Terrorism Potential

It is important that entertainment and sport event managers know their spectators and recognize the potential for threats to the safety of all the spectators, entertainers, and staff. Since 9/11, terrorism has become a distinct possibility at any event attracting large numbers of spectators. It is important to recognize potential terrorist situations. Managers must educate their personnel about the common terrorists indicators. There seven key terrorist indicators identified by Kennedy (2006) and supported by Hall et al. (2012): (1) people who appear to be watching the facility (surveillance), (2) people who are attempting gain information about event and facility security operations (elicitation), (3) people trying to access unauthorized areas (testing the security), (4) reports of missing explosives or individuals purchasing large amounts of explosive material(s) (acquiring supplies), (5) suspicious people, (6) trial run before the attack, and (7) deploying assets people and supplies for the financial stability.

Crowd Management Personnel

The management of crowds is an integral and vital component of managing a public assembly facility. IAVM (2013) has developed guidelines for public assembly facility managers regarding the job competencies and recommended training for crowd management staff. These guidelines in no way supersede or should conflict with state and local law, statutes, ordinances, licensing, or training requirements for event personnel. Thus, each facility manager must be responsible for ensuring the local and state regulations are followed and ensure that training programs address the legal and political environment in which the facility operates.

The guidelines can be used by facility managers to design and implement in-house training and also may be used as a requirement for agencies providing contract staffing for event services. Attendees acknowledged that formal facility training sessions are an important source of education, but that on-the-job training, orientation, briefing/debriefing sessions, mentoring, and use of job aids also are essential for developing an effective event staff.

The IAVM has established four levels of crowd management responsibility that should be adopted by public assembly facility managers (IAVM, 2013):

1. Crowd assembly facilitator (CAF)—front-line event staff providing direct services to patrons. Example job titles are usher, ticket taker, parking attendant.

2. Crowd assembly supervisor—During an event, CAFs report to the crowd assembly supervisor, who oversees activities of CAFs during an event.

3. Crowd management administrator—Professional staff person with necessary experience and expertise to design and implement all facility security, crowd management, and emergency preparation activities.

4. Crowd management instructor—A crowd management professional, trained under an IAAM-endorsed curriculum, who has the knowledge and skills to develop and conduct in-facility training programs for crowd assembly facilitators and crowd assembly supervisors. Instructors may be regular staff or consultants.

Crowd Management Planning

The most effective crowd management plan clearly delineates areas of responsibility and authority and especially underscores the need for cooperation and communication between public and private parties. When those elements are absent, problems can arise at an event.

Crisis/Emergency Management Planning

Crisis/emergency management is the process of servicing, containing, and bringing order to any natural (earthquakes, floods, hurricanes, tornadoes, blizzards, and thunderstorms) or man-made (criminal acts, accidents such as train derailments and plane crashes, fire, bomb threats, and terrorism) traumatic incident. It includes planning, recognition, assessment, emergency response, intervention, and follow-up procedures. The planners also need to be able to predict situations, position the facility in the best possible way, prevent man-made incidents, persevere by following the plan in times of stress, and evaluate the overall plan before and after an incident.

Checklist for Crisis/Emergency Management Plan

A crisis is anything that has the potential to significantly impact an organization. Organizations with crisis management plans are better able to

- work effectively with local emergency responders city, state and federal agencies in responding to events,

- promptly attend the needs of those affected,

- assist investigating agencies without jeopardizing the company's legal position,

- form working relationships with media and elected officials that will help assist the facility's message to the public,

- prepare for possible litigation and claims,

- provide accurate and timely information,

- minimize the diversion of corporate executives,

- contain financial exposure, and

- minimize the incident' effect on the reputation of the facility (Coleman, 2011; Association of Corporate Counsel, 2013).

According to Hall et al. (2012), crisis/emergency management has four objectives: reducing tension during the incident, demonstrating commitment and expertise, controlling the flow and accuracy of information, and managing resources effectively. Further, the major elements of effective management planning include the identification of a crisis/emergency management team (CEMT), an assessment of the most likely crisis scenarios, the development of a crisis/emergency management plan (CEMP) document, periodic crisis training exercises, adherence to crisis communication guidelines, and continual review and refinement of the plan.

The following are the steps, according to Hall et al. (2012), the following steps should be taken when developing a CEMP:

Step One

Create a Crisis/Emergency Management Team (CEMT) and assess potential crises. The CEMT team can include legal counsel, investigators, public relations personnel, investor relation's personnel, risk manager, financial personnel, marketing personnel, employee relation's personnel, and technical personnel.

Step Two

Develop CEMT plans to protect spectators, employees, and the facility. The primary objective of any plan is to set up a flexible structure that is capable of responding to any type of crisis quickly, decisively and in a coordinated manner. The CEMP should establish relationships, responsibilities and continuity. It should include a notification system with a specific and up to date listing of current contact information on the team members, chain of command, outside relevant agencies.

Step Three

Establish guidelines for gathering information and internal investigations. The CEMT should be prepared to initiate the investigation, determine the facts, potential liability and available defenses. The team should implement policies that promote the fact-finding process.
- Identify who has the authority to initiate an investigation,

- Establish who will determine the scope of the investigation,

- Identify an attorney or investigator that is qualified to head the investigation,

- Formulate a preliminary list of employees and management with knowledge about particular crisis risks,

- Develop guidelines that establish an initial schedule for the investigation and identify the information needed, and

- Determine which team member will evaluate the results and what will be done with them.

The CEMT should take efforts to maximize protections provided by legally recognized privileges, including attorney-privilege, work-product immunity doctrine, and self-evaluative privilege.

Step Four

Provide periodic crisis training evaluation is an important component of the CEMP. The best way to ensure that everyone understands his or her roles in the plan is to have training on managing a crisis. The training will help address legal issues before they occur, develop investigation procedures and identify systems and equipment needed during a crisis and develop good media relation's skills.

Step Five

Develop guidelines for crisis communications is essential to the CEMP. Good communication is the heart of any crisis management plan. Communication should reduce tension, demonstrate a commitment to correct the problem, and take control of the information flow. Crisis communications involves communicating with a variety of constitutes: the media, employees, neighbors, investors, regulators, and lawmakers. Public relations in the single most important element of the crisis communication response plan. The planners should create guidelines for designated spokesperson covering how working with the media and community leaders. Prepare templates for communicating with various scenarios. Attorneys on the crisis management team should review media statements and proposed answers to protect against privilege waivers and potential admissions than can be used in litigation.

References

Association of Corporate Counsel. (2013) Checklist for Crisis Management Planning. Retrieved from http://www.acc.com/vI/public/QuickReference/loader.cfm?csModule=security/getfile&pageid=16744.

Beer Institute. (2013). Alcohol Management. Retrieved from http://www.beerinstitute.org

Coleman, T. S. (2011). *A practical guide to risk management.* Saratt Rickmansworth Hertfordshire, UK: The Research Foundation of CFA Institute.

Cotton, D. J., & Cotton, M. B. (2012). *Waivers and releases of liability* (8th ed.). Statesboro, GA: Sport Risk Consulting.

Crowd Management Strategies. (2013). Successful Crowd Management Strategies. Retrieved from http://www.crowdsafe.com/taskrept/chapter6.html.

Fay, J. (2010). *Contemporary security management* (3rd ed.). Burlington: MA: Butterworth-Heinemann.

Hall, S.A., Cooper, W. E., Marciani, L., & McGee, J. A. (2012). *Security management for sports and special events.* Champaign, IL: Human Kinetics, Inc.

Hopkin, P. (2012). *Fundamentals of risk management (2nd ed.).* Philadelphia, PA: Institute of Risk Management.

International Association of Venue Managers. (2013). Retrieved from http://www.iavm.org/cvms/crowd_management.asp.

Kennedy, D. B. (2006). A précis of suicide terrorism. *Journal of Homeland Security and Emergency Management, 3*(4).

Ortmeier, P. J. (2012). *Introduction to security: Operations and management* (4th ed). Saddlebrook, NJ: Prentice-Hall.

Sennewald, C. A. (2011). *Effective security management* (5th ed). Burlington, MA: Butterworth- Heinemann.

Serving Alcohol Inc. (2007). *Selling and Serving Safely.* Retrieved from http://www.servingalcohol.com.

U.S. Department of Homeland Security. (2009). *Sport event risk management.* Retrieved from www.rems.ed.gov/docs/EMHETraining_STATX08_StadiumSecurity.pdf .

PART II

Communication and Media Relations

CHAPTER 7

Communication Principles

Michael G. Hypes

Morehead State University

Introduction

Communication is something that we all do. It is a dynamic process that involves everything from what we say, what we write, the use of silences, to the way we look. Communication occurs at various levels throughout an organization. The sport manager communicates with supervisors, peers, employees, clients, sponsors, vendors, and the public in general. Effective communication involves more than simply talking. It also involves listening, speaking, delivering, selling, giving and receiving information. To be an effective manager, a person must be able maximize communication. Communication has been identified as both an art and a science and is a critical skill for the sport manager.

Models and Definitions

Communication is a process or system of exchange and interaction that is directed at conveying meaning and achieving understanding. It occurs within (internal) and outside (external) to the organization. The mode of communication can be verbal, nonverbal, written, sensory, or demonstrative. Most models of communication involve a sender of a message, a message, the channel through which the message is sent, noise, a receiver, and feedback.

The sender is the person who initiates the communication process. The sender develops the message that he wants to send to the receiver. There has to be the desire or intent to communicate and then an encoding process of what it is to be said.

The message is perceived to be the most important element in the communication process. It is the object of the interaction between the sender and the receiver. Messages can take many forms. The message may be verbal (either overt or hidden meaning), nonverbal, written (memos, letters, e-mails), and symbolic.

The channel is the way in which the message is sent. It can take the form of an e-mail or memo to employees, face-to-face meetings with an individual or group, a presentation or webinar, or even over the phone. Many have identified the flow of communication to include downward, upward, and lateral communication.

Downward communication refers to a one-way communication from upper level managers to the middle and lower levels of the organization. This type of one-way path of communication eliminates the opportunity to receive valuable information and feedback from others in the organization.

Upward flow allows the manager to receive information from below whether it be from subordinate employees or club members. This will allow the manager to receive necessary feedback from the stakeholders in order to make possible changes to operating procedures and to evaluate the direction of the organization.

Lateral communication refers to the flow between individuals and groups at the same level of management. Lateral communication can decrease duplication and provide a platform to foster employee involvement.

The receiver of the message perceives the incoming information and must decode or interpret what is being communicated. "Feedback is a reaction given by the receiver (initially) which tells the sender that the message was understood, or was unclear and clarification is needed."

Noise is anything that is not part of the communication that interferes with the sending and receiving of a message. Noise, if not properly addressed, can lead to ineffective communication, misunderstanding, or improper interpretation of the message that was sent.

Functions of Communications

Communication can be used for a variety of purposes. It is a dynamic process that involves different people and may require change and revision to be effective. The following are commonly identified as functions of communication (Schwartzman, 2012; Williams, McQuitty, & Tracey, 2012):

- Persuasion/Influence
- Information Sharing
- Social/Expressive
- Command/Instruct
- Conflict Resolution

The sport manager can increase communication quality and effectiveness by understanding the role of communication and some of the barriers associated with ineffective communication. When attempting to communicate with others, the sender needs to speak or write at the level of his audience. It should be the manager's purpose to share ideas with others and to do so while being cognizant of the emotional aspects of the communication. The following are commonly known as the six Cs of effective communication (Shockley-Zalabak, 2011; Solomon, 2011):

- Clear (language and messages should be unambiguous)
- Concise (being succinct and concise minimizes misinterpretation)
- Correct (effective communication is correct communication)
- Complete (the communication cycle should be complete for a message to be fully understood)
- Courteous (being courteous and considerate of receivers and their needs enhances communication)
- Convincing (to be effective, communication should be convincing in its logic and reasoning)

Miscommunication is a breakdown in the process and the result is that the intended message is not the message that is received. Miscommunication can result through the sender improperly encoding the message, the message may be ambiguous, the channel may not be the best choice for the message, the noise may be too intrusive, there can be misinterpretation of the message by the receiver, or inadequate or inappropriate feedback. For the manager to improve at communication, he needs to practice and understand some of the barriers to communication.

Barriers to Communication

Shockley-Zalabak (2011) has identified three distinct categories of barriers to communication: (1) linguistic barriers, (2) psychological barriers, and (3) environmental barriers. By attempting to minimize these barriers, the manager can enhance the communication process. Other barriers of communication have been identified, such as the sender, receiver, and group. These behaviors or barriers are separated below (Schwartzman, 2012; Solomon, 2011):

Sender

- Prejudging the receiver

- Avoiding the real and immediate concerns of the receiver

- Having disorganized thoughts

- Having strong emotions

- Trying to share too much information at one time

- Using inappropriate language or nonverbal signs

- Mismatching communication style with receiver

Receiver

- Prejudgment of the sender

- Poor listening skills

- Defensiveness

- Strong emotions

- Incorrect assumptions

- Different connotations for words and intonations

- Mismatched communication style with sender

Group

- A lack of cohesiveness

- A lack of openness to opposing views

- A lack of willingness to talk

- Unacknowledged cultural differences

- Biases inherent within the group

- Ineffective leadership

Communication in Presentations

There are four things audiences will not forgive speakers for not being prepared, comfortable, committed, and interesting. If the speaker concentrates on being prepared, committed, interesting, and making others comfortable, he/she will become an accomplished communicator in formal speeches as well as in interpersonal communications.

Be prepared. Preparation is essential because whenever a speaker talks to other people, the audience must have absolute confidence that the speaker knows what he/she is talking about. Solomon (2011) suggests the listeners (1) must have confidence that you know what you are talking about, (2) should feel that you know more about the subject than they do, (3) will feel that you spent time preparing your subject and analyzing your audience, (4) must feel there is a purpose to your message, and (5) must understand that you are prepared to face a hostile or skeptical audience. Table 7.1 shows a preparation checklist that will save you time in preparing your next speech.

Be comfortable. It is essential to make others feel comfortable. But, first, you must be comfortable with yourself and your surroundings. People who are confident are usually comfortable with themselves. Others take their cues from you; so, relax, keep things in perspective, and do not overreact. Maintain your sense of humor and take your work seriously but not yourself.

Table 7.1
Speech Preparation Checklist

Speech preparation
- Evaluate the audience.
- Consider the occasion.
- Determine the length of the talk.
- Determine the purpose of your speech-to entertain, inform, inspire, or persuade (good speeches often combine elements of all four).
- Decide on a central theme (If you cannot write your theme on the back of a business card, it is too complicated).
- Develop background knowledge.
- Gather facts.
- Consider the makeup of the audience.
- Find a good opening line or story that relates to the speech (If it does not interest you, it will not interest your audience).
- The speech can be in either the past, present, or future (Write down three to five questions the audience might ask you and answer them as the body of the speech).

Speech outline
- Introduction (Tell them what you are going to tell them).
- Body (Tell them).
- Close (Tell them what you have told them and close the door).

Speech delivery
- Be interesting; use some memorable phrases and quotes.
- Support statements with facts and examples.
- Practice speech out loud in front of a mirror (Also use either a tape recorder or video recorder.).
- Time speech (Add 20 seconds for actual delivery)
- Consider size of audience and room (Adjust volume).
- Take your time to get audience's attention.
- Concentrate on good eye contact.

Be committed. It is important for the speaker to be committed to the message. This is crucial. Very few speakers freeze up when they feel strongly about something. If you know what you are saying, why you are saying it, and care about what you are saying, you will say it well.

Be interesting. A speaker must be interesting. It is vital to the health of the audience. It is difficult to be interesting if you are not committed and vice versa. No audience will forgive you if you are boring.

Committees

The primary function of a committee is to contribute to the efficient operation of an organization. In most cases, a committee is concerned with the communication of information and with assisting the leadership in the decision making process by providing needed information.

A committee can be one of the most productive tools an organization has to work with. Whether you are chairing a committee or are a committee member, you face the challenge of becoming involved in the work the committee was formed to accomplish.

Your contribution and your participation on the committee will determine its success or failure. If you participate, become involved, and encourage others on the committee to do so, the committee will be successful. Enthusiasm is contagious.

The findings of a committee have a direct impact on the decisions made by the officers and the board of directors of the club. The energy you put into your work on the committee has a direct influence on the direction your club takes.

Committees are clearly one of the most important tools available to executives. More than any other managerial area, management is charged with the responsibility for representing, involving, and serving a vast number of members. A staff that attempts autocratically to establish policy and procedure and to plan is doing a disservice to itself and to the organization.

A committee can provide a vital link with the attitudes of members and the world of actual practice. Committee members can keep personnel attuned to realities of the industry or profession and committees are an excellent training ground and screening device for budding leaders.

The following is a generally accepted sequence, or order of business, that is observed for a meeting (Solomon, 2011):

- Call the meeting to order.

- Roll call (sometimes omitted).

- Minutes of the previous meeting.

- State the purpose of the meeting.

- State briefly the program for the meeting.

- Discuss and resolve agenda items as they appear.

- New business.

- Adjourn the meeting.

One of the real measures of a committee is the report and recommendations that end up trying to communicate the extensive involvements and investigations of the committee. Care should be given to the report lest it become the weak link in a strong chain. No matter how thorough and effective the committee's work has been, it is going to have to be made understandable to the uninitiated.

Meeting minutes are invaluable. Usually, the minutes are kept by the committee secretary or organization staff. Minutes nail down committee decisions, assignments, and become a permanent record for continued reference. Minutes should be prepared for approval immediately following a meeting and distributed promptly to all committee members and, in some cases, to the governing body for review. Briefly, minutes should include date, time, place of meeting, members present, presiding officer's name, names of guests or outside consultants, decisions reached and follow-up action decided upon, formal motions (indicating members making and seconding motion), and their outcomes (passage or defeat), summary of discussions to justify decisions, information on the next meeting, and signature of the committee secretary.

Communications in the 21st Century

Electronic communication has changed as the technology has advanced. Also a "green approach" has drastically reduced the number of organization memos and other correspondences being printed on a piece of paper. We now have e-mail, instant messaging and texting as options to communicate with others. It is important to understand that e-mail is a formal means of communication. It is not texting or instant messaging. The e-mail that is sent not only represents the sender but also the organization he/she represents. Some basic guidelines regarding the use of e-mail are provided (Sklar, 2001; Proakis & Salchi, 2004; Williams et al., 2012):

- E-mail is a formal means of communication.

- Don't say anything in an e-mail that you would not say in person.

- Use proper grammar.

- Always check spelling.

- Always include a subject in your e-mail.

- Delete e-mails without subjects.

- E-mail Signature

  - Have a business card.

  - Include information for other contacts (i.e., phone, FAX, etc.).

  - Avoid long sayings or quotes.

- Be concise of replying, replying all, or forwarding.

- Follow proper Netiquette.

  - www.albion.com/netiquette

  - www.fau.edu/netiquette/net

In some cases, you may have multiple e-mail addresses. Keep your professional and personal e-mails separate. You do not want to send a potential client or donor an e-mail from an address that does not reflect well upon you and the organization. Do not send an e-mail while mad. Once it is sent there is no taking back what you said. Compose the e-mail and then review with a cool head before you send.

Social Networking

Social media is taking the world by storm. Using social media for business is also a hot new trend that you cannot afford to miss out on. Use these basic dos and don'ts of social media for business to position your organization for virtual success: (Sklar, 2001; Williams et al., 2012)

- Do use a future-oriented approach.

- Do update regularly.

- Do use pictures, video and music.

- Don't send mixed messages.

- Don't forget to analyze your stats.

Using social media for business is becoming a basic necessity in the virtual world. These dos and don'ts will help you develop a well-rounded approach to using social media, and your business can reap many rewards as a result.

References

Proakis, J. G., & Salchi, M. (2004). *Fundamentals of communication systems.* Upper Saddle River, NJ: Prentice-Hall/Person.

Schwartzman, R. (2012). *Fundamentals of oral communication* (2nd ed.). Dubuque, IA: Kendall Hunt Publishing.

Shockley-Zalabak, P. S. (2011). *Fundamentals of organizational communication* (8th ed.). Upper Saddle River, NJ: Pearson.

Sklar, B. (2001). *Digital communications: Fundamentals and applications* (2nd ed). Upper Saddle River, NJ: Prentice-Hall/Pearson.

Solomon, M. G. (2011). *Fundamentals of communications and networks.* Sudbury, MA: Jones and Bartlett Learning.

Williams, R.W., McQuitty, D. L., & Tracey, B. S. (2012). *The fundamentals of speech communication in the digital age.* Dubuque, IA: Kendall Hunt Publishing.

CHAPTER 8

Media Relations Principles

Julia Ann Hypes

Morehead State University

Introduction

In today's modern society, consumers are bombarded by millions of words, pictures, videos, and publications. This often leads to information overload and missed messages. For those who are not familiar with mass communications, the media may appear to be no more than a source of information and entertainment. An organization's relationship with the media must be built over time and include trust, respect, and honesty. Three terms not often associated with mass media.

There exists a conflict between physical activity organizations and the media. The media want news and the organization wants publicity. This basic tenant often sets up an adversarial relationship between the organization and the press. It has been suggested that each group has a predisposition about the wants and needs of the other.

Mass communications organizations must seek programming that is new, appealing, and of interest to their audiences. Their job is to sell subscriptions, advertising, or time in this highly competitive business. For the news to be interesting and effective, it must contain human interest stories, personal items of success and failure, new programs, and reports on rare or unusual events. Therefore, the manager must be creative enough to develop stories that meet the needs and wants of the mass media.

Sport Journalism

Sport journalism in the media has been around for more than 200 years. It began as a complement to news and politics of the day in daily newspapers. Most newspapers today devote an entire section to sport. Newspapers and magazines dominated the delivery of sports information for more than 150 years with the main source of information devoted to covering sport events. The Industrial Revolution created an avenue to deliver messages using sound and sight. The new forms of communication transformed media relations into the multi-billion dollar industry it is today (Hall, Moynahan, Nicholas, & Taylor, 2006).

Mass communications involves the process by which the media delivers written, audio, and visual messages to a large audience. This audience is diverse, invisible, and unknown in many respects. Feedback occurs more slowly than in other forms of communication (Schultz, Caskey, & Esherick, 2010).

With the growth of the media, clubs, recreation and sport organizations have found it necessary to depend upon media relations departments/personnel to address the growing impact of the media in and on our organizations. There are a number of terms that might be used to title those professionals who direct the functions of media relations; Media Relations Director, Sports Information Director, or Public Relations Director. The size and scope of the organization will determine if a separate unit is warranted to deal specifically with media relations.

Types of Media

A communication outlet must contain four elements to be considered mass media.

1. Commercial in nature

2. Audience

3. Content of mass media

4. Delivery by a media organization

Mass media is commercial in nature with an aim to make money. They make this money by supplying an audience for advertisers. Subscriptions do not pay for the publication or broadcast. The audience should be large, heterogeneous, widely dispersed, and anonymous to the media organization and other audience members. There must be a message that is delivered by a media organization to the mass audience. The message is the words, sound, and/or pictures.

The primary methods for information delivery are print and electronic. Traditional print media includes newspapers and magazines. Organizations also utilize newsletters and fan publications to communicate within a more immediate circle of consumers and employees. Magazines have transitioned toward special interest publications that are published with detailed information for the media relations professional and/or the hard-core fan. A story published in a specialty magazine, such as *Street and Smith Sport Business Journal*, can provide prestige for an organization and spark fan interest. Professional teams and independent operators sponsor fan magazines. These publications contain statistics, features, game previews, and reviews as well as promotions, ticket information, and contests. The editorial content is usually favorable toward the team or organization (Hall et al., 2006).

Electronic media is continuing to expand and includes radio, television, and the Internet. Technology has allowed audience interaction not only to the content provider but with each other through blogs, social networks, and online communities. Consumers have more choices and options on how to receive, share, and interact with information now than ever before. Today's reporters must incorporate electronic content, such as video and posting web information, to accompany their print stories (Schultz et al., 2010).

Role of the Media Relations Director

In the 1930s and 1940s, promotion specialists were known as press agents or publicity men. Today, the title may be PR director, press director, director of communications, media director, or director of community relations. Just being in love with sports is no longer a qualification for professional employment in this field. The millions of dollars invested in personnel and the billions of dollars allocated to facilities and broadcasting are proof that skilled professionals are required (Helitzer, 2000).

A career in media relations requires that the professional have strong skills in communication and control of that communication. Schultz et al. (2010), lists five necessary skills for a sport information specialist:

1. "Effective writing skills

2. Keen visual skills

3. Strong speaking and interviewing skills

4. Effective problem solving skills

5. Good interpersonal skills (p. 86)."

The information that you present to the media reflects the image of the organization as well as your professional integrity. The media relations professional must accurately and effectively convey the organization's message through game notes, press releases, feature stories, interviews, and web content. It is essential that information be accurate and states the message as intended. Visual skills can aid in delivery of the message through layout and design. In our visual, global environment, audiences are bombarded with information and messages can easily be overlooked or misinterpreted. Designing a visual component so your message is seen and interpreted correctly is an important quality in media relations professionals.

Speaking and interviewing skills are utilized during press conferences and as the official spokesperson for the sport organization. The professional may be asked to speak at a civic organization meeting, in front of the international media, or convince the media to run a feature story. Interviewing skills are necessary to write and publish feature stories, biographies, and coordinating interviews for organization personnel.

When the unexpected happens, the media relations director is utilized to communicate the official message for the organization. Crisis management and the ability to think on your feet will aid in the rapid response to any stressful, exciting, and/or unexpected situation. Teamwork and the ability to coordinate with others are vital to a successful media relations program. The media have publication and broadcast deadlines that may not always coincide with the organization activities. The media relations professional does not work in isolation. It may be impossible for one person to handle all necessary interactions and duties; so, the professional must be skilled in cooperation, teamwork, and delegation of duties.

The Media Relationship

The media not only provides information but interpretation of that information for the audience as a method of entertainment. This type of entertainment connects the consumer of the selected information a part of an experience, the lives of the entertainer, as well as images and ideas. Media content is presented and re-presented, edited, and controlled before it is delivered to the consumer. Each of the editors, directors, writers, technicians, etc. who come in contact with that information has their own interest and point-of-view which shapes the end message. Television programming has planned images and "soap opera" coverage of sport events to heighten dramatic content and provide more entertainment value for the consumer (Coakely, 2014).

The media has goals that will allow it to thrive as a business entity. As sport event coverage has increased and the consumer has been more influenced by the media messages, the lines between "reality" and "entertainment" have been blurred. Consumers feel they are part of an organization, event, or the personal life of a professional athlete. This sense of belonging provides an opportunity for the consumer to feel entitled to provide input on the decisions an organization or individual has made. The media has taken "talk radio" to a new level. Coakely (2014) lists five goals of the media:

1. "Make profits

2. Shape values

3. Provide a public service

4. Build their own reputations

5. Expressing themselves in technical, artistic, or personal ways (p. 137)."

The effect of these goals can be seen in the impact the media has on sport scheduling. The multibillion-dollar broadcast contracts hold sport hostage to the media schedule. TV timeouts, delay in broadcast, extending/shortening half-time, schedule modification, just to name a few have all impacted how sport is delivered consumers. The impact is not all negative. The media has provided global exposure for sport and allowed for increased advertising dollars which in turn provides larger broadcast contracts for sport organizations.

The media want news and the sport organization wants publicity. It is important to remember that advertising is paid for by the organization that will control the message. Publicity, on the other hand, is free and the organization has no control over what is written or said. This basic tenet often sets up an adversarial relationship between the sport organization and the press. Most sport organizations fortunate and have so much mass appeal that media organizations are compelled to cover them on a regular basis. This popularity creates a "pull" affect from the media. Most other industries have to "push" their information to the media and hope to receive publicity for their efforts (Masteralexis, Barr, & Hums, 2014). The desire of the consumer to know all they can about their favorite team and player is turned into dollars by selling more newspapers and advertising. Thus, it is important that the media possess the most current information possible about the daily activities of a sport organization and be able to deliver that information to the consumer quickly.

Press Release

A steady stream of press releases to media outlets helps keep the sport organization in the public consciousness. Journalists depend on contacts within the community and sport organizations to inform them of newsworthy events, remind them of upcoming events, and suggest news stories. Most content analyses indicate that half of the stories in daily newspapers, and more in smaller papers, contain information from news releases (Shultz et al., 2010).

The press release is written in common hard news format called the inverted pyramid. It includes the 5 Ws: who, what, when, where, and why of the story and the H: how of the story.

- Most important information or element
- Summary of 5 Ws and H
- Less important information
- Least important information .
- No conclusion

In opposition to traditional story writing, the main point of information is given to the reader of the release first. This is to catch the eye of the journalist and draw them in to read the remainder of your press release. The details will then follow. The press release is usually short, to the point, and does not contain fluff or suspense (See a sample press release in the Appendices available in the student and faculty resource center at www.sagamorepub.com). Schultz et al. (2010), identifies eight common errors that arise in press releases:

1. "Lack of newsworthy
2. Lack of objectivity
3. Too many superlatives and interpretive adjectives
4. Self-serving quotations
5. Emphasis on the obvious
6. Lack of a local tie (out-of-town releases)
7. Unnecessary background
8. Wordy (p. 97)."

The media relations office should be careful not to overwhelm the local media with releases, especially when they regularly cover the organization. It is important to know when to pick up the phone and call a reporter or editor.

Press Conference

Planning a news conference is a team effort that may involve administrators, coaches, and sports information staff. The media relations director must work with administrators to create a chain of command and a roster of responsibilities for the news conference.

Press conferences should occur only when circumstances warrant it. Too many times a press conference is called to disseminate information which should properly go into a press release. This causes the press to be wary of press conferences. It must be remembered that a press conference takes a great deal of time out of a reporter's day therefore the information must warrant it.

When a press conference is held, the following guidelines should be implemented in the following order (Hall et al., 2006):

1. **"Establish a check-in desk.** You should know who did and did not accept your invitation to the press conference.

2. **Arrange to have a photographer on hand.** Announce to all that photographer's services are available at given times. Arrange to have the photos delivered immediately after the press conference. The advances in digital photography have made this process more efficient as the images can be sent via email.

3. **Newspaper and television photographers should be given full courtesy.** If possible, assign a representative of the media relations staff to each photographer to help contact and properly identify subjects for the photographs.

4. **Know the deadlines for newspapers that are most important to your organization.** When possible, schedule the press conference a minimum of four hours before the media deadline to assure the story will make it into the paper or broadcast (p. 167).

Heitzer (2000), offers a list of news events that usually deserve a press conference:

1. A major change in personnel

2. A major change in the status of a star player

3. An important event is scheduled

4. A major investigation

5. Change in a major facility

6. Award presentations

7. Crisis developments

8. Postgame interviews

9. The sport banquet speaker

10. The introduction of a new product (or service)

11. A new rule that is complex or controversial (p. 157)."

A press kit should be prepared in advance for all who attend the conference. This should contain a news release about the main subject of the conference, a full text of any explanation or statement that is to be delivered at the conference, any important photographs, and historical reference material. After the press conference, a press-kit should be sent to the press members who were invited but did not appear.

Clubs, recreation, and sport organizations usually avoid calling attention to negative news. The handling of controversial issues, especially involving athletes, is tricky. The Family Educational Rights to Privacy Act prohibits release of information a personal nature. It is also difficult to management a negative announcement in a way that reinforces the positive image the sport organization wants to foster. An organization may set up a news conference to quell rumors, dispel false information, or demonstrate how well it is handling a serious problem (Schultz et al., 2010).

References

Coakely, J. (2014). *Sports and society: Issues and controversies* (11th ed.). New York, NY: McGraw-Hill Publishers.

Hall, A., Moynahan, P., Nicholas, W., & Taylor, J. A. (2006). *Media relations in sport* (2nd ed.). Morgantown, WV: Fitness Information Technology, Inc.

Helitzer, M. (2001). *The dream job: Sports publicity, promotion and marketing* (3rd ed.). Athens, OH: University Sports Press.

Masteralexis, L., Barr, C., & Hums, M. (2014). *Principles and practice of sport management* (5th ed.). Sudbury, MA: Jones and Bartlett Publishers, Inc.

Schultz, B., Caskey, P., & Esherick, C. (2010). *Media relations in sport* (3rd ed.). Morgantown, WV: Fitness Information Technology, Inc.

CHAPTER 9

Public Relations Principles

Thomas H. Sawyer
Professor Emeritus, Indiana State University

Michael G. Hypes
Morehead State University

Introduction

A public relations program is designed to influence the opinions of people within the targeted market through responsible and acceptable performance based on mutually satisfactory two-way communication. It has been noted that Abraham Lincoln once said, "Public sentiment is everything. With public sentiment, nothing can fail; without it, nothing can succeed." In order to gain public sentiment, programs must familiarize not only customers/clients but the public in general with all aspects of the services, products, and programs offered. An effective public relations program will open communication lines with the various publics and effectively utilize the media in a manner that competently presents the objectives of the organization to the public at large. Further, it will modify the attitudes and actions of the public through persuasion and integrate them with those of the organization.

Public Relations

Public relations is an all-encompassing term. It is commonly defined as the planned effort to influence opinion through good character and socially responsible performance based on mutually satisfactory two-way communication.

Krotee and Bucher (2007) identify a public as a group of individuals drawn together by common interests who are in a specific geographical location, community, or area or are characterized by some other common feature (e.g., age, interest, lifestyle, marital status, motivation, opinion). All publics possess common elements to which public relations and marketing efforts must be sensitive. Each public (e.g., internal, external, immediate, associated) usually needs to belong, wants to have input, and desires to be included in order to maintain its interest and enhance its reputation.

Wilcox and Cameron (2011) indicate a sport organization's public relations program should include, but not be limited to

- serving as an information source regarding organization services, products, and activities;

- promoting confidence that the services, products, and activities provided by the organization are useful and assist people in maintaining, gaining, or regaining their health and fitness;

- gathering support for the organization's programs and fund-raising appeals;

- stressing the value of active lifestyles and the positive impact they have on health and fitness;

- improving communication among customers/clients, staff, parents, and the surrounding community;

- evaluating the organization's services, products, and activities; and

- correcting myths, misunderstandings, and misinformation concerning the organization's services, products, and activities.

Steps in Developing a Public Relations Program

It is important to first agree that a public relations program is necessary for the organization. Once it is agreed that a public relations program is necessary, than resources to develop and implement a public relations plan must be provided. The primary resources are human, financial, facility space, equipment (e.g., computers, printers, and scanners), and materials (e.g., funds for duplication, phones, postage, printing, software, etc.).

Initially, a public relations program planning committee should be established with representation from all facets of the organization. Krotee and Bucher (2006) and Wilcox and Cameron (2011) suggest this committee should follow the ensuing steps in the development of a public relations program plan:

- Develop a philosophy statement that encourages the foundation for any good public relations program is outstanding performance.

- Establish a mission statement that encourages the establishment and maintenance of two-way lines of communication with as many related publics as possible.

- Develop a sound uniform public relations policy (i.e., all communication with the public will be handled through the public relations office).

- Establish a set of principles to guide the development of the public relations program, such as:

  - Public relations must be considered internally before being developed externally,

  - The public relations program plan will be circulated to all members of the organization for meaningful input and buy in,

  - The persons selected by the sport organization to implement the public relations plan must have a thorough knowledge of the professional services to be rendered, the attitudes of members of the profession and organization represented, and the nature and reaction of the consumers and all the public directly or indirectly related to the organization's services, products, or programs, and

  - The public relations office must be kept abreast of the factors and influences that affect the program, and develop and maintain a wide sphere of contacts.

- Identify the services, products, and programs that will yield the greatest dividends.

- Define the various related publics.

- Obtain facts regarding consumers'/clients' and other publics' knowledge level about the organization's services, products, and programs.

- Determine the following before drafting the program plan:

- Is there a handbook or manual of guidelines, or a newsletter to keep members of the organization informed (internal communication)?

- Is there a system for disseminating information to the media?

- Is there access to the Internet and if so, does the organization have a Web homepage?

- Is there a booklet, flyer, or printed matter that tells the story of the organization?

- Do the members (customers/clients) and staff participate in community activities?

- Does the organization hold open houses, clinics, seminars, or workshops?

- Are there provisions for a speakers' bureau so that civic and service clubs, schools, and other organizations may obtain someone to speak on various topics relating to the organization's services, products, or programs?

- Does the organization have an informational video?

- Is inter- and intra-organizational electronic mail utilized to its fullest capacity?

- Determine appropriate time lines for implementation and who or what group is responsible for the completion of the task.

- Establish a regular evaluation process for the plan.

After the public relations committee completes the public relations plan, it is important for the committee to determine what the steps are to gain publicity for the organization. Every organization should have established a strategy for publicizing its programs and services. The basic tenet in effective publicity is developing a positive image for the organization and linking with other organizations with a similar philosophy. For example, a youth organization would not be wise to align itself with an alcohol or tobacco industry in sponsoring its events.

The primary objective of publicity is to draw attention to a person, the organization, or an event. An effective publicity program is required to obtain an individual's attention. Publicity will not sell tickets, raise funds, win supporters, retain members, or sell merchandise; however, publicity can be helpful in conveying ideas to people so that these ends can be more easily attained.

Effect of Publicity

Sebellin-Ross (2011) and Wilcox and Cameron (2011) indicate publicity should be planned with these guidelines in mind: (1) too much publicity can be poor public relations, because often at a given point people tend to react negatively to excessive publicity, (2) the amount of publicity absorbed is important, not the amount released, (3) the amount of publicity disseminated does not necessarily equal the amount received or used, (4) the nature of the publicity eventually tends to reveal the character of the organization it seeks to promote, for better or worse, (5) some publicity an organization receives originates from outside sources, and (6) not all public relations activities result in publicity. Figure 9.1 outlines some basic steps for effective publicity.

Finally, Sebellin-Ross (2011) and Wilcox and Cameron (2011) suggest a few general pointers that should be considered regarding the interrelationship between the media and the organization's publicity practices:

- It is nice to know someone in the media, but it is not necessary to get free publicity. Editors have numerous pages and hours to fill, and in many instances your news release may be very helpful to them. Therefore, do not hesitate to send materials to a media source.

- The key to success with the media is to package the news release in such a way it attracts attention, allowing for a more in-depth examination by the editor.

Publicity is free; however, a sound plan for publicity does not happen by accident. It requires planning and careful execution. Consistent media attention is the overall goal of the publicity plan. Sebellin-Ross (2011) and Wilcox & Cameron (2011) indicate there are a number of guidelines that should be followed when developing publicity materials for the media and others including, but not limited to the following:

- Focus the materials on specific objectives.

- Create materials that are interesting to the editors and the reader and are creative in nature.

- Make the materials newsworthy.

- Ensure the materials are accurate and neat.

- Fashion materials so they look professionally complete.

- Furnish background material regarding the submission.

- Provide artwork, graphics, or photographs with the submission.

- Focus manuscript (text) on intended audience.

- Develop and respect all relationships with media contacts.

- Reinforce all relationships with the media contacts by expressing appreciation for their efforts.

Figure 9.1. Steps to Effective Publicity

- The best way to communicate with the media is by mail or electronic mail. Avoid using the telephone unless it is an emergency or to return a call.

- It should be understood that publicity efforts do not have to appear in the most influential media to be worthwhile.

Principles of Good Publicity and Media Relations

The sports manager can develop confidence and respect by adhering to some basic principles. Sebellin-Ross (2011) and Wilcox and Cameron (2011) suggest these include the following: (See a Sample Public Relations Plan in the Appendices available in the student and faculty resource center at www.sagamorepub.com).

1. Be honest.

2. Do not try to block the news by use of evasion, censorship, pressure, or trickery.

3. Be cooperative at all times; be accessible by telephone or in person at all times.

4. Be candid; do not seek trouble, but do not try to hide from it either.

5. Use facts, not rumors, although initially they may be more detrimental than the rumors. Remember, facts limit the story, rumors tend to remove all boundaries.

6. Do not pad a weak story; this practice tends to weaken credibility.

7. Do not stress or depend upon off-the-record accounts. Remember, the job of the reporter is to obtain facts and report the story. Asking the reporter to abide with off-the-record requests is unfair and costly.

8. Give as much service to newspapers as possible. When news occurs, get the story out expeditiously. Hot news is desired by newspaper reporters, so one must be willing and able to supply newspapers with the stories, pictures, and statistics they wish, as they want them prepared, and on time.

9. If a reporter uncovers a story, do not give the same story to another reporter. Treat it as an exclusive right.

10. Since news is a highly perishable commodity, remember that newspapers want news, not publicity.

Sports managers must become acquainted with the publishers, the highest ranking officer (the executive editor), the editor, the editorial page editor, and finally, the managing editor who is the working head of staff engaged in handling news. In addition to these individuals, a close working relationship is necessary with the sports editor, Sunday desk editor, and society editor. Of course, it is advantageous to also know the editors for the amusements, arts, and business sections.

Positive reinforcement is as important in public relations as it is in sports. One should act promptly to commend all persons involved in carrying a special story, promotional activity, or unusual action. Copies of the commendation should be mailed to all relevant members of the newspaper.

Difference between Internal and External Public Relations

Internal public relations is communicating openly and often with personnel and members. The best promotion for an event can be negated if one of the employees or members gives a disgruntled response to the media. The best promoters of an organization are its employees and members.

External public relations are communicating with the outside publics external to the organization and its employees and members. This communication is done directly with the public(s) and through the media. These are prospective new members.

Outlets for Public Relations

Wilcox and Cameron (2011) suggest there are numerous avenues for getting the message out to the internal and external publics, including, but not limited to: "(1) printed media, (2) pictures and graphics, (3) radio, (4) television, (5) video, (6) posters, (7) exhibits, (8) brochures, (9) billboards, (10) public speaking opportunities, (11) electronic mail, (12) Internet, (13) direct mail, and (14) telemarketing (p. 236)."

The news release can be distributed using a variety of electronic equipment and other means: (1) FAX machine, (2) computers, (3) newswire services, (4) handouts, (5) messenger, (6) express mail, and (7) telephone.

The media directories most often used include the following:

- *Bacon's Publicity Checker* reports on the content of 5,000 trade and business periodicals in over 100 different categories.

- *Broadcasting Yearbook* lists every licensed radio and television station in the United States, Canada, and Central and South America.

- *Burrelle's Special Groups Media Directory*, an annual list of newspapers, periodicals, and electronic media classified by Black, European Ethnic, Hispanic, Jewish, Older Americans, Women, Young Adults, and Activists.

- *Communications Guide*, an annual guide published by local chapters of the Public Relations Society of America. It includes area broadcasts, print media, news bureaus, community publications, college publications, and special interest magazines.

- *Editor and Publisher Yearbook*, an encyclopedia of the newspaper industry.

- *Gale Directory of Publications*, an annual listing of over 20,000 publications including daily and weekly newspapers and all major trade and specialty magazines.

- *Standard Periodical Directory*, a guide to more than 65,000 U.S. and Canadian periodicals.

- *Working Press of the Nation* lists editorial staffs in newspapers, magazines, syndicates, broadcast news, and major free-lance writers and columnists.

- *PR Newswire and BusinessWire* provides listing of subscribers in all types of media.

What is Necessary for Preparing Radio and Television Public Service Announcements (PSAs)?

Radio and television media are powerful and well worth the money spent for public relations. The largest obstacle is obtaining free time, known as public service announcements. The idea of public service will influence some station managers to grant free time to an organization. This may be in the nature of an item included in a newscast program, a spot public service announcement (PSA), or a public service program that might range from 15 to 60 minutes.

Sometimes, a person must take advantage of the media on short notice. Therefore, it is important for an organization to be prepared with written plans that can be put into operation immediately. Sebellin-Ross (2011) suggests the following are a few guidelines for preparation:

- "Know the organization's message.

- Know the program (i.e., style, format, audience participation, time).

- Know the audience (i.e., seniors, teens, upscale, non-consumers, gender).

- Tailor the message and presentation to the audience interests.

- Practice-speak in lay terms and be brief and concise (p. 167)."

What Are the Four Essentials of a Great Communicator?

There are four areas in which audiences will not forgive speakers: not being prepared, comfortable, committed, and interesting. If the speaker concentrates on being prepared, committed, interesting, and making others comfortable, he or she will become an accomplished communicator in formal speeches as well as in interpersonal communications.

Preparation is essential. According to Stodlt, Pratt, and Dittmore (2007), your listeners (1) must have confidence that you know what you are talking about, (2) should feel that you know more about the subject than they do, (3) will feel that you spent time preparing your subject and analyzing your audience, (4) must feel there is a purpose to your message, and (5) must understand you are prepared to face a hostile or skeptical audience (p. 87). Figure 9.2 shows a preparation checklist that will save you time in preparing your next speech.

It is important for the speaker to be committed to the message. This is crucial. Very few speakers freeze up, unable to speak on what they feel strongly about. If you know what you are saying, why you are saying it, and care about what you are saying, you will say it well.

A speaker must be interesting. It is vital to the health of the audience. It is difficult to be interesting if you are not committed and vice versa. No audience will forgive you if you are boring. It is essential to make others feel comfortable, but you must first be comfortable with yourself and your surroundings. People who are confident are usually comfortable with themselves. Others take their cues from you, so relax, keep things in perspective, and do not overreact. Maintain your sense of humor and take your work seriously but not yourself.

Speech preparation
- Evaluate the audience.
- Consider the occasion.
- Determine the length of the talk.
- Determine the purpose of your speech-to entertain, inform, inspire, or persuade (good speeches often combine elements of all four).
- Decide on a central theme (If you cannot write your theme on the back of a business card, it is too complicated).
- Develop background knowledge.
- Gather facts.
- Consider the makeup of the audience.
- Find a good opening line or story that relates to the speech (If it does not interest you, it will not interest your audience).
- The speech can be in either the past, present, or future (Write down three to five questions the audience might ask you and answer them as the body of the speech).

Speech outline
- Introduction (Tell them what you are going to tell them).
- Body (Tell them).
- Close (Tell them what you have told them and close the door).

Speech delivery
- Be interesting-use some memorable phrases and quotes.
- Support statements with facts and examples.
- Practice speech out loud in front of a mirror (Also use either a tape recorder or video recorder.).
- Time speech (Add 20 seconds for actual delivery)
- Consider size of audience and room (Adjust volume).
- Take your time to get audience's attention.
- Concentrate on good eye contact.

Figure 9.2. Speech Preparation Checklist

Public speaking, if done well, can be an effective medium for achieving good public relations. Addresses should be made regularly to civic and social groups, schools, professional meetings, government entities, and general gatherings.

Radio and television media are powerful and well worth the money spent for public relations. The largest obstacle is obtaining free time. The idea of public service will influence some station managers to grant free time to an organization. This may be in the nature of an item included in a newscast program, a spot public service announcement (PSA), or a public service program that might range from 15 to 60 minutes.

There are four areas in which audiences will not forgive speakers: not being prepared, comfortable, committed, and interesting. If the speaker concentrates on being prepared, committed, interesting, and making others comfortable, he or she will become an accomplished communicator in formal speeches as well as in interpersonal communications.

Public Speaking: A Key to Achieving Good Public Relations

The sports manager needs to understand that public speaking, if done well, can be an effective medium for achieving good public relations. Addresses should be made regularly to civic and social groups, schools, professional meetings, government entities, and general gatherings. If the organization is large enough, a "speakers bureau" should be formed and a number of qualified employee speakers recruited. Once the bureau has been established, a list of topics should be circulated and distributed to civic and social groups, schools, churches, and other interested parties. The bureau and speakers need to prepare a number of topic areas with appropriate overheads, slides, and videos. Finally, the bureau should prepare younger professionals to become effective and accomplished speakers.

Legal Aspects of Public Relations

The sport manager, when dealing with public relations, may become involved in legal matters in two ways: first with regard to what is written by and about the sports organization by outside sources and second in the dissemination of information about a sport participant by the public relations office, coaches, or administrators of the organization. A situation may arise where an official of the organization may be asked to comment on a particular participant, coach, or employee. It is precisely this situation which requires careful thought and planning on the part of sport managers.

Occasionally, material written by the news media can constitute defamation which generally involves a communication that causes damage to an individual's good name or reputation. Defamation includes both libel and slander. Libel most frequently refers to communications which are written, printed and seen. Included in this area are electronic media as well as the print media. Slander, on the other hand, involves messages that are spoken and heard. Regardless of the medium of conveyance, defamation occurs when false information is communicated to at least one other person and causes damage to the subject of the statement. The First Amendment of the U.S. Constitution provides for freedom of speech but does not extend to defamatory remarks.

In 1964, the U.S. Supreme Court (*New York Times v. Sullivan*) set a precedent for contemporary writers. The court ruled that for a written statement concerning a public official to be libelous, it must be shown that actual intent to cause harm (malice) existed. Further, if a reporter was found to have lacked intent to cause harm, the libeled person could not recover damages.

This case was also concerned with the legal interpretation of the term public official. In cases subsequent to Sullivan, the concept of public official has been expanded to cover public figures. In sports organizations, the term public figures have been shown to include players, coaches, and administrators. The finding was based on the rationale that since sport exhibitions are provided for public enjoyment, legitimate criticism and comment can be made regarding the performance of the coach, team, or players. The opinions of sports writers and commentators are covered by the First Amendment of the U.S. Constitution which protects freedom of the press.

This broad coverage of the First Amendment to public officials extends only to their public activities. Their private lives do not fall within the same broad coverage as do their professional activities as a public figure. The balance between a sports figure's privacy and the public's right to know is not always clear.

The constitutional protection surrounding this right becomes important to the sports organization in two circumstances. First, it can apply to what the media write and say about members of the organization and secondly, it pertains to what the public relations department produces. It should, therefore, be noted that the writers in a sports organization's public relations department have to be as careful about violations as the media professionals.

According to the Sullivan ruling, any written material produced about public figures by the public relations professional must be shown to have actual malice to be found libelous. If, on the other hand, the individual cannot be shown to be a public figure, considerable restraint must be exercised.

The spoken word in public relations can also encounter legal difficulties. However, because the spoken word is less permanent than the written word, the courts have made it more difficult for the injured party to prove damages.

Sport managers are often involved with the distribution of photographs (still or motion) of the sports figures in their organization. This raises the issue of an image of an individual as personal property. It is generally illegal to use a person's name or likeness without consent by another to advertise its products, add luster to its name, or for any of its other business purposes. This issue has generated several implications for schools and universities, amateur sports bodies, and fitness centers. Before any sport organization uses any picture of its participants or clients, the public relations director should be certain to secure photographic releases.

Sebellin-Ross (2011) suggests the wording of such a release might be similar to the following such as:

"I hereby give those acting on behalf of right and permission to copyright and/or use, re-use, and/or publish, and republish photographic pictures of me. I do hereby waive any right to inspect and/or approve the finished photograph. This consent is given for any photographs which have been taken, are about to be taken, or will be taken.

These statements should be required of all athletes, coaches, and administrators in the athletic department. It is also a good idea for all sports organizations to require such releases from employees, club members, or administrators. The sport manager should keep these on file should any question arise concerning the legality of the reproduction of a photograph by the organization.

Finally, several lawsuits have been filed regarding access of reporters to locker rooms. Generally speaking, the press has no right to gather information in places not open to the public. Considerable thought should be given to the development of policies relating to access to locker rooms. These policies should be distributed to all reporters in advance of sport competitions and should be strictly enforced (p. 123)."

Seeking a Public Relations Agency

Wilcox and Cameron (2011) suggest the following 10 questions are commonly asked before an organization contracts with a public relations agency:

- "Does the agency have experience in the health, fitness, physical activity, recreation, and sport industries?
- Do the account executives have experience in these industries?
- Does the agency have a good reputation?
- Will the agency give you a list of references?
- Will you get senior-level management attention?
- Do they know the industries' publications and have media contacts at each?
- Are they a full-service agency with public relations, advertising, direct mail, and promotional capabilities?
- Are they creative? Ask to see other public relations campaigns completed for other organizations in the same or related areas.
- Are they result-oriented?
- Are they good listeners (p. 145)?"

Once the questions have been answered and analyzed, it is time to narrow the field of prospective agencies to the top three to five. These agencies should be requested to make a presentation to the selection committee. After the presentations have been completed the committee should make a recommendation ranking the agencies and providing a narrative explaining the ratings for each agency.

References

Krotee, M. L., & Bucher, C. A.(2007). *Management of physical education and sport* (13th ed.). New York, NY: McGraw-Hill.

Sebellin-Ross, S. J. (2011). *Public relations.* Amazon Digital Services, Inc.

Stodlt, G. C., Pratt, C., & Dittmore, S. (2007). Public relations in the sport industry. In J. Parks (Ed.), *Contemporary sport management* (3rd ed.). Champaign, IL: Human Kinetics.

Wilcox, D. L., & Cameron, C.T. (2011). *Public relations: Strategies and tactics* (10th ed.). Old Saddle River, NJ: Pearson.

PART III
Financial and Marketing Fundamentals

CHAPTER 10

Financial Principles

Morehead State University

Introduction

The term *finance* can mean different things to different people. Often, those not trained or educated in finance will include any activity that deals with dollars or dollar production in the definition. This sweeping brush stroke could include everything that occurs within an organization since our decisions, more often than not, have a monetary impact. Those trained and educated in finance have a more focused scope that addresses the concepts and techniques that we use to make organizational decisions. According to Longley (2008) and Brooks (2012), finance generally refers to two primary activities of an organization:

1. How an organization generates the funds that flow into an organization,

2. How an organization allocates and spends these funds once they are within the organization.

Therefore, the concept of finance is not so much about where money enters the organization; but, how it is allocated to insure maximum return. The revenue generated should optimally aid the organization in

Managers of physical activity organizations have many tools and resources available to assist them in making decisions. Sound financial decisions require information from a wide variety of sources such as staff, accountants, consultants, sales representatives, boards of directors, and customers. There are several financial tools that managers can use to aid in the decision making process beginning with documents used on a daily basis, such as balance sheets and profit and loss statements. Utilizing financial data, management must develop a financial plan that will provide the basis for a successful operation for the next fiscal period. That financial plan is the operating budget.

In addition to the operating budget, another budget that must be prepared is the capital development budget. This is a budget plan that prioritizes what the organization intends to acquire or build that is nonrecurring in nature and generally has a life span of at least 10 years. Examples of capital budget projects would be expanding existing physical activity spaces through building expansion, renovating the watering system on a golf course, purchasing new vehicles, or purchasing land for future expansion purposes.

This chapter will review financial principles that address the budget process, preparation of budgets, revenues and expenditures, as well as sound financial planning.

Financial Planning

The goal of financial planning or management is to maximize the current value of the organization. This is often represented as maximizing the current value per share of the existing stock. The financial planner for a physical activity organization needs to link the organization's goals and objectives with the short and long-term financial plan. Financial planning can help provide appropriate solutions for many of the problems that a physical activity organization may face every day (Brigham & Houston, 2014; Sawyer, Hypes, & Hypes, 2004).

Financial planning allows an organization to make decisions in a proactive manner rather than a reaction to unplanned situations. This reduces risks and the organization's competitiveness is increased. Effective financial planning is the foundation upon which an organization can build a successful future. (Brigham & Ehrhardt, 2013; Horine & Stotlar, 2013).

It is much easier for decisions to be made in a proactive manner rather than as a reaction to unplanned situations. Risks are reduced and the organization's competitiveness is increased (Horine & Stotlar, 2013).

An organization must develop a sound strategic plan which includes establishment of the organization's objectives, design of the organization's structure, recruitment and selection of qualified employees, inducing individuals and groups to cooperate, and determining whether or not the organization's objectives have been obtained. Financial planning is an integral part of any strategic plan.

A strategic plan specifically for financial planning should be developed to integrate into the overall organizational strategic plan. All revenue and expenditures need to be planned for well in advance in order to ensure success of the organization.

When planning for financial success, the manager must consider many facets of finance, including cash planning, profit planning, capital budgeting, long-term planning, short-term financing, asset management ratios, forecasting, evaluating the environment, and risk management. The manager must be able to determine revenue streams and flow in order to cover expenditures in a timely fashion.

Financial planning, according to Block, Hirt, and Danielson (2010), can also help provide appropriate solutions for many of the problems that a business may face every day, such as

- funding of capital projects,
- developing new products and services,
- retiring products and services,
- selling assets,
- purchasing assets,
- protecting assets,
- moving an organization to a new location, and
- covering tax liabilities.

The financial staff's task is to acquire, and then help, employ resources so as to maximize the value of the organization. Some specific activities (Brooks, 2012) include

- forecasting and planning,
- major investment and financial decisions,
- coordination and control,
- dealing with the financial markets, and
- risk management.

The Financial Manager

A common feature among all large sport entities is that the owners (the stockholders) are usually not directly involved in making decisions, particularly on a day-to-day basis. Instead, the corporation employs managers to represent the owner's interests and make decisions on their behalf. Those managers would include, but not be limited to general manager, facility and grounds manager, concessions manager, human resource manager, risk manager, and financial manager.

The financial manager has the responsibility to answer key questions (Block et al., 2010; Brooks, 2012), including the following:

- What long-term investments should the organization consider?

- What lines of business will the organization be in?

- What sorts of facilities, machinery, and equipment will the organization need?

- Where will the organization secure the long-term financing to pay for investment?

- Will the organization bring in additional investors?

- Will the organization borrow the funds needed?

- How will the organization manage everyday financial activities such as collecting from customers, paying suppliers, and meeting payroll?

The financial management function is usually associated with a top officer of the firm such as the chief financial officer (CFO) or the vice president of finance. The top financial officer may have two key subordinates called controller and treasurer. The controller's office handles cost and financial accounting, tax payments, and management information systems. The treasurer's office is responsible for managing the firm's cash flow and credit, its financial planning, and its capital expenditures. In small organizations the responsibility for financial accountability, budgeting, and planning becomes the duty of the executive director or general manager.

The Role of Financial Analysis

An organization must review and revise its financial status just as it reviews its programs and facilities. Through financial analysis, managers can review financial statements, assess cash flow, and determine if the organization is financially sound. There is no real difference in reviewing your own personal finances and the finances of an organization. An organization will have more and different categories to review, but the purpose of the analysis is the same.

Financial analysis allows an organization to determine when, and if, capital projects may be undertaken, as well as take advantage of investment opportunities. Capital projects are often defined as a major building project, building acquisition, or major equipment purchase. Missed opportunities or great financial risk can result from poor financial analysis. Budget reductions often occur during economic downturns and knowing and understanding your financial status is essential in maintaining organizational solvency.

When analyzing financial statements, it is essential that good judgment prevails. It is more appropriate to compare the financial statements of similar organizations to obtain realistic information for present and future financial growth. The current performance of an organization should be compared with its performance in previous years. This will aid the manager in setting realistic goals and objectives for future growth.

Evaluating the Environment

Evaluating the environment in which your organization competes is vital to its long-term financial stability. From terrorist activities that may affect event planning to advances in food preparation for concession sales, the competitive environment in which an organization operates must be monitored to avoid missed opportunities as well as financial disaster.

There are numerous ways to evaluate the environment of an organization. The manager must first look internally for components that may be easily altered to bring about a more profitable future. Internal aspects may include employee benefits, workloads, staffing, and policies. All of these areas work together to provide a pleasant work environment, which, in turn, increases productivity. By reviewing benefit expenses, it can be determined, for example, if less expensive health coverage could be provided to save both the organization and the employee money without reducing services. Workloads may be reassigned or new staff hired to reduce overtime and tension of overworked employees. Policies may need to be altered as an organization grows both in size and as its financial status changes. All of these components are controlled within the organization and requires little effort to monitor, evaluate, and change.

The external environment in which an organization operates is not as easy to monitor and therefore necessary change may be slow; however, its importance is vital to the future financial success of an organization. The international political environment such as terrorism, war, and government stability must be monitored to determine if events must be moved or canceled. The marketing environment for sports products and services must be analyzed so opportunities in the marketplace will not be lost.

Demographics and geography should be reviewed to determine new market potential and current market change. Such information can be found in census reports conducted by the government. Market research is the foundation for reviewing the environment in which an organization operates.

Forecasting Sales

Financial planning is often based on the successes and failures of previous years' sales. Along with the present market analysis, managers can use previous sales to forecast future sales. A market analysis will include a strengths, weaknesses, opportunities, and threats, (SWOT) analysis of the organization and its competition. When properly conducted, a SWOT analysis can show the position of a product within the market and can help the manager realize future market potential and opportunities within the market place. Strengths and weaknesses are internal components that can be controlled and corrected within the organization whereas opportunities and threats are external factors that are influenced by areas such as the economy, trends, fads, culture, and the environment. By realistically forecasting sales, an organization can better plan for cash flow and conduct both short- and long-term planning.

Financial Risk Management

As sports enterprises become increasingly complex, it is becoming more and more difficult for the sports manager to know what problems might lie in wait. The sports manager needs to systematically look for potential problems and design safeguards to minimize potential damage. There are 12 major sources of risk common to sports organizations including business partners (e.g., contractual risks), competition (e.g., market share, price wars, antitrust), customers (e.g., product liability, credit risk, poor market timing), distribution systems (e.g., transportation, service availability, cost), financial (e.g., cash, interest rate), operations (e.g., facilities, natural hazards, internal controls), people (e.g., employees, independent contractors, training, staffing inadequacy), political (e.g., change in leadership, enforcement of intellectual property rights, revised economic policies), regulatory and legislative (e.g., antitrust, licensing, taxation, reporting and compliance), reputations (e.g., corporate image, brand), strategic (e.g., mergers and acquisitions, joint ventures and alliances, resource allocation, planning), and technological (e.g., obsolescence, workforce skill-sets).

Preparing a Financial Plan

When preparing a financial plan, the manager must review all aspects of the organization and make decisions for its future stability and profitability. Financial planning will allow an organization to sustain itself through inflation, recession, cash flow shortages, and other economic situations that can be devastating to any business.

Building the Case

Without a sound financial plan, investors and lenders will not place their trust and resources into an organization. Research should be conducted by looking at both past and present budgets, revenue generation resources, and capital outlay projects. This research of both internal and external factors will provide the manager with an overview of the past and current financial condition and help to make future decisions for improved financial stability.

The Balance Sheet

The balance sheet, income statement, and cash flow statement all summarize some aspect of an organization's finances at a given point in time. The balance sheet summarizes the financial position of an organization at a particular point in time and is considered one of the most important financial statements. According to Parkhouse, Turner, and Miloch (2012), and Brock (2010), the four main uses of the balance sheet are that it shows (1) changes in the business over a period of time, (2) growth or decline in various phases of the business, (3) the business's ability to pay debts, and (4) through ratios, the financial position.

The balance sheet is a snapshot of the firm. It is a convenient means of organizing and summarizing what an organization owns (its assets), what an organization owes (its liabilities), and the difference between the two (the organization's equity) at a given point in time.

Accountability

According to Brigham and Houston (2014) and Brooks (2012), accountability is defined as the state of being accountable, subject to the obligation to report, explain, or justify something; responsible; and answerable. Most academicians use a narrow definition that involves the nonprofit answering to a higher authority in the bureaucratic or inter-organizational chain of command.

The public and the media tend to use a broader definition of accountability. Generally, this definition holds the organization accountable to the public, media, donors, customers/clients, stockholders, and others. The public and media have a greater expectation that the organization will have a certain level of performance, responsiveness, ethics, and morality.

The organization's views on accountability will play a key role in developing an organization's standards of accountability. The manager should answer two questions when defining accountability for the organization: To whom is the organization accountable? For what activities and levels of performance is the organization held responsible?

Auditing

Auditing is a field of accounting activity that involves an independent review of general accounting practices. Most large organizations employ their own staffs of internal auditors.

Brooks (2012) notes that internal auditing is an independent, objective assurance and consulting activity designed to add value and improve an organization's operations. It helps an organization accomplish its objectives by bringing a systematic, disciplined approach to evaluate and improve the effectiveness of risk management, control, and governance processes.

Block et al. (2010) suggest that internal control is a process affected by the board of directors, senior management, and all levels of personnel. It is not solely a procedure or policy that is performed at a certain point in time; but rather, it is continuously operating at all levels within the organization. The board of directors and senior management are responsible for establishing the appropriate culture to facilitate an effective internal control process and for continuously monitoring its effectiveness; however, each individual within an organization must participate in the process. The main objectives of the internal control process can be categorized as follows (Block et al., 2010; Brooks 2012):

- efficiency and effectiveness of operations (operational objectives)

- reliability and completeness of financial and management information (information objectives)

- compliance with applicable laws and regulations (compliance objectives)

Brigham and Houston (2014) indicate operational objectives for internal control pertain to the effectiveness and efficiency of the bank in using its assets and other resources and protecting the organization from loss. The internal control process seeks to ensure that personnel throughout the organization are working to achieve its objectives in a straightforward manner without unintended or excessive cost or placing other interests (such as an employee's, vendor's, or customer's interest) before those of the organization.

Information objectives address the preparation of timely, reliable reports needed for decision-making within the organization. They also address the need for reliable annual accounts, other financial statements, and other financial-related disclosures including those for regulatory reporting and other external uses. The information received by management, the board of directors, shareholders, and supervisors should be of sufficient quality and integrity that recipients can rely on the information in making decisions. The term reliable, as it relates to financial statements, refers to the preparation of statements that are presented fairly and based on comprehensive and well-defined accounting principles and rules.

Compliance objectives ensure that all business of the organization is conducted in compliance with applicable laws and regulations, supervisory requirements, and internal policies and procedures. This objective must be met in order to protect the organization's reputation.

Internal control consists of five interrelated elements (Brooks, 2012):

- management oversight and the control culture

- risk assessment

- control activities

- information and communication

- monitoring activities

The problems observed in recent large losses at organizations can be aligned with these five elements. The effective functioning of these elements is essential to achieving an organization's operational, informational, and compliance objectives.

Although the board of directors and senior management bear the ultimate responsibility for an effective system of internal controls, supervisors should assess the internal control system in place at individual organizations as part of their ongoing supervisory activities. The supervisors should also determine whether individual organization management gives prompt attention to any problems that are detected through the internal control process.

Financial Accountability

The financial manager makes the following assertions regarding the execution and summarization of financial transactions that are found in various financial reports.

Existence and Occurrence

The assets and liabilities actually exist at the report date and transactions reported actually occurred during the reporting period covered. There is physical security over assets and transactions are valid.

Completeness

All transactions and accounts that should be included in the reports are included and there are no undisclosed assets, liabilities, or transactions.

Rights and Obligations

The organization owns and has clear title to assets and liabilities, which are the obligation of the organization. Transactions are valid.

Valuation and Allocation

The assets and liabilities are valued properly and the revenues and expenses are measured properly. Transactions are accurate.

Presentation and Disclosure

The assets, liabilities, revenues, and expenses are properly classified, described, and disclosed in financial reports.

Internal Control

Since employees and management involved with financial processes are making (implying) the above representations (assertions), management, at various levels, needs internal controls to ensure that financial data compiled is not false, misleading, incomplete, or inaccurate. Users have every reason to believe the data and reports you give them are accurate and reliable. These minimum financial reporting objectives therefore become the objectives used in designing an effective system of internal control that ensures reliable financial reporting. The uniquely designed internal control procedures within the organization are there to achieve these objectives.

Everyone in the organization has some responsibility for internal control even though it is often supervisors and/or managers who design the internal control procedures within their area of influence. This is true from two perspectives. First, almost all employees play some part in effective control. They may produce information used in the control system or take other actions needed to affect control. Any weak link in the organization's structure can create a weakness in the control system. Second, all employees are responsible to communicate problems in operations, deviations from established standards, and violations of the organization's financial policy.

By definition, internal control is a process designed to provide reasonable assurance regarding the achievement of the organization's financial reporting objectives. Within this definition there are fundamental concepts relating to internal control, including (a) it is not one event, but a process or series of actions that permeate the organization's activities and are inherent in the way business is transacted; (b) it is affected by the people of the organization in what they do and say and they must therefore know their responsibilities and the limits of their authority; (c) it provides reasonable, not absolute, assurance regarding the achievement of objectives and should be cost effective; and (d) it is geared to the achievement of the organization's objectives.

Components

In determining the control procedures to achieve the objectives, the process usually starts with a management-directed self-evaluation at the business operation cycle level and applies the "objectives" to groups of similarly processed transactions (types of transactions). The objectives for each group are achieved by a judiciously determined mix of procedures from the following five major components of internal control. The mix may be different for each type of transaction within a financial area based on the relative risk and significance of the amounts involved. Also, some components cover a number of transaction types. The overriding purpose is that there is not a high risk of significant errors getting through the accounting process that would not be caught by a control procedure performed by an employee performing his or her regular duties.

The process used to fulfill responsibilities and determine the level of internal control necessary should adhere to the following steps and be documented.

- Control Environment

  It is the responsibility of the financial manager to establish an environment that encourages integrity and ethical values. The financial manager's leadership philosophy, competence, and management and operating style communicate to the employees a sense of control conscious-ness in the organization.

- Risk Assessment

  Risk assessment is the process of identifying financial risks and the consequences of such risks as related to control activities.

- Control Activities

  Control activities are those procedures designed to see that objectives are met and the risks identified in step two are reduced to a reasonable level. These techniques include procedures to ensure that transactions are:

  - These executed in accordance with management's general or specific authorization, and

  - These properly recorded to permit the preparation of financial reports in confor-mance with generally accepted accounting principles and to maintain accountability for assets.

- Information and Communication

  Surrounding the control activities are information and communication systems. These enable the organization's employees to capture and exchange the information needed to conduct, manage, and control operations. A large part of the communication system is the accounting system, which consists of methods and records established to identify, assemble, analyze, classify, record, and report the organization's transactions in accordance with generally ac-cepted accounting principles and maintain accountability for recorded assets and liabilities. At a minimum, the system must be able to:

  - identify types of transactions executed (revenues, expenses, assets, and liabilities),

  - accumulate (record) economic events in the appropriate accounts at the correct amounts, and

  - record the economic events in the correct accounting period.

- Monitoring

  The entire process must be monitored and modified as necessary to react to changing condi-tions. The monitoring process should be performed at several levels. A supervisory review of activities should be on a regular basis as part of the normal management function. Periodic special reviews should be by management, internal auditors, and external auditors.

Nonprofit Organizations' Accountability

Nonprofit organizations are defined as private, self-governing organizations that exist to provide a particular service to the community (e.g., American Legion Baseball, AAU Basketball, Boys Clubs, Community Soccer Leagues, Girls Clubs, Little League Baseball, YMCA, YWCA, and many more). The word *nonprofit* refers to a type of organization that operates without the purpose of generating a profit for owners. As government continues to decline in providing services due to legal and budget constraints, nonprofits have been filling the void by providing these needed services; but unlike government agencies, nonprofits have not always been held to the same public scrutiny.

As scandals over nonprofit accountability (e.g., American National Red Cross, United Way, and others) make their way to the headlines of widely read newspapers, nonprofit credibility wanes. As a result, nonprofit organizations' images suffer, causing much of the public to decrease donations to all nonprofit organizations; although, many of the accusations against nonprofits are spurious. Today, nonprofits face powerful accountability pressures and are asked by donors and the public to justify their delivered services and operations.

During hard economic conditions, society is especially concerned with accountability of nonprofit organizations. Donors want to be assured that their limited resources are being utilized in the most efficient and effective manner possible. They want to "see" how their donations are being utilized and identify how a difference is being made for those in need

Budgets

Budgets are an integral part of financial planning. They are designed to help guide an organization through a financial calendar year, budget cycle, or a fiscal year. Budgets can aid an organization in utilizing its available resources in the most efficient and effective manner possible.

The Role of the Budget

The budget is a part of the foundation upon which an organization justifies its mission. It establishes financial parameters through which the organization can determine its objectives and attain its goals. The mission statement for the organization establishes guidelines that help construct the budget.

It is the statement of purpose for the organization that establishes goals that the organization wants to achieve. Without a mission statement, an organization would not function in an effective and efficient manner. There would be no direction, goals, or means of obtaining those goals. An organization without a budget could be likened to someone setting out on a cross-country road trip to visit relatives without a map or plan for which direction to drive first. A budget is an estimate of revenue and expenses for a given period of time, usually one to two years.

Budgets anticipate or predict cash flow as well as control cash flow. Effective cash flow budgeting involves estimating when income and expenses occur to ensure that no times arise when a shortage of income means that an agency is unable to pay its expenses (Howard & Crompton, 2013). In sport, there are many periods when an organization may not be generating income sufficient to cover expenses. Monthly bills continue to become due and renovation projects are often undertaken during this off-season period. When cash flow problems are anticipated and planned for within the budget, the organization can easily attend to routine monthly bills as well as continue with maintenance schedules and renovation projects.

The budget of the organization is determined by the organization's goals and objectives. Essentially, the budget is a restatement of the organization's goals and objectives in financial terms.

The Budget Process

A fitness, physical activity, recreation, or sport organization must develop objectives to guide the program decision making process. An operating budget is used for projecting and quantifying these program objectives. Organizations might use the terms production, sales, or service objectives in lieu of program objectives. A budget can also be considered a plan that uses dollars in both revenue (income) and expenditures to project what an organization can do in the coming year. In the case of capital budgets, these projections would be over a period of five or more years.

There are five steps, according to Horine and Stotlar (2013), that are commonly used in the budget process:

1. "Collecting data relative to the needs, strengths, and resources of the organization then applied to the mission of the organization, and goals of the previous year.

2. Analyzing the data collected, comparing it to past experiences and present requirements.

3. Identifying other factors that may impact operations.

4. Preparing the document according to stipulations and requirements of the organizations governing budget including reviewing the document for accuracy and feasibility. Soliciting a third party to review the draft document, and preparing for questions during the formal budget review.

5. Implementing the approved budget and auditing the budget at the conclusion of the fiscal year (p. 172)."

When collecting data for budget preparation, sport managers should use a variety of resources. Statistical information should be considered when preparing a budget. Statistics that a manager needs are:

1. How income and expenses compare for a given period of time (variance analysis),

2. Usage and participation data,

3. Program evaluation reports,

4. Inventory levels, and

5. Other sources as appropriate.

Management must also look to employees for input on budgetary needs. Since employees are users of equipment and supplies, they are knowledgeable in what is most effective and efficient in the production of goods and services. Management should provide all workers with the opportunity to share their knowledge and experience and contribute to budgeting decisions (Sawyer, Hypes, & Hypes, 2004).

Past budgets should be examined to attempt to identify financial trends that have developed. A comparison of current financial statements with previous will reveal revenue and expenditure trends, potential problem budget areas, as well as opportunities that may lead to future revenue.

To build a budget, management must be able to forecast, or predict with some degree of confidence, what expected revenues and expenses will be for the next fiscal period. Forecasting must be done for both existing programs as well as anticipated new programs.

There are factors that do not come directly from previous budget data and can impact operations and therefore, budget preparations. These factors can be classified as internal or external. Internal factors are those occurrences that come from within an organization. Such internal factors may include cost of living increases for employees, changes in organization policies, changes in management structure, change in management personnel, and other factors that may be unique to the organization. External factors are those that occur outside an organization and over which the organization has little or no control. Some examples of these factors would be program trends, changes in law, the economy, changes in the tax base, or even the weather.

After all data have been collected and analyzed, dollar amounts should be calculated and applied to various accounts. Expenses should be based on input from the three methods of forecasting (i.e., employee, statistical, and managerial input). Income can be forecast using those same methods. Most managers estimate expenses based on anticipated increases in the cost of living and/or suppliers forecasts for price increases. Income, on the other hand, us usually projected to be somewhat less than actually hoped.

When the budget has been completed at a given level but before it is presented for approval at the next higher level, it must be reviewed and interpreted with as much staff involvement as possible and practical. It is important that the staff understand what the financial picture for the organization will be for the coming year. Management must be satisfied that the budget numbers appear to be reasonable and justifications for decisions are clearly stated. In the end, the operating budget is most often the result of experience and a combination of the "best guess" based on available data and a "gut" feeling of where the organization should be going financially.

Once a budget is established, it becomes a tool to monitor and control expenditures. Through this control, management is kept honest. This is especially important for a public agency whose primary source of revenue is tax dollars.

Revenue Generation

There are three major categories of revenue generation for physical activity organizations and sport programs, including public, private, and a combination of public and private sources (Sawyer, Hypes, & Hypes, 2004). Within these categories, the primary sources of revenue generation are (Brooks, 2012; Sawyer, Hypes, & Hypes, 2004):

1. Membership fees

2. Tax revenue

3. Ticket sales

4. Admission fees

5. Concession sales

6. Sponsorship

7. Licensing

There are five concessions that impact club, recreation, and sport programs: food service, merchandising (i.e., pro shop, souvenir stand), beauty shop, child-care, and parking. A concession is a privilege granted by a government, company, or organization such as the following (Howard & Crompton, 2013):

1. "The right to use land for a specified purpose.

2. A government grant of land forming a subdivision of a township.

3. The right or a lease to engage in a certain activity for profit or the lessor's premises (i.e., a refreshment, parking, merchandising, fireworks, child-care, or beauty care concession).

4. The land, space, etc. so granted or leased (p. 216)."

Sponsorships are partnerships with corporations who assist financially with a particular project or event in order to gain a higher public profile. For the organization, sponsorships are a way to obtain funding to operate their programs and events. For the corporations, sponsorships provide a method to get their product in the minds of the consumer. A sponsorship must serve the interests of four constituent groups, including the following (Sawyer, Hypes, & Hypes, 2004):

1. "The business interest of the sponsoring company.

2. The best interests of the event and participants.

3. Serve as a positive influence on the sponsor's direct customers.

4. Benefit the customer who buys the products (p. 193)."

Licensing is defined as a contractual agreement whereby a company may use another company's trademark in exchange for a royalty or fee (Sawyer, Hypes, & Hypes, 2004). Licensing affords the organization an opportunity to generate revenue through the commercial use of its name, logo, or slogan. Consumer demand for logoed apparel has provided an opportunity for organizations to grant a second party the right to produce merchandise bearing their logos. A royalty fee is paid to the organization for the use of their name, logo, or slogan.

There are a number of other revenue generating sources. Fitness, physical activity, recreation, and sport programs are always seeking ways to generate additional revenue. Without adequate revenues, an organization cannot meet its financial commitments and eventually will have to close its doors. Examples of additional revenue sources are: advertising profits, donations, franchising receipts, fund-raising dollars, league/conference revenue, leasing revenue, broadcasting contracts.

Expenditures

Expenditures are costs, or money paid out, that an organization encounters. Costs are those factors associated with producing, promoting, and distributing the sport's product (Shank, 2014). There are three types of costs: fixed, variable, and total. Expenditures have been consumed in the process of producing revenue and are often called expired costs or expenses (Sawyer, Hypes, & Hypes, 2004).

Fixed costs are those that do not change or vary in regard to the quantity of product or service consumed. A fixed cost used in break-even analysis is that cost that remains constant regardless of the amount of variable costs. For example, fixed costs include insurance, taxes, etc. Variable costs are those costs that are going to increase or decrease based on the increase or decrease in a product or service provided. For example, variable costs include utilities, postage, merchandise distribution, advertising, etc. The total cost for operations is arrived at when the fixed costs (expenses) and the variable costs (expenses) are added together (Sawyer, Hypes, & Hypes, 2004).

Total Cost = Fixed Costs + Variable Costs

Costs are considered to be internal factors that can be largely controlled by the organization; however, they can have an external or uncontrollable factor. The cost of raw materials, league imposed salary minimums, and shipping of products is controlled by external factors. When establishing a budget, the sport manager must review the total operating expenses considering both internal and external factors to forecast expenditures for the upcoming year (Sawyer, Hypes, & Hypes, 2004).

Income Statements and Balance Sheets

The financial success of an organization is ultimately dependent on the difference between revenues and expenses. This difference is call profits or income. Profits can be increased by increasing revenues, decreasing costs, or both. An income statement is the financial statement that summarizes an organization's revenues, expenses, and profits over a given period of time.

The balance sheet summarizes the financial position of an organization at a particular point in time and is considered one of the most important financial statements. According to Parkhouse et al. (2012), the four main uses of the balance sheet are that it shows the following:

1. Changes in the business over a period of time

2. Growth or decline in various phases of the business

3. The business's ability to pay debts

4. Through ratios the business's financial position

The balance sheet is a snapshot of the firm. It is convenient means of organizing and summarizing what an organization owns (its assets), what an organization owes (its liabilities), and the difference between the two (the organization's equity) at a given point in time (Sawyer, Hypes, & Hypes, 2004).

Capital Budgets

Capital budgeting deals with investment decisions involving fixed assets (e.g., equipment, buildings, accumulated depreciation for equipment and buildings). The term *capital* is defined as long-term assets used in production and budget means a plan that details projected inflows (amount of dollars coming into the organization) and outflows (amount of dollars leaving the organization to cover expenses) during some future period. Thus, the capital budget is an outline of planned investments in fixed assets and capital budgeting is the process of analyzing projects and deciding which ones to include in the capital budget.

Capital budgets provide for expenditures to purchase assets that have service life of at least five years. In the case of buildings, the expectancy is usually 10 years or more. Capital budgets require physical and financial planning. Careful physical planning is essential because of the long-term service associated with capital projects. A mistake involving a capital project will be around for many years. Physical planning involves more than design considerations. In the case of new construction, improper selection of the building site that causes disruption of traffic flow or prohibits expansion might well be a mistake that cannot be corrected after construction has begun.

Equipment is most often replaced by regularly placing funds in a depreciation account. When equipment reached the end of its service life, the money to replace the equipment should be in hand. The depreciation account assures those funds will be available for the replacement of equipment and not used for other capital projects. Capital projects may have to be funded through loans, bonds, stock sales, or other means.

Cash Planning

Determining the amount of cash needed at a particular point in the budget year can be accomplished by gathering data from both internal and external sources. Internal data are generated by the organization itself and may include areas such as past budgets, sales records, and human resources reports. This type of data is primary data. The organization generates the data, analyzes it, and compiles reports from the data gathered within the organization. Internal data can also be gathered from personal observation or conversations as well as customer and employee surveys.

External data may be gathered from resources outside of the organization to help determine the impact of factors such as the local, state, national, and world economy and demographic and geographic information. These external factors may impact sales and trends within the industry and the organization must be able to respond to the changing consumer needs. External data are often referred to as secondary data because such compilations have been published by another organization.

Because the nature of a sport is seasonal, the manager should utilize previous budget records to determine how much cash will need to be on hand during particular points in the budget year. During times of revenue prosperity, cash should be held back to pay for expenditures during the off-season or other low revenue points. Cash planning should also include capital projects, those projects that require large sums of money to complete, as well as daily operation expenses. Cash is any medium of exchange that a bank will accept at face value including bank deposits, currency, checks, bank drafts, and money orders.

Cash Flow

While it may seem impossible, an organization shows a profit on its income statement and may not have enough money available to pay bills. Cash flow refers to the flow of cash in and out of an organization over a given period of time. Outflow of cash is measured by the payments that will be made for expenses such as salaries, suppliers, and creditors. The inflows are the revenues brought in from customers, lenders, investors, and sponsors. A successful organization will always have cash on hand to cover operating expenses and labor costs.

In sport, cash flow is of particular importance because of each sport's unique revenue status at the collegiate level. Some sports can be quite profitable and assist in funding other sports within the organization. A sport manager must always prepare for weak revenues from those peak-generating sports. Weather and negative win-loss records can affect revenue generation and therefore have devastating effects on cash flow.

It is important to note that cash flow does not tell the manager the financial condition of the organization, nor does it show profits or losses of the organization. It merely sows how much cash has come into an organization and how much is going out (Parkhouse et al., 2012). The sport manager must be certain that the available funds are being used wisely for both short and long-term financial planning.

The cash activities of an organization can be summarized by a simple formula:

Cash flow from Assets = Cash flow to creditors + Cash Flow to Owners

Operating Cash Flow

Operating cash flow is an important number because it tells the sport manager whether or not an organization's cash inflows from its business operations are sufficient to cover its everyday cash outflows. For this reason, a negative operating cash flow is often a sign of trouble.

Cash Flow Budget

The cash flow budget is a forecast of cash receipts and disbursements for the next planning period. The cash flow budget is a primary tool in the short-run financial planning. It allows the sport financial manager to identify short-term financial needs and opportunities. Importantly, the cash flow budget will help the manager explore the need for short-term borrowing. The concept behind a cash flow budget is simple. It records estimates of cash receipts (cash in) and disbursements (cash out). The result is an estimate of the cash surplus or deficit.

Profit Planning

Profit is the sum remaining after all costs, direct and indirect, are deducted from the revenue of an organization. In general, revenue is the amount charged to customers for goods or services sold to them.

There are alternative terms used to identify revenue including sales, fees earned, rent earned, or fares earned. The bottom line for an organization is the ability to generate revenue at such a pace that continued growth could be both sustained and achieved. If an organization has shareholders, this growth should include rewards, or dividends, for those shareholders.

While making a profit is the ultimate goal of any business, the mission, goals, and objectives of the organization should not be forsaken in order to obtain profit. By determining the short- and long-term goals of an organization and keeping them in mind during all phases of financial planning, resources can be better allocated to achieve these goals. Short-term goals are those goals that you want to achieve in the near future. The time frame for short-term is no more than one to two years. Long-term goals are priorities that are set for a 3- to 5-year period in the future and they often require more time and resources to bring to reality. These goals should move to the short-term goal list as their deadline approaches and resources become available. By properly planning where an organization's profits will be allocated, the manger can allocate funds for these various short- and long-term projects.

To properly plan for where and when profits will be spent, a person must first know where they are obtained and how stable that revenue generation will be over a longer period of time so the manager can better determine the profit margin. Revenue generation is not the only area of concern when determining profits. The manager must also forecast costs and plan for unforeseen emergencies in order to determine profit margin.

There are several commonly used measures of profitability. These include profit margin on sales, return on total assets, return on common equity, and return on investment. Profit margins, gross and net, are determined by dividing profits by revenue. Net profit margins use net income or income after taxes and interest and gross profit margin uses earnings before taxes and interest have been paid. Margin is the difference between the cost and the selling price of goods produced and services rendered. This is sometimes called a margin on sales or sales margin. Profit margin is a profitability measure that defines the relationship between sales and net income. The result is a percentage of profit. Some items have a high percentage of profit margin and others have a lower percentage. The sport manager uses the profit margin measure to determine what the price of the service or product should be to be competitive and allow the organization to make a profit.

Common equity is the sum of the par value (i.e., the principal amount of a bond that is repaid at the end of the term), capital in excess of par, and accumulated retained earnings. Community equity is usually referred to as an organization's book value or net worth.

Return on assets (ROA) is another profitability measure of profit per dollar of asset. The ROA is determined by dividing profits by average assets for a given reporting period. The average assets (i.e., an average of an organization's assets over a prior period of time) can be located on the balance sheet. The return on investment (ROI) is often referred to as the ROA because it reflects the amount of profits earned on the investment in all assets of the firm. These terms are interchangeable.

The return on common equity (ROE) is similar to the ROA; however, it is concerned with stockholder equity. The ROE is determined by dividing the net income by the average stockholders' equity in the organization. The ROA and the ROE can be effective in comparing the financial statuses of businesses of similar size and interest.

The balance sheet is a snapshot of the organization. It is a convenient means of organizing and summarizing what an organization owns (i.e., assets), what is owed (i.e., liabilities), and the difference between the two (i.e., equity) at a given point in time. If the difference between assets and liabilities is positive then the organization is profitable. The ROE is yet another profitability measure of how the stockholders did during the year. It is the true bottom-line measure of performance.

A fixed or permanent asset is one that is long-lived. These assets are tangible in nature, used in the operations of the business, and not held for sale in the ordinary course of the business. They are classified on the balance sheet as fixed assets.

Long-Term Planning

Long-term planning is considered any type of planning that is at least five years into the future. All sport managers need to establish a long-term plan for the organization. This plan can be 5 to 15 years in length. The plans need to be revised annually and extended for one additional year into the future. Each department within the organization needs to be involved in the long-term plan and each department's plan needs to be an integral part of the overall organization's long-term plan. Those organizations that do not plan well into the future generally are not around for the long haul. An organization cannot plan too much. Planning must be an integral part of the organization's culture.

Short-Term Financing

Most sport organizations in the private sector use several types of short-term debt to finance their working capital requirements, including bank loans (e.g., line of credit, revolving credit agreement, promissory note), trade credit (i.e., accounts payable), commercial paper (e.g., unsecured promissory note issued by the organization and sold to another organization, insurance company, pension fund, or bank), and accruals (i.e., accrued assets). Short-term credit is generally much less expensive, quicker, and more flexible than long-term capital; however, it is a riskier source of financing. For example, interest rates can increase dramatically and changes in an organization's financial position can affect both the cost and availability of short-term credit.

References

Block, S., Hirt, G., & Danielson, B. (2010). *Foundations of financial management* (14th ed.). NY: McGraw-Hill.

Brigham, E. F., & Ehrhardt, M. E. (2013). *Financial management: Theory and practice* (14th ed.). Mason, OH: South-Western Cengage Learning.

Brigham, E. F., & Houston, J. F. (2014). *Fundamentals of finance management, concise* (8th ed.). Mason, OH: South-Western Cengage Learning.

Brooks, R. M. (2012). *Financial management: Core concepts* (2nd ed.). Upper Saddle River, NJ: Prentice-HHall

Horine, L. (2013). *Administration of physical education and sport programs* (5th ed.). New York, NY: McGraw Hill.

Howard, D. R., & Crompton, J. L. (2013). *Financing sport* (3rd ed.). Morgantown, WV: Fitness Information Technology.

Longley, N. (2008). *Financial and economic principles applied to sport management*. Sudbury, MA: Jones & Bartlett Publishers.

Parkhouse, B., Turner, B., & Miloch, K.S. (2012). *Marketing for sport business success*. Dubuque, IA: Kendall Hunt Publishing.

Sawyer, T., Hypes, M., & Hypes, J. (2004). *Financing the sport enterprise*. Urbana, IL: Sagamore Publishing.

Shank, M. D. (2014). *Sports marketing: A strategic perspective* (5th ed.). Upper Saddle River, NJ: Prentice Hall.

CHAPTER 11

Purchasing and Inventory Control Principles

Michael G. Hypes

Morehead State University

Introduction

The purchase of sports equipment and supplies involves an intricate process that is generally controlled by institutional or organizational policies and regulations. The ultimate goal of the purchasing process is to provide the organization with the best product at the best price. Purchasing may be controlled through a central purchasing office or by independent agencies.

Monczka, Handfield, Giunipero, and Patterson (2011) suggest the purchasing process involves: 1) the selection process, 2) needs assessment, and 3) procurement (p. 56). The selection of sport equipment and supplies is one of the most important responsibilities of a sport manager. The selection process is an integral component for the organization to provide quality programs and facilities.

A needs assessment should be completed to determine the needs of the program that begins with a simple overview of the situation. Is the program new or pre-existing? Is the program educational, recreational or competitive? In each circumstance, it is important to understand the scope, variety and nature of the program(s) to be offered. The procurement process provides a means to provide consistency in the selection and purchase of equipment and supplies. The procurement process usually begins with a purchase request and ends with a purchase order, delivery and payment of the invoice. The institution or organization, according to Murphy and Boffey (2012), should establish a process that ensures that equipment and supplies that are purchased will 1) meet program needs, 2) provide quality, 3) be acquired following an organizational established procedure, 4) be properly accounted for, and 5) be maintained for future safe use (p. 76).

Equipment is identified as items that are nonconsumable, which implies they will be used over a period of years. Supplies, on the other hand, are consumable materials such as paper, pens, and athletic tape.

What is the Role of Purchasing?

No matter what type of purchasing system is used, there are common principles and guidelines which apply. The following are common components of any purchasing program (Harris, 2000):

- "Standardize

- Quality

- Prompt payment

- Early-bird ordering

- Professional and personal relationships with vendors (p. 87)."

Businesslike Approach

Standardization of ordering equipment and supplies should be based upon conservative items that would be well received when personnel change. The sport manager does not want to incur additional costs by reordering equipment or supplies because of new personnel feeling it necessary to have a different brand or style. The selected products chosen to standardize, should be somewhat generic in nature and provide effect use for any personnel.

Purchasing quality equipment can be very economical in the long run even though the organization may have to pay higher initial costs. Proper security, storage, and maintenance along with initial high quality can increase the longevity of many products.

An organization should only order items that can be afforded and should be able to pay bills in a timely fashion. Failure to do so can result in damage to the professional reputation of the organization.

Early-bird ordering provides a means of having inventory available when it is needed. In many cases, there are discounts available when ordering early or prepaying.

Develop both a professional and personal relationship with the vendors that are most commonly used. A good working relationship allows both parties to provide assistance for the other. For the organization, there are opportunities for discounts, information on new products, trial use, group rates, and the possibility to expedite orders. The vendor has the opportunity to improve image, get repeat orders, and have a valuable reference.

Regardless of the vendor or order, purchasing should be done in a professional, businesslike manner following organizational procedures with checks and balances. Ultimately, the sport manager is striving to get the highest quality for the best price.

The following factors are commonly considered in developing the needs assessment for the selection and purchase of equipment and supplies. AEMA (2013), Monczka et al. (2011), and Murphy and Boffey (2012) suggests these factors include:

- Available space and facilities—Some equipment is limited to indoor use. Safety and circulation around equipment should be considered before purchase.

- Desired activities—Certain activities cannot be properly conducted without unique equipment.

- Safety and health of the participants—Attempts to reduce costs through reduced safety is unjustifiable.

- Number of participants—The number of participants who will use the equipment greatly affects the amount required.

- Costs—Will the equipment purchased fulfill the needs of the organization?

- Staff and supervision—The personnel required to safely supervise the use of the equipment should be considered during the selection process.

- Instructor/coach input—Consultation with those individuals directly involved with the administering of programs provides thorough feedback in the selection of equipment.

- Continual learning—Technological advances occur every day. Up-to-date knowledge of what equipment functions well under given circumstances, what vendors are currently available, and the drive to get better products should influence the selection process.

- Storage—Proper storage can enhance the longevity of the products. Obtain storage requirements from the manufacturer to ensure the life of the product (temperature control, humidity, orientation)

- Age of participants—The equipment provided for a group should be appropriate for that age group.

- Gender of participants—All male, all female, and coed teams provide unique challenges for the equipment manager. Selections will be based in part to the rules developed by the governing body (size of basketball to be used by men and women).

- Skill of participants—The skill level of the participants has a major impact on the equipment selected.

- Physical and mental abilities

- Type of organization—If the organization purchasing the equipment is a school, there may be league or conference requirements on what equipment can be used.

- Length of season—The number of days per year that the equipment can be used may prohibit the purchase of large amounts.

- Geographical location—The location, climate, and local environment are major factors in determining program needs.

- Fit—Properly fitted equipment, especially protective equipment, is essential.

- Inventory—Comparison of current needs of an existing program should be made first. An inventory should not just include the number of items but also sizes and condition of the existing products.

- Prioritizing—Prioritize your wish list from the "must haves" to the "nice to haves". Participant and spectator safety should be top priority.

- The program should be the determining factor in selecting the equipment and supplies needed. As previously stated, it is much better (and economical) in the long run to purchase high-quality equipment.

- Guidelines for selecting equipment and supplies

In addition to the selection variables identified above, specific standards have been developed regarding sport and fitness equipment. The National Operating Committee on Standards for Athletic Equipment (NOCSAE) and the American College of Sports Medicine (ACSM) have established standards that should be of first considerations made when considering the purchase of athletic equipment. NOCSAE was formed to meet the need for nationally approved and accepted standards for activity and sport. These additional guidelines for the selection of equipment and supplies have been identified as useful, according to ACSM (2013), AEMA (2013), and IHRSA (2013):

- Determine purchasing power (how much money is available),

- Begin and maintain a "wish list" of needed and wanted equipment,

- Determine organization needs,

- Determine quality desired,

- Consider whether the product is both budget and maintenance friendly, and is manufactured by reputable companies,

- Consider whether old equipment can be reconditioned successfully or whether new equipment should be purchased,

- Purchase must be based on program goals, objectives, and budget,

- Determine the priority need and amount of funds available for purchase,

- Consider those persons with disabilities,

- Consider only equipment that meets safety standards,

- Obtain product information from various and diverse vendors, organizing the information by category and type, and each specific company,

- Consider the guarantee, whether or not replacement parts are accessible, the ease of maintenance, and whether or not it fits properly,

- Evaluate the usability of the equipment, making certain that it is adjustable, is state-of-the-art in terms of both design and safety, and is user friendly for all persons,

- Evaluate companies in terms of service record, scientific merit of claims, dependability record, amenities offered, and price, and

- Consider trends in equipment and supplies.

Guidelines for Purchasing Equipment and Supplies

It is important for managers to develop specific guidelines for the purchasing of equipment and supplies. These guidelines enable the manager to standardize equipment and supplies, supervise the entire process of selection and purchase, maintain an inventory, secure bids for larger ticket items, test the items received, and decide on a plan for distribution. The following specific guidelines, according to Monczka et al.(2011) and Murphy and Boffey (2012), should be implemented by any organization when considering the purchase of equipment and supplies including the following:

- All purchases should meet the organization's requirements and have management approval,

- Purchasing should be done in advance of need,

- Specifications should be clear,

- Cost should be kept as low as possible without compromising quality,

- Purchases should be made from reputable business firms,

- Central purchasing can result in greater economy,

- All requests must have purchase requisitions,

- Local firms should be considered,

- Competitive bids should be obtained (for large purchases),

- All purchases must be accompanied by a purchase order, and

- Purchase requisitions are requests to purchase items. The purchase request is a check measure that allows the manager to determine if funding is available from the desired budget line and to ensure that there is not unnecessary replication of items to be purchased.

The purchase order (PO) is an official request from the organization to the vendor to deliver a specific item at a specific price. The purchase order is usually synonymous with voucher (See sample purchase order in Figure 11.1).

Both the purchase request and the purchase order should contain the following , according to AEMA (2013) and IHRSA (2013):

	To:			Ship/Bill To:		
	FlagHouse			Julia Ann Hypes		
	Physical Education & Recreation			Dept. of Health, Physical Education		
	601 FlagHouse Drive			and Sport Sciences		
	Hasbrouk Hts., NJ 07604-3116			Morehead State University		
				201 Laughlin Health Building		
				Morehead, KY 40351		

Purchase Order Number: 014325
Account Number: 10-15320-201
Date: June 4, 2015

Quantity	Item	Units	Description	Unit	Total
5	G11655	Ea.	Wilson Impact Rubber Basket-ball Size 7	14.00	70.00
10	G5786	Ea.	Rawlings "RWW" Leather Basket-ball Size 6	56.00	560.00
3	G5976	Ea.	Thera-Brand Dumbbell Roller	20.00	60.00
10	G11970	Doz.	Spalding Top Flight Series X-Out Golf Balls	10.00	100.00

Subtotal   790.00
Shipping   40.00
Balance Due 830.00

_____   _____
Requestor   Approved by
Special Delivery Instructions: Ship via UPS Ground.

Figure 11.1. Sample Purchase Order

- Name and contact information for person submitting request (return address)
- Name and contact information of the vendor
- Date
- Account Number
- Department
- Amount
- Quantity
- Unit
- Description
- Unit Price
- Special Terms: date for delivery, substitutions, discount
- Requestor's signature
- Supervisor's signature

The formal purchase order will also contain a purchase order number for tracking and bookkeeping purposes. Once the purchase order is approved, it will be sent to the vendor for filling the order.

Upon receipt of the merchandise, the accounting office will approve payment to the vendor. Figure 11.1 provides a sample purchase order. The organization/agency should provide a blank purchase order form in the policy and procedures manual.

Evaluating Equipment before Purchase

Every organization should have a plan for a comprehensive evaluation of equipment before purchasing. Before the final selection is made, the manager should as the following questions regarding the equipment to be purchased.

What are the Safety Issues Relevant to the Equipment?

Is the equipment safe to be used or are there obvious design flaws that increase the risk to the user? Are there backup electronic circuits? Does the nature of the use of the equipment require putting body parts in a position where they may go beyond the normal range of motion? Can more than one person safely use the equipment at one time?

Are There Special Considerations for Using the Equipment?

Is the equipment self-instructing? Does the use of the equipment necessitate the assistance of a spotter? Is the equipment easy to use? Easy to learn? Does the equipment provide a means to motivate the user through a feedback system? Does the equipment have capabilities to accommodate individuals of different body types? Does the equipment have capabilities to accommodate individuals of differing ability levels? Does the equipment have capabilities to accommodate for individuals with disabilities? Is a comprehensive ownership manual provided with the equipment? Is the product aesthetically pleasing? Is the product space efficient and appropriate for your facility?

Does the Product Meet Your Needs?

Does the product perform the task for which it was intended? Does it operate quietly and with precision? Is the product built to last? Is the product composed of high quality components? Does the product possess surface treatments which are durable?

What is the Warranty?

How long is the product warranty? Does it include parts and labor? Are parts kept in stock by the dealer? Will the manufacturer provide replacements? Is there an option to purchase an extended warranty?

What Do You Know about the Manufacturer?

How long has the product been available? What is the past history of the manufacturer? Is the manufacturer likely to be around in the next three to five years? Will the manufacturer provide instruction? Does the manufacturer or dealer provide setup/installation?

Miscellaneous Questions to Ask Yourself

Have your participants requested the product? Is it desirable? Is the product a fad? Will the product become obsolete quickly? Do you have first hand experience with the product? Will the manufacturer provide a list of users to be contacted as references for the product?

The manufacturer will, in many cases, provide written documentation regarding the product. Everything from maintenance procedures to safety features and warranty information must be catalogued. You may have to request this information from the manufacturer. Trade journals and magazine articles also can be a source of valuable information during the purchasing process.

The Procurement Process

The procurement process is that part of the purchasing process that begins with the purchase request and ends with the purchase order and payment of the invoice. The primary goal of the procurement process is to obtain the desired, high-quality equipment and/or supplies, on time, and at the lowest possible price. AEMA (2013) and Murphy and Boffey (2012) suggest the most common steps involved in the procurement process include:

- Need established
- Management consultation
- Initial request submitted
- Request reviewed
- Determine if funds are available
- Preparation of specifications
- Receipt of bids
- Comparison of bids
- Recommendation of appropriate bid for purchase
- Purchase order to supplier
- Follow-up, receipt of goods
- Payment authorized

The Bid Process

Most governmental units, such as schools and universities, restrict direct purchasing. The school system, college/university, or agency places a dollar limit ($1,000) on direct purchases. Many managers do not have a choice whether to direct purchase or bid. There may be regulations or laws that prohibit direct purchasing over a certain amount and require the use of a bid process. The bidding process usually involves the intention to purchase, identification of specifications, vendors deciding upon cheapest price at which to sell, and the submission of this figure as an official bid on the product.

The following disadvantages and advantages of the bid process have been identified (Monczka et al., 2011; Murphy and Boffey, 2012):

Disadvantages
- Quality can suffer.
- The bid system sometimes adds to equipment costs if the item is rather inexpensive but the process is complex.
- The system is slow.
- The process can discourage purchasing from local vendors.
- The process can generate competition among vendors to see who can "cut the most corners".
- Many times the product delivered does not meet the specifications but is used because it is needed immediately.

Advantages
- Can result in lower costs through honest competitive selling.
- Can result in on-time deliveries.
- It can stimulate the vendor to include warranty information and reliable service.

- Shares the wealth. Purchases are spread across a number of vendors.

- It will ensure favoritism and friendship is not the basis of the purchase.

- Reduces the chance of mistakes regarding the technical quality of the product.

There are different types of bid systems available. The competitive sealed bid is the most frequently used system. The specifications are advertised for a set time, usually seven to twenty-one days, for open bidding. Competitive negotiation is similar to sealed bidding but is not as specific. Rather than provide technical specifications, the competitive negotiation describes what the product is to accomplish. Competitive negotiation after competitive sealed bidding is a method that can be used if the product bids are expected to exceed available funds. The purchasing agent can negotiate with the vendors once it is determined that all bids exceed available funds. Noncompetitive negotiation is used when there is not time to bid. This could be utilized for replacement parts or if the product is needed to match existing products.

The typical bidding process includes the following (AEMA (2013); Monczka et al., 2011; Murphy & Boffey, 2012):

- Writing specifications for approved items to be purchased

- Advertise for bids from vendors

- Receive bids

- Evaluate bids to ensure all specifications have been met

- Choose vendors

- Submit the purchase order

- Receive equipment

- Pay invoice after equipment or supplies are verified

- Writing specifications

Writing a clear, well-defined, and complete set of specifications is the most important step in assuring what is ordered is in fact what is delivered. Developing written specifications helps to guarantee fair comparisons of bids when alternatives are proposed. The specifications need to be stated clearly and concisely and should be well defined so that the burden of responsibility for providing the product that meets the user's needs falls on the shoulders of vendor. In general, written specifications include clear descriptions of the product being ordered, quantity, quality, size, color, material, brand, model number, catalog number, performance characteristics, any assembly or installation requirements, delivery requirements, and acceptable alternatives, if any. The following specific suggestions that should be considered when writing accurate specifications (See sample specifications document in Figure 11.2).

Clothing. It is important to include the following when ordering clothing:

• Manufacturer or name brand	• Colorfastness
• Style number	• Sizing
• Fabric content	• Special cuts
• Shrinkage factor	• Lettering
• Color	• Numbering

Shoes. The purchaser needs to include the following:

- Manufacturer or name brand

- Style number

Incomplete	Worth BW8 Powercell Baseball Bat or equivalent (does not specify length requested and allows vendor to make judgment on substitution)
Complete (without substitutions)	Worth BW8 Powercell Baseball Bat, 35" Length, 32 ounce weight, 2 5/8" diameter – No substitutions or alternatives
Complete (with substitutions)	Worth BW8 Powercell Baseball Bat, 35" Length, 32 ounce weight, 2 5/8" diameter Or Easton LK8 Magnum Bat, 35" Length, 32 ounces weight, 2 5/8" diameter Or Louisville Slugger "YB-17" Baseball Bat, 35" Length, 32 ounce weight, 2 5/8" diameter

Figure 11.2. Writing Specifications Modified from http:www.slideshare.net (2010)

- Shoe material
- Color

Protective equipment. When purchasing protective equipment the following should be considered.

- Manufacturer or brand name
- Material content
- Certification standards
- Accurate sizing

Playing equipment. The purchaser needs to consider the following:

- Manufacturer or brand name
- Equipment model number
- Material content
- Size
- Weight

Scheduling the Purchase of Equipment and Supplies

If the organization is involved in purchasing sport equipment and supplies in needs to be understood that the bidding process can take between four and six weeks before the purchase order is released. Add on to this the possibility that another six to eight weeks can pass before the product is delivered. Therefore, it is necessary to plan ahead. It is recommended to allow six to twelve weeks for the product to be delivered onsite.

The following are recommendations regarding a purchase schedule for sports equipment:

Sport Season	Order Date	Delivery Date
Early Spring	October 1	February 1
Late Spring	December 1	March 15
Fall	May 1	August 1
Winter	July 1	October 15

Purchasing Fitness Equipment

The process of outfitting a fitness club with the newest equipment does not have to be a chore. It is important for purchasers to know the right questions to ask dealers/sales personnel whose products catch the purchaser's attention. Ask equipment dealers the following questions before purchasing or leasing any of their machines (National Strength and Conditioning Association [NSCA], 2013):

- How many machines are needed?

- Do you sell or lease?

- What is the length of the warranty?

- What is contained in the warranty?

- Will you install/set up the equipment?

- Where can the machine be serviced?

- What is the worst feature of your product?

- Do you have references?

- Who has purchased your equipment?

- What has been the biggest complaint received about your equipment?

- What kind of discounts are you offering?

- Do you offer a test model?

Planners must devote a significant amount of time ensuring that a facility's exercise equipment space is functional, well-stocked, and affordable. The planners should consider the use of a three-phase process.

Phase I: Identification of Preliminary Factors

There are two main factors that exist prior to equipment selection—total space and budget available for the equipment purchase. When calculating space the planners can use the following average square foot requirements: weight-stack resistance—60, free-weight resistance—70, plate-loaded resistance—60, and cardiovascular equipment—55. The average equipment costs are weight-stack—$2,800, free-weight—$ 1,000, plate-loaded—$ 1,600, and cardiovascular equipment —$3,400.

Phase II: Selection Criteria

The following should be considered when selecting equipment— goals and objectives, availability of funding, commercial grade equipment, accommodation rate (user to unit), total body workout, manufacturer history (years in business, customer service record, reputation, and client list), product history (years in production, product warranty, service program, maintenance schedule, and product's special requirements), purchase options (30 days, monthly, or annual), and lease options (at the end of the leasing program, a buyer has the following options: purchase for agreed upon amount, return the equipment, extend the lease, and establish a new leasing program for a new list of equipment).

Phase III: The Action Plan

The list below summarizes the main tasks to consider during the equipment selection.

- Identify any existing preliminary factors concerning the amount of space and funds available;

- if limitations exist with the total space or funds available, identify the amount of equipment that can be acquired based on the limitations;

- choose the type of equipment to be included in the exercise equipment area;

- develop a list of criteria to use during product and manufacturer reviews;

- conduct product and manufacturer review;

- make final equipment selections;

- determine the purchasing option that best fits your financial situation; and

- purchase equipment.

Considerations When Purchasing a Complete Fitness Program

Putting together classes and routines can be a lonely and time-consuming process unless the purchaser reaches out and taps into the ever-growing pool of industry resources. Music suppliers and program licensers offer a multitude of different types of music and fitness programming that are current and well re-searched. Before deciding to purchase fitness programming, ask the following seven questions (IHRSA, 2013):

- What different types of programs are available?

- Can my staff handle the programming?

- Are promotional materials, instructional manuals and videos, other program materials and supplier support included in the programming?

- How much will it cost, initially and on an ongoing basis?

- Do I have to purchase a franchise to be involved in the program?

- Do the benefits of purchasing programming outweigh the advantages of putting it together in-house?

- Are other facilities like mine using the program successfully?

Value of Used Equipment

If you have evaluated your five-year-old or older strength training equipment and found it is no longer attracting the same interest among new or renewing members, you are probably facing some hard questions about what to do next. Turning aging equipment into reconditioned equipment, or into dollars toward new equipment, starts with appraising the equipment.

The following questions, developed from information from Monczka et al. (2011) and Murphy and Boffey (2012), can be used as a value-appraisal tool for equipment. The higher the score on the value-rating tool indicates a greater number of options for the owner. This tool will provide a general idea of the equipment's marketability.

1. How old is the equipment?

    0-12 months = 10 points; 13-24 months = 8 points; 25-36 months = 6 points; 37-48 months = 4 points; 49+ months = 2 points

2. How marketable is the line?

* Survey the industry to estimate how widespread the use is of lines of equipment similar to yours among other clubs nationwide.

* Among the top three most common lines, and is a late model $=10$ points; Among the top three but is an older model $= 7$ points; a widely used line, not top three, but late model $= 7$; a well-known line that is less-frequently seen in clubs $= 3$-5; well-made, but little-known, selected line $= 3$; plate-load machines and free-weights $= 3$.

3. Aesthetic appeal?

   Chrome, paint, pads: excellent $= 5$; very good $= 4$; good $= 3$; fair $= 2$; and poor $= 1$.

   Add one point if paint is silver, white or gray. Subtract one point if paint is red, blue, brown, tan, green, etc.

4. Total score:

   21-25 points $=$ an excellent value rating; 16-20 $=$ good; 11-15 $=$ fair; 10 or below$=$ poor.

Inventory Control

There are six general guidelines that should be considered when developing equipment control procedures (Monczka et al., 2011):

1. "All equipment and supplies should be carefully inspected upon receipt,

2. equipment and supplies requiring organization identification should be labeled,

3. procedures should be established for issuing and checking in equipment and supplies,

4. equipment should be maintained and stored in good repair,

5. equipment and supplies should be inventoried and stored properly, and

6. garments should be cleaned and cared for properly (p. 93)."

The following management principles should be considered for a well-managed system of inventory, control, and accountability (AEMA, 2013; Murphy & Boffey, 2012):

* A system (computerized if at all possible) of inventory must be established and followed (the system should include an emplacement function, a listing of items including dates of purchase, an evaluation system, an updating system).

* All equipment and supplies must be counted into the inventory.

* All items that are in use must be officially checked out.

* Personnel who sign for equipment and materials are held accountable for same.

* All equipment must be coded and labeled upon arrival.

* Old or damaged items that are being eliminated from stock should be removed only by authorized equipment management personnel. Removal of items must be noted in the inventory records, and equipment should be properly disposed.

* Written procedures must be followed by all persons.

* Systematic inventory checks and continual updating must be conducted.

* Instruction must be provided on the proper use and care of the equipment.

* Equipment must be returned in the condition it was in when issued.

* The equipment room lock should only be accessed by authorized personnel and should not be on the master.

- All warranties and safety documentation from the manufacturers should be filed appropriately.

- An inspection form should be developed to inspect of equipment that is either freestanding or attached to the facility and a regular inspection schedule should be adopted by the organization.

- A maintenance record should be maintained for all equipment.

Labeling Systems

The labeling system should be well organized and simple. There are many effective methods of marking equipment and supplies, and every imaginative manager develops personalized techniques. The following marking suggestions are offered:

1. felt tip pen, laundry pen (ideal for fabric items),

2. indelible pencil (for leather products),

3. branding irons (for wood, plastic or leather goods),

4. stencils (fabric),

5. decals (items that have little wear),

6. processed numbers (fabric items by manufacturer), and

7. rubber stamps (leather and rubber items).

Space Requirements for an Equipment Room

When facilities are constructed, five areas have a tendency to be reduced in size—custodial or maintenance space, locker rooms, office and lobby areas, storage spaces and equipment areas. All these spaces are critical to the efficient operation of any health, fitness, physical activity, recreation, or space facility. College and university facilities should be approximately 3,000 square feet. Others have suggested equipment storage space should be approximately 20% of the total usable facility space. The American Entrepreneurs Association (AEA) suggests that for every 10,000-100,000 people there should be 1,000-3,000 square feet, 100,000-200,000 people there should be 1,500-4,000 square feet, and 200,000-4000 people there should be 2,000-10,000 square feet.

The equipment room should be located near locker rooms and multipurpose activity areas. The main entrance into the equipment room should be at least 6 feet wide and 8 feet high. A roll-up door might be more efficient than double-wide doors. The room itself should contain storage shelves, movable interlocking storage units, a repair area, racks, folding tables, a space to store larger pieces of equipment, laundry equipment (commercial washers and dryers), a small office, distribution counter, and a space to hang equipment from the ceiling. Further, all the cabinets, office, repair space, laundry area, and main entrance need to be secured with appropriate alarms. Finally, the area needs to have installed appropriate environmental controls to maintain the entire area at 70° F with 50% humidity if possible. The area also needs to be well ventilated.

Management of the Equipment Room

Depending on the size of the organization, it may be necessary to employ personnel to manage the equipment operation. The qualities that an individual(s) should possess are (AEMA, 2013; Lipsey, 2006):

1. good interpersonal skills,

2. knowledge of equipment,

3. good judgment maturity,

4. integrity,

5. basic accounting skills,

6. basic management skills,

7. computer skills in word processing and spreadsheets,

8. knowledge of equipment care,

9. an understanding of purchasing and bidding procedures, and

10. knowledge of fitting equipment.

The equipment room operation should have the following as priorities (AEMA, 2013):

1. proper fitting of equipment,

2. maintenance of equipment,

3. accountability,

4. practice coordination and cooperation,

5. permanent and daily assignments,

6. cleanliness, and

7. helping each other.

The Athletic Equipment Managers Association (AEMA) announced in 1990 it contracted with Columbia Assessment Services to establish its certification program. AEMA has established the following areas that should be included in an equipment manager's job description:

1. purchasing,

2. fitting equipment and clothing,

3. maintenance,

4. administration and organization,

5. management, professional relations, and education, and

6. accountability for equipment. The association has established an educational program that will give equipment managers a certain level of proficiency in these six areas.

References

American College of Sports Medicine (ACSM). (2013). Retrieved from http://www.acsm.org.

American Equipment Managers Association (AEMA). (2013). Retrieved from http://www.equipment-managers.org.

Harris, G. L. (2000). *Fundamentals of purchasing.* New York: American Management Association.

International Health Racquet and Sportsclub Association (IHRSA). (2013). Retrieved from http:///www.ihrsa.org.

Lipsey, R. A. (2006). *The sporting goods industry: History, practices, and products.* Jefferson, NC: McFarland.

Monczka, R. M., Handfield, R. B., Giunipero, L. C., & Patterson, J. L. (2011). *Purchasing and supply chain management.* Stamford, CT: Cengage Learning.

Murphy, H. D., & Boffey, L. F. (2012). *The fundamental principles of purchasing.* Whitefish, MT: Literary Licensing, LLC.

National Operating Committee on Standards for Athletic Equipment. (2013). NOCSAE Standards. Retrieved from http://www.nocsae.org/standards/documents.html.

National Strength and Conditioning Association (NCSA). (2013). Retrieved from http:///www.nosca.org.

CHAPTER 12

Revenue Streams

Thomas H. Sawyer
Professor Emeritus, Indiana State University

Darrell L. Johnson
Grace College

Introduction

Physical activity and sport entities that are successful year after year have a variety of revenue streams. These revenue streams are used to support construction of new facilities or remodeling older facilities as well as operations support. The good manager understands how to develop new revenue streams, manage all revenue streams, and retain all the revenue streams that have been secured. The revenue is generated through four common sources including bonding instruments, public sources, private sources, and joint public and private ventures. This chapter will focus on understanding the revenue streams available to physical activity and sports managers. Many of the examples used throughout this chapter relate to professional and collegiate sport entities; however, the information provided can easily be used by clubs, community centers, YMCAs, and medical fitness centers. The medical fitness centers often use three party payment streams to fund construction loans for fitness facilities.

Public Revenue Streams

Since 1961, professional sports venues for Major League Baseball, National Basketball Association, National Football League, and National Hockey League franchises have cost, in 2015 dollars, approximately $32.4 billion (Johnson, 2014; Sawyer, 2006). The projected costs for major stadiums and arenas will amount to $8.3 billion (2010-11)(Johnson, 2014; Sawyer, 2006). This is equal to 28% of what has been spent since 1961 in only two years. The public sector's share of this amount has been approximately $17.5 billion, which represents 59% of the total (Johnson, 2014; Sawyer, 2006). Prior to 1950 the venues were almost totally built by use of private dollars.

Venue development has evolved through five joint private and public funding eras. It is clear that the public (tax payer) is growing weary of supporting venue construction for billionaire owners and multimillionaire players (Sawyer, 2006). The future funding for facility construction will require substantially more private funding. This evidenced by stadiums constructed in New York for the Giants and Jets, Mets, and Yankees, where the city and state have limited their investments to infrastructure construction. In Dallas, the new football stadium was financed by the owner (SportsBusiness Research, 2014).

Sample Financing Packages from the Majors to the Minors*

*These samples have been prepared using information from Street and Smith's *Sports-Business Journal* (2012).

Majors

Cardinals Stadium (Glendale, Arizona)

The total project cost was $448 million. The tenant is the Arizona Cardinals of the NFL. The state authority was responsible for $344 million, which was funded primarily from bond proceeds. Additional amounts were derived from construction sales tax recapture, investment earnings, equipment lease-back, and other funding sources. The bonds will be repaid through a new 1% hotel/motel room tax, a 3.25% care rental tax, a stadium-related sales tax, and income taxes on professional football players and Cardinal employees as approved by Maricopa County voters. The Cardinals will contribute $104 million to the project plus any cost overruns.

National Park (Washington, D.C)

The total project cost was $700 million. The tenant is the Washington Nationals of the MLB. The city will sell $610.8 million in bonds and the Washington Nationals will pay $5.5 million in annual rent for 30 years. The bonds will be retired through in-stadium taxes on tickets, concessions, and merchandise, new taxes on businesses with gross receipts of $3 million or more, and rent from the Washington Nationals. The team will retain all stadium revenue, naming rights revenue, and founding partner revenue in exchange for the annual rent. The District will be responsible for all cost overruns.

Lucas Oil Stadium (Indianapolis, Indiana)

The total project cost was $723 million. The primary tenant is the Indianapolis Colts of the NFL. The Colts will provide $100 million. The city will cover the remainder plus all overruns. The city will sell bonds to cover the cost and retire those bonds from revenue from the following taxes: 45% from the Marion County food and beverage tax, 22% from hotel tax, 14% from an existing sport development tax, 6% from sporting event tickets, 6% from restaurant tax in Marion County and neighboring counties, 5% from car rental tax, and 1% from the sale of Colts license plates. The Colts will retain all revenue from naming rights, founding partners, sponsorships, and advertising.

New York Mets and Yankees (New York City)

The total cost of these two separate projects $1.4 billion ($600 million for the Mets Stadium and $800 million for Yankee Stadium). The tenants will be the New York Mets and the New York Yankees of the MLB. The city will pay for infrastructure expansion and replacement ($135 million) and the state will pay for three parking garages ($75 million) both will sell tax-exempt bonds and the state will retain all revenue from the garages. Neither MLB club will pay rent and will retain all in stadium revenues generated.

Minors

Frisco Soccer (Frisco, Texas)

The total project cost was $80 million for the soccer complex, which was part of a $300-million community sport development. The tenants are Dallas Burn (professional soccer) and Frisco Independent School District (football). The public contribution is capped at $55 million with revenue sources derived from the school district ($15 million), city ($20 million), and county ($20 million). The team owner, Hunt Sports Group, is responsible for the remaining $25 million and all cost overruns. The city designated the entire community development area (95 acres) as a Tax Increment Financing (TIF) development. The owners will pay $100,000 annually to rent the stadium for 20 years, will retain all stadium-generated revenue including naming rights, and will be responsible for all operating expenses. The stadium is part of a larger development that includes 17 community soccer fields, Embassy Suite hotel, Class AA Baseball Park, training facility for the NHL Dallas Stars, a convention center, and the Kurt Thomas Gymnastics Center.

First Horizon Park (Greensboro, North Carolina)

The total project cost was $20.5 million. The tenant is the Class A Greensboro Grasshoppers. This project is 99.8% privately funded. The city contributed $35,000 for infrastructure work.

Wells Fargo Arena (Des Moines, Iowa)

The total project cost was $116.6 million. The tenant is the Iowa Stars of the AHL. This new arena is part of a larger public project which includes a convention center and auditorium. The entire project was $217 million. The State of Iowa provide $40.8 million, the county contributed $75.8 million, and Wells Fargo signed a 20-year naming rights contract for $11.5 million.

ARVEST Ballpark (Springdale, Arkansas)

The total project cost was $50.9 million. The tenant is Northwest Arkansas Nationals of the Independent Baseball League. The owners will pay $1.4 million plus an annual rent of $350,000 for 20 years. The city will provide the remaining funding plus cost overruns using a voter approved 1% sales tax to generate the revenue. The owner is responsible for all game-day expenses and retains all in stadium revenue that is generated including the naming rights.

Parkview Ballpark (Fort Wayne, Indiana)

The total project cost was $30.6 million. The tenant is the Fort Wayne Tin Caps of the Class A Midwest League. The facility was funded by team money and city funding. The team is responsible for all game-day expenses and retains all in stadium revenue that is generated including naming rights.

Gwinnett Stadium (Gwinnett County, Georgia)
        The total project cost was $64 million. The tenant is the Gwinnett Braves of the Triple-A International League. The facility was funded by the Atlanta Braves and the Gwinnett County Board of Commissioners. The team is responsible for all game-day expenses and retains all in stadium revenue that is generated including naming rights. The County used a 2% hotel and restaurant tax to pay the bonds sold for the project.

Taxes

There are a variety of taxes that can be levied by local governments. These taxes provide revenues to pay the public's share of costs for sports facilities. There are two categories that these taxes fall under: hard taxes and soft taxes.

Hard Taxes

Hard taxes commonly include the following (Johnson, 2014; Sawyer, 2006):
* Local income
* Real estate
* Personal property
* General sales
* Wheel

These taxes require government and often voter approval. There have been incidences (i.e., Seattle, WA and Portland, OR) where voters have voted to reject the tax. The problem with these taxes is that they never go away after the debt has been paid. The following are details regarding these taxes.

Local income tax. A local government can levy a tax on income earned. Not all states allow this practice. Most income taxes require voter approval.

Real estate tax. Local government (i.e., cities, counties, school districts, and in some states community college districts) for generations has been dependent on real estate tax revenue to cover operational and capital costs. (Johnson, 2014; Sawyer, 2006) Generally, real estate taxes are based on the value of land and improvements. The current value increases annually but generally is only reassessed every three to five years. Every time the owner improves the land or buildings, he or she is required to report the improvements to the local tax assessor generally through a building permit process.

All property owners are required to pay the real estate tax except for nonprofit organizations (e.g., churches, charitable organizations, educational institutions, other government agencies, cemeteries, hospitals, and historical properties). The real estate tax is generally considered a benefit tax. Its revenues are used to finance local government expenditures for services that benefit the common good of property owners and increase the value of the property.

Personal property tax. The personal property tax includes tangible property (e.g., furniture, machinery, automobiles, jewelry, artwork, etc.) and intangible property (e.g., stocks, taxable bonds, and insurance) (Johnson, 2014; Sawyer, 2006).

General sales tax. Johnson (2014) and Sawyer (2006) indicate that the general sales tax is the largest single source of state tax revenues and the second largest source of tax revenues for local governments after the real estate and local income taxes. It is also considered a regressive tax, which bears more heavily on lower income groups than on higher income groups.

The general sales tax has been used, in part, to finance sport entities and facilities since the early 1990s. In most jurisdictions, a voter referendum is required since the burden is borne by all residents.

Wheel tax. Often counties assess a wheel tax on vehicles to raise funds for road development and repair. The tax is collected on each vehicle based on the number of wheels on the vehicle. It is collected from motorcycle owners as well.

Soft Taxes

Soft taxes include the following (Johnson, 2014; Sawyer, 2006):

- car rental,
- gaming taxes and lotteries,
- hotel-motel,
- limousine and taxi,
- parking,
- player,
- restaurant,
- sin (excise),
- sport district,
- ticket, and
- tourist development.

The beauty of soft taxes is that they borne by a select and relatively smaller portion (e.g., generally tourists) of taxpayers and are easier to levy. These taxes generally do not require a voter referendum.

Car rental taxes. Many local governments have instituted a car rental tax to finance sport entities and recreational facilities. This mechanism has increased in popularity over the last two decades (Sawyer, 2006).

Gaming taxes and lotteries. Johnson (2014), Mikesell (2009), and Sawyer (2006) suggest states have applied portions of proceeds from gaming taxes and lotteries to finance investments in sport facilities.

Hotel-motel and restaurant taxes. This is a very common. It is most commonly applied as tourist tax by local governments. Many communities use a portion of this revenue to support the development and operations of sports venues. The hotel-motel tax was originally called a bed tax.

Limousine and taxi tax. The limousine and taxi tax is similar to the car rental tax. The tax is calculated into the final fare the rider pays to the bus/cab/limo/shuttle driver.

Parking taxes. According to Johnson (2014) and Winfree and Rosentraub (2012), several local and state governments have implemented a parking tax. This usually is calculated as a percent of the parking price. That price is added to the cost of parking similar to a sales tax.

Player tax. When professional athletes began earning large salaries local and state governments saw an opportunity to gain additional revenue by taxing player salaries based on the per game income earned by the player. This tax is levied against both home and visiting players. This practice began in the early 1990s. Currently, there are 43 states that have imposed player taxes (Johnson, 2014). It is sometimes referred to as the "jock tax." Some have suggested this is an unfair tax.

Restaurant (food and beverage) tax. According to Mikesell (2009) and Johnson (2014), a tax on food and beverage consumption sold in bars, pubs, and restaurants has emerged as a popular tax to support the public sector's investment in sport facilities as well as other facilities such as parks.

Sin (excise) taxes. There are five common sin taxes imposed on the sale of alcohol, gambling, marijuana, prostitution (Nevada only), and tobacco. These taxes have partially been used to assist in financing the development and operations of sports facilities.

Sport district taxes. according to Johnson (2014), Rosentraub (2010), and Sawyer (2006), this type of financing is similar to tax increment financing. Johnson (2014) indicated the State of Indiana created a sports tax district to support the building of Bankers Life Fieldhouse in Indianapolis. Like tax increment funding, state income and sales taxes resulting from activity within the geographic boundaries created to designate the special tax district were deflected to assist in the repayment of the bonds sold to finance the construction of the new arena. Johnson (2014) and Rosentraub (2010) suggest taxes were not directly increased, but existing revenues were deflected to repay the bonds sold to build the facility. The cost or impact of this financing method was on what the state of Indiana either could not fund as a result of the deflection of the taxes or the increases in statewide taxes to meet Indiana's budget needs (Johnson, 2014).

Ticket taxes. Several local governments, according to Johnson (2014) and Winfree and Rosentraub (2012), have implemented an amusement or ticket tax. This is calculated as a percent of the event price or as a flat figure. The price is added to cost of a ticket just like when paying the sales tax on any purchase.

Tourist development taxes. These are taxes imposed primarily on tourists. They include the cost of occupying a hotel or motel room and the cost of renting a motor vehicle. These taxes are easy to impose and cities are always ready to tax people who will not be there to take advantage of the taxes paid. Some might view this, like our forefathers did in Boston, as "taxation without representation."

Tax Abatement

Another tax strategy, according to Johnson (2014) and Sawyer (2006), used by governments to stimulate private sector investment and create employment in the community is to offer property tax abatements. Abatement programs typically are awarded whenever they are requested. Therefore, they often are part of a city's incentive package in negotiations with professional franchises. Tax abatement will exempt an organization's assets from property taxation for a given period of time. It may be for all or a portion of the tax. The length of time varies according to the state enabling legislation.

Grants. Additional sources beyond taxes and bonding available from the public sector include state and federal appropriations and public grants. These can be applied for through city, county, or state. They typically are not used to finance sport facilities, but rather to provide for parking lots or structures, roadways, sewer and water lines, and sidewalks.

Private funding sources. Most stakeholders, as a result of declining public monies and questionable economic impacts, prefer private sector investment. Private sector investments take on a variety of forms and degrees of contribution. Johnson (2014), Sawyer, Hypes, and Hypes (2004), and Winfree and Rosentraub (2012), indicate that the private sector regularly contributes to financing of sport facilities in ways such as the following:

- Cash donations

- In-kind contributions. An organization, business, or craftsman donates equipment or time to the project in return for a tax deduction

- Naming rights. Corporations vie for the right to place their name on the professional sport venue for a specific sum of money for a specific number of years. It is also becoming more common for corporations to purchase naming rights for college sport facilities. Johnson (2014), Sawyer, Hypes, and Hypes (2004), and Sawyer (2006) suggest the key elements of a naming rights agreement includes length of contract, signage rights and limitations, installation costs, marketing rights, termination upon default, reimbursement, and renewal option.

- Concessionaire exclusivity. Companies purchase the exclusive rights for all concessions within a spectator facility for a specific number of dollars over a specific time period.

- Food and beverage serving rights.
- Premium restaurant rights.

- Sponsorship packages. Large local and international firms are solicited to supply goods and services to a sporting organization at no cost or at substantial reduction in the wholesale prices in return for visibility for the corporation.

- Life insurance packages. These programs solicit the proceeds from a life insurance policy purchased by a supporter to specifically benefit the organization upon the death of the supporter. This type of private funding is done most often with colleges and universities as well as private high schools.

- Lease agreements. These agreements are with other organizations during the off-season. It could also include spaces within the facility not used for the sporting activity, such as office space or retail space.

- Luxury suites (i.e., skyboxes). Luxury suites are commonly found in professional sport facilities; however, over the past decade, many universities have added these spaces as well as some private high schools. They are a dominant and universal feature in every new or remodeled stadium or arena. Johnson (2014), Sawyer, Hypes, and Hypes (2004), and Sawyer (2006) note that luxury seating first became commonplace in arenas and stadiums in the early 1990s the Astrodome was the first to have this type of accommodations. The luxury suite generally includes amenities such as carpeting, wet bar, restroom, seating for 12 to 24 guests, computer hook-ups, cable television, telephones, and an intercom.

- Premium seating (i.e., club seating). This is VIP seating located within the club seating areas of the arena or stadium, which are the most expensive seats in the facility. This seating is one step below the luxury seating mentioned above.

- Personal seat licenses (PSL). Sawyer, Hypes, and Hypes (2004) and Johnson (2014) state that personal seat licenses became a widespread practice in sports venues in the early 1990s. A seat license is to the individual as the luxury suite is to the corporation. This license requires an individual to make an advance payment to purchase the right to secure a particular seat in the venue. After making the one-time payment, the buyer is provided with the opportunity to purchase a season ticket to that seat for a specified period of time.

- Power or loaded tickets (food and beverage credits) became popular in the early 2000s, which includes dollar credits embedded for concessions.

- Single-game rental cabanas (group sales), which includes ticket price and concession credits.

- Parking fees. These fees are generated from parking lots that surround the spectator facilities. In the early 2000s, professional venues became more creative and added luxury car lots (i.e., Cadillac, Lincoln, Mercedes, etc.) with a free shuttle to the arena or stadium. These lots often include roofs to protect the cars. Other amenities include car detailing, oil changes, and more. Many universities actually sell spaces for motor homes for multiple years to increase the luxury of game day tailgating. For example, Atlanta's Turner Field and Miami's Office Depot Center, with the backing of area Lexus dealers, are carved out sections of preferred parking reserved for those fans who drive Lexuses. This new twist on sponsorship may be called exclusionary or elitist, but in the competitive marketplace, it should be classified as creative thinking.

- Merchandise revenues. This income is generated by the sale of shorts, hats, pants, T-shirts, sweatshirts, key rings, glassware, dishware, luggage, sports cards, balls, bats, and other licensed goods.

- Advertising rights. Rights are sold to various entities that wish to advertise to the spectators within the sports facility. These rights are sold as part of a sponsorship package or an advertising package outside of a sponsorship package. All professional venues as well as universities and high schools are selling advertising from billboards, to score boards, to cup holders and more.

- Vendor or contractor equity. The vendor or contractor returns to the owner a specific percentage of the profit generated by the firms during the construction process.

- Bequests and trusts. Agreements are made with specific individuals that upon their deaths a certain amount of their estates will be given commonly to universities and private high schools. Rarely are these sought by or given to professional teams.

- Real estate gifts, endowments, and securities. Agreements are made with specific individuals to give to a university or private high school real estate, stocks, or mutual funds to support an endowment for a specific project. Only the annual income returned by the endowment could/would be used, not the principle.

- Project finance. Johnson (2014), Sawyer, Hypes, and Hypes (2004) and Sawyer (2006) noted in 1993, the Rose Garden (Portland, Oregon) was the first facility financed using a new mechanism called project finance. Project finance is the Wall Street term that refers to the type of financing used to build arenas such as the Rose Garden, Delta Center, SBC Park, American Airlines Arena, and the St. Louis Cardinals' new home. The word "project" is used because traditionally this type of loan has been used to finance utility plants, factories, and other large enterprises. These entities have guaranteed revenues that provide comfort to the insurance companies and pension funds that lend the money. The recent Rose Garden bankruptcy case may leave insurance companies and pension funds reluctant to finance sports venues in the future.

- Founding partners. Johnson (2014) indicates these are partners (firms) who have signed five- to eight-year contracts to put their names on gates, corners, suite levels, club lounges, and other real estate. In the case of the Indianapolis Colts, who signed 14 founding partners, they were worth in total between $10 million and $12 million annually exceeding the naming rights for the stadium. Further, the Washington Nationals successfully secured five founding partners. Universities and private high schools do this as well. They will most often have more founders for less money.

- Party suites. Johnson (2014) suggests party suites are becoming very popular in all venues. The Baltimore Oriels were one of the first professional teams to over this type of suite. These suites are rented by groups for a single game with sitting for 50–100 guests. They have become very popular for fundraising events for many non-profit organizations. Food services are included in the rental price. The number of party suites ranges from 1–15 in sporting venues. The Washington Nationals' Park has 78 suites including 10 party suites.

- Private equity investment. Rosentraub (2010) and Johnson (2014) suggest private equity firms that control large pools of professionally managed money are looking for places to invest if they can turn the sport property around and resell the property with a profit for the firm. It could be a short term financial opportunity for the private equity firm. This can be good or bad for the sport entity. Some private equity firms will bleed the cash from the sport entity and then sell it

Private and Joint Public-Private Funding

Over the past two decades, public-private partnerships have been developed to construct large public sports facilities. Typically, the public sector lends its authority to implement project-funding mechanisms while the private partner contributes project-related or other revenue sources. The expanded revenues generated by the facilities and their tenants have resulted in increases in the level of private funding. Recent examples of partnerships include the Alamodome (San Antonio), Coors Stadium (Denver), and Big Stadium (Saint Denis, France).

Broadcast Rights

There are 10 common types of broadcast media including networks as outlined in Table 12.1. The sale of broadcast rights is major revenue source for professional sports, Division I intercollegiate sports, and many interscholastic tournaments. Television contracts are multiyear contracts worth millions of dollars to leagues and teams. For example, the National Football League has a seven-year deal with ABC, CBS, ESPN, and FOX worth $17.6 billion, Major League Baseball has a five-year agreement with ESPN and FOX for $3.35 billion, National Basketball Association has a five-year contract with ESPN, ABC, and Time Warner for $4.6 billion (SBR Net, 2012).

Table 12.1
Ten Common Types of Broadcast Media

- ABC, CBS, NBC, FOX, Westinghouse Broadcasting, and Public Broadcasting Service
- Ultra High Frequency (UHF) Channels
- Superstations (namely, WGN in Chicago and WTBS in Atlanta)
- Cable Channels (e.g., TNT in Atlanta and USA Network in New York City)
- Sports Channels (e.g., Entertainment and Sports Programming Network [ESPN],
- Sportsvision and Sports Channels in Chicago, St. Louis, Ohio, and Orlando, Prime Network in Houston, Prism in Philadelphia, and Sunshine Network in Orlando)
- Independent Producers
- Local TV Stations (local Very High Frequency [VHF])
- Cable Franchises
- Pay-Per-View
- Local AM and FM Radio Stations *(SBR Net, 2012)*

The National Hockey League has a five-year contract with ABC and ESPN for $600 million; NCAA Men's Basketball has an 11-year contract with CBS for $6 billion, NCAA Football has a five-year contract with ABC for $500 million, and Professional Golf Association has a 4-year contract with ABC, CBS, ESPN, and NBC for $107 million.

Broadcasting executives will couple audience size and revenue together. This combination is used when deciding whether or not to broadcast a sporting event. The larger the audience size, the higher the potential for revenue production from advertising. Broadcasters seek programming that will appeal to larger, more valuable audiences.

The contract for broadcasting rights is based on the potential for generating advertising and gaining high TV ratings. The greater the advertising revenue and the higher the average TV rating (e.g., the average five-year TV ratings for the NFL was 11.2, MLB was 2.8 for regular season, 12.4 for the World Series, NBA was 2.75, and NHL was 1.1), the greater the value will be for the short-term contract for the sporting entity (SBR Net, 2012).

Financial Team

All building projects need to assemble a proper financial team in order to design, organize, and finance a public, private, or public-private facility. A successful financial team should include the owner, facility manager, feasibility consultant, examination accountant, business plan consultant, financial advisor, facility consultant, architect, cost estimator, contractor, construction manager, senior underwriter, bond council, and the owner's legal counsel. The financial team must work together to develop the goals and objectives of the community and/or owner. Successful facility financing is a partnership among the regional community, the owner, government, the financial institutions, and the investors.

Essential points of a financial plan. The following are essential points of a financial plan, and these points should be broken down for each year of the financial plan (Sawyer, 2006):

- the mission, goals, and objectives for the overall plan;

- an analysis of the organization's current financial situation;

- an analysis of revenue projections versus expense projections, including dollars obtained through private fund raising and government resources;

- an analysis of capital projections throughout the time period of the plan broken down into needs versus ideals; and

- specific information regarding the intended financial state at the end of the time period.

Mechanisms for financing debt. Cities, counties, and states invest in capital projects by borrowing substantial amounts of money over an extended period of time. The loans or bond issues secured are backed by tax revenue streams such as real estate, personal property, personal income taxes, general sales tax, hotel-motel and restaurant taxes, sin taxes, and others. The downside, like personal loans to individuals to spreading out payments over a 15- to 30-year period, is the amount of interest incurred. However, politically debt financing is a desirable approach and from an equity perspective, long-term debt financing makes good sense. The primary source for governments to secure long-term financing is through bonds. Bank loans are used for short-term loans of less than five years.

Bonds

The issuing of bonds is the most common way for a city or county to generate the needed money for recreation and sports facilities. A bond is defined as an interest-bearing certificate issued by a government or corporation, promising to pay interest and to repay a sum of money (the principle) at a specified date in the future. A bond can also be a promise by the borrower (bond issuer) to pay back to the lender (bond holder) a specified amount of money, with interest, within a specified period of time. Bonds issued by a government or a subdivision of a state are referred to as municipal bonds. Municipal bonds are typically exempt from federal, state, and local taxes on earned interest. Bond buyers can include individuals, organizations, institutions, or groups desiring to lend money at a predetermined interest rate. However, bonds are not a panacea for recreation and sports facility development for two primary reasons—debt ceiling or capacity and tax-exemption concerns by the public.

Tax-exempt bonds issued by government entities. Sawyer (2006) suggests there are basically two types of government bonds—full-faith and credit obligations and nonguaranteed. A general obligation bond is a full-faith and credit obligation bond. The general obligation bond refers to bonds that are repaid with a portion of the general property taxes. There are two key disadvantages to issuing general obligation bonds—it requires voter approval and it increases local debt (Sawyer, 2006).

The second type of full-faith and credit obligation bond is a certificate of obligation. The certificate(s) is secured by unlimited claim on tax revenue and carries a low interest rate. Its greatest advantage to politicians is that the certificate(s) does not require a voter referendum.

Nonguaranteed bonds including revenue bonds, tax increment bonds, and certificates of participation have been the most common type of bonds used in funding sports facilities construction and operations (Sawyer, 2006). These bonds are sold on the basis of repayment from other designated revenue sources. If revenue falls short of what is required to make debt payments, the government entity does not have to make up the difference. There are three main advantages for using this funding mechanism: voter approval generally is not required, debt is not considered statutory debt, and those who benefit the most from the facility pay for it.

Sawyer (2006) notes revenue bonds can be backed exclusively by the revenue accruing from the project or from a designated revenue source such as hotel-motel tax, restaurant tax, auto rental tax, or a combination of these taxes and others. Revenue bonds normally carry a higher interest rate compared to general obligation bonds (i.e., approximately 2%).

Certificates of participation are third-party transactions. It involves a nonprofit public benefit organization or government agency borrowing funds from a lending institution or a group of lending institutions to construct a new facility. Once the facility is completed, the organization or agency leases the facility to a public or private operator. This operator, in turn, makes lease payments to retire the certificates. There is no need for a voter referendum.

Taxable bonds issued by private entities. According to Sawyer (2006), there are two types of taxable bonds—private-placement bonds and asset-backed securitizations. Private-placement bonds are sold by the sporting entity. The security for these bonds is provided by a lien on all future revenues generated by the sport entity. Asset-backed securitizations are also sold by the sporting entity. Its security is provided by selected assets that are held by a bankruptcy proof trust.

In the mid- to late 1990s, local governments were inclined to provide less and less support for the construction and operation of sport facilities. Therefore, the private sector began developing a number of other financial strategies including luxury suites, premium or club seating, premier restaurants (i.e., high-class restaurants), naming rights, and private-placement bonds. Facilities initially using the private-placement bonds included the Fleet Center (Boston) for $160 million, First Union Center (Philadelphia) for $142 million, and the Rose Garden (Portland) for $155 million. These private-placement bonds were issued for a long term (20–30 years) with a fixed-interest-rate (6 to 9%) bond certificates to a large number of private lenders (e.g., insurance companies and venture capitalists). The private-placement bonds are secured by revenues generated from premium seating, advertising, concessions, parking, and lease agreements (SBR Net, 2012).

The asset-backed securitizations (ABS) are a variation of the private-placement bonds. The ABS is the newest debt financing mechanism in the private sector. It is secured by selling future cash flow through bundling such revenue streams as long-term naming rights agreements, luxury suite leases, concession contracts, and long-term corporate sponsorship deals. The following sports facilities have used ABS as financing mechanisms: Pepsi Center (Denver) and Staples Center (Los Angeles)(SBR Net, 2012).

Tax-increment bonds. Sawyer (2006) notes that over half the states now have enabling legislation authorizing tax increment financing (TIF). TIF is available when an urban area has been identified for renewal or redevelopment. Real estate developed with the use of TIF is attractive to stakeholders as tax increases are not necessary. The tax base of the defined area is frozen and any increases in the tax base are used to repay the TIF bonds. The economics of any TIF are dependent on the development potential of a chosen site and its surrounding land.

Special bonding authority. According to Sawyer (2006), special authority bonds have been used to finance stadiums or arenas by special public authorities, which are entities with public powers (e.g., Georgia Sports Authority, Lubbock Sports Authority, Maryland Stadium Authority, Nashville Metropolitan Sports Authority, Oregon Sports Authority, San Jose Sports Authority, and Stadium Authority of Pittsburgh) that are able to operate outside normal constraints placed on governments. Primarily, this has been used as a way to circumvent public resistance to new sports projects (e.g., Georgia Dome, Oriole Park at Camden Yards, or Three Rivers Stadium) and construct them without receiving public consent through a referendum. Without having to pass a voter referendum, the authorities float the bonds that are sometimes guaranteed or accepted as a moral obligation by the state.

References

Johnson, D. L. (2014). Understanding the revenue streams. *Journal for Facilities Planning, Design, and Management, 2*(2), 85–103.

Mikesell, J. (2009). *Fiscal administration: Analysis and applications for the public sector.* Boston: Wadsworth Publishing.

Rosentraub, M. S. (2010). *Major league winners: Using sport facilities and cultural centers for economic development.* New York: CRC Press/ Taylor & Francis.

Sawyer, T. H. (2006). Financing facilities 101. *Journal of Physical Education, Recreation, and Dance, 77*(4), 23–28.

Sawyer, T. H., Hypes, J. A., & Hypes, M. G. (2004). *Financing the sport enterprise.* Urbana, IL: Sagamore.

SportsBusiness Research Net (SBR Net). (2014). Retrieved from http//:www.sbrnet.com

Winfree, J. A., & Rosentraub, M. S. (2012). *Sports finance and management.* New York: CRC Press/Taylor & Francis.

CHAPTER 13

Marketing Principles

Julia Ann Hypes
Morehead State University

Thomas H. Sawyer
Professor Emeritus, Indiana State University

Introduction

Marketing consists of all activities designed to generate and facilitate any exchange intended to satisfy human needs or wants. More simply put in business terms, activities designed to plan, price, promote, and distribute products or services to target markets. Further, marketing is a fact of life. There are so many businesses in so many categories, how will you persuade potential customers to come to you?

Mullin, Hardy, and Sutton (2014) notes that marketing is a total system of interacting business activities designed to plan, price, promote, and distribute programs, products, and services to meet the needs of present and potential customers. Marketing is comprised of all activities designed to meet the needs and wants of consumers through an exchange process. Sport marketing has developed into two major thrusts: the marketing of products and services directly to consumers (e.g., a professional team, college/university team, fitness club), and marketing of other consumer and industrial products and services (e.g., automotive companies, a beer company, or cola companies) through the use of sport promotions.

Sport consumers are involved in sport through playing, officiating, watching, listening, reading, and collecting (Mullin et al., 2014). Fitness and recreation consumers are involved in fitness and recreation through involvement in fitness activities and a variety of recreational endeavors. Through the marketing planning process, we will be able to determine how to best meet the variety of consumer needs.

Blackshaw (2012) notes advertising is a form of communication that typically attempts to persuade potential customers to purchase or to consume more of a particular brand of product or service. Many advertisements are designed to generate increased consumption of those products and services through the creation and reinforcement of "brand image" and "brand loyalty." For these purposes, advertisements sometimes embed their persuasive message with factual information. Every major medium is used to deliver these messages, including television, radio, cinema, magazines, newspapers, video games, the Internet, and billboards. Advertising is often placed by an advertising agency on behalf of a company or other organization.

Promotions is a catch-all category for any one of a variety of marketing efforts designed to stimulate consumer interest in, awareness of, and purchase of the service, product, or program. Shank (2013) suggests promotion is the vehicle that (1) carries the message about the services, products, and programs; (2) positions them in the market; and (3) develops the appropriate image for the services, products, and programs. Promotions, according to Shank (2013) include the following forms of marketing activities: (1) advertising; (2) personal selling (i.e., any face-to-face presentation); (3) publicity; (4) sales promotion (i.e., a wide variety of activities including displays, trade shows, free samples, introductory free classes, coupons, giveaways, and exhibitions); and sponsorships (p. 138).

Shank (2013) suggests sponsorship is a form of advertising in sports, music, broadcasting, and the arts. Sponsorship became a major source of finance for sports in the 1970s, and takes several forms. (See Sample Sponsorship and Licensing Agreements in the Appendices available in the student and faculty resource center at www.sagamorepub.com). Many companies sponsor fitness, recreation, and sporting events, while others give money to individuals who wear the company's logo or motifs while performing. Advertisers also commonly sponsor concerts, although some performers refuse in principle to endorse a product in this way. Large companies will also sponsor museum exhibitions, a form of corporate funding for tax deductions.

In the United States, radio broadcasts were sponsored by consumer goods and television companies. This sponsorship continued as television programs became the prime mode of home entertainment. Sponsors often seek to associate the name of their product with a particular show, event, or personality, thus enhancing the product's image.

Marketing

Marketing is a method of communicating to people that the company, product, or service exists. It's no use having the best product in the world if nobody knows about it or about you. Marketing is an ongoing process of planning and executing the marketing mix (Product, Price, Place, Promotion often referred to as the 4 Ps) for products, services, or ideas to create exchange between individuals and organizations.

Marketing tends to be seen as a creative industry, which includes advertising, distribution, and selling. It is also concerned with anticipating the customers' future needs and wants, which are often discovered through market research. Essentially, marketing is the process of creating or directing an organization to be successful in selling a product or service that people not only desire, but are willing to buy. Therefore good marketing must be able to create a "proposition" or set of benefits for the end customer that delivers value through products or services.

There are many methods of marketing, from simple to elaborate and from inexpensive to extremely costly. All or only some of these may be applicable to your business, but you can choose the ones that are and create a powerful marketing strategy. The following list outlines some common marketing and communication methods used by millions of press releases and public service announcements in newspapers (Lough & Sutton, 2011; Parkhouse, Turner, and Miloch (2012):

- Print advertising in newspapers, magazines, business journals, community newsletters, etc.

- Sales flyers, brochures, or newsletters for distribution to potential customers.

- Attend trade shows or exhibitions related to your industry, product, or business.

- Press releases and public service announcements in newspapers. Usually free and good exposure.

- Cooperative marketing efforts (in advertising, etc.) with a business that complements yours.

- Join community networking groups such as your local chamber of commerce or business committee.

- Join professional associations through your industry, business, or personal credentials.

- Internet marketing is an exciting and inexpensive method of regional, national, or global marketing.

- Telemarketing to potential customers off a list or out of the telephone book.

- Direct marketing with written correspondence using a list to mail or fax marketing literature.

The American Marketing Association (AMA, 2011) indicates a market-focused or customer-focused organization first determines what its potential customers desire, and then builds the product or service. Marketing theory and practice is justified in the belief that customers use a product or service because they have a need or because it provides a perceived benefit.

Two major factors of marketing, according to the AMA (2011), are the recruitment of new customers (acquisition) and the retention and expansion of relationships with existing customers (base management). Once a marketer has converted the prospective buyer, base management marketing takes over. The process for base management shifts the marketer to building a relationship, nurturing the links, enhancing the benefits that sold the buyer in the first place, and improving the product/service continuously to protect the business from competitive encroachments.

The AMA (2011) notes that in order to be successful, in a marketing plan, the mix of the four "Ps" must reflect the wants and desires of the consumers or shoppers in the target market. Trying to convince a market segment to buy something it does not want is extremely expensive and seldom successful. The AMA (2011) suggests marketers depend on insights from marketing research, both formal and informal, to determine what consumers want and what they are willing to pay for. Marketers hope that this process will give them a sustainable competitive advantage. Marketing management is the practical application of this process. The offer is also an important addition to the 4Ps theory.

The American Marketing Association (AMA) states, "Marketing is an organizational function and a set of processes for creating, communicating, and delivering value to customers and for managing customer relationships in ways that benefit the organization and its stakeholders" (AMA, 2011).

Managing the Strategic Marketing Process

In the theory of managing the marketing process, Fetchko, Roy, and Clow (2012) and Mullin et al. (2007) identify five strategic components of the marketing management process:

1. Visualize and position the organization vis-à-vis the market.
2. Clarify your goals and objectives.
3. Develop a marketing plan.
4. Integrate the marketing plan into a broader strategic allocation of resources that ensure success.
5. Control and evaluate the plan's implementation.

An organization cannot begin to develop a strategy until the organization establishes the environment in which it operates as well as your place within that market. The organization must have a mission and understand its core vision. In marketing, planning and operating decisions must be in line with the goals established by the organization (See Table 13.1). An organization must be goal oriented and directed by those goals to be effective as well as efficient. An organization cannot be all things to

Table 13.1

Marketing Plan Components

A complete marketing plan must answer these eight questions:

- **Objectives:** What are we trying to accomplish?

- **Target audience:** Who are we trying to reach?

- **Research:** What do we know about our target audiences, competition, pricing?

- **Themes and messages:** What communications will persuade our target audience to do, think or act in a manner we would wish them to?

- **Action plan:** What are we going to do?

- **Evaluation:** How do we judge the success and/or value of what we do?

- **Resources:** What allocation of time, people and money will be required to implement the program?

- **Priorities and responsibilities:** Who will do what, within what time frame?

(Modified from Shank, 2013)

all people; therefore, a step-by-step process will aid you in developing the best marketing plan possible. As you can see, marketing does not just "happen." It is strategically planned (see Business Plan for Marketing in the Appendices available in the student and faculty resource center at www.sagamorepub. com). An organization must understand where it is in the marketplace before it can decide where it wants to go or how to get there (Mullin et al., 2014).

Basic Marketing Principles

The marketing of fitness, recreation, and sport is often associated with promotional activities. It is important to remember that promotions are only a part of the marketing process. An organization meets the wants and needs of consumers and achieves its objectives through a coordinated set of elements called the strategic marketing mix. This marketing mix consists of the product, price, place, and promotion. Marketing managers have control over each of these elements and can manipulate decisions and components of each to meet the needs of their specific consumer.

Products and services are developed, revised, or maintained to meet consumer needs and eliminated by managers when weak. The three consumers we consider in clubs, recreation, and sport organizations when making marketing decisions are the spectator, the sponsor, and the participant. Decisions must be made regarding licensing, branding, merchandising, and packaging products and services offered to consumers. Services offer unique challenges. With services, the experience cannot be repeated. Once that experience has happened, the perception of the quality of the service is imprinted in the mind of the consumer. While consumers may agree to a second experience, the first experience, positive or negative, is always there for comparison.

Pricing affects our marketing strategies when we establish ticket prices, membership fees, PSL fees, recreational sport program costs, etc. Pricing objectives must be developed prior to selecting a pricing technique. The marketer must also be prepared to make adjustments to pricing over time. There are commonly three times when prices should be increased (Shank, 2009): (1) announcement of a major new improvement to the facility or a plan to purchase new equipment, (2) completion of the major improvement or the new equipment has been installed, and (3) during the peak activity season. Marketing managers must be sensitive to consumers and understand that pricing is one of the most critical components of marketing. You can have a good product/service, a method to get the product/service to the consumer, and effective advertising campaigns. If the pricing of the product/service is not acceptable to consumers, they will not purchase, even if product/service is what they want.

How distribute products and services to consumers in sport and physical activity includes issues such as, where to locate a new facility and the methods we will use to sell event tickets. The most efficient and effective method for delivering products and services to consumers is a high priority for marketing managers.

The Exchange Process

A marketing strategy relies on the exchange process for success. A buyer will have something of value that they will offer to the seller in return for goods and/or services.

According to Shank (2013), there are several conditions that must be satisfied for an exchange to occur:

- There must be at least two parties.
- Each party must have something of value to offer the other.
- There must be a means for communication between the two or more parties.
- Each party must be free to accept or decline the offer.
- Each party must believe it is desirable to deal with the other(s).
- Tangible and intangible benefits.

Fitness, Recreation, and Sport Products

A fitness, recreation, and sport/or product is a good and/or service that provides benefits to a consumer of fitness, recreation, or sport. These benefits are considered to be tangible or intangible. When we can see, feel, and touch a product, it is tangible. If we can go back and look at a product and it has not changed, it is considered tangible. For example, a ticket to a sporting event is sold when actually the event is the product. When we look at the ticket purchased for a Super Bowl, it stirs emotion and feelings for the event, but it does not change physically. Intangible components of a product and/or service are those feelings and emotions that the consumer associates with the product/service. Within the sport industry, something tangible is often linked with an intangible aspect of the product and/or service so the consumer might reflect and remember the experience.

Market Segmentation

Market segmentation consists of taking the total, heterogeneous market for a product or service and dividing it into several submarkets, each of which tends to be homogeneous in all significant aspects. This division of the market becomes useful when an organization sells the same product or service to different markets through the use of different advertising appeals designed specifically for each homogeneous market. More often, however, market segmentation is accompanied by product or service differentiation by developing a different product for each market segment to meet the market's need.

Segmenting the market into target markets has emerged as the dominant features of marketing. Organizational resources can be focused to meet the wants and needs of a specific group. Each target market is made up of individuals who share similar demographics (e.g., age, occupation, education, income, etc.), geographics (e.g., urban, suburban, countries, states), psychographics (e.g., lifestyle, personality, attitudes, self-concept), and/or behaviors (i.e., grouping consumers according to their responses to the features of specific products/services).

Determining how narrowly to segment a market can be a challenge. There are four questions that should be answered when selecting a target market (Shank, 2013):

1. Is the segment measurable?
2. Is the segment large enough?
3. Is the market reachable?
4. Is the market responsive?

The manager should rate each target market on the basis of these criteria. The most desirable segments would be those that elicit a positive answer to all four questions.

Further, a target segment must have a sufficient number of potential customers to permit a profitable sales volume. Competition and possible market share must also be considered. Some factors for segmentation are easily identified and measured (e.g., age, gender, income level, educational background, occupation) and some are not (e.g., lifestyles, attitudes, and self-concepts).

One common trap that marketers fall into with respect to the size of the potential market is known as the majority fallacy. The majority fallacy assumes that the largest group of consumers should always be selected as the target market. The biggest market may be the best choice; however, the competition is the fiercest for this group of consumers (Shank, 2013).

All identifiable target segments are potentially reachable. However, the manager must ask two questions before proceeding with segmentation: (1) How can you communicate with the specific target segment? (2) How much will it cost to communicate with the market segment? If the target market does not have the potential to be profitable, it should not be pursued.

To determine the responsiveness of a target market segment, it is necessary to ask two questions: (1) Are the people in the target segment willing to buy the product or service?, and (2) Can the organization develop marketable products or services and a strategy for promoting the products or services? The main challenge is to identify what consumers in the target market need and want and then provide it to them at a price they are willing to pay.

Advertising

Parkhouse, Turner, and Miloch (2012) suggest advertising is a form of communication that typically attempts to persuade potential customers to purchase or to consume more of a particular brand of product or service (See Table 13.2, Top Fitness, Recreation, and Sport Advertisers). Many advertisements are designed to generate increased consumption of those products and services through the creation and reinforcement of "brand image" and "brand loyalty." For these purposes, advertisements sometimes embed their persuasive message with factual information. Every major medium is used to deliver these messages, including television, radio, cinema, magazines, newspapers, video games, the Internet and billboards (e.g., stationary and mobile). Advertising is often placed by an advertising agency on behalf of a company or other organization (See Table 13.3 Advertising Agency Involved in U.S. fitness, recreation, and/or sport industries). Shank (2013) indicates there are nine common rules for making the most of sports property or ad agency relationships (See Table 13.4 for details).

Advertisements are seen on the seats of shopping carts, on the walls of an airport walkway, on the sides of buses, and are heard in telephone hold messages and in-store public address systems. Advertisements are often placed anywhere an audience can easily or frequently access visual, audio and printed information.

While advertising can be seen as necessary for economic growth, it is not without social costs. Because of the social costs criteria are needed for deciding whether or not to advertise (See Table 13.5). Unsolicited Commercial Email and other forms of spam have become so prevalent as to have become a major nuisance to users of these services, as well as being a financial burden on Internet service providers. Advertising is increasingly invading public spaces, such as schools, which some critics argue is a form of child exploitation.

Table 13.2
Top Fitness, Recreation, and Sport Advertisers

General Motors
Anheuser-Busch Cos.
AT&T
Ford Motor Co.
Coca-Cola Co.
Visa
Miller Brewing Co.
Procter & Gamble
Nissan North America
IBM
Pespi Cola
Toyota North America
(SportBusiness Research, 2012)

Table 13.3
Advertising Agency Involved in U.S. Fitness, Recreation, and/or Sport Industries

Advertising Conglomerates	BBDO Worldwide
AEGIS	Bravo Group
HAVAS	Bromley Communications Group
Inter Public Group	Campbell-Ewald
Omnicom Group	Carat
Publicis Groupe	Cramer-Krasselt Company
WPP	Crispin Porter & Bogusky
Other Advertising Agencies	Cutwater
Aguilar/Girard Agency	Dailey & Associates
Almighty	DDB Worldwide
Anomaly	Deutsch
Arnold Wordwide	DeVita/Verdi
Bartle Bogle Hegarty	Dieste Harmel & Partners
Berlin Cameron United	Doner
Boathouse Group	Element

(SportBusiness Research, 2012)

Table 13.4

Rules for Making the Most of Sports Property or Ad Agency Relationships

- The consistency of consumer products breeds marketing constancy. The opposite is true of teams and leagues.
- The business arrangements are not the norm.
- Branding should precede advertising.
- Advertising sports products is not the same as advertising sport properties.
- Campaigns for sports properties that promise performance will invariably under-perform.
- Team and league campaigns are under scrutiny that belies their normally paltry media budgets.
- Sports consumers know their product far better than other consumers, so respect their knowledge.
- Sell the brand first — everything else will follow.
- Sports are social currency; spend it wisely.

(Street and Smith's SportBusiness Journal, Volume 10:22, September 24–30, 2007, 24–28.)

Table 13.5

Criteria for Deciding Whether or Not to Advertise

Advertising works best when the seller wishes to inform many people quickly (e.g., change in hours, a special sales promotion, or a new credit policy). There are five criteria that should be considered when deciding whether or not to advertise:

- The primary demand trend for the product or service should be favorable.
- There should be considerable opportunity to differentiate the product or service.
- The product or service should have hidden qualities.
- Powerful emotional buying motives should exist for the product or service.
- The organization must have sufficient funds to support an advertising program adequately.

(Mullin et al., 2014)

The Function of Advertising

Advertising consists of all the activities involved in presenting to a group a nonpersonal, oral or visual, openly sponsored message regarding a service, product, or program. This message, called an advertisement, is disseminated through one or more media and is paid for by the identified sponsor.

There is a significant distinction between advertising and an advertisement. The advertisement is simply the message itself. Advertising is a process. It is a program or a series of activities necessary to plan and prepare the message and get it to the intended market. Another point is that the public knows who is behind the advertising because the sponsor is openly identified in the advertisement itself. Further, the payment is made by the sponsor to the media that carry the message. These last two considerations differentiate advertising from propaganda and publicity.

Fundamentally, the only purpose of advertising is to sell something—a service, product, or program. The intent may be to generate a sale immediately or at some time in the future. Nevertheless, the basic objective is to sell. Stated another way, the real goal of advertising is effective communication; that is, the ultimate effect of advertising should be to modify the attitudes and/or behavior of the receiver of the message.

The general goal of advertising is to increase profitable sales, but this goal is too broad to be implemented effectively in an advertising program. It is necessary to establish some specific objectives that can be worked into the program. A few examples of these more limited aims are listed here (Parkhouse et al., 2012; Shank, 2013):

- Support personal selling program

- Reach people inaccessible to salesman

- Improve dealer relations

- Enter a new geographic market or attract a new group of customers

- Introduce a new product or a new price schedule

- Increase sales of products

- Expand membership sales

- Counteract prejudice or substitution

- Build goodwill for the organization and improve its reputation by rendering a public service through advertising or by telling of the organization behind the service, product, or program

How Is the Advertising Budget Developed?

According to Kahle and Close (2010) and Lough and Sutton (2011), The advertising program budget is developed by taking into consideration the following components:

- **Expenses**
1) The number and size of printed advertisements (internal and external sources)
2) The number and length of radio spots
3) The number and length of television spots
4) The number of billboards in use
5) Personnel
6) Office expenses
- **Income**
1) Advertisement space sold
2) Trade outs (It is possible to increase the advertising schedule for a program on a noncash basis [trade outs—tickets or memberships for free advertising] if the attraction and manager are willing to allow a radio station [it is less common for television and the printed media to enter

into trade out agreements] to be the program's official media sponsor. Never allow a media sponsorship to be construed as a sponsorship exclusive. Offer the media sponsor a promotional exclusive and clearly retain the right to advertise anywhere else it is appropriate).

The annual budget should include funds each year to advertise the schedule of services, products, and programs in local newspapers in a format which people can clip out and retain on a month-to-month basis. Many organizations also publish a weekly or monthly in-house newsletter which is used as a direct-mail piece as well as a handout at the facility.

Depending on the organization's philosophy, advertising can generate income by selling space for advertising in a variety of media throughout the organization's facility(ies). Kahle and Close (2010), Mullin et al. (2014), and Wakeland (2011) suggest the possibilities include, but are not limited to 1) scoreboard systems, 2) concourse display cases, 3) lobby displays, 4) point-of-sale displays, 5) Zamboni, 6) in-house publications, 7) message centers, 8) outdoor marquees, 9) upcoming program display cases, 10) membership packages, 11) concession product containers, 12) indoor soccer wall boards, 13) baseball/softball outfield fence, 14) scorer tables, and 15) contest programs. There are a number of potential advertisers for these spaces and, in particular, for concession products. Concession product vendors are willing to advertise their names and products on concession containers. This coupled with discount sale promotions will increase food and beverage sales for the organization as well as its vendors.

What Are the Steps to Selecting the Media for Advertising?

Advertising strategy varies from program to program and season to season depending on the nature of the anticipated audience or market. Where to place an advertisement is governed generally by funds available.

Management must determine what general types of media to use—newspapers, magazines, radio, television, and billboards? If newspapers, local or regional? If television is selected, will it be local, national network, or spot telecasting?

Objective of the advertisement. Media choices are influenced both by the purpose of a specific advertisement and by the goal of an entire campaign. If an advertiser wants to make last-minute changes in an advertisement, or if he or she wishes to place an advertisement inducing action within a day or two, he or she may use newspapers, radio, or television. Magazines are not so good for this purpose, because the advertisement must be placed weeks before the date of publication.

Media circulation. Media circulation must match the distribution patterns of the service, product, or program. Consequently, the geographic scope of the market will influence the choice of media considerably. Furthermore, media should be selected that will reach the desired type of market with a minimum of waste circulation. Media used to reach a teenage market will be different from those used to reach mothers with young children.

Requirements of the message. Management should consider the media that are most suitable for the presentation of the message to the market. Meat products, floor coverings, and apparel are ordinarily best presented in pictorial form; thus, radio is not a good medium for these lines. If a product, such as insurance, calls for a lengthy message, outdoor advertising is poor. If the advertiser can use a very brief message, however, as in the case of salt, beer, or sugar, then billboards may be the best choice. Television can be used to show pictures, but not detailed ones.

Time and location of buying decision. The advertiser should select the medium that will reach the prospective customer at or near the time and place that he or she makes his buying decision. For this reason, outdoor advertising is often good for gasoline products and hotels/motels. For this reason, outdoor advertising (billboards) is often good for gasoline products and hotels/motels. Grocery store advertisements are placed in newspapers on Thursday nights or Friday mornings in anticipation of heavy weekend buying.

How Are Advertisements Created?

Before creating the advertisement, the people concerned should remember that the main purpose of advertising is to sell something and that the advertisement itself is a sales talk. The advertisement may be a high-pressure sales talk as in a hard-hitting, direct-action advertisement; or it may be a very long-range, low-pressure message, as in an institutional advertisement. In any case, it is trying to sell something. Consequently, it involves the same kind of selling procedure as a sales talk delivered by personal salespersons. That is, the advertisement must first attract attention and then hold interest long enough to stimulate a desire for the service, product, or program. Finally, the advertisement must move the prospect to some kind of action. The desired action may lie anywhere within a virtually un-limited scope of possibilities ranging from an immediate change in overt behavior to a slowly changing attitude or thought process.

Creating an advertisement involves the tasks of writing the copy, selecting illustrations to be used, preparing the layout, and arranging to have the advertisement reproduced for the selected media. The copy in an advertisement is defined as all the written or spoken material in it, including the headline, coupons, and advertiser's name and address, as well as the main body of the message. The illustration, whether it is a photograph, drawing, reproduction of a painting, cartoon, or something else, is a pow-erful feature in an advertisement. Probably the main points to consider with respect to illustrations are 1) whether they are the best alternative use of the space and 2) whether they are appropriate in all respects to the advertisement itself. The layout is the physical arrangement of all the elements in an advertisement. Within the given amount of space or time, the layout artist must place the headline, copy, and illustrations. Decisions are made regarding the relative amount of white space and the kinds of type to be used. A good layout can be an interest-holding device as well as an attention- getter. It should lead the reader in an orderly fashion throughout the entire advertisement.

What Is Important to Consider When Selecting an Advertising Firm?

If the organization is unable to maintain an in-house advertising operation, it is advisable to in-terview and select a local agency to serve the organization. If an outside agency is engaged, the per-formance must be constantly monitored so that more than simple advertisement placement is accom-plished.

The agency should advise the organization of the most appropriate advertising media plan for the organization. Finally, the agency should have a good sense of promotion and public relations. The aver-age charge by an outside agency is a 15% commission for each advertisement placement.

Promotion

Many people consider advertising, selling, and marketing to be synonymous terms. However, advertising and selling are only one of the many components of marketing. Advertising is an activity of attracting public attention to a product or business, as by paid announcements in the print, broadcast, or electronic. Selling is the personal or impersonal process of assisting and/or persuading a prospec-tive customer to buy a commodity or a service or to act favorably upon an idea that has commercial significance to the seller.

Promotion is a form of selling but is the all-inclusive term representing the broad field. Selling suggests only the transfer of title or the use of personal salesmen while promotion includes advertising, personal selling, sales promotion, and other selling tools.

The two most widely used methods of promotion are personal selling and advertising. Mullins, et al. (2014) and Shank (2013) suggest other promotional methods/strategies are 1) sales promotion, which is designed to supplement and coordinate personal selling and advertising efforts (e.g., store displays, trade shows and exhibitions, and the use of samples or premiums); 2) mail-order advertising and selling; 3) automatic vending; 4) auctions; 5) telemarketing; 6) product differentiation; 7) market segmentation; 8) trading up; 9) trading down; 10) use of trading stamps or frequent flyer miles; and 11) branding a product or service.

The Promotional Campaign

A promotional campaign is a planned, coordinated, and integrated series of promotional efforts built around a single theme or idea and designed to reach a predetermined goal. The first step in developing the campaign is establishing the goals and determining the campaign strategies. Mullins et al. (2014), Schwarz, Hunter, and LaFleur (2012), and Shank (2013) indicate the manager should answer the following questions when developing the campaign strategies:

- What is the relative emphasis to be placed on primary versus secondary demand stimulation?

- What balance is desired between the immediacy of the action-response and the duration of the response?

- Does the organization influence everyone a little bit or a few people intensively?

- At what point is the management targeting the organization's emphasis on the spectrum between brand awareness and brand insistence?

- What issues, products, or services (e.g., both the organization's and the competitor's) will the organization stress?

Early in the course of planning the campaign, management should decide what selling appeals will be stressed. This decision will be based to a large extent upon the specific objectives of the campaign and the research findings concerning the buying motives and habits of the customers.

Most campaigns revolve around a central theme. This theme should permeate all promotional efforts and tends to unify the campaign. A theme is simply appeals dressed up in a distinctive, attention-getting form. As such, it is related to the campaign's objectives and the customers' behaviors. It expresses the product's benefits. Frequently the theme is expressed as a slogan (e.g., Nike's "Just Do It;" or Ford's "Quality Is Job One").

The key to success in a campaign depends largely on management's ability to activate and coordinate the efforts of its entire promotional task force and the physical distribution of the product or service. In a successfully implemented campaign, the efforts of all involved should be meshed effectively. The advertising program will consist of a series of related, well-timed, carefully placed ads. The personal selling effort can be tied in by having the salesperson explain and demonstrate the products or services benefits stressed in the ads. Sales-promotional devices such as point-of-purchase display materials need to be coordinated with the other aspects of the campaign. Personnel responsible for the physical distribution activities must ensure that adequate stocks of the product are available prior to the start of the campaign.

Determining the Promotional Mix

Determining the promotional mix (i.e., advertising, personal selling, sales promotions) can be difficult for management. However, Shank (2013) says should management take into consideration such areas as 1) the factors that influence the promotional mix (e.g., money available for promotion, nature of the market [geographical scope, concentration, and type of customers], nature of the product or service, and stage of the product's or service's life cycle); 2) the questions of basic promotional strategy in order to illustrate the effect of the influencing factors (e.g., When should advertising and personal selling be main ingredients, when should promotional efforts by retailer be stressed, when should manufacturer-retailer cooperative advertising be used, is retailer promotion needed when manufacturer emphasizes advertising, if a retailer emphasizes personal selling, does he or she need to advertise, and should promotional activity be continued when demand is heavy or exceeds capacity); and (3) the quantitative data from a research study to show the practical applications of the analytical material.

References

American Marketing Association. (2011). Retrieved from http://www.ama.org .

Blackshaw, I. S. (2012). *Sports marketing agreements: Legal, fiscal, and practical aspects.* The Hague, The Netherlands: ASSER Press.

Fetchko, M., Roy, D., & Clow, K. E. (2012). *Sports marketing.* Upper Saddle River, NJ: Prentice-Hall/Pearson.

Kahle, L. R., & Close, A. G. (2010). *Consumer behavior knowledge for effective sports and event marketing.* New York: Routledge/Taylor & Francis Group, LTD.

Lough, N. L., & Sutton, W. A. (2011). *Handbook of sport marketing.* Morgantown, WV: Fitness Information Technology.

Mullin, S. D., Hardy, S., & Sutton, W. A. (2014). *Sport marketing* (4th ed.). Champaign, IL: Human Kinetics.

Parkhouse, B., Turner, B., & Miloch, K. S. (2012). *Marketing for sport business success.* Dubuque, IA: Kendall Hunt Publishing.

Schwarz, E.C., Hunter, J. D., & LaFleur, A. (2012). *Advanced theory and practice in sport marketing.* New York: Routledge/Taylor & Francis Group, LTD.

Shank, M. D. (2013). *Sports marketing: A strategic perspective* (5th ed.). Upper Saddle River, NJ: Prentice Hall/Pearson.

SportsBusiness Research. (2012). Retrieved from http://www.sbrnet.com.

Staff. (2012). Rules for making the most of sports property or ad agency relationships. *Street and Smith's SportBusiness Journal,* 10:22, 24–28.

Wakeland, K. (2011). *Team sports marketing.* New York: Routledge/Taylor & Francis Group, LTD.

CHAPTER 14

Retail Principles

Thomas H. Sawyer
Professor Emeritus, Indiana State University

Tonya L. Gimbert
Indiana State University

Fitness, recreation, and sport organizations have known for years that retail operations can generate a significant and consistent revenue stream. If the retail operations are run well and selling the right products at competitive prices, they should be turning a handsome profit and saving the clientele money.

The most dramatic change for the food and beverage concession industry came in 1987 with the opening of Joe Robbie stadium. Joe Robbie Stadium started the luxury suites and club seats era. The owners of Joe Robbie Stadium offered its customers a new level of service never before available in a sports facility: waiter and waitress service at their seats and a fully air-conditioned and carpeted private concourse featuring complete buffets from gourmet sandwiches to homemade pasta and freshly carved prime rib. A new level of culinary expertise would now be required of the concessionaire, and the concessionaire's skill would be instrumental in the success of the customer's total entertainment experience at the sport's venue.

Gibbs (2012) suggests that successful retail operations accomplish the following: (1) feature prominent locations that require clientele to pass through the various sites, (2) offer personalized service and competitive pricing, (3) print catalogues for clients to share with friends, (4) merchandise their goods/products (i.e., displaying goods/products in an appealing way), (5) consider themselves retail outlets, (6) sell innovative goods/products, (7) concentrate on apparel, accessories, beverages, and food, (8) stock regularly needed convenience supplies, and (9) sell licensed merchandise.

The box/ticket office is the heart of a sport enterprise that fields teams. Its management is the key to financial success. Selling tickets to events is a major financial resource for any sporting team whether at the interscholastic, intercollegiate, or professional level. It is vital for sport managers to book a well-rounded schedule of events to satisfy the desires of the market and to ensure a major portion of the annual operating revenue.

Retail Operations

Retail operations within a fitness, recreation and sport organization can include concessions including beverage (i.e., alcoholic and nonalcoholic), fast food, and parking found when attending most sporting events, licensed and convenience products, and full-service restaurants. Some operations (i.e., state and national parks) extend their offerings beyond products to include services including rentals (e.g., bicycle, watercraft, ski equipment, golf equipment), downhill ski facilities and services, equestrian services, golf courses and services, photography services, marina services, shuttle bus services, theater productions, vending machine services, and aquatic facilities. Retail operations must stretch the discretionary income of the clientele. Some operations provide the organization a source of operating revenue separate from, but in addition to, a subsidy provided by the media rights and ticket sales. Others operate on a break-even basis and serve strictly as a service to clientele.

Concession Operations

The food and beverage concessions can be a gold mine if handled appropriately. Many stadia and arenas are expanding their options from the traditional concession stand to include favorite fast food options (i.e., Burger King, McDonald's, Pizza Hut, Papa John's, Hardees, Taco Bell, Long John Silver, Kentucky Fried Chicken, Ballpark Franks, TCBY yogurt, Krispy Kreme donuts, TGIFriday's-Miller Park, Outback Steakhouse-PNC Park, Hard Rock Café-SkyDome, etc.) as well as the traditional hot dog, popcorn, peanuts, pretzels, and beer concessions. All stadiums have added, along with their luxury suites and club seats, full-service premium restaurants. Numerous concession companies have added regional favorites including a micro-brewery and Rocky Mountain oysters in Denver, fish tacos in San Diego, cheesesteaks in Philadelphia, and dog bone-shaped chocolate chip cookies in Cleveland. The greatest amount of profit in the food concessions business is from soda drink sales followed by popcorn, hot dogs, tacos and cheese, candy, and beer.

A food concession open from dawn to dusk must be flexible, offering breakfast, lunch, and dinner favorites that are fast and convenient. People expect to pay more at a food concession than elsewhere because of the convenience factor. The food concession will be successful if the customers' needs and wants are known and a clean, fresh atmosphere with friendly, convenient, and fast service is provided.

The food concession must be conveniently located to the customers. Many stadia and arenas are now using portable concession stands as well as the permanent locations to provide more convenient service to the customers. The food concession area should have plenty of counter space, hot and cold running water, adequate electricity to operate popcorn popper, microwave, refrigerator and freezer, a warming unit, and storage space. The floor and walls should be tile. The floor should have numerous drains for cleaning. On the customer side, there should be plenty of space to accommodate a large number of people quickly and efficiently.

The seven major concessionaires in the food service industry are (SportsBusiness Research, 2012):

- Aramark (largest concession company in North America),
- Compass (European, largest concession company in the world)
- Fine Hosts Corporation,
- Global Spectrum,
- Sodexho (European),
- Sportservice Corporation (Buffalo), and
- Volume Services America (VSA) now known as Centerplate (Spartanburg).

Food Concession Guidelines

It is important for any food concession system to have operation guidelines. The recommendations address and include employee appearance, training goals, maintenance goals, operation goals, regulations, inspections, safety certification and sanitation, patron comforts, guest relations, professional signs and pricing, decorations, and food handler's guidelines.

National Organizations for Concessionaires

The sport manager should be aware of the two national organizations that deal with food and beverage concessions. The first is the National Association of Concessionaires, which can be found on the web at http://www.NAConline.org. This organization offers a concession manager certification course and an executive concession manager certification course. The programs for these courses include these topics: management, profit planning, cost control systems, menu planning/branding, and event planning. The basis of the course and the textbook it is based on are also part of the curriculum at the School of Hospitality Management at Florida International University in Miami and the School of Human Sciences, Department of Nutrition and Food Science at Auburn University in Alabama. The second organization is the National Association of Collegiate Concessionaires whose URL address is http://www.nacc-online.com. Finally, a third organization is the Outdoor Amusement Business Association (OABA) that can be reached at http://www.oaba.org. The OABA have guidelines for food and game concessions.

Alcohol Management

The focus on patron safety relating to alcohol consumption began in 1983 with the *Bearman v. University of Notre Dame*. The Indiana Supreme Court determined that Notre Dame had a "duty" to its paid patrons. This was a landmark case because the court determined that intoxicated persons could pose a general danger to other patrons. This determination flew in the face of previous decisions that placed the responsibility of duty of care on the individual or group, not on the event organizers. The Court determined that foreseeability dictated that Notre Dame had a duty to protect its patrons from the potentially dangerous actions of intoxicated third parties. This case set the standard for duty of care for the management of alcohol at events.

In a number of states, there are dram shop statutes that allow injured plaintiffs to bring suit against restaurants, bars, and other establishments that allow the defendant to become drunk. In some states, the court allows recovery through common negligence actions. There are a few states that allow recovery using both methods.

In addition to the dram shop statutes, there is another liability of which to be aware exists known as the social host liability. This statute provides the injured plaintiff an opportunity to sue based on a social host knowingly serving alcohol to a minor who becomes intoxicated and causes injury or damage to property. In the jurisdiction where this line of thinking is embraced, the venue manager should be aware of this type of liability.

Alcohol Management Plan

Venue managers should have in their liability tool bags an alcohol management plan. This plan should be coordinated with the crowd control management plan. The plan should include procedures to check age restrictions, restrictions on the number of beers served, terminating beer sale at a specific point during the event (i.e., basketball, end of third period, football, beginning of third quarter, ice hockey, end of the second intermission, and baseball, end of the seventh inning), deploying trained personnel to watch for trouble, and incorporating a designated-driver program.

Alcohol Sales Strategies

In 1992, Miller Brewing Company, in combination with previous research and encouragement from its legal department, provided the following suggestions regarding an effective alcohol sales strategy, which is still used currently:

- Decide whether or not to sell alcohol and if the decision to sell alcohol is made, then an alcohol management plan must be developed.

- Develop procedures to stop outside alcohol from entering the venue.

- Establish crowd management procedures for alcohol management for day and evening events and for weather.

- Install appropriate signage to enlightened patrons about responsible and irresponsible drinking and its consequences.

- Establish a strong ejection policy.

- Do not promote or advertise drinking during the event.

- Make sure that security personnel are aware of the demographics of the crowd in each section of the venue (e.g., gender, white-collar, blue-collar, families, senior citizens, under 21, etc.).

- All staff (not just security and servers) should complete regulated alcohol management training.

- Establish consumption policies (e.g., number of beers per patron at one time, termination of sales prior to conclusion of the event).

- Tailgating only permitted in parking lots under strict supervision of security personnel.

- Establish non-alcohol sections within the venue (i.e., family sections).

- Develop a designated-driver program.

Parking Concession

The parking concession can be profitable but it has its liabilities. Fisher (2010) and Lewis and Dart (2010) indicate the manager, before charging for parking, must ensure that the following have been accomplished: (1) purchase adequate liability insurance, (2) provide adequate surfacing for the proposed traffic, (3) ensure safe entrance and exit areas, (4) provide adequate lighting, (5) plan for immediate snow and ice removal, (6) establish an emergency plan for the space, (7) ensure that adequate supervision and security is available, (8) provide for the safety of the pedestrians, (9) plan a graphic system that makes it easy to find customers' cars at the conclusion of the event, and (10) provide an adequate number of cashiers and attendants. After the manager has accomplished the above, it is time to decide how many spaces will be allotted for the handicapped (i.e., review state and federal handicapped guidelines for actual number of spaces), VIPs, and regular customers. The greatest amount of money will be made from VIP parking.

According to Fisher (2010) and Lewis and Dart (2010), the following controls should be implemented to ensure a smooth operation: (1) sensors or loops buried in each entrance line, (2) a single pass lane, (3) a cashier or checker watching the sellers and authorizing passes, (4) spot checks on sellers, (5) different colored tickets for different events, days, or hours, (6) cash registers, (7) TV monitors, and (8) clean graphics and signs indicating special entrances.

The parking operation is second only to the box office in terms of direct contact between the facility and the patron. A well-designed and managed parking operation will ease crowd tension and allow for sufficient time for patrons to buy a snack, enter the venue, and still be in their seats on time. There is no question that the ease of access and parking is a major factor in increased public acceptance and attendance at events.

Mercantile Operations

These are the stadium or arena gift or souvenir shops. They deal with licensed products and convenience items needed by patrons while attending a sporting event.

Finding a Retail Niche

Fisher (2010) and Gibbs (2012) indicate that finding customers who value what you offer is difficult at best. Achieving customer approval is especially demanding in these uncertain times. It takes regular and consistent cultivation on several fronts. Every community is overwhelmed with retail shopping locations and merchants offering everything imaginable. What makes your business emerge from the masses as distinctive? Developing a niche and working it could be the long lost answer.

The following questions are crucial to your success. Record your answers and you are sure to hit pay dirt. Fisher (2010) and Gibbs (2012) suggest the following questions tell who your customers happen to be and, more importantly, who they should be:

- How is my store special and unique?

- What groups of people would most benefit by what I offer?

- How have I physically set up my store to be user-friendly in a concerted effort to serve this group of people?

- Is my advertising targeted to the customers I desire to serve?

- What products do I like?

In the effort to add value, a pitfall to avoid is that of adding the value that is desired, rather than the value of niche customers want. The organization must become market driven, rather than product driven, by listening to your customers' needs, wants, and desires. Do this, and the organization will be rewarded with greater profitability than you have ever enjoyed before.

Using Cutting-Edge Retail Strategies in Merchandising and Buying

The world of retailing is changing at breakneck speed. These changes are driven by busy people who have too little time to shop, consumers who have new economic priorities, and the fact that too many stores are selling the same merchandise. All this is having a profound impact on when, where, and how merchandise is sold.

There are nine steps to being a good buyer. Fisher (2010), Lewis and Dart (2010), and Gibbs (2012) have put the nine steps under the umbrella of **B-U-Y W-I-S-E-L-Y** as follows:

- **B**e specific in defining needs, identifying performance, and results.

- **U**nderstand the options that are available prior to purchasing the item(s).

- Tell the supplier, It's **Y**our move. Tell me why you can meet my needs better than anyone else.

- Aim for a **W**in-win situation between you and the seller.

- **I**mpose deadlines and conditions when necessary.

- **S**eek assistance from an outside consultant when in doubt about a purchase.

- **E**ducate the seller about your special needs.

- **L**ook for after-sale service.

- **Y**ell for help when necessary.

The Four Ms in Retail

According to Fisher (2010), Gibbs (2012), and Lewis and Dart (2010), operating a successful retail establishment comes down to the four "Ms": merchandising, markups, marketing, and methodology. The basis for any success in a retail business comes down to merchandising the items placed on the shelves. Failing to carry what the customers want and need, they will breeze right past on their way to their destination; but capture their interest and you have won dedicated customers.

Merchandise must be visible. If no one sees what merchandise is available, the store manager is setting him/herself up to fail. The store should be positioned in a high-traffic area where the customers must pass by on their way to activities. If merchandise is not in the customers' line of sight, they will probably not be enticed to enter the store. Keeping goods in a high-traffic space will also discourage shoplifting.

Basic Store Merchandise

The retail store does not require a great deal of space. Some of the most popular elements that will enable an organization to start even the most basic store are outlined in Table 14.1.

Most retailers agree that you should promote your retail store by offering clothes with the organization's logo. Embroidered items go so much faster than anything else. People like to wear items that look good and are crisp, sharp, and classy. Even with a really nice T-shirt, embroidery dresses it up.

Table 14.1
The Building Blocks

Clothing

T-shirts	*Shorts*	*Hats*
Socks	*Sweatshirts*	*Tank tops*
Bike Shorts	*Gore-Tex running suits*	*Coolmax singlets*

Retail Store Design

The retail manager needs to carefully plan the layout of the retail store. The store layout is as much a marketing tool as are the catalogues and merchandise on the shelves. The manager needs to work with a consultant and visit other employee stores before making the final decisions regarding store layout, space needs (including storage), and overall design.

Effective Store Layout

When customers enter an employee store, what do they see? Do they see a store that is cluttered and disorganized, or one that is clean, attractive, and interesting? Do they see too much merchandise or too little? Do they see merchandise that is poorly displayed, or do they see a well-designed store that shows off the merchandise at its best? Do they find it difficult to locate specific merchandise, brands, styles, sizes, and colors, or do they find a store with merchandise that is logically organized on racks and shelves so that it is easy to find and buy? Do they experience a dynamic shopping environment or just another store where they can occasionally buy a few items because it is convenient and the prices are pretty good?

Customers expect more from every kind of store, whether it is located in the mall or where they work. Influencing employee customers' buying decisions means knocking their socks off with a creative shopping environment where the merchandise is the star. Further, Gibbs (2012) and Lewis and Dart (2010) suggest three main keys to an effective store layout: maximizing the space, controlling and directing traffic flow, and maximizing exposure.

Maximizing the space. The key is to create an exciting, comfortable, and dynamic retailing environment for customers by using innovative layout and design software tools. The well-designed store maximizes every square foot of selling space. The manager needs to fine-tune the layout to minimize or eliminate "dead spots" and maximize a store's "hot spots" where almost anything will sell.

Controlling and directing traffic flow. The customer's experience starts in "the decompression zone." This is the all-important space at the very front of the store where customers first enter and sometimes stop for just a few moments to become acclimated. During the first few moments after customers enter, they begin to get a feeling for the store, even those who may have been in the store many times before. If everything stays the same month after month and year after year, the customer simply breezes in, buys what he wants, and leaves, never seeing all of the other merchandise. Therefore, it is important to remerchandise and change the location of the merchandise frequently.

Further, it is important that the customers feel as though the store is comfortable, inviting, easy to shop, and they are welcome. While it is nice to showcase new merchandise in the front of the store, it is more important to give customers a little space when they first enter the store to begin to feel comfortable.

After years of observing customers, researchers have discovered that more than 70% of the time when people enter a store they will either look or walk to the right. The simple explanation is that we have become a "right-handed" society. Researchers say even left-handed people frequently look or turn to the right. What merchandise will customers find in the store when they look or turn to the right? Is there merchandise on the left side that is being ignored? Are the displays in the front of the store changed frequently so customers do not just come in and look past the merchandise?

Another important research finding is that customers prefer shopping in stores where the aisles are wide enough to easily accommodate two or three people going in opposite directions. A growing number of the nation's most successful retail chains are discovering that wider aisles mean more sales and more satisfied customers.

Maximizing exposure. Are departments easy to find and identified clearly with appropriate signs? Are the fixtures and displays arranged in nice, neat, symmetrical rows, or are they angled to create open spaces that allow customers to see most of the merchandise? It is recommended by many retailers to arrange fixtures and displays at 45% angles, creating soft corners that maximize customer exposure to merchandise. Fixtures placed at 45% angles and rounded corners are being used to display all types of merchandise.

The proper use of fixtures will make your life easier and your bottom line greater, especially if you keep four things in mind: flexibility, convertibility, ingenuity, and simple common sense. A totally inflexible fixture should be used only for products that are sold in fixed quantities throughout the entire year (e.g., greeting card cases).

Further, the use of slatwall panels, wall systems, and fixtures like spinners, four-ways, and A-frames permit the use of a seemingly endless array of slatwell accessories. In addition, using slatwall as a component in a fixture can totally change its function. Put a slatwall on the back of a window display, and you have just created a two-sided fixture.

Steel shelving is found everywhere, usually with flat shelves. Yet you can create entirely new departments by removing the flat shelves and replacing them with a wide variety of inserts. They range from simple peg hooks and hang bars to spinner displays, units with glass doors, computer demo shelves, and even inserts for such items as fishing poles.

One of the simplest ways to incorporate flexibility into fixtures is to put them on casters. You can then alter traffic layout, move fixtures into position for seasonal promotions, or even take them out of the store for special sales. There are ready-to-assemble fixturing systems available that can be reconfigured depending on the need.

The following are a few useful tips offered by Fisher (2010) and Gibbs (2012) to maximize sales dollars per square foot:

- Look at that empty space between the top of your wall fixtures and the ceiling.
- Use box displays of various sizes, stacking them in different configurations.
- Jamming as much as possible into a limited space is not always wise.
- Gridwall is a simple and inexpensive way to add display capacity.
- If the customer cannot find it, she cannot buy it.
- The simplest way to maximize the use of space is just to clean up the store.
- Research what is successful in other stores.
- Use conservative numbers when estimating future sales.
- Use logic when estimating how much money will be made.

Table 14.2 displays 15 questions offered by Gibbs (2012) that should be used as a checklist for store managers to answer when preparing store layouts.

Table 14.2
Effective Store Layout Checklist

Would you answer yes, no, or needs improvement to these questions about the store?

- If I were one of your customers, would I enjoy shopping in the store?
- Is the store always clean and well maintained?
- Are the shelves always stocked with merchandise?
- Do the in-store signs clearly communicate the information the customers need and expect?
- Is the store laid out so that it is easy for customers to move around and find the merchandise they want?
- Are merchandise displays dynamic, attractive, fun, and interesting?
- Is the merchandise frequently rearranged to take advantage of seasonal events?
- Is the store regularly remodeled to keep it fresh and inviting for customers?
- Do display fixtures fit the overall decor of the store?
- Is the exterior of the store attractive and inviting?
- Has management done everything within the budget to make the interior and exterior of the store more attractive and inviting?
- Is the store bright and colorful?
- Are all the merchandise display possibilities taken advantage of in order to make the store a pleasant and enjoyable place to shop?

Table 14.2 (cont).

- Are the merchandise displays fresh and interesting, and are seasonal themes used to create excitement and keep customers coming back?

- Does the lighting in the store show merchandise at its best?

(Information gathered from Fisher, 2010; Gibbs, 2010; Lewis & Dart, 2010; Reese, 2012)

The Most Common Mistakes Made by Retailers

A successful retail store is the outcome of constant planning and setting realistic goals. Yet, many business people run their businesses without any direction. The following are the 10 most common mistakes suggested by Lewis and Dart (2010) and Reese (2012) that retailers should avoid.

- No business plan.

- No marketing plan.

- No sales plan.

- No advisory board.

- No cash reserve or real cash flow.

- Ignoring the numbers.

- Not being automated.

- Not knowing your customer.

- Ignoring employees.

- Being a lone ranger, or going it alone.

The Vending Machine

What could be more low maintenance than a retail effort that requires minimal staff? How about something that involves no store staff at all? Many facilities are finding that an effective way to sell small retail products such as convenience items, health foods, and beverages is by positioning at least one vending machine in a prominent spot in the employee services area.

Cameron (2012), Mazzola (2010), and Tomasso (2012) suggest there are two ways to become involved with the vending option: own or lease the machine or contract with a vending company for a commission. The first option, that of owning or leasing a machine or a number of machines, is the most profitable and the ultimate way to go. However, it can become labor intensive and requires an up-front investment in merchandise. Further, merchandise can take up valuable storage space. In contrast, the second option requires no labor or any investment in merchandise. The commission covers the cost of electricity, floor space, and the store's percentage of the net income.

A vending machine location, according to Mazzola (2011) and Roncevich and Primm (2011), is accessible and unattended 24 hours a day, seven days a week. Another benefit is that vending machines virtually eliminate theft and facilitate inventory control. It is possible to vend such items as vitamins, minerals, protein supplements, sport drinks, socks, shirts, headphones, and almost anything else that will fit in a vending machine.

Staffing the Retail Store or Concession Stand

The dwindling pool of candidates, especially for sales positions, is of grave concern to all retailers and concessionaires. Store or concession managers are looking for a special type of retail salesperson who can perform a variety of tasks and build relationships with revisiting customers. To attract this type of person, you should know that surveys of employees show that the opportunity to do meaningful work, the feeling of being appreciated, and a sense of job security are as important to workers as the hourly salary and benefits. Of course, you should check to see what other stores are paying and offer as much as you can afford in order to attract the best candidates; but, you must look beyond money and benefits to create jobs that people will enjoy.

Where to Find Valuable Employees

Kramer (2008) and Reese (2012) suggest most applicants discover retail positions by reading the classified ads section of a newspaper. To attract applicants in today's labor market, ads must be larger (which can be quite expensive) and more enticing. An effective ad should romance the job and the excitement of working in your store. Be sure to mention the salary and benefits, if they are attractive, and specify the experience and skills required for the position.

Colleges, technical schools, and local high schools often have placement offices that will post employment listings. Many schools even provide internship programs which allow students to earn credit hours for time on the job. Students placed with a store as part of a course in retailing business may be interested in permanent placement in the future.

The community may have a program for retirees looking for part-time work. Senior citizens often make excellent employees. The sport manager should network with friends and coworkers for potential candidates.

One of the best ways to advertise a job opening is to post a notice on the store door or prominently within the store. Customers who have shown an interest in the store and its merchandise may know someone who would like to work in the store. However, Gibbs (2012), Rabolt and Miler (2008), and Reese (2012) say to avoid broadcasting the organization is short-staffed or that an employee just quit and, out of respect for the current staff, do not post an hourly wage on the job opening notice. This is a matter that can be discussed with applicants later or mentioned in a memo attached to the application form. Also including a job description and the hours required in this memo will help applicants understand what type of experience and availability are necessary for the position.

Job Sharing

Gibbs (2012) and Reese (2012) suggest considering having employees job share all specialized job functions such as bookkeeping, stocking, and managing the store. The store and the employees will benefit from this flexible arrangement and essential store responsibilities will not come to a halt if someone is ill or on vacation. Staff members will have someone to share the workload while parents can enjoy being home when children return from school or if a child is sent home ill from school. Usually those sharing a job build a close rapport, developing their own division of tasks, and even setting their own schedule.

Typical Payroll Costs

The following are the typical payroll costs associated with retail operations and food and/or beverage concessions (SportsBusiness Research, 2012):

Concession Stand Workers	8-12% of concession sales
Food and Beverage Vendors	15-20% of vending sales

Catering/Restaurant Workers   18-30% of catering/restaurant sales
Sports Souvenir Vendors   12-17% of sports souvenir sales

Financial Risk Management

An adverse event that is planned, or unplanned, can potentially impact an organization, operation, process, or project. It is usually defined, in negative terms, as an outcome. If a risk has a positive outcome, it will be an opportunity. However, if it has a negative outcome, it will be a problem or loss.

If the activity is planned (i.e., defined, analyzed, and controlled), countermeasures can then be in place before the risk materializes. If unplanned, the risk can result from minor consequences to severe catastrophes. The probability of outcome is part of the analysis as well as the financial impact.

Bonding

Roncevich and Primm (2011) indicate bonding is an insurance agreement guaranteeing repayment for financial loss caused to the covered organization by the act or failure to act of a third person. Bonding is used to protect the financial operations of organizations. For purposes of the sporting enterprises, bonding is intended to protect the organization from losses caused by acts of fraud or dishonesty by officers, employees, or other representatives.

To Catch a Thief

Shrinkage (theft) happens to retailers, large and small. According to Christman and Sennewald (2006) and Richards and Giljazova (2011), there are the top five ways of minimizing the damage:

- **Lock it up.** Sounds obvious, but often at the end of the day, every item must be stored securely away behind a gate or glass.

- **Play traffic cop.** Positioning the employee store in a high-traffic area not only encourages impulse shopping, it also discourages sticky fingers.

- **Watch who cleans up** after the employee store closes.

- **Encourage employees.** Establish an incentive program for employees that financially rewards them for low shrinkage.

- **Keep an eye on the future.** Technology is constantly changing in both equipment and in security. For those willing to make an investment, new practices similar to ink tags and computer chips can help prevent merchandise from leaving the store.

Ticket Sales and Box Office Operations

For sport organizations that depend on fan participation to generate revenue, the box office becomes a vital operation. If the box/ticket office is not operated efficiently and effectively, it could cause a serious financial dilemma for the organization. The box office is also the point of entry for your new and older reliable fans. The impression the ticket personnel leave with the customer is like a first impression at a job interview. Return purchases by fans can and will be influenced by the box office staff.

The Importance of Ticket Sales or Memberships

Reese (2012) suggests the importance of ticket sales varies greatly from one professional league to another and from one collegiate division to another (i.e., Division I-A to Division III). The media-rich NFL (i.e., long-term contracts with ABC, Fox, NBC, ESPN, and TNT) is the only professional league for which ticket sales is not the most prominent revenue source. Washo (2010) indicates the amount of ticket revenue generated by sport organizations is dependent on two interrelated factors: the number of tickets sold and the unit cost of each ticket sold. The mission of the sport manager relating to ticket sales is to determine the optimal ticket prices that will maximize total cash flow per seat (i.e., general admission, club or premium seats, and luxury box seats). Pricing, in the past, has been based on the best, informed guesses of management. In the future, a successful sport manager must establish ticket prices based on market research, which provides an understanding of sport consumers' expected price threshold or their willingness to pay. The manager must be knowledgeable about marketing techniques and strategies to effectively sell the product(s) to the general public.

While the mission of managers in club settings (i.e., golf, racquet, health and fitness, and multi-sport) focuses on developing optimal membership programs, selling and retaining memberships is the lifeblood of the sport club sector. The key challenge facing sport club managers is to sustain membership levels in the face of growing competition such as watching television, including cable and satellite, Internet access, renting a video tape or DVD, rent a PlayStation 2 cartridge, attending a movie, purchasing a CD, going out to dinner, attending a rock concert or Broadway play, or going to your child's sporting or other event. In the future, sport club performance will be based on how effectively clubs recruit and retain members as well as their ability to maximize income return from each member.

The challenges of selling tickets to sporting events for the athletic director at any level or president of a professional sport enterprise are very similar to those faced by the sport club manager mentioned above. Both groups of managers must sell their products to the general public more effectively than the competitors. Further, they must retain the customer from year to year or event to event, in order to be successful.

The Product of a Box Office

The primary product of the box office is the ticket. According to Reese (2012) and Washo (2010), when selecting a ticket and the method by which the ticket will be sold, there are a number of factors to consider, including the physical characteristics of the facility, seating plans, ticket system, ticketing software (e.g., BOCS, Data Factors, Haven Systems, Folio Box Office Management, Nortech Software, Smart Box Office, Software4Sport, and Tickets.com), outsourcing ticketing (e.g., TicketMaster, TicketWeb, 800BuyTickets), online ticketing, pricing structure, credit card service, group sales, discounted prices, advanced sales, and sales incentive plans utilized.

The ticket is a product. It is a souvenir for the patron. It can also be used to notify patrons of dangers by the inclusion of a warning on the backside of the ticket. Further, the backside of the ticket could include a safe harmless clause with the warning. This alerts the patrons to known dangers (i.e., when purchasing a ticket for a hockey contest, it could warn patrons seated in rows 10 and higher of the possibility of being hit by a puck).

Printing of Tickets

Tickets can either be purchased from an outside organization or printed internally in the ticket office through a computerized system. General admission tickets are easily controlled and can be purchased at any print shop, office supply, Walmart, or K-Mart.

Reserved tickets are more complicated. If the box office is not computerized, tickets must then be purchased for every seat for each event. If the tickets are not sold, the remaining tickets must be destroyed. If there are 10,000 seats in the sporting facility and there are 15 home games, the box office then needs to store 150,000 tickets for the season. The tickets need to be stored by each event and seat. This requires a large area and a number of cabinets with appropriate shelving to secure the tickets. Once tickets are received from the printer, they all need to be checked and inventoried. The tickets sold must be checked off the master-seating chart to avoid duplicating sales. This system is labor intensive, costly, time-consuming, and exposing the box office to seating errors.

In a computerized box office, there is no need for ticket storage and purchase of tickets from an outside vendor. The computer will generate the tickets and automatically record the sale. The manager will need to purchase ticket stock on a regular basis. Internal printing also enables the ticket manager to control how many tickets are printed for each event. This reduces waste and the need for storage space. Further, the computer will allow the box office personnel to print complete season-ticket packages with mailing labels. The tickets are separated for each season order, placed into envelopes for mailing, and mailing labels are attached. Printing tickets internally and in packages is preferable for the organization than affording a computerized system. Many organizations cannot afford this cost and continue to use the manual reserved system or sell all seats as general admission.

Finally, one of the biggest problems for sport managers is a counterfeit ticket. The manager needs to consider the best method for reducing or preventing counterfeiting. Including the any of the following within a ticket design can do this: bar codes, computer chips, watermarks, or holograms.

Types of Tickets

Typically, sport organizations use one or more of the following types: reserved, general admission, season ticket, mini-season plans, individual event, complimentary, student, or rain check. What tickets are available depends on the organization (e.g., interscholastic, intercollegiate, or professional sports). The larger more established organizations will offer all types of tickets.

The season ticket provides a guaranteed source of income before the season starts and does not depend on variable factors including weather, quality of opponents, or team record. The season ticket involves the sale of a particular seat and location in the stadium or arena for an entire season for a one-time fee.

The mini-season plans allow fans to purchase tickets for a portion of the season. These plans offer a lower financial commitment to individual game ticket holders who wish to become more active fans but are not ready to purchase season tickets. The plans are designed to encourage individual event purchasers to move up to a multi-plan with hopes of making them season-ticket holders.

Individual tickets are tickets that are available for walk-in purchases the day of the event. The purchasers are generally in town for a convention, a business meeting, or visiting friends or relatives and want to experience a game.

Complimentary tickets (comps) are those given to individuals (e.g., visiting dignitary, politician, local hero, donor, key clients, family and friends of players and coaches, etc.) or groups (e.g., Boy Scouts, Girl Scouts, youth sport teams, elementary school teams, etc.). There are two key strategies behind complimentary tickets (a) to increase crowd size and (b) the organization hopes the "free" experience will be so positive that fans will want to return as paying customers.

Universities and colleges generally allocate seats for students. These tickets are often discounted, but not always. Many institutions require students to pick up their tickets early to control crowd size and to allow the athletic department to sell unclaimed student tickets.

Rain checks are tickets given to patrons when an event is canceled due to weather or other reasons. The patron can return to the next event without paying an admission fee. Some organizations require the patrons to notify the box office one week prior to the event to control crowd size and to determine what additional tickets can be sold.

The Event

Before an event goes on sale, the ticket manager gathers important information about the venue, the organization, and the event itself and provides this information to all points of sale including individuals selling tickets on consignment. The ticket manager should be familiar with all aspects of the event that affect the patron. The ticket manager should visit the venue ahead of time, sit in different locations in the house, attend a rehearsal or performance, and be ready to offer feedback on the event based on first-hand experience.

Event Information

You will need to give the following information, as noted by Reese (2012), Schneider and Ford (1999), Washo (2010), to box office managers and ticket outlets so that they are able to answer patron inquiries:

- Information obtained from the producer.

- A description of the event including featured performers.

- Number and length of intermission(s).

- Will any of the performances be ASL (American Sign Language) interpreted?

- Instructions for writing checks.

When running an independent ticket operation, checks should probably be written to the producing organization. When selling tickets through an established box office or ticket outlet, they will provide the following instructions to the patron (Reese, 2012; Schneider & Ford, 1999; Washo, 2010):

- Your organization's tax ID number.

- Any information regarding connected events such as a black tie opening, pre or post event receptions, or lectures.

- Websites with information about the event or producing organization.

  - A statement from the producer regarding the suitability of the event for children.

  - Description of the event. At the point of sale, the ticket seller may be asked to volunteer information about the performance or the performing group to aid the patron in their decision-making process.

  - Information obtained from the representative of the venue.

- Directions to the venue both by car and public transportation.

- Parking options.

  - Information for patrons in wheelchairs regarding parking, access to building, the house, the box office, restrooms, and location of wheelchair seating in the house.

- Is there a TTY phone line at the box office? Does the venue have assisted listening devices?

- The seating capacity and seating chart of the house. When using an established box office, it may already have this information.

- Websites with information about the venue.

- Information obtained from the stage manager.

  - An estimated running time for the event.

Setting Policies and Parameters

The following guidelines offered by Schneider and Ford (1999) and Washo (2010) should be established in consultation with the producer, ideally two months in advance of the event.

Seating configuration. General admission (unreserved) tickets are easier to sell and account for. They also make house management simpler. Remember to inform patrons that seating is on a first-come, first-served basis.

Reserved seating is used in special circumstances. It restricts seating options for patrons and house management, requires more work for the box office and usher staff working the event, and often delays the start time of an event.

Discounting ticket prices. Discounting tickets for special groups of people (e.g., students, seniors, disabled, etc.) can assist in filling the house and provide a nice community service. The discounted tickets can be used as a means of penetration marketing into a new customer base or to fill seats that may not be filled for the event. It is important for the manager to determine what number of individuals constitutes a "group". Further, it is important to decide prior to the season whether or not there will be discounted preseason games for all patrons.

It is the producer's responsibility to consider both the positive and negative impact of any special offers on the overall event budget. Special deals should be geared toward people who would not otherwise attend the event and for performances that would otherwise be undersold.

On sale date. Tickets for undergraduate events generally go on sale one month before the event. Do not publicize or advertise an event before tickets are on sale. If necessary, the On Sale Date should be included in press releases, brochures, and "save the date" postcards.

Tickets to be held. Before tickets are on sale to the public, the ticket manager and producer should discuss how many and which tickets should be withheld from sale. This is a good time to determine the best and worst places to sit. If an event is reserved seating, sit in several different seats to determine what the view of the stage is like from different sections of the house. Reasons for holding tickets include the following (Reese, 2012; Washo, 2010):

- *House seats/trouble seats.* These are seats that are kept off-line for last-minute problems. The house manager may need to use these seats if an error leads to a show being oversold or, in a reserved seating house, a seat being "double sold." They may also be needed if there is damage or a spill that makes another seat in the house unusable. House seats are also kept available so that the producer can accommodate last-minute ticket requests from VIPs.

- *Usher seats.* Consult with the house manager on how many and which seats need to be held for ushers.

- *Obstructed seats.* The placement of lighting and sound equipment or the need for cameras and other video equipment in the house often necessitates removing seats from the capacity because the equipment is placed in the seating area. These decisions need to be made early so that the appropriate number of tickets can be pulled. In the case of a reserved seating house, the exact placement of such equipment must be established before a show can go on sale.

- *Obstructed view seats.* Some seats may offer particularly bad sight lines to the stage or have views that are obstructed by architectural elements or production equipment. The producer and ticket manager should use discretion in deciding whether to pull these seats or to sell them at a reduced price. Patrons must be informed by the ticket seller and by the text on the ticket that they are purchasing an obstructed view seat.

- *Seats required for performers.* A performer may need a seat if s/he is being "planted" in the house. Events with multiple performing groups may allow performers to sit in the audience for part of the performance.

- *VIP seats.* A producer will often decide to make complimentary tickets available to performers, production crew and VIPs such as college staff and faculty, donors, and other special guests. The ticket manager should have a list of such individuals. The producer and ticket manager should be very selective in offering complimentary tickets. If you offer someone a free ticket to one event, they are likely to expect free tickets to your next event. Set a policy as to when unclaimed complimentary tickets will be released for sale. Inform all recipients that their tickets will be released at the door for sale if these tickets are not picked up 30 minutes prior to the advertised start time.

VIPs should be given a special invitation by the producer and asked to RSVP. The ticket manager can develop a list of VIPs for whom tickets should be held ahead of time and submit it to the box office. Producers and ticket managers may offer performers and production crew a certain number of complimentary tickets. Since the core audience for most student shows is comprised of friends and family of the performers and production crew, be aware that a generous complimentary ticket policy will diminish your primary income source.

It is recommended that you create and use a complimentary ticket voucher that cannot be easily duplicated for cast and crew. Complimentary ticket vouchers simplify the process of complimentary ticket distribution for the ticket manager especially for multi-performance events. Complimentary tickets for cast and crew are usually offered on an "as-available" basis, unlike VIP seats, which are actually pulled from the pool of tickets put on sale.

- *Latecomer seats.* Think about latecomers before you put tickets on sale. If you decide that it is unsafe or impractical to admit latecomers at all, you need to include a "no latecomer policy" in your advertising and press releases. If you decide that latecomers can be admitted only to a particular area of the house, you'll need to pull those seats before an event goes on sale.
- *Waiting line policy.* When an event sells out, the ticket sellers should inform the patrons that a waiting line will be established at the door. It is not recommended to start a waiting list either by phone or for friends who did not buy a ticket in time. A clearly established policy set ahead of time should clarify when and where the waiting line will begin and at what time tickets will be released. It should be well marked and be out of the way so that it does not interfere with other patron traffic. If tickets can be released, start releasing them at fifteen minutes before curtain.

Schneider and Ford (1999) and Washo (2010) suggest that people in the waiting line may be admitted only if

- complimentary tickets are unclaimed,
- unpaid reservations are unclaimed,
- standing room is available, and
- the producer and house manager decide to release house seats.

Preparing the Box Office for an Event

For each event, there is a beginning and an end. The beginning commences after the event is scheduled and the tickets are offered for sale. The ending is after the books are closed and all sales are finished. The length of an events promotion depends on the promoter. It could be as few as two weeks or as long as six weeks.

Pre-event preparations. Each ticket seller is assigned a specific number of tickets and a small bank in order to make change. The seller confirms the number of tickets and the amount of money in the bank by signing the section of the ticket sellers audit sheet. Each organization has a different set of audit or reconciliation forms as directed by the organization's controller.

During the event. There should be a will-call window for spectators to pick up prepaid tickets, complimentary tickets, press passes, and tickets being held for someone. The ticket seller at this window will not have separate tickets to be sold or a bank. The seller should have a list with the names of the people assigned to the tickets. Once a person identifies him or herself with appropriate identification, tickets should be signed for on the master sheet. Finally, this seller would also be the troubleshooter to assist other ticket sellers with questions or complaints.

Post event. At the conclusion of the event, the ticket sellers will reconcile their banks and cash, checks, and credit card receipts received for the tickets they were assigned. The head ticket seller will verify everything is in order before allowing the ticket seller to leave. The head ticket seller will prepare a final event sales report and deposit the cash, checks, and credit card receipts in the bank. The final event report will include the total number of tickets sold, number of complimentary tickets provided, number of press passes provided, number of season patrons attending, total amount of income received, and the total number of people in the audience paid and non-paid.

The head ticket taker will confirm with the head ticket seller the total number of patrons present at the event. The ticket takers will collect the tickets and count all those that were collected or scan them into a small computer. If tickets are collected, they should be torn in half with half being retained by the patron (as a souvenir). If the ticket is scanned, the entire ticket can be given to the patron.

Box Office Design

The box office is the initial contact office for most patrons. Sales windows should be located on all sides of the facility and a drive up window should also be considered for customer convenience. The box office manager can decide which window areas should be open on a daily and event basis.

This space should be easily accessible to all patrons. It must be compliant with the Americans with Disabilities Act (ADA) sections dealing especially with facility accessibility.

Schneider and Ford (1999), Washo (2010), and Reese (2012) suggest the main box office space should be large enough to accommodate such areas as office spaces for personnel, sales windows (at least 10) for walk-in traffic and a drive up facility, storage area for office supplies and ticket paper stock, a small conference room, and rest rooms. The smaller sales areas should have a minimum of six windows for sales and "will-call" tickets. These spaces should be protected from the elements and have a depth of at least 15 feet. All smaller auxiliary ticket sales areas should be facing the outside of the facility. The main ticket area should have inside and outside windows. The windows should be shatter proof. Computers to all sites should be networked to each other and to the main office computer. The tickets spaces should have environmental controls and telephone communication. The main office should have a safe built into the wall to store funds safely.

References

Bearman v. University of Notre Dame, 453 NE2d 1196, Ind: Court of Appeals, 3rd, September 22, 1983.

Cameron, A. (2012). *How to start a vending business.* New York: CreateSpace.

Christman, J. H., & Sennewald, C. A. (2006). *Shoplighting: Managing the problem.* Alexandria, VA: ASIS International.

Fisher, M. (2010). *The new science of retailing: How analytics are transforming the supply chain and improving performance.* Cambridge, MA: Harvard Business Review Press.

Gibbs, R. J. (2012). *Principles of urban retail planning and development.* Hoboken, NJ: John Wiley and Sons.

Kramer, A. (2008). *Retail development handbook.* Washington, DC: Urban Land Institute.

Mazzola, J. O. (2010). *Vending machine book: How to start a vending machine business: A real business with over a 100-year track record.* New York: CreateSpace.

Mazzola, J. O. (2011). *Vending machines: The complete business book.* New York: CreateSpace.

Lewis, R., & Dart, M. (2010). *The new rules of retail: Competing in the world's toughest marketplace.* New York: Palgrave McMillian.

Rabolt, N. J. & Miler, J. K. (2008). *Concepts and cases in retail and merchandise management.* New York: Fairchild Publishing.

Reese, J. (2012). *Ticket operations and sales management.* Morgantown, WV: Fitness Information Technology

Richards, R., & Giljazova, A. (2011). *The most effective shopping reduction strategies.* Amazon Digital Services.

Roncevich, T., & Primm, S. (2011). *Vending machine business.* New York: CreateSpace.

Schneider, R. E., & Ford, M.J. (1999). *Theater management handbook.* Cincinnati, OH: Better Way Books.

SportsBusiness Research. (2012). Retrieved from http://www.sbrnet.com

Tomasso, C. (2012). *Vending business 101: What you should know before getting into full line vending.* New York: CreateSpace.

Washo, M. (2010). *Break into sports: Through ticket sales.* Gaithersburg, MD: MMW Marketing

http://www.NAConline.org

http://www.nacc-online.com

http://www.oaba.org

CHAPTER 15

Sales, Sponsorships, and Licensing Principles

Thomas H. Sawyer
Professor Emeritus, Indiana State University

Julie Ann Hypes
Morehead State University

Introduction

Sales are the lifeblood of any organization as well as sport entities. Sport entities sell advertising, club seats, luxury suites, merchandise, media rights, signage, and sponsorships. The word *sales* or the term *salesperson* often equates to images of hucksters, who are people who use persuasion to talk customers into buying products they might not want at prices they sometimes cannot afford.

Sales generate the revenue streams to keep the doors open and the sport entity profitable. The components of sales include salesperson, sales department, sales-oriented organization structure, telemarketing, direct mail, personal selling, customer retention, and lifetime value.

Over the past two decades, the amount of money spent on sport and special-event sponsorships has grown in number and dollars dramatically. Sponsorships include a wide variety of activities associated with communications process that is designed to use sport and lifestyle marketing to send messages to a targeted audience.

Licensed products are those items of clothing or other products bearing the name or logo of a popular sport organization. The value of licensing to a sport organization has grown by leaps and bounds. It has become a significant revenue stream for most sport organizations.

This chapter has been designed to assist the prospective sport manager in understanding the importance of sales, sponsorships, and licensed products to the sport entity. Further, it will provide an introduction to each of these very significant revenue streams for most sport organizations. Finally, the reader will begin to understand the impact and relationship of these three linked marketing tools.

What are Sales?

The simple definition of sales is it is the revenue-producing element of the marketing process. Battersby and Simon (2012), and Shank (2013) suggest there are four components of selling: (1) identifying potential customers; (2) linking the potential customer to the product being sold; (3) increasing the customer's awareness and interest in the product, program, or service; and (4) persuading the customer to act on that interest or desire to purchase the product. Sales do not end with the purchase of the product by the customer. It is the beginning of a relationship which opens the door to retaining the customer for future purchases.

However, unlike food, clothing, and shelter, sport is not a necessity of life. It is a want rather than a need. It requires the customer to spend discretionary income which is reduced as the economy declines and inflation increases. As such, value is more important than price. Yet, unlike the majority of purchases consumers make, sport purchases ask them to invest their time, money, and emotion. Knowing this, when developing a sales plan the developers should consider defining what value the customer is receiving in exchange for their investment. The sales plan should not just be about being the low-cost provider but about being the best value no matter how expensive the product.

What Makes a Good Salesperson?

A good salesperson is a person who has the following common traits: good listening skills, is comfortable speaking to people, an attitude to succeed, is user-friendly, has a competitive spirit, enjoys people, maintains a good sense of humor, and has common sense. A good salesperson has qualities such as belief in the product, a belief in him- or herself, a willingness to knock on old doors, asking anyone and everyone to buy, following up after the sale, and seeing a large number of customers. Finally, the successful salesperson not only sells a product but builds a relationship with the customer for future sales.

What are the Key Elements of a Successful Sales-Oriented Organizational Structure?

There are eight accepted elements in determining the overall success and impact of the sales department. Fetchko, Roy, and Clow (2012), Irwin, Sutton, & McCarthy (2008), and Shank (2013), suggests these elements are the reporting structure, the relationships between the various departments within the organization, the organizational philosophy, the sales development process, the composition of the sales force, the strengths and weaknesses of the sales team or its individual members, the training of the sales staff, the sales staff have the resources it needs to accomplish the established goals, and the compensation mix (incentive structure) for the sales staff.

What are the Items Commonly Known to be Sport Products?

Over the past two decades, sport inventories have changed dramatically and continue to evolve as time passes. Fetchko et al. (2012); Mullin, Hardy, and Sutton (2014); and Shank (2008) suggest the inventories include the following:

- Concessions (e.g., beverage rights, beer rights, standard food concessions, premium food concessions, premium restaurants)

- Community programs (e.g., awards, banquets, camps, clinics, golf tournaments, kick-off luncheons and dinners, school assemblies)

- Electronic (e.g., broadcast [radio and television], e-newsletter, Web-page)

- Hospitality (e.g., parties, special events, stadium/arena clubs)

- Merchandise (e.g., licensed goods and products)

- Naming rights (e.g., arena, stadium, practice facility, team office complex)

- Parking (e.g., general parking, VIP parking, luxury car parking lots, car services [e.g., detailing, waxing, wash only])

- Print (e.g., game programs, media guide, newsletter, roster sheets, scorecards, ticket backs, ticket envelopes)

- Promotions (e.g., contests, Diamond Vision™, on-floor promotions, pre/postgame entertainment, premium items)

- Signage (e.g., blimps, boards [i.e., dasher, matrix, message, score], concourse, floor/field/ice, LED signage, marquees, medallions, turnstiles)

- Tickets (e.g., advance sales [charitable, outlet, phone, telemarketing, and volunteers] [20%], club seats [2%], community promotional tickets and family packages [2%], group [20%], PSLs, season [i.e., full or partial plans][50%], suites [1%], and walk-up and day-of-game sales [5%])

  - Assets related to ticket sales (e.g., ball boy/ball girl opportunities, clinics, court/ice/field time, fan tunnels and high-five lines)

- Miscellaneous (e.g., fantasy camps, off-season cruises and trips with players, road trips)

What is Telemarketing?

Telemarketing is a marketing approach that utilizes telecommunications technology as part of a planned, organized, and managed marketing program. This approach can be one- or two-dimensional. The one-dimensional approach is handling inbound calls from customers inquiring as a response to advertisements, catalogs, promotional campaigns, or other sources. While the two-dimensional approach is an outward-oriented approach to prospecting, among cold, warm, or hot prospects, following up leads, or soliciting existing customers for repeat or expanded business volume. Most authorities suggest telemarketing offers considerable possibilities for enhancing the productivity of the sales force by permitting more specification by account type and better focus on high-yield accounts. Finally, it is valuable in terms of sales support (e.g., checking the status of the customer, conducting surveys, providing customer service, and scheduling sales calls and deliveries).

What is Direct Mail?

Direct mail is another form of direct marketing. It is characterized as being flexible, measurable, personal, targeted, and testable. According to Battersby and Simon (2012), Fortunato (2013), and Sims (2011), the advantages are that the message can (a) appeal to certain groups of consumers that are measurable, reachable, and sizable enough to ensure meaningful sales volume; (b) be personalized; (c) be measured for effectiveness; (d) be tested for offers, formats, prices, and terms; and (e) be flexible (e.g., color, format, shape, size, and timing).

What is Personal Selling?

Battersby and Simon (2012) and Sims (2011) indicate personal selling is a technique or art of convincing a customer to purchase a product through face-to-face selling. Personal selling is just that—personal, one-on-one—It is more effective than telemarketing or direct mail; but, it is much more expensive. Even though is it more costly than telemarketing or direct mail, personal selling can be more precise, enabling marketers to closely target the most promising sales prospects. Finally, developing and maintaining a strong sales force can be the most expensive part of the sales department. However, the return on investment in the sales force may be well worth the cost.

Personal selling is the delivery of a specially designed message to a prospect by a seller, usually in the form of face-to-face communication, personal correspondence, or a personal telephone conversation. Unlike advertising, a personal sales message can be more specifically targeted to individual prospects and easily altered if the desired behavior does not occur. Personal selling, however, is far more costly than advertising and is generally used only when its high expenditure can be justified. For example, the marketing of a sophisticated computer system may require the use of personal selling, while the introduction of a new product to millions of consumers would not. Two other forms of personal selling that are not used with high-end products are door-to-door selling and home demonstration parties. These two personal selling methods are primarily used for personal care products, cosmetics, cookware, encyclopedias, books, toys, food, and other items of special interest to homemakers. Ideally, personal selling should be supported by advertising to strengthen its impact.

Consumer Behavior

Managers need to know and understand what motivates consumers to buy certain products/services. According to Fetchko et al. (2012), consumers prefer to patronize stores where they perceive they are maximizing money, service, and product benefits while minimizing risks as perceived in terms of the product price, acceptability of the product/service offerings, and required time and effort to purchase. Patterns should be researched and analyzed in when people buy, how people buy, and who does the buying.

Managers should be able to answer questions about when people buy products/services (the season, day of the week, and time of day). If seasonal buying patterns exist, the manager should try to extend the buying season. Promotional programs will often smooth out the seasonal fluctuations. When people buy influences the planning, pricing, and promotional phases of an organization's marketing program.

Fetchko et al. (2012) and Irwin et al. (2008) suggest an organization should consider two factors with respect to where people buy: (1) Where is the buying decision is made? (2) Where does the actual purchase occur? The organization's promotion program must be focused to carry the greatest impact at the place where the buying decision is made. If the decision to buy is made in the club, then attention must be devoted to packaging and other point-of-purchase display materials. If the primary decision to buy is made at home, a substantial promotional effort must be devoted to such advertising media as newspapers, magazines, radio, and television.

The *how* part of consumer buying habits includes several areas of behavior. Some people are highly price conscious and will select only the lowest priced item regardless of brand. Others will buy the lowest priced product as long as it is a known brand, while others willingly pay a higher price to get the service they desire, and still others believe you get what you pay for.

Who does the family purchasing is three-fold. First the manager must understand who actually makes the physical purchase. Second, the manager must understand who makes the purchase decision. Third, the manager must understand who uses the product being purchased. Understanding each of these will allow the manager to develop a marketing plan that will identify the most effective channels of distribution and promotion.

What is the Customer's Lifetime Value?

The customer's lifetime value is defined as the present value of expected benefits (gross margin) minus the burdens (direct cost of servicing and communicating) associated with the customer. It should be obvious that customers have different value levels to an organization depending on the amount of revenue the customer contributes, the costs of the serving the customer, and the estimated length of time they are projected to be with the organization. For example, a season ticket holder of four club seats is of much more valuable to the organization then the day-of-game and walk-up customers.

What is Customer Retention?

Retaining current customers is the key to success. Customer retention minimizes the number of new sales that must talk place to be profitable and establish a stable base that can help attract new customers through referrals. Finally, customer retention maximizes the customer's lifetime value to the organization.

The following, as suggested by Fetchko et al. (2012), Irwin et al. (2008), Mullin et al. (2014), and Shank (2013), are the factors that affect the retention of ticket-plan purchasers:

- Customer service
    - Feeling valued by the organization
    - Appreciated by the organization
    - Quality of customer information
    - Problem resolution
    - Ease of problem resolution
- Performance of the team
- Satisfaction with seat location
- Demand for tickets in the marketplace
- Satisfaction with beverage and food concessions
- Satisfaction with merchandise and souvenirs
- Enjoyment in attending the games
    - Game programs
- Satisfaction with the price/value relationship of the purchase
    - Ease of use of the benefits and amenities included in their purchase
- Convenience factors relating to attending in person
    - Ease of parking
    - Expense of parking

Promotional Licensing

Promotional licensing is the umbrella term that encompasses sponsorship, while sponsorships is the acquisition of rights to affiliate or directly associate with a product or event for the purpose of deriving benefits related to that affiliation or association. Sponsorship programs are one element of promotional strategies; but, it can affect the entire marketing mix.

There are five basic reasons suggested by Fetchko et al. (2012), Mullin et al. (2007), and Shank (2008) for an organization to become a sponsor: (1) to demonstrate good citizenship, (2) to increase sales, (3) to generate positive visibility for the sponsoring organization, (4) to generate positive media interest and publicity, and (5) to meet competition threats. Before contacting potential sponsors, the marketer must develop a sponsorship proposal. This proposal will provide the sponsor with information on exactly what they will receive for their sponsorship investment.

Nearly four decades ago, the business world discovered the best vehicle to reach a new customer base and expand their previous markets. That vehicle was sports. Once the public and sport governing bodies accepted the commercialization of sport promotional licensing and sponsorships, agreements began to skyrocket.

The sponsor uses the business relationship to achieve its promotional objectives or to facilitate and support its broader marketing objectives. The rights derived from this relationship may include entitlements, hospitality, purchase of media time, and retail opportunities.

Sponsorship

A sponsorship is when a company or organization pays a promoter or organization a fee for the right to associate itself and its products with an event. Sponsorships come in all sizes and shapes as companies and organizations look to achieve vastly different objectives within their sponsorship budgets.

Benefits of a Sponsorship to a Sponsor

Fortunato (2013), Irwin et al. (2008), and Sims (2011) suggest that for a sponsor, an event can do the following:

- Create positive publicity
- Heighten visibility
- Set sponsor apart from its competition
- Complement other marketing programs
- Enhance image
- Drive sales
- Shape customer attitudes
- Improve customer relations
- Sell or sample products/services directly
- Drive traffic
- Increase employee morale/quality of life
- Contribute to community economic development
- Combat larger advertising budgets of competitors
- Promote image of sponsor as a good corporate citizen
- Reach specifically targeted markets

Fortunato (2013) and Sims (2011) and suggest there are three key benefits to a sport sponsorship including exclusivity, heightened communication, and publicity. By marketing through sport, a corporation attempts to reach target consumers through their lifestyles. Corporations are sold on marketing through sport and spend a great deal of energy doing serious research and strategic planning before investing large sums of dollars in purchasing a sponsorship.

Further, there are additional benefits, for example, including product exclusivity, 30-second commercial spots, on-premises signage, tickets to each session, hotel accommodations, free or reduced parking, VIP parking, invitations to all social activities, point-of-sale displays, on-site promotion, name and logo on materials produced, radio spots, player appearances, and an ad in the event program.

A word of caution regarding sponsorships: Be careful about what benefits are provided for each type of sponsorship and make sure that the price for a sponsorship is high enough to cover all sponsor benefits as well as provide for a nice margin of profit for the event. Finally, make sure the contract is clear to all parties.

A Typical Sponsorship Package

Fortunato (2013), Sims (2011), and Skildum-Reid (2012) indicate a sponsorship package includes, but, is not limited to the following:

- exclusivity

- television

- signage

- entertainment

- display/merchandise

- promotions/public relations

- advertising

- sponsor benefits

- cost

- term of contract

- option to renew

Levels of Sponsorship

There are commonly four types of sponsorships offered. They are title (primary or exclusive) sponsor, presenting (secondary) sponsor, media sponsor, and official product sponsor. There is another category called associate, partner, or other levels. The title sponsor is the lead sponsor of the event.

The presenting sponsor is the second biggest sponsor of the event. This sponsorship costs less and proportionately fewer sponsor benefits are provided. The third type of sponsorship is official product sponsors. This category has the greatest opportunity for corporate clutter. For example, Coca-Cola (soda category), Verizon (telecommunications), UPS (shipping), Miller (beer), Ben & Jerry's (ice cream), Kodak (film), Wells Fargo (banking), etc. Too many sponsors can kill the golden goose. These sponsors receive approximately a third less than presenting sponsors, who receive about 25% less than the title sponsor (Mullin et al., 2014).

The media sponsors usually provide a predetermined amount of advertising support for the event. They may also provide some cash support and publicity. Finally, they may provide celebrities for the event. The committee should consider selecting three media sponsors including print, radio, and television.

Another sponsorship category includes associate, partner, and specialty sponsorships. An associate sponsorship might fall in between the title and presenting sponsors. A partner sponsorship might be at the title level with multiple title sponsors. Finally, a specialty sponsorship could be what is often found at golf tournaments such as hole sponsors, cart sponsors, and beverage/refreshment cart sponsors.

Competitive Threats to Be Concerned About

One objective of sponsorship is to meet competitive threats. Many corporate sponsors indicate that they are not interested in investing in sponsorship opportunities; however they cannot afford to pass them up. If they do not take the sponsorship opportunity, their competition will. A specific example of this competitive threat is the rivalry between Coke and Pepsi. These companies consistently battle for the competitive advantage in the sport market.

A sponsor can be harmed by competitors that use ambush marketing strategies. Ambush marketing is a planned effort by an organization to associate indirectly with an event to gain at least some of the recognition and benefits that are associated with being an official sponsor. The most effective method for event organizers to block out unauthorized advertising is to negotiate deals with stadium owners. These agreements allow organizers to fully control advertising on the premises. The organizer may also require that the stadium be renamed for the duration of the event.

Commercial Sponsorship

Fetchko et al. (2012), Mullin et al., (2014), and Sims (2011) indicate that commercial sponsorship is financial support in the form of cash, in-kind products, or services in exchange for exposure or recognition to an audience. It is the act of providing assistance, funding, goods, or services to an organization's event by an individual, agency, company, corporation, or other entity for a specific time in return for public recognition or advertising promotions. The goal of a commercial sponsorship is to meet the specific measurable goals of the entity or brand by building a link in the target audiences' minds between the sponsor and a valued organization or event. Table 15.1 outlines the top 10 sponsorship categories in major U.S. sports properties.

Table 15.1
Top 10 Sponsorship Categories in Major U.S. Sports Properties

- Credit cards
- Automobiles
- Wireless
- Beer
- Apparel
- Quick service restaurant
- Hotel/resort, soft drink, footwear, airline
- Sport drinks
- Snack
- Insurance, internet service, financial services

(SportsBusiness Research, 2012)

Types of Commercial Sponsorship

According to Sims (2011), there are two common types of commercial sponsorship: solicited and unsolicited. A solicited sponsorship is one that is sought by an entity for a specific event. The entity prepares a request for proposal indicating sponsorship availability, which is a formal solicitation. Once all proposals are reviewed, negotiations take place with the accepted sponsor.

An unsolicited sponsorship is one where the sponsor makes the first contact based on general knowledge, hearsay, or third-party reference as to the availability of an event and the opportunity to sponsor.

Commercial Sponsorship Options

Fetchko et al. (2013) and Sims (2011) suggest there are three common types of sponsorship options including direct financial support, direct in-kind support, and combination package of financial and in-kind support:

- Direct financial support—cash contribution
- Direct in-kind support—gift certificates, refreshments, prizes, sponsor product giveaways, transportation, uniforms, costumes, sports and leisure apparel, medals, and trophies.
- Combination package—cash contribution and in-kind contributions

Commercial Sponsorship Success

Selling sponsorships, according to Fetchko et al. (2013), is not a matter of buying a mailing list of potential buyers, writing a direct mail letter, putting together a "package," mailing everything out, and waiting for the telephone to ring with people offering you money. Before getting started, the organization must have a clear definition of sponsorship, such as a sponsorship is an investment, in cash or in kind, in return for access to exploitable business potential associated with an event or highly publicized entity.

Fetchko et al. (2013) indicates the keywords in this definition are "investment," "access to," and "exploitable." The first word, *investment,* means constantly looking at sponsorship as an investment opportunity, where there is a viable payback; no longer are you talking to someone about a payment of cash or money. Rather, use the word investment, which automatically implies that value will be returned to the investor. Second, *access to* means the ability to be associated with a particular offering (event, sport, festival, fair ... you name it). Lastly, *exploitable*, is a positive word that means "to take the greatest advantage of" the relationship. In other words, allowing the sponsor to make the greatest use of their investment and capitalize on their relationship.

With this definition in mind, the entity goes forward. There are 12 basic steps that will assure success in sponsorship endeavors. Fortunato (2013), Irwin et al. (2008), Mullin et al. (2014), Shank (2008), and Sims (2011) suggest they include the following:

Take inventory. The entity's event have value to the sponsor including (Shank, 2013):

- Radio, TV and print partners
- Retail outlet
- Collateral material ... posters, flyers, brochures
- Banners
- Tickets: quantity for giving to sponsor plus ticket backs for redemption
- VIP seating
- VIP parking
- Hospitality ... for the trade, for customers, for employees
- On-site banner exposure
- Booth
- Audio announcements
- Payroll stuffers
- Billboards
- Product sales/product displays
- Celebrity appearances/interviews
- Internet exposure

Develop media and retail partners. Next, approach media and retail partners.

They should be treated the same way as all other sponsors, with the same rights and benefits. Here is what is important to these two key partners.

Media. The entity's event offers the media an opportunity to increase their non-traditional revenue (NTR). The event has an audience, sampling opportunities, sales opportunities and multiple media exposure that the media people can offer to their own advertisers. Many times an advertiser asks for additional merchandising opportunities from the media. The event offers them that opportunity. The media can sell a sponsorship for the entity in return for the air time or print coverage.

Retail. A retail partner, such as a supermarket, drugstore, or fast food outlet, might offer some additional benefits that can be passed on to sponsors. And with a retail outlet, the entity can approach manufacturers and offer them some of these benefits. For example, once the entity has retail partners, the following opportunities exist (Fortunato, 2013; Sims, 2011; and Skildum-Reid, 2012):

- End cap or aisle displays

- Register tape promotions

- In-store displays

- Store audio announcements

- Inclusion in weekly flyers

- Weekly advertising

- Cross-promotion opportunities

- Bag stuffers

- Placemats (fast food outlets)

- Shopping bags

As with the media, treat the retail outlet as a paying sponsor. They are providing terrific benefits that can be passed on to your other sponsors, a tremendous value in attracting retail products. And, as with the media, have them provide you with documentation of their support … samples of bags, flyers, inserts, etc. In return, the organization will provide them with a post-event report, documenting the benefits they received and the value of those benefits.

Develop the sponsorship offerings. Now put together the various components of the sponsorship offerings to be prepared to offer valuable sponsorships. Do not use gold, silver, and bronze or use industry-specific terms the buyer might not understand. Simply have title, presenting, associate, product-specific, and event-specific categories. They are easy to understand and easy to sell. Of course, title is the most expensive and most effective. Think of the Volvo Tennis Classic or the Virginia Slims Tennis Classic. The minute the name of your event is "married" to the sponsor's name, the media have to give the whole title and provide the entity with great exposure for the title sponsor.

The first step in preparing for the initial sponsor contact is to prepare a one-page fact sheet that clearly and succinctly outlines the basics of the event (the who, what, where, when of the property) and highlights the various benefits of being associated with that event (radio, TV, print, on-site, etc.).

Research the sponsors. Learn about the potential sponsors. Get on the Internet, read the annual reports, do a data search on the company, use the Team Marketing Report sourcebook … find out what the companies are currently sponsoring, what their branding strategies are, what their business objectives are. Become an expert on the prospects. The more that is known about them the better prepared one will be for their questions and the easier it will be for to craft a sponsorship offering that meets their specific needs.

Do initial sponsor contact and secure the appointment. Pick up the telephone and try to reach the proper person. When the correct person is reached, do not launch right into a sales pitch. Rather, ask them several questions about their business that will indicate whether or not they are a viable sponsor for your project.

Be creative and make the sale. Once in front of the sponsor, be prepared. Demonstrate knowledge of their business by offering a sponsorship that meets their specific needs. Help them come up with a new and unique way to enhance their sponsorship beyond the event. For example, if it's a pet store, come up with a contest that involves the customers and their pets. Or devise a contest where people have to fill out an entry form to win something. Think about hospitality opportunities, such as rewards for leading salespeople, special customer rewards, incentives for the trade. Be prepared to offer these ideas, and more, to help the sponsor understand how this sponsorship offers him/her great benefit.

Keep the sponsor in the loop. Once the sales process is complete, keep the sponsor involved before and through the event. See if their public relations department will put out a press release on the organization's involvement. Show them collateral as it is being developed to make sure they are happy with their logo placement. Make sure they are kept up to date on new sponsors, new activities, whatever is happening. The more you involve them in the process the more involved they become.

Involve the sponsor in the event. Make sure the sponsor is involved in the event. Do not let a sponsor hand over a check and say, "Let me know what happens." The entity is doomed to failure. Get them to participate by being on site, walk around with them, discuss their various banner locations, the quality of the audience, the lines at their booth, whatever is appropriate to their participation.

Provide sponsors with a postevent report and renew for next year. Provide sponsors with complete documentation of their participation. This should include copies of all collateral material, affidavit of performance from your radio and TV partners, tear sheets, retail brochures, tickets, banners, press stories. This should all be included in a kit, with a written postevent report that lists the valuation of the various components, and presented to the sponsor with a certificate of appreciation for their participation.

Commercial Sponsorship Agreement Provisions

Fetchko et al. (2012), Fortunato (2013), Irwin et al. (2008), Mullin et al. (2014), Shank (2008), and Sims (2011) suggest commercial sponsorship agreements may include, but are not limited to, the following provisions and benefits (See Sample Sponsorship Agreement in the Appendices available in the student and faculty resource center at www.sagamorepub.com):

- The right to use a logo, a name, a trademark, and graphic representations signifying the purchaser's connection with the product or event.

- The right to use in advertising, promotion, publicity, or other communication activities employed by the purchaser.

- The right to media coverage –

  - Local

  - Regional

  - National

  - International

- The right to sponsorship status within a product or service category, such as the following:

  - Title sponsor

  - Major sponsor

  - Exclusivity

  - Established

  - Long-term involvement

  - Co-sponsor

  - In-kind supplier

  - Team

  - League

- The right of entitlement to the following:

- Event
  - League championship
  - Regional championship
  - National championship
  - Tournament
- Facility
  - Arena
  - Stadium
  - Team offices
- The naming rights to a facility.
- The right to use various designations or phrases in connection with the product, event, or facility such as official sponsor, official supplier, official product, or presented by.
- The right of service.
- The right to use the purchaser's product or service in conjunction with the event or facility.
- The right to conduct certain promotional activities.
- The right to conduct in-store promotions and create point-of-purchase displays.
- The right to preferred ticket packages.

The following are additional components, according to Fortunato (2013) and Sims (2011), of an agreement for sponsorship:

- identify the parties involved,
- term of the contract,
- description of the event,
- site,
- date,
- sponsor benefits,
- obligations of the sponsor,
- warranties,
- indemnity,
- insurance,
- assignment,
- waiver,
- employer/employee relationship,
- notices,
- confidential terms of the contract,
- governing law,
- severability,
- force majeure, and
- option for renewal.

What are the objectives commonly influencing the decision to enter in to a sport sponsorship agreement? According to the Fortunato (2013) and Sims (2011), the following are the objectives that most often influence the decision to enter into sport sponsorship agreements to:

- Increase public awareness

- Alter or reinforce public perception

- Involve the corporation with the community

- Identify the company with a particular target market

- Build connections among the various decision makers

- Generate media benefits

- Achieve corporate sales objectives

- Showcase unique product features, technologies, or advantages

- Create an advantage over competitors through association or exclusivity

- Gain unique opportunities in terms of hospitality and entertainment

- Secure entitlement

- Obtain naming rights of a facility or portions of a facility

Each objective(s) selected by a corporation should provide it with a return on investment that might be in a monetary form or a return on objective that should also be measured through the media (number of impressions) and the ability to exclude competitors.

Sponsorship Lists

It is important to carefully develop a prospective sponsorship list. The committee should start with a list of categories and companies that could be interested in sponsoring the event. Further, the committee needs to spend time researching the various companies. In developing the list, the following questions should be proposed for each prospective sponsor. Fortunato (2013) and Sims (2011) suggest those prospects that receive a "yes" to all probably would be the most likely to become involved:

- Does the prospective sponsor sell or operate in the event's host community?

- Does the prospective sponsor's history include past or present sponsorship? If so, what kind?

- Does the prospective sponsor advertise in the host community?

- Does the prospective sponsor maintain a high profile in the host community?

- Is the prospective sponsor's name mentioned with some frequency in the news media? (Is it mentioned for positive or negative reasons?)

- Does the prospective sponsor provide a commercial function that is customer-or client-driven?

- Is the prospective sponsor noted for the support of at least some altruistic or community betterment efforts?

The following is a sponsorship checklist outlined by Irwin et al. (2008), Sims (2011), and Fortunato (2013) for the event organizers:

- Seek sponsorships aggressively.

- Develop a sponsorship proposal.

- Design a marketing and sales strategy to sell the sponsorships.

- Determine the competition for sponsorships.

- Concentrate on building relationships.
- Determine the optimal number of sponsorships in each category developed.
- Research potential sponsors.
- Develop a plan for advertising and promotion that will add value to the sponsor's participation in the event.
- Make sure the final contract protects all parties.

Licensed Products

To understand this area of marketing, we must first understand the definition of licensed products and branded merchandise. Battersby and Simon (2012) explain that licensed products are those items of clothing or products bearing the name or logo of a popular collegiate or professional sport team. Branded merchandise includes products featuring the name of the manufacturer, most notably apparel. Sales of these items produce revenues in the billions of dollars worldwide.

Marketers contract with companies such as Nike, Reebok, Electronic Arts (EA), and Pinnacle to use a brand name, logo, symbol, or character. The brand name may be a sport franchise (college or professional) or a sporting event. These products are usually apparel such as team hats, shirts, jackets, or jerseys. Organizations transfer the right to use their names, marks, and logos to other companies so products may be produced. A licensing fee will be paid to the organization that owns the trademarked name and/or logo. A name and/or logo must be registered with the U. S. Patent and Trademark Office to be considered a trademark. Licensing enables schools and teams to generate brand recognition and interest while increasing revenues with little financial risk (See Sample Licensing Agreement, in the Appendices at available in the student and faculty resource center at www.sagamorepub.com).

Electronic and technology products are a growing portion of licensed merchandise sales. The NFL Films produces DVDs of extraordinary accomplishments of NFL teams. EA Sports dominates the sport games market with earned revenues in the billions (SportsBusiness Research, 2012). Cellular phone companies offer official fight song ring tones for as little as 99 cents.

A full-time licensing director is becoming more common in organizations. According to Battersby and Simon (2012), the following three items will determine the need and staff size for a licensing program: (1) market size, (2) number of products licensed, and (3) number of licensees.

References

Battersby, G. J., & Simon, D. (2012). Basics of licensing. Colorado Springs, CO: Kent Press.

Fetchko, M., Poy, D., & Clow, K. E. (2012). *Sports marketing.* Old Saddle River, NJ: Prentice-Hall/Pearson.

Fortunato, J. A. (2013). *Sports sponsorships: Principles and practices.* Jefferson, NC: McFarland Publishing.

Irwin, R. L., Sutton, W., & McCarthy, L. (2008) *Sports promotion and sales management.* Champaign, IL: Human Kinetics.

Mullin, S. D., Hardy, S., & Sutton, W. A. (2014). *Sport marketing* (4th ed.). Champaign, IL: Human Kinetics.

Shank, M. D. (2013). *Sports marketing: A strategic perspective* (5th ed.). Upper Saddle River, NJ: Prentice Hall/Pearson.

Sims, B. (2011). *Sports sponsorship: A professional's guide.* Plymouth, MI: Icon Publishing, Inc.

Skildum-Reid, K. (2012). *The corporate sponsorship toolkit.* Tempe NSW Australia: Freya Press.

SportsBusiness Research. (2012). Retrieved from http://www.sbrnet.com

CHAPTER 16

Fund-Raising Principles

Thomas H. Sawyer
Professor Emeritus, Indiana State University

Tonya L. Gimbert
Indiana State University

Introduction

All organizations have the need for additional funds beyond the normal revenue sources (i.e., membership fees, ticket sales, guarantees, postseason opportunities, radio and television contracts, concessions [food, merchandise, and parking], franchising, licensing agreements, sponsorships, etc.). There are, of course, many legitimate and logical reasons why additional funding is needed to support programs, such as program expansion, facility renewal or expansion, inflation, changing priorities, increase in unemployment with markets, and a decrease in the purchasing power of the consumers within the markets. Without successful fund-raising programs, exciting promotions, and an excellent public relations program, the organization could be forced to reduce or eliminate marginal programs and sport teams, layoff personnel, reduce hours of operation, or close facilities. Therefore, it is imperative for sport managers to develop strong programs in fund-raising and promotions. An effective, efficient, and successful fund-raising program will allow the organization to grow and prosper in today's very competitive financial environment. Fund-raising is the art of soliciting money for charitable organizations, schools, colleges/universities, political parties, and many other worthy projects and organizations. Many organizations define fund-raising as anything that increases revenue, including concessions, deferred giving, donations, grants, merchandising, licensing, promotions, and sponsorships.

Guidelines for a Fund-Raising Program

One of the biggest errors made by novices as well as experienced fund-raisers is to seek something new, different, and unique when it would be far better to adopt a program that has been successful. Why reinvent the wheel? The challenge should not be to originate activities but to be creative in the implementation of those things that have produced results elsewhere .There are a multitude of events and projects that are appropriate for fund-raising activities.

Sargeant and Shang (2010) and Heyman (2011) indicate it is vital that an overall plan for fund-raising be developed using the following guidelines: (1) fund-raising must be program specific; (2) a prospect list must be developed; (3) an accounting system must be established; (4) an acknowledgement and follow-up system must be devised; (5) a timetable must be established; (6) the organization will do better if it is classified as a nonprofit 501 (c)(3) tax-exempted corporation; (7) a board of directors must be formed and a legal binding contract be drawn requiring the board to review and monitor funds periodically; (8) the overall plan should have short- [one to two years] and long-range [three- to five-year] goals and objectives; (9) the goals and objectives (projects) should be prioritized; (10) all activities, policies, and procedures should be kept simple; (11) an attorney and certified public accountant should be involved in the early phases of the fund-raising program; (12) in selecting projects, choose those that are cost-effective and appropriate for the organization to sponsor; and (13) a training program should be established for staff and volunteers to prepare them for the tasks and a formal and informal means of appreciation needs to be established for all volunteers and community members.

Addressing Preliminary Issues

A fund-raising program is a major commitment for any organization. Heyman (2011), Lindahl (2009), and Sargeant and Shang (2011) suggest it is very important for the manager to be able to answer the following questions in detail:

- Is there a definable financial need?

- Can fund-raising activity meet the program's needs?

- Is this the only way, or the best way, of meeting the needs?

- Is the program itself worthy of support?

- Is there adequate and competent leadership activity?

- Are there sufficient volunteers?

- Is there an organization support infrastructure capable of achieving the successful conclusion of the fund-raising effort?

- Is there a support organization in existence?

- Could this organization be recognized as the official representative of the athletic program in terms of fund-raising?

- Is there a positive reputation and image of the support organization in the eyes of the various constituencies?

Other questions, according to Heyman (2011) and Sargeant and Shang (2010), to be considered include the following:

- How much will it cost to raise the desired amount?

- What are the downside risks and liabilities?

- Will the program be cost effective in terms of money, time, effort, personnel, and other resources?

- Are the necessary resources available?

- What are the requirements in terms of time to reach the objective(s)?

- Can the objectives be reached in that time?

- What legal matters will be of concern (i.e., incorporation, tax-exempted status, mailing permit, taxes, special permits, insurance, etc.)?

- Can the end results stand up to close scrutiny of various constituencies?

- Is the financial and political climate conducive to success?

Resources Necessary to Conduct a Successful Fund-Raising Program

Fund-raising, if not planned properly, can be a resource drag. There are a number of resources necessary for conducting any fund-raising project. Lindahl (2009) and Sargeant and Shang (2010) indicate these usually include the following:

- time, personnel (i.e., internal/external and paid/volunteer)

- equipment (i.e., computers, printers, fax machine, filing cabinet)

- supplies (i.e., paper, stationery, envelopes, file cards, file folder, postage)

- facilities, reputation and image of the organization, the organization's past accomplishments and achievements, seed funding to start projects, and other nonpersonnel (i.e., members, students, parents, community members, friends of the organization)

Key Components of a Fund-Raising Program

There are seven components of a fund-raising program. Each of the components must be integrated in order to develop a successful program. The components outlined by Sargeant and Shang (2010) include the following.

What

The establishment of a mission, purpose, and function statements, development of short- and long-term goals and objectives, and prepare appropriate strategies to implement the action plans within a suitable time frame.

Where

Fund-raising should take place in many venues inside as well as outside the organization (see Table 16.1).

Why

No fund-raising program or project should be developed unless there are justifiable needs that can be utilized in the development of the case statement (a case statement is an embellished need statement).

When

Fund-raising, like fruit, is time sensitive and there are good times and bad times in every community to mount a fund-raising campaign, a time should be carefully chosen that allows for maximum penetration into the community, the campaign should be designed in time-sequenced events that follow an established priority of importance, and the most commonly implemented fund-raising efforts are one-time events, repeatable projects, and annual events that are either one-time or repeatable projects.

Table 16.1

Common Models Used in Fund-Raising

- Person-to-person solicitation
- Single-person cultivation
- Door-to-door solicitation
- Telephone solicitation (telemarketing)
- Contest of chance (i.e., 50/50 drawing, raffle
- Lottery, casino nights)
- Direct mail solicitation

(Modified from Sargeant & Shang, 2010)

By Whom

A key to any fund-raising program's or project's success is the people involved. There must be involvement of paid staff, volunteers (i.e., members, students, parents, community leaders, friends of the organization), and other external sources.

Categories or Vehicles of Giving

Heyman (2011) suggests there are a number of categories utilized in fund-raising projects, including the following:

- major donor programs, capital programs (i.e., building campaign)
- annual scholarship appeals
- annual giving campaigns for the total program, annual special events or projects
- annual giving campaigns for special purposes
- annual giving campaigns on an unrestricted basis
- deferred/planned giving (i.e., proceeds from life insurance or wills), memorial giving programs (i.e., in memory of someone)
- gifts-in-kind (i.e., donations of professional time or equipment)
- general endowment programs

Feasibility

The manager and fund-raising committee need to develop an assessment process for evaluating all projects or events to determine: how successful a project or event might be, whether or not to proceed with the project or event, and what should be done to improve the project or event before it is repeated.

Committees Used in Fund-Raising Projects

Not many fund-raising projects are undertaken without a number of key committees, particularly to support public school and not-for-profit fund-raising efforts. These committees may be composed of both paid staff and volunteers .The most commonly utilized committees, according to Lindahl (2009) and Heyman (2011), are (1) site selection, (2) publicity and promotion,(3) equipment and supplies,(4) finance, (5) refreshments and hospitality, (6) invitation and program, (7) ticket, (8) decorations, (9) prizes, (10) security, (11) cleanup, and (12) project assessment.

Examples of Fund-Raising Events

There are many events that can be used for fund-raising by organizations; the only thing that limits a manager is his/her imagination. Following is a list of possible fund-raising events offered by Heyman (2011), Lindahl (2009), and Sargeant and Shang (2010):

- athletic contests
- clinics/workshops
- youth sport camps/clinics
- fun nights
- team/individual athlete photos
- flea markets/consignment sales
- car washes
- swim-, walk-, run-, bike-a-thons
- invitational tournaments
- novelty athletic events (i.e., Harlem Gobletrotters, King and His Court, donkey baseball/soft-ball)
- craft and hobby shows/sales
- rummage/white elephant/garage sales, shows (i.e., baseball cards, musicals, etc.)
- exhibitions, bazaars, festivals, fairs, and carnivals
- rodeos
- celebrity and regular golf tournaments
- hole-in-one contests
- card and board games
- excursions
- house/garden tours
- fashion shows
- professional wrestling events
- haunted houses
- Christmas and Santa Claus workshop
- ghost dinners
- celebrity roasts
- dances
- sponsoring camping, boating, or recreational equipment shows
- athletic hall of fame

- auctions
- road races
- meet the coaches lunch/breakfast
- Monday night football club
- wine and cheese/ice cream socials
- reunion of championship teams
- alumni games
- pancake breakfast/fish fry
- meet the team night with a barbecue and annual pig roast

Fund-Raising Support Groups

Fund-raising support groups, such as athletic or band booster clubs, are very useful tools in the fund-raising arsenal. These groups are composed of members, parents, and community supporters who are all volunteers.

Heyman (2011) and Sargeant and Shang (2010) indicate there are seven steps in the establishment of support groups, including (1) recognition of the need for such a group; (2) communication with management, board members, and/or appropriate school officials; (3) consultation with representative of various internal and external constituencies; (4) establishment of general principles and guidelines for the support group; (5) recognition of potential pitfalls that should be avoided (i.e., overzealous boosters, selecting proper accounting methods, establishment of priorities, relationship between support group and organization, planning for continuity); (6) dissemination of information about the organization and its purpose; and (7) determination of the organizational structure of the group through the establishment of articles of incorporation, bylaws, and rules of operation.

Contributors to fund-raising usually receive some kind of benefit for their donations. According to Heyman, 2011, Lindahl (2009), and Sargeant and Shang (2010), these benefits might be any of the following or a combination of the following:

- preferred parking
- complimentary or reduced ticket prices or the privilege to purchase tickets in a particular location
- special event ticket priority
- dinner and banquet seating priority, plaques or other gift items to recognize donors
- invitations to special events
- VIP lounge privilege membership card, periodic newsletters, press guide(s), and other publications
- mention and recognition in game programs
- away game ticket priority
- travel with specific teams
- access to press box or special areas for special teams and/or events
- specific apparel to identify donors and contributors

- a private booth for home contests or events
- auto decals
- free golf at college/university course
- free or reduced membership in college/university health/wellness center
- scholarship named after donor, building named after donor, dinner to honor donor
- perpetual award given in donor's name

References

Heyman, D. R. (Ed.). (2011). *Nonprofit management 101: A complete and practical guide for leaders and professionals.* San Francisco, CA: Jossey-Bass.

Lindahl, W. E. (2009). *Principles of fund-raising: Theory and practices.* Sudbury, MA: Jones & Bartlett Publishers, LLC

Sargeant, A., & Shang, J. (2010). *Fund-raising principles and practices.* San Francisco, CA.

CHAPTER 17

Customer Retention Principles

Thomas H. Sawyer
Professor Emeritus, Indiana State University

Tonya L. Gimbert
Indiana State University

Introduction

Retaining current customers is the key to success. Customer retention minimizes the emphasis on securing new customers that must take place to be profitable and establish a stable base that can help attract new customers through referrals. Finally, customer retention maximizes the customer's lifetime value to the organization.

The following, offered by Buttle (2008), Kahle and Close (2010), and Liraz (2013) are factors that affect the retention of ticket-plan purchasers for entertainment and sporting events:

- Customer service
  - Feeling valued by the organization
  - Appreciated by the organization
  - Quality of customer information
  - Problem resolution
  - Ease of problem resolution
- Performance of the team
- Satisfaction with seat location
- Demand for tickets in the marketplace
- Satisfaction with beverage and food concessions
- Satisfaction with merchandise and souvenirs
- Enjoyment in attending the games
  - Game programs

- Satisfaction with the price/value relationship of the purchase
  - Ease of use of the benefits and amenities included in their purchase
- Convenience factors relating to attending in person
  - Ease of parking
  - Expense of parking

Why Do Customers or Fans Decide Not to Renew Their Memberships or Season Tickets?

It is not hard to understand that the campaign to retain customers begins the day a person joins a club or purchases a sport ticket. The critical time period is the first year of membership or the first few games attended by a fan. This period of time is when most people decide whether they will stay with the club or sport team or let their membership lapse (see Tables 17.1 and 17.2).

Table 17.1
Why Customers Drop Out

- Failure to receive enough attention
- Failure to receive appropriate guidance during the first year of membership
- Failure to lose weight as quickly as perceived
- Failure to transform their body composition overnight
- Failure not to get into physical shape as quickly as perceived
- Lack of proper orientation for using the facilities, equipment, or personnel
- Failure to see results from the program designed
- Club does not meet expectations
- Poorly maintained facility or equipment
- Does not feel as though he/she belongs
- Loss of motivation to continue program
- The visit to the club was not enough
- The club does not cater to his/her needs
- Not a family affair
- The benefits do not outweigh the costs
- Employees are not personable or friendly

(Modified from Buttle, 2008)

Table 17.2
Why Sport Teams Lose Fans

- They did not feel as though they were important
- Cost outweighs enjoyment
- Dirty facilities
- Boring food service
- Poor seating
- Inconvenient parking
- No luxury seating
- No picnic areas
- No nonsmoking areas
- No nondrinking areas
- No place to change young children
- No daycare facilities
- No playground for young children
- Souvenirs too expensive
- No other entertainment but the game itself
- Team is not exciting
- Team fails to win consistently
- No opportunities to meet the players

(SportsBusiness Research, 2012)

How to Gather Knowledge from Current Customers or Fans to Guide the Renewal Process

Kahle and Close (2010), and Liraz (2013) offer the following questions to assist the sport manager in knowing the customer or fans: Does he/she know how old they are? Their level of income? Their family structure? The specific needs? Does he/she know why they come to this fitness club or sport team? Why do some of them come more often than others? Why do some stop coming altogether?

Many club or sport managers actually know very little about their customers. Some, however, have learned to gather, retain, and organize information on their customers and how to use this information to increase and maintain business. Getting this type of information does not have to be expensive. A sophisticated computer system and special software are not needed. An expensive consultant is not required. The sport manager does not need to be a mathematician or an expert at consumer research. All that is needed is an understanding of a few simple points about a very simple and effective business tool. A customer survey can be used to provide management information about the customer base.

Customer surveys, such as the Customer Profile System described on the next page, are a key tool used by thousands of businesses to provide the kind of information they need to increase business, introduce products or services that will meet with a strong consumer response, determine why some never "got off the ground," and ascertain what kinds of customers currently belong or attend so similar customers can be sought and added to the customer base.

Customer Profile System

A Customer Profile System (CPS) assists in making sure the participants or ticket holders are satisfied customers—and loyal members or fans. A CPS is an after-marketing strategy to assist managers in retaining customers. It is important to create a CPS that enables the organization to develop and maintain personal relationships with the customers. The CPS serves as a type of dialogue between the actions and interests of the consumer and the organization. The potential of what can be accomplished through the establishment of a CPS and related marketing efforts depends upon two factors: (1) what information will be compiled in the CPS, and (2) how consistently and aggressively this data will be used. There are four important features in developing the CPS database: (1) addressability—ensures that the CPS provides communication with every identifiable customer and enables the organization to communicate with all current customers, (2) consumer purchasing histories—enables the marketer to monitor attendance patterns and purchasing behaviors of the various customer groups, (3) flexibility— the CPS must be flexible enough to be able to segment customers for specifically designed/targeted communications, and (4) accountability—a quantifiable way to assess the number of people who are members or customers.

A CPS software program can easily be stored on a single personal computer. The CPS program can be developed by the organization by using Lotus 1-2-3 or any other data base software program. Storage and utilization are dependent upon the size of the organization and the number of individuals who will be accessing the information simultaneously or during the course of an average work day. The data obtained for the CPS should be updated annually by using a Customer Profile Sheet completed by all customers at time of purchase.

After building the database, the organization can begin after-marketing. Its appli-cations are only limited by the manager's imagination. A few uses for the data base could be customer satisfaction surveys, analyzing customer groups, promoting other and special events, tracking members' purchasing and attendance habits, and to set a benchmark or reference point for future analysis.

(Modified from Buttle, 2008)

Kuranchie (2011) and Rai (2012) suggest the business survey can be used to (1) increase business, (2) introduce new programs to customer base, (3) determine why existing programs are not getting the attention they were designed for, (4) ascertain more about the existing customer base to encourage renewals and go out and prospect for similar customers, and (5) determine why customers have decided not to renew membership or season tickets.

However, Kuranche (2011) and Rai (2012) warn surveys will not (1) fully identify best prospects' characteristics, wants, and needs; (2) determine why elements of a program are working or not working; (3) monitor how perceptions of the facility, equipment, and services are changing over time; or (4) explain why some programs are successful and others are failures.

Yet, Kuranche (2011) and Rai (2012) suggest surveys can assist in (1) effectively defining the market and help marketing dollars go further, (2) becoming more familiar with the existing and potential customers, (3) determining how customers perceive the facilities, equipment, programs, and services,

(4) positioning or repositioning facility among other competitors in the same marketplace, and (5) identifying the kinds of program benefits that can be converted into advertising that sells.

When does the sport manager need to conduct a survey? It depends on what you need to know and whether that information is available from any other source, such as marketing magazines, trade magazines, or research journals. Before deciding to conduct a survey, Kuranchie (2011), Rai (2012), and Liraz (2013) indicate the sport manager should ask the following questions:

- What do I need to know?

- Why do I need to know?

- How much do I want to know?

- When do I need the information?

- How much is the information worth to me?

- Can I afford to make an uninformed decision?

Once the sport manager has decided to use a survey, he/she needs to determine the best type of survey to utilize. According to Kuranchie (2011) and Liraz (2013), there are three types of surveys, including (1) a mail survey where the respondent is asked to read, interpret, and answer the questions posed, (2) a telephone survey executed by trained operators who ask the questions and are also available to explain ambiguous queries, and (3) a personal survey conducted face-to-face by trained interviewers who are also available for interpretation of questions. Mail surveys are the easiest and most cost effective to prepare, as well as the most common.

How many customers or prospects should be surveyed? The answer to the question depends to a large degree on the information to be gathered. If it is existing customers, then the manager will select what he/she is comfortable with. For example, if it is decided a decision can be made with 1,000 responses, and felt that a 20% response rate can be obtained, then it would be necessary to mail 5,000 surveys chosen randomly from the 10,000-member customer base. If the response rate was only 10% then 10,000 surveys would have to be mailed. If the manager wants to know more about the people who are not current customers, the manager will need to rely on a purchased list or a list of prospects that the organization has gathered.

The actual preparation of the survey instrument is the most difficult part of conducting a survey. However, Kuranchie (2011), Rai (2012), and Liraz (2013) indicate a sport manager can do it effectively, if aware of a few simple points, including the following:

- Wording must be simple and easy to understand. The instrument must be easy to read.

- Frame questions so that they can be answered in a straightforward fashion. Avoid open-ended questions (e.g., "What do you think about the proposed water aerobic program?") because they result in a wide variety of responses that can be difficult to categorize and quantify. Instead, frame the question in the following way—"How would you rank your interest in the water aerobics program?"—and then give a series of responses that provide brief descriptive phrases so that respondents can simply check their choice (also known as a forced-answer item). Do not forget to include an "others" category.

- Do not ask leading questions—"Would you be interested in registering for the water aerobics program if it were held every Wednesday at 7 p.m.?"— but, rather, ask the question this way—"When would you be interested in registering for a water aerobics program?"—followed by a list of days and times for the respondent to select from.

- When would you be interested in registering for a water aerobics program:

| Monday | 5 p.m. |
| Tuesday | 6 p.m. |

Wednesday	7 p.m.
Thursday	8 p.m.
Friday	6 a.m.
Saturday	12 noon

- Do not make the survey look too complicated or time-consuming. The survey should not be more than two pages, preferably only one. A simple, one-page survey that is easy to read will receive a higher rate of return.

- Make the survey look important by attaching a cover letter on the organization's letter head and the survey printed on quality paper.

- The use of premiums has been found to greatly increase response rate. The two most commonly used are money/gift certificates and ball point pens. When choosing a premium, make sure that it is something the respondent will find desirable, something that does not introduce a bias, small and light enough to be easily delivered, and not so expensive as to make the cost of conducting the survey prohibitive.

- Encourage a quick response by providing an additional premium for those who return the survey within five days.

- Offer respondents a check off for a copy of the results. This has been shown to significantly increase response.

- Plan on sending a follow-up reminder with a survey two weeks after sending the initial mailing, and a postcard reminder two weeks after the first follow-up.

- Avoid confidential areas and technical jargon.

- Include a brief cover letter from the manager describing the purpose of the survey and its importance.

- Protect the respondents' confidentiality.

- Provide a self-addressed, postage-paid return envelope.

- Finally, checking on bias is an extremely important step in assuring accuracy in the responses to the survey. Determining bias can easily be accomplished by selecting a small sample of non-respondents and use a telephone interview to get their responses to a small number of survey questions. Then, compare their answers to the original respondents. If you find contamination, use other data or switch the method from mail survey to either telephone or personal interviews or discard the contaminated data.

Retaining Memberships

Extending memberships is a constant challenge for club operators. Without a doubt, members are the foundation of the club industry. Experts maintain that the campaign to keep members must begin the day the person joins the club and it must be ongoing. The first year is the most critical year. Table 17.3 describes a number of tips for better member retention.

According to Kahle and Close (2010), and Liraz (2013) the successful clubs in membership retention have four fundamental strategies that play a critical role in maintaining high levels of membership satisfaction as discussed below.

Table 17.3
Membership Retention Tips

- Adopt a club-wide retention philosophy and appropriate action strategies.
- Give the members what they want and need.
- Assimilate new members right away.
- Target high-risk members (e.g., low-use members, general fitness members).
- Develop and implement program with retention in mind.
- Seek and select with retention in mind (people pleasers).
- Offer incentives to your members.
- Operate according to the fun factor vs. the pain factor.
- Get the staff involved with retention.
- Divide retention responsibility among personnel.

(Modified from Kuranchie, 2011)

Quality programming. The club management must regularly and consistently implement creative and enjoyable programs that everyone in the club can participate in—from club to individual competitions. The personal touch (TPT) is a necessity. Seek and select personnel who have good interpersonal skills and can establish a rapport with the members. Make sure the front-desk staff and on-floor trainers and instructors know members, greet them by name, and ask about their workout and progress. While it is helpful to select personnel knowledgeable about fitness, employees with people skills may be preferable. People skills are hard to teach, but fitness knowledge can easily be gained. Finally, call members regularly to see how they are doing or ask why they have not been working out lately. Show that management is really concerned about the well-being of the members. Concerned and happy employees translate into happy comfortable members.

Club atmosphere. The management should implement regular special events and socials (e.g., Easter party for kids, St. Patrick's Day social event, Halloween party for kids, New Year's Eve social) to create and maintain a friendly and caring club atmosphere. Further, the management should consider selling clothing and other merchandise with club logo and publishing a regular club newsletter. All of these opportunities assist the people to identify with a club. It is more likely for those members who identify with the club to maintain their annual memberships.

Staying informed. It is extremely important to solicit membership input regarding all aspects of the club operations. Use focus groups or a suggestion box at the front desk to solicit members' concerns or complaints. Ask all personnel to carefully listen to members, especially the maintenance staff. Or go into the sauna or steam room yourself and listen to what members are saying.

Understanding the positive influences. Retention largely depends on understanding the positive influences before the negative consequences are realized. One way a manager can improve retention is by identifying the areas which he/she can control, such as instructors, safety, fun, appropriate classes, atmosphere, group unity, rewards, and cleanliness of the facility (see Table 17.4).

Table 17.4

How to Motivate Customers to Renew

Motivating current customers to renew their club memberships or season tickets is much more cost effective than seeking new members. The secret to a high renewal rate is frequently a highly satisfied and motivated staff. The following 10 management guidelines will assist in boosting membership retention.

- Seek, select, train, and retain highly qualified and motivated employees.
- Direct all sales personnel to call new customers within the first few days afterclosing the sales to inquire about the instructional staff, locker accommodations, guest utilization and general satisfaction with the club or team.
- Send all new customers a thank you card (salesperson).
- Prepare and send a personal welcome letter from the club manager to all new members.
- Maintain all club and team operations, including membership, on a computer.
- Send birthday and anniversary cards to customers.
- Develop a number of customer incentives (e.g., 50% discount on a first massage or free court time and group instruction for those novices who have never tried racquetball).
- Implement special annual promotions with incentives for renewals in the off season.
- Develop good programming for the social, instructional, and recreational needs of the members (e.g., club/team-organized activities, such as vacation trips, week end getaways, cruises, card games, movies, dances, contests, fund-raisers, lecture series, or introductory classes in scuba diving, windsurfing, dancing, tennis, hiking).
- Guarantee all members a well-managed, well-maintained facility with good programming and proper incentives.

Finally, there are a number of personal and program factors that influence customer retention rates that the manager must consider. The personal factors that influence customer dropout rates include the following:

- smoking
- inactive leisure time
- inactive occupation
- blue-collar worker
- Type-A personality
- increased physical strength
- extroverted

- poor credit rating
- overweight/overfat
- poor self-image
  - depressed
  - anxious
  - introverted
  - low ego strength

The program factors include the following:
- inconvenient time/location
- excessive cost
- high intensity
- exercise
- lack of exercise variety
- exercises alone
- lack of positive feedback or reinforcement
- inflexible exercise goals,
- low enjoy ability ratings for running the programs
- poor exercise leadership.

Other factors include such things as
- lack of spousal support
- inclement weather,
- excessive job travel
- injury
- medical problems
- job change/loss

Source: Kahle and Close (2010), Rai (2012), and Liraz (2013)

The most powerful bonds for retaining members are established by instructors in a club setting. According to Kennedy-Armbruster and Yoke (2009), a good dance exercise leader (or any instructor for that matter) will use the following customer strategies: "(1) show a sincere interest in the customer; (2) be enthusiastic during instruction and cheerfully provide guidance; (3) develop a personal association and relationship with all customers and learn their names; (4) consider the various reasons why a person exercises and allow for individual differences; (5) initiate customer follow-up when several unexplained absences occur in succession; (6) participate in the exercise sessions, honor special days (e.g., birthdays, anniversaries, special holidays) or exercise accomplishments with extrinsic rewards such as T-shirts, ribbons or certificates, attend to orthopedic and musculoskeletal problems; (9) counsel customers on proper exercise clothing and foot apparel; and (10) motivate to make long-term exercise commitments (p. 147)."

Costs of Recruiting New Customers

The cost of recruiting new customers or fans varies from organization to organization. The components of the cost are similar, but the actual cost attributed to each component varies. According to Buttle (2008), Kahle and Close (2010), Rai (2012), and Liraz (2013), the cost components include (1) advertising in print, over the radio, and on the television; (2) telephone calls to follow up with potential clients; (3) sales commissions; (4) sales and processing time; (5) development of cold prospect lists (i.e., people who are in target market but not stake holders in the club); (6) direct mailings to target market; (7) printing direct mailing pieces; and (8) telemarketing. These costs can range from as little of 15% of the membership fee to well over 45%. The cost of renewing a membership is minimal in comparison.

Staff Training to Maintain Customers or Fans

Management and customer or fan retention are so intertwined, yet many organizations leave membership in the hands of sales personnel who are only interested in new weekly sales numbers. Before relying on this method of sales, however, it is important to carefully examine the costs of acquiring new customers as well as the market the customers are drawn from. Instead of actively seeking new customers, why not look at attracting renewals?

Renewals are cost effective because they are proven buyers who are already satisfied customers or ticket buyers. In addition, very few clubs have such a large base of new customers that they can afford to overlook renewals as a real source of income. The key to customer retention is developing highly motivated employees who enjoy people and their jobs. Sport managers who establish good management policies resulting in highly motivated employees are likely to be those who have high membership retention rates or very loyal fans.

The sport manager should develop a regular in-service program for a staff and an orientation program for all new personnel. These programs, according to Buttle (2008), Liraz (2013), and Kahle and Close (2010), should include how to (1) answer the phone (*Good morning, XYZ Fitness Club or Terre Haute Rex, how may I direct your call?*); (2) welcome customers or fans (*Hello, how are you today?*), (3) respond to customers or fans questions; (4) deal with complaints; (5) assist customers with their programs; (6) maintain equipment and facilities; (7) clean locker rooms, spas, saunas, steam rooms, and equipment; (8) create an enjoyable experience (People do not just join a club, they join a lifestyle, and are looking for reliability, assurance, and responsiveness); (9) be reliable and responsive; (10) small talk with customers or fans (*How are you? How is the workout going? How is the game? Happy birthday! Happy anniversary!*); and (11) do something special for the customer (shining shoes in the locker room, offering water to customers during the workouts, handing out towels in the weight room, suggesting the best seating available, telling regular fans of any special promotions coming in the future).

Staff Preparation and Motivation for Customer Retention

Recognizing that there is a large source of potential revenue in current and past customer lists is the beginning of good management. However, employing staff who have good personal skills and can establish a rapport with customers is a key to success. After completing the hiring process, the sport manager should develop an in-service training program to prepare staff for the task of customer retention. Buttle (2008), Kahle and Close (2010), Rai (2012), and Liraz (2013) outline the ensuing steps will create a reasonable set of goals to motivate employees to increase customer retention:

- The management, in consultation with the staff, should develop a plan for customer retention. The management should establish bimonthly meetings that are informative, well-researched, and exciting for all to attend. Allow time for staff customers to present new retention ideas.

- The sport manager should maintain (a) a positive attitude in these meetings to further excite and elicit good ideas from the staff and (b) good leadership and direction.

- Communication should be the keyword for all management and staff. Courtesy should be demanded of all employees, not just toward customers but toward each other. Being courteous can have a remarkable effect on attitudes and camaraderie and can help foster a positive team attitude.

- Establish a specific set of goals regarding customer retention for all employees. This should be an overall or long-term goal to be reached through small, evenly paced steps that are reasonably attainable, yet require moderate effort on everyone's part. This allows for vision and accomplishment with a sense of achievement.

- Along with the goals there should be a reasonable level of expectation for success. If you expect more, you get more. When you expect less, you get less than expected.

- Consistency is sorely needed in any endeavor for it to be successful. Slight manipulation and rethinking should be the norm when expectations are not met. Overhauls should be avoided at all costs.

- A well-designed employee incentive plan based on customer retention can be an extremely effective tool in enlarging not only gross sales, but net sales as well.

- A staff needs to understand not only anatomy but also how to communicate with customers of all different ages, skill levels, personalities, schedules, and interests. People respond to people. Retention is about keeping people happy and active.

- Finally, the wise sport manager will make sure the front-desk staff and on floor trainers and instructors know customers, greet them by name, and ask about their workout. While it is helpful to hire individuals knowledgeable about fitness, employees with people skills may be more preferable. Fitness knowledge can be taught; but, people without natural people skills find it extremely difficult to modify their attitudes and personalities to become people oriented.

Customer Retention Strategies

Once the sport manager has developed an effective staff that is motivated and responsive, Buttle (2008), Kuranchie (2011), Kahle and Close (2010), Rai (2012), and Liraz (2013) suggest the following should be accomplished:

- The sales personnel should call new customers within the first few days after closing the sale to inquire about contact with instructional staff, locker needs, guest utilization, and general satisfaction with the organization. This is the beginning of the creation of a sales/customer relationship that should not only spin off new referrals but also cement the customer's commitment to the facility for future renewals.

- Good retention programs include group programming that runs six to eight weeks—with a beginning and end. These programs must have a leader, an achievement recognition system, and a mechanism to track results. The most important ingredient for group programs is an instructor who creates a fun environment.

- The wise manager gets the staff involved with customers. Staffers should play an active role in a program in which customers accumulate organization points or "dollars" that can be put toward special premiums. Staff can collect, distribute, and answer questions regarding club points, making employees more approachable to customers. Staff involvement gives customers a reason to go up to staffers and talk to them. Communication is essential to retention.

- Organizations are selling a service and no one likes to be forgotten right after the sale. In addition to follow-up calls, a personalized note of thanks from the salesperson to a new customer is a nice thought.

- Within the first week of membership, the new customer should receive a welcome call from the manager.

- Once a customer joins, the staff has a period of 30 days to fully integrate that person into the club. Providing fitness assessments is an important part of that integration process. And as with any type of health analysis, customers must feel comfortable providing personal information to the club staff. If the customer is comfortable with the staff, it can help to create a bond between the customer and the staffer.

- Offering customers fitness assessment and body composition analysis builds a strong relationship between clients and club staff and, therefore, serves as a valuable retention tool.

- The key to maintaining a strong customer and staff relationship is to periodically retest and reevaluate customers to make sure they are on track. In this way, the staffer can offer the feedback customers need to stay motivated in their fitness programs.

- The new customer's name, address, phone number, e-mail address, birthday, anniversary, wife's birthday, children's birthday, and other dates of interest should be entered into the computer. The personal touch: Notices can be sent to the customer on these special occasions, cards can be sent to remind customer of customer renewal dates, congratulation notices can be sent when the customer has received an honor from work or a family customer has received an honor or the customer has met a predetermined goal, etc. Computer software can be purchased that will allow front-desk personnel to run a customer's card through the computer card reader and if it is the customer's birthday, the computer plays happy birthday.

- Ascertain customers' interests and link them to the interest areas or services available.

- Buddy new customers with established customers or a member of the staff.

- Doing so will help make the organization more personalized and make the customer feel wanted.

- Organize a "welcome" party periodically for the new customers to introduce them more thoroughly to the facilities, staff, and other customers.

- Special incentives can be provided to new customers, including a 50% discount on the first massage, free court time, 10% discount in the pro shop, annual promotions with incentives for renewals during a specified time period (months before they are due).

- Organize activities, such as vacation trips, weekend getaways, cruises, card games, movies, dances, Halloween party, Christmas Party, Easter Party, contests, fund-raisers, lecture series, or introductory lessons in nutrition, scuba diving, windsurfing, dancing, tennis, massage, or hiking, are just the tip of the iceberg.

- Make sure the facilities are attractive, clean, safe, and well-maintained.

- Be sure the equipment is not broken, and it is clean, safe, and well maintained. Add new equipment periodically to increase customer interest.

- Implement creative and enjoyable programs that everyone in the club can participate in. Good programming for the social, instructional, recreational, and competitive needs cannot be overlooked. Each program needs a marketing plan, a goal, and a budget to succeed. Programming is about marketing to the customer who already has bought you. It has to include sociability, camaraderie, fun, leadership, direction, and constant service. People are more likely to work out on their own if they are receiving programming that makes them happy on a consistent basis.

- Use focus groups or a suggestion box at the front desk to gain input from customers regarding concerns or complaints. Ask maintenance staff what they are hearing in the locker room. Deal with problems before they turn customers off.

- Club atmosphere: Run special events and socials regularly to create and maintain a friendly atmosphere. Consider selling T-shirts, caps, water bottles, jackets, sweat suits, sweat shirts, key chains, glasses, mugs, and other items bearing the club's logo. Publish a regular club membership, making sure customers' names appear. The more people identify with a club, the more likely they are to stick with it over time.

- Multiple visits with a trainer who can assess a customer's fitness level and design a program are necessary early on. Reevaluation opportunities are a necessity. Trainers on the floor need to be accessible and know when and when not to approach customers.

- Offer customers who encourage an existing customer to renew $4 off of the monthly dues for up to one year. On slow months, double the dues offer to $8.

- Initially, show new and deconditioned customers only four strength-training machines (one for each muscle group) and one cardiovascular machine. When the new customer visits the club 15 times, he is shown how to use more machines. This strategy keeps the customer from being overwhelmed with all the new equipment but is still getting a good workout. The new customer's goal becomes learning the other machines.

- Offer a discount for all renewals, increasing the discount for length of longevity.

The Fan (Consumer) Comes First

Retaining sport fans is a challenging task in this day of high technology and multiple entertainment opportunities that can be enjoyed in one's own living room (See Table 17.5). What makes the sport fan want to return to the ball park, stadium, court, or rink, contest after contest? Sport teams are well-oiled entertainment businesses built by hard-driving sport entrepreneurs. These entrepreneurs have a deep respect for their customers. They offer amenities including changing tables in restrooms for mothers and fathers with young children, more restroom facilities for women to reduce wait time, day-care centers for mothers and fathers with young children, nonsmoking and non-drinking seating areas, handicapped areas, barbershops, specialty foods, expensive restaurants, highly recognized fast food establishments (e.g., Pizza Hut, Taco Bell, McDonald's, Hardees, Burger King, Subway),luxury boxes, mini-malls (e.g., souvenir shops, clothing shops, shoe stores, etc.), reasonably priced souvenirs and other licensed products, entertaining scoreboards, reasonable and accessible parking, health and fitness centers, playgrounds and entertainment rides, free parking for season ticket holders, car washing service for fans as they watch the game, assigned parking for fans, and picnic areas.

Table 17.5
How Can I Increase the Audience or Memberships?

- Pre-event entertainment
- Youth games at half-time
- Special group promotions (i.e., Girl Scouts, Boy Scouts, mother-and-son outing, father-and-daughter dance)
- Special rates for groups (i.e., senior citizens, ladies night, honor students)
- Giveaways (i.e., small basketballs, small footballs, small baseball bats, baseball or painter caps, T-shirts)
- Scheduling doubleheaders
- Reduced membership fees
- Shoot-out contest at half time
- Event buses
- Special days (i.e., hometown day, specific town day, specific school day)
- Student athletes visiting schools as role models
- Clip-out coupons
- Radio giveaways to listeners (i.e., tickets, free memberships)
- Use of a pep band at events
- Team color night (i.e., offer half-price admission to anyone dressed in team's colors)
- Face-painting contest (i.e., encourage students to come early and face-paint each other in an area separate from the event area and judge the painting jobs providing prizes to the winners at halftime).

Further, they provide special entertaining promotional activities, including periodic fireworks, celebrities during opening ceremonies or halftime, contests for the fans prior to games or during halftimes, children wearing any kind of sport uniform will get in free, hat or bat night, team picture night, and family picture with your favorite player. These are all examples of how a sport manager can encourage his or her fans to continue their loyalty to the team.

References

Buttle, F. (2008). *Customer relationship management* (2nd ed). Burlington, MA: Elsevier, Ltd.

Kahle, L. R., & Close, A. G. (2010). *Consumer behavior knowledge for effective sports and event marketing.* Florence, KY: Routledge/Taylor and Francis Group.

Kennedy-Armbruster, C., & Yoke, M. (2009). *Methods of group exercises instruction.* Champaign, IL: Human Kinetics.

Kuranchie, F. K. (2011). *Customer retention and relationship management.* Saarbrucken, Germany: Lambert Academic Publishing.

Liraz, M. (2013). *Build customer loyalty: Identify customer needs.* Seattle, WA: Amazon Digital.

Rai, R. P. (2012). *Consumer retention and satisfaction in business management.* Nottingham, UK: Koros Press.

SportsBuisness Research. (2012). Retrieved from http://www.sbrnet.org.

PART IV

Facility Design, Event Management, and Facility Operations and Maintenance

CHAPTER 18

Programming for Success

Thomas H. Sawyer
Professor Emeritus, Indiana State University

Tonya L. Gimbert
Indiana State University

Introduction

The term *program development* as used in this chapter refers to the total learning experiences provided to consumers to achieve the objectives of health, fitness, physical activity, recreation, and sport. It is concerned with the component parts of all the programs in each of the five areas as well as with the resources (e.g., facilities, financial, human, and technological) involved in implementing those learning experiences. According to Sawyer (2009), the overwhelming trend in American society today is to provide carefully planned programs based on the following considerations:

- "the abilities, needs, and wants of the customer/client;

- the needs of society in general;

- the practical usefulness of the various knowledge bases and physical skills;

- the social-psychological aspects of society that influence learning; and

- the marketability of the products or services developed to meet the needs and wants of the customer/client (p. 236)."

Program Development

The responsibility of program planning falls on the shoulders of a number of people and organizations. The planners include, but are not limited to management personnel, staff, professional organizations, customers/clients, parents, community leaders, and other professionals such as medical personnel, lawyers, architects, and corporate leaders.

The management personnel play a vital role in the planning process. Rossman (2012) offered they serve as the (1) creators of the catalytic force that sets the planning in motion, (2) facilitators for the planning process, and (3) sustainers of the development process. Further, they provide the leadership that encourages and stimulates interest in providing optimal experiences, clears the barriers (e.g., time, place, space, and resources) that might impede the accomplishment of the task, and implements the appropriate recommendations for a program plan. Finally, management is responsible for pulling together a team who can work cooperatively and effectively together, provide them with a charge or challenge, and supply them with the necessary motivation as well as adequate financial, human, and technical resources to accomplish the task of designing a quality program.

The staff members are at the grassroots level of program development. They will be key members of the team that develops programs. The staff member contributes experience and knowledge and provides data to support the directions of program development. Staff input and perceived ownership are necessary before a program is designed and implemented.

The professional organizations are the many groups and agencies that can help in program planning. These groups may provide program guides, consulting services, and advice that will prove to be invaluable in the planning of any program. Before embarking on a program development adventure, you should first consider what professional groups or agencies can be of assistance and contact them early on in the process. There is no need to reinvent the wheel. The old wheel may only need a small amount of adjustment to meet your needs.

The customers/clients should play a part in program development. Their collective thoughts on what constitutes desirable activities for program delivery are important. Customers/clients today are more actively involved in expressing their program needs or desires. They want to be heard and identified as part of planning the various activities and experiences that a quality program should provide to its customers/clients.

The parents and community leaders can assist in communicating with the public what an organization is trying to achieve. These two groups can make significant contributions by supplying information regarding desired outcomes. It is important to include representation from these two groups in order to develop any program in an effective and efficient manner.

Program Development Elements

Rossman (2012) and Sawyer (2009) suggest there are 11 elements that either directly or indirectly influence program development: (1) climate and geographical considerations; (2) economic and social forces, (3) population demographics; (4) the community; (5) federal, state, and local legislation and regulations; (6) professional organizations; (7) attitudes of managers and consumers; (8) staff; (9) research; (10) facilities and equipment; and (11) competition.

Components of the Planning Process

Mull, Forrester, and Barnes (2012) and Rossman (2012) suggest the components of the planning process for effective program planning are (1) establishing that a need exists for program development, (2) appointing a diverse planning team to specify the areas of need, (3) organizing for planning, (4) identifying program objectives, (5) generating program solutions, (6) selecting the program design, (7) implementing the program design, and (8) evaluating the program.

Steps in Program Development

Mull et al. (2012) and Rossman (2012) indicate the major steps involved in program development include (1) determining the objectives, (2) analyzing the objectives in terms of the program, (3) analyzing the objectives in terms of activities, (4) providing program guides, and (5) assessing the program based on predetermined outcomes.

In determining the objectives, the planning team should consider studying such factors as the nature of society, developmental program trends, needs and wants of the consumers, competitors' programs, and technological advances so that objectives may be clearly formulated to meet market demands. According to Mull et al. (2012), Rossman (2012), and Sawyer (2009), every program should consider the following four goals or purposes when determining program objectives:

- Self-realization goals include the inquiring mind, speech, reading, writing, numbers, sight and hearing, health knowledge, health habits, recreation, intellectual interests, aesthetic interests, and character.

- Human relationship goals consist of respect for humanity, friendships, cooperation, courtesy, appreciation of home, conservation of the home, home-making, and democracy in the home.

- Economic efficiency goals concern work, occupational information, occupational choice, occupational efficiency, occupational adjustment, occupational appreciation, personal economics, consumer judgment, efficiency in buying, and consumer protection.

- Civic responsibility goals embrace social justice, social activity, social understanding, critical judgment, tolerance, conservation, social applications of science, world citizenship, law observance, economic literacy, political citizenship, and devotion to democracy.

After the objectives have been determined based on the understanding of the consumers' characteristics, needs, and wants, they should be analyzed in terms of the program and activities. The analysis should consider the various constraints associated with the objectives and assign relative emphases to the various phases of the program. Further, the analysis must focus attention on the activities needed to achieve the set objectives. Do these activities allow for the objectives to be met?

Each program developed needs to have a program guide for its participants and its marketing endeavors. Program guides offer opportunities to achieve objectives. Further, they provide opportunities for marketing products/services to the organization's various markets.

All programs need to be assessed based on predetermined outcomes. Evaluation represents the culmination of the program development process. It defines the end result of the program and compares it with what the program expected to achieve during the developmental stages. Evaluation, like program development, is a dynamic process that helps to determine the progress being made in meeting program objectives. It should identify strengths, weaknesses, and omissions and show where needed resources or emphases might be shifted in order to improve the program. Further, it assists the consumers in determining their own progress within the program and is useful to the management for interpreting and reporting program outcomes to its consumers and board.

Five Common Program Approaches

Mull et al. (2012), Rossman (2012), and Sawyer (2009) suggest there are five common approaches to programming including programming by (1) objectives, (2) desires of the participants, (3) perceived needs of the participants, (4) cafeteria style, and (5) external requirements.

Programming by Objectives
- A contemporary approach
- This approach to planning should be based on the following four planning principles.
    - The needs of the consumer,
    - Life enhancement
    - Evaluation
    - Participant readiness

- Manager is –
  - able to conceptualize the activity process
  - skilled in writing performance objectives
- Objectives must consistent with the objectives of the participants
- Program is evaluated by whether or not the program has realized the objectives

Programming by Desire of Participants

- A consumer/participant involvement approach
- Desires of the participant groups are ascertained
- Manager is –
  - able to understand which activities meet which desires in most individuals
  - able to know when desires have been met or satisfied.
- Planning principles involved in this approach are:
  - all programs should be designed to meet the needs and interests of the consumer/participant
  - all programs should encompass a variety and balance in substance and organizational patterns
  - all programs should be set in a safe environment

Programming by Perceived Needs of the Participant

- Programming by a professional programmer approach
- This approach uses the following programming principles:
  - All programs should be designed to utilize creatively all facilities and areas available
  - All programs should be efficiently organized and planned so that maximum participation is available
  - All programs should be nondiscriminatory
  - All programs should be staffed by competent personnel
  - All programs should have an interrelationship and progress sequences from one level to another

Programming Cafeteria-Style

- The compromise approach
- Guiding principles to employ with this approach are:
  - programs should include all possible resources available
  - programs should provide an opportunity for new, creative experiences
  - programs should be compatible with the economic, social, and physical abilities of the potential consumers/participants

Programming by External Requirements (Standards)

- The external standards approach
- Guiding principles to employ with this approach are:
  - If the external standard is met, the program is good
  - Those persons involved in setting the standards are able to make quality judgments about the local situation
  - Standards generally represent minimums; therefore, to exceed the standard would indicate higher quality in the program experience

The guiding principles of programming by external requirements are the following (Mull et al. 2012; Sawyer, 2009):

- All programs should have diversity and internal balance.
- All program planning should adhere to carefully developed standards for both design and administration.
- All programs should be delivered through a system of highly qualified leadership.
- All programs should utilize the full resources available to the planning agency.

Components of Program Evaluation

The programming team/programmer must complete a thorough evaluation of the program(s) developed on a regular basis. The following questions need to be answered prior to embarking on the evaluation journey (Mull et al., 2012; Rossman, 2012; Sawyer, 2009):

- What is the philosophy behind the program developed?
- What personnel and customer/client behaviors represent the minimum acceptable competence for the program?
- Can you verify that all of the personnel make safety a priority?
- Do the personnel maintain appropriate, proper, and accurate records?
- Are the facilities safe, adequate, and cost effective for the program offerings?
- Is equipment maintained, distributed, collected, and stored properly and safely?
- Does the program offer equal access to all people regardless of gender, race and ethnicity, and socio-economic status?
- Are the program offerings the best use of financial resources?

The approach taken in evaluating the program(s) should be dictated by the needs of the organization and its customers/clients. Effective and efficient program evaluation requires careful planning. There are six steps that will lead you to a successful evaluation (Mull, et al., 2012; Rossman, 2012; Sawyer, 2009):

1. Reflect on organizational philosophy(ies).
2. Identify key roles.
3. Assess evaluation needs.
4. Develop an evaluation plan.
5. Implement the evaluation plan.
6. Review and revise the evaluation plan.

Process for Expanding or Reducing/Eliminating a Program

The programming team/programmer, after completing the evaluation, has a number of options regarding the future existence of the program. These options include maintaining, expanding, reducing, or eliminating the program. According to Appenzeller and Appenzeller (2008), Mull et al. (2012), and Sawyer (2009), before any of these options can be selected, the following must be determined regarding availability and impact:

- human resources

- financial resources

- facility resources

- equipment resources

- the effects on other related or tangential program offerings

- the effect on overall programming

- the effect on the customer/client base

Any time a program is modified in any way, it has a domino effect on all other activities within the organization. It may appear to be a simple modification on the surface; but, it could cause major problems with other related and non-related activities within the organization. Any recommendation for modification must be reviewed carefully in the context of the whole organization, not merely the area of suggested change.

Scheduling

It is important for the programming team/programmer to understand the calendar patterns of the customer/client who the organization serves. Appenzeller and Appenzeller (2008) and Sawyer (2009) suggest scheduling has at least four distinct and different patterns: (1) seasons; (2) block periods such as 2-, 3-, 4-, or 8- to 10-week periods; (3) monthly or weekly; and (4) daily time frame, such as sessions held during the early morning (6 to 9 a.m.), morning (9 a.m. to 12 noon), early afternoon (12 to 3 p.m.), late afternoon (3 to 6 p.m.), early evening (6 to 9 p.m.), and late evening (9 to 11 p.m.).

Considerations When Scheduling the Facility or Event

Sawyer (2009) observes that a standard procedure should be established for requesting use of facilities. The organization should create and adhere to a standard request form and establish priority guidelines for authorizing use. According to Appenzeller and Appenzeller (2008) and Sawyer (2009), Table 18.1 provides an example of a priority list commonly used in higher education.

Table 18.1
Priority Listing for Facility Usage

- scheduled academic classes

- scheduled nonacademic classes

- recreational sports

- athletic practices and contests

- other campus groups—academic

- other campus groups—nonacademic

- off-campus groups

Strict adherence to priority guidelines and request protocol should be stressed to all groups using facilities. In smaller organizations, scheduling may be less complicated and how the organizations, scheduling may be less complicated; however, there is still a need for protocol and proper authorization for facility use. Computer programs for facility management are available to assist in scheduling and they are very useful.

Effective scheduling is a distinguishing characteristic of every successful sports program, whether it is at the youth, interscholastic, intercollegiate, or professional level. Scheduling impacts every aspect of the sports program. It is extremely important that a high level of agreement between the mission of the organization and the schedule generated is obtained. The success level of each team within a sports program rests, in a great part, on the construction of a well-planned schedule.

According to Appenzeller and Appenzeller (2008), and Sawyer (2009), the following questions should be used as a guide for the development of successful and competitive schedules for all teams involved in a sports program:

- What is the standard of competition sought for each sport? What is the expected level of success for each team?

- What is the participation level? How should participants be grouped—by age, gender, experience, size, or skill?

- What are the financial parameters governing the construction of the schedule?

- What geographical/travel limitations exist? Are there conference affiliations to be considered?

- What is the policy governing the mode of transportation utilized for trips?

- Is it necessary or desirable to arrange schedules to enable two different teams from the same institution to travel together to a common opponent?

- Relative to some sports, is there a limit on how many contests per week are academically permissible? How many contests can be played during one day? Is there a difference or a preference for weekday versus weekend day contests? Can contests be played on Sunday?

- Are contests permitted to be scheduled during vacation periods which fall within a sport's season?

- Are teams who qualify permitted to participate in postseason tournament competition? What are the ramifications if postseason participation falls during examination periods or after the academic year is concluded?

- What considerations are given to vacation periods—Christmas, New Years, Easter, summer?

If an institution is a member of a conference, there will most certainly be guidelines and agreements relative to scheduling that should be understood by those making the schedules. Likewise, it is quite important for the sports director/coordinator to be aware of scheduling parameters set forth by the national or state governing bodies to which the institution belongs (e.g., American Legion Baseball, Little League Baseball, Miss Softball America, etc.).

Appenzeller and Appenzeller (2008) and Sawyer (2009) stress that once a scheduling policy has been established and adopted by the organization, other questions need to be considered before the scheduling team/scheduler can draft the schedule:

Facility Considerations
- What facility considerations exist?

- Is the facility shared with others?

- If the facility is shared, what priorities for usage have been established so that equity exists and conflicts can be avoided?

Program Considerations

- What are the goals of the program?

- How many contests, if any, should be scheduled in different divisions?

- If scheduling against a lower-division opponent, how strong is the opponent?

- What effect would a defeat to a lower or higher-division opponent have on the morale or team ranking?

- Is Monday a good day to schedule a contest if it follows a weekend of no competition or practice?

- Which opponents should be scheduled early in the season?

- How should the strong opponents be spread throughout the season?

- What kind of home and away balance is desired?

- How does a long trip affect the next competition?

- •What are the considerations of a long trip and how should long trips be balanced from year to year?

- How many contests should be played during a long trip?

- What considerations exist for contest starting times?

Sales Considerations

- What days of the week are preferred for scheduling of contests?

- Is spectator attendance an important factor and how is it affected by day or time of contest?

- Should contest days and times be consistent from week to week?

Academic or Religious Considerations

- Do the participants on the team tend to have one day per week when it is better not to schedule contests because of academic reasons?

- Does the organization have a policy about scheduling a contest on a religious day (e.g., Friday, Saturday, or Sunday)?

- Are there participants who cannot play on certain religious holidays or days?

- When should away trips be scheduled (e.g., short trips during the week and longer trips over the weekend)?

- What are the vacation periods and holidays that fall during the season (e.g., Thanksgiving, Christmas, New Years, Easter, spring break, summer)?

External Considerations

- When is the first permissible contest date of the season?

- What national or state sport organizations' rules may impact noneducational institution scheduling?

A Good Sport Schedule

According to Appenzeller and Appenzeller (2008) and Sawyer (2009), a good schedule is the end result of meeting the stated philosophy and policies of the organizationand the following is an example of a reasonable educational institution schedule:

- Includes all members of the conference if possible number wise (if the institution belongs to a conference)
- Contains a few nonconference games that encompass
  - at least one probable win,
  - at least one ranked team, and
  - at least one respectable opponent with name recognition and the possibility of a toss-up competitive situation.
- Allows for a 50/50 split between home and away contests.
- Generates maximum financial rewards.
- Tolerates no more than two games at home or two on the road consecutively.
- Creates fan interest.
- Gives a fair chance to
  - have a winning season and
  - gain postseason opportunities.
- Is reasonable in terms of travel.
- Is comprised of opponents who have reasonably similar academic standards.
- Maximizes geographical, institution, and individual player(s) exposure.

Mechanics of a Sound Schedule

Organization is the key to success in almost any administrative function, and scheduling is no exception to the rule. Scheduling at best is a complex task requiring a great deal of patience. The greatest assets a schedule team/scheduler must possess are patience, the ability to negotiate, and attention to detail.

The following records must be kept regarding the schedule: records of ideas, thoughts, phone calls, correspondence, past schedules, future schedules, agreements to play, contest contracts (e.g., actual contracts, when sent, received, and returned), officials' contracts, officials' roster, and details of successes and concerns.

All contests within a schedule should have contracts or agreements, even in youth league operations. According to Appenzeller and Appenzeller (2008) and Sawyer (2009), the following is a checklist of items that should be found in a scheduling agreement:

- dates the agreement is entered into
- site of the contest
- date of the contest
- time of the contest
- eligibility regulations of participants
- financial agreements, if any
- auditing requirement, if required

- complimentary ticket arrangements for both teams
- number of sideline passes for both teams, if appropriate
- number and location of visiting teams
- number of seats for team parties
- admission of band and cheerleaders, if appropriate
- control of ticket prices
- admission of game workers
- media agreements
- programming concession rights
- game officials
- special event rights (e.g., Band Day)
- additional games to be played as part of the original contract agreement
- conditions of failure to comply with the contract
- terminations of the contract clause
- additional miscellaneous agreements (e.g., meals, lodging, guarantees, etc.)

The development of a good schedule requires good sound planning, good communication, and attention to detail. The greater the number of sports to be placed on the calendar, the more important these elements become. It is possible for a scheduling team/scheduler to accomplish this task well, especially if a reasonable timetable is established early in the process.

Fundamentals of Booking Events

Micocci (2008) and Sawyer (2009) suggest a facility without a schedule of events has little purpose. A public facility has an obligation to provide for scheduling community events. A private facility may limit charitable and nonprofit activities. Regardless of the facility's purpose and mission, its manager is encouraged to book a well-rounded schedule of events geared to satisfy the desires of the market. Since rental income is such a major portion of annual operating revenue, this is an extremely important process.

Booking is the act of engaging and contracting an event or attraction to be held at the facility on a specific date. Scheduling is the reservation process and coordination of all events to fit the facility's annual calendar. According to Micocci (2008) and Sawyer (2009), there are two types of reservations: *tentative* indicates that an organization requested a specific date and time on a tentative-hold basis, and *confirmed* refers to an organization that has placed a deposit for the agreed-upon date and time (contracted reservation).

Facilities that are successful in scheduling events have made a good first impression on the tenants and the ticket-buying public. These facilities are clean, well-maintained, well-lit, environmentally comfortable, and staffed by friendly, courteous, and professional people. Miocci (2008) and Sawyer (2009) suggest there are a number of fundamentals to be considered when attracting, booking, and scheduling a facility, including the following (Appenzeller, 2008; Micocci, 2008):

- Developing a level of confidence others have in the quality of services available at the facility.

- Establishing trust on the part of the promoter and the ticket-buying public in the professionalism of the facility manager and staff.

- Advertising the facility in various trade publications such as *Amusement Business, Variety*, and *Performance.*

- Attending appropriate trade and convention functions and networking with other facilities.

- Maintaining visibility with local and national promoters.

- Producing a facility informational brochure detailing the specifications of the building, staff, types of events, and event suitability.

- Preparing and making available a current financial report for the facility.

- Assigning responsibility of booking and scheduling to one person.

- Preparing contracts for the event and follow up to make sure the contracts are executed and returned with the necessary deposits and certificates of insurance.

Types of Tournaments and Selecting a Particular Type of Tournament

This will be a brief description on how to organize a successful tournament. For greater detail, refer to *Organizing Successful Tournaments* (Byl, 2013). There are also numerous software programs available, such as Tournament Pro (See Tournament Brackets – www.printyourbrackets.com/).

The selection of a tournament is based on the goals of the program. The programming team/programmer should answer the following questions before selecting a particular type of tournament (Byl, 2013):

- "Should all players or teams play an equal number of contests?

- Does it matter whether the number of contests is the same per player or team?

- Should all the contests to be closely contested?

- Does it matter if there are a few lopsided contests?

- How important is it to know who comes in first, second, third, fourth, or fifth? (p. 113)."

The common types of tournaments used in programs are single elimination, double elimination, round robin, and extended. There are variations to these such as multi-level, round robin-double split, -triple split, and -quadruple split.

Single Elimination Tournament

The single elimination tournament is best used for postseason competition after the completion of a round robin tournament. The advantages of a single elimination tournament are that the format is easy to use and understand, it accommodates a large number of entries, it requires few games, and it requires few playing areas. The disadvantages are that each participant is guaranteed only one game, accurate seeding is crucial, and it does not maximize use of multiple playing areas.

Double Elimination Tournament

The double elimination tournament is best used when time and playing areas are limited and final standings are important. The advantages of a double elimination tournament are that each participant is guaranteed two games, so a participant who loses once can still win the championship; it requires few playing areas; and it is a better measure of ability than a single elimination tournament. The disadvantages are that some players participate in many games and others in few, it takes many rounds to complete, and it does not maximize use of multiple playing areas.

Round Robin Tournament

A round robin tournament is best used for league play and whenever standings are essential. The advantages of a round robin tournament are that all players play each other so true standings result, seeding is unimportant, it uses multiple playing areas effectively, and no one is eliminated. The disadvantages are that it requires many games and several games may be lopsided.

Extended Tournaments

Extended tournaments are best for individual sports in recreational settings. The advantages of extended tournaments are that they can be conducted over any length of time, the number of games per entry can be limited, they require little supervision, and no one is eliminated. The disadvantage is the number of contests depends upon participants' initiative in challenging.

References

Appenzeller, H. & Appenzeller, T. (2008). *Successful sport management* (3rd ed.). Durham, NC: Carolina Academic Press.

Byl, J. (2013). *Organizing successful tournaments* (4th ed). Champaign, IL: Human Kinetics, Inc.

Micocci, T. (2008). *Booking performance tours: Marketing and acquiring live arts and entertainment.* New York: Allworth Press/Skyhorse Publishing, Inc.

Mull, R. L., Forrester, S. A., & Barnes, M. L. (2012). *Recreational sport management* (5th ed.). Urbana, IL: Sagamore Publishing, LLC.

Rossman, J. R. (2012). *Recreation programming: Designing and staging leisure experiences* (6th ed.). Urbana, IL: Sagamore.

Sawyer, T. H. (2009). *Facility management for physical activity and sport.* Urbana, IL: Sagamore.

CHAPTER 19

Planning Facilities
Master Plan, Site Selection, and Development Phases

Thomas H. Sawyer
Professor Emeritus, Indiana State University

Michael G. Hypes
Morehead State University

Tonya L. Gimbert
Indiana State University

Anyone who has been involved in facility planning and development understands that errors are common during the planning and development process. The challenge is to complete a facility project with the fewest number of errors. Before becoming too deeply involved in the planning and development process, it is important to review some of the common errors that have been made in the past. Flynn (1985), Horine and Stotlar (2013), Sawyer (1999, 2002, 2005, 2013), Fried (2009), NIRSA (2009), Puhalla, Krans, and Goatley (2010), and Long (2012) suggest these errors include, but are not limited to (1) failure to provide adequate and appropriate accommodations for persons with disabilities throughout the facility; (2) failure to provide adequate storage spaces; (3) failure to provide adequate janitorial spaces; (4) failure to observe desirable current professional standards; (5) failure to build the facility large enough to accommodate future uses; (6) failure to provide adequate locker and dressing areas for both male and female users; (7) failure to construct shower, toilet, and dressing rooms with sufficient floor slope and properly located drains; (8) failure to provide doorways, hallways, or ramps so that equipment may be moved easily; (9) failure to provide for multiple uses of facilities; (10) failure to plan for adequate parking for the facility; (11) failure to plan for adequate space for concessions and merchandising; (12) failure to provide for adequate lobby space for spectators; (13) failure to provide for an adequate space for the media to observe activities as well as to interview performers; (14) failure to provide for adequate ticket sales areas; (15) failure to provide adequate space for a loading dock and parking for tractor trailers and buses; (16) failure to provide adequate numbers of restroom facilities for female spectators; (17) failure to provide adequate security and access control into the facility and within the facility; (18) failure to provide adequate separation between activities (buffer or safety zones) in a multipurpose space; (19) failure to provide padding on walls close to activity area, padding and/or covers for short fences, on goal posts, and around trees; (20) failure to plan for the next 50 years; (21) failure to plan for maintenance of the facility; (22) failure to plan for adequate supervision of the various activity spaces within the facility; (23) failure to prepare a financial plan including public and private partnerships; and (24) failure to plan to plan.

Planning Facilities/Venues for Health, Fitness, Physical Activity, Recreation, and Sports

According to Sawyer (2013), the planning process defined in this chapter should be used for planning any of the following facilities/venues:

- stadiums for baseball, football, soccer, softball, or track and field,

- arenas for basketball, football, or ice hockey,

- gymnasiums for public and private schools, colleges and universities, YM/WCAs, or Boys' and Girls' clubs,

- natatoriums (indoor aquatic centers),

- outdoor aquatic centers,

- municipal parks and recreation areas,

- skateboard parks,

- adventure areas, including rope courses, challenge courses and climbing walls, and

- combative areas (p. 4).

Flynn (1985) and Sawyer (2013) suggest the process should include a planning committee, a master plan, pre-development review, a facility checklist, site selection, and development phases.

Development of a Master Plan

Master planning is a decision-making process that promotes changes that will accommodate new and revised needs and search for ways to improve existing conditions. The master plan is very critical during periods of excess and limited resources. The process of planning can and does change attitudes about the needs and utilization of current assets, as well as provides a way for communicating with the stakeholders (Sawyer, 2013, p. 4).

The master-planning process requires coordination, organization, and integration of program, financial, and physical planning. Such planning is cyclical in nature and requires the development of procedures and schedules implemented by the expertise of architectural firms, strategic, and master planning staff to ensure that the various activities occur in the proper sequence (see Figure 19.1). Another important characteristic of the master-planning process is its ability to respond to changing needs. It must be a flexible and dynamic plan so that it is easy to amend, taking into consideration future projections as reflected by the realities of the present and the absolutes of the past. This means the process will be more important than the eventual product (Sawyer, 2013, p. 4).

Master planning is a process structured to promote cost-effective development decisions that best serve the goals and objectives of the organization. The process operates on the premise that the development of facilities and their ongoing management can best serve specific program needs if the organization's standards of space planning, facilities programming, design, and construction management are closely linked (Sawyer, 2013, p. 4).

Typical Phases of a Master Plan

The master plan can be used to answer three common questions often raised: Where are we? Where do we want to go? How do we get there? This approach is flexible to allow the individual organization to reflect local conditions, priorities, and emphases (Sawyer, 2013, p. 4).

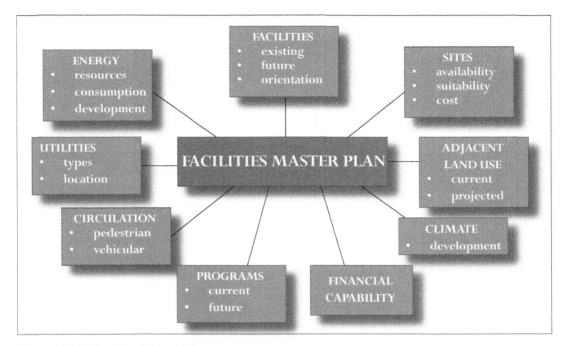

Figure 19.1. Facilities Master Plan (*Source:* White & Karabetsos, 1999; Sawyer, 2013)

Establishment of an Ad Hoc Program Committee and a Plan for Planning

The organization's ad hoc planning advisory committee (sometimes called the program committee), according to Sawyer (2013) should be composed of the following members:

- program specialists,
- end users,
- financial consultants,
- maintenance personnel,
- community representatives,
- management representatives,
- facility consultants, and
- risk management and safety consultants (Sawyer, 2013, p. 4).

The role of the planning advisory committee includes representing all of the organization's constituencies, overseeing and reviewing the ongoing work, communicating with the various stakeholders about the work in progress, findings, and results, validating the process, resolving unsettled issues, and endorsing the results and forwarding the master plan for approval (Sawyer, 2013, p. 6).

The committee should be assisted by the office staff within the organization, which should keep the senior administration advised of the ongoing work, coordinate and schedule the planning efforts, serve as committee recorder, assist in communicating the ongoing work to the stakeholders, and represent the committee at planning work sessions and related meetings (Sawyer, 2013, p. 6).

Organization Briefings and Initiation of Organization Master Plan Studies

According to Flynn (1985) and Sawyer (2013), the committee should organize and schedule information meetings to (a) notify the organization and the community of the organization's planning activity, purpose, method, and schedule; (b) solicit immediate concerns, comments, and suggestions; (c) encourage participation in the planning process and identify organization or community issues; and

(d) identify the planning staff who will be available for further discussions of these and related matters (Sawyer, 2013, p. 6).

Identification and Confirmation of the Organization's Goals and Objectives

Now detailed planning can begin with three concurrent studies: development of an organization profile, identification of capital improvements, and analysis of existing conditions. The development of the organization's program statement is intended to generally describe the organization's niche (see Figure 19.2). The statement should include, but not be limited to a brief history of the organization; the organization's mission; the organization's programs, products, and services; the administrative structure; critical issues and strategic responses; goals and objectives for the organization; details about clientele; an outline of short-range planning, mid-range planning, and long-range planning; and other programmatic features that help describe the organization as a distinctive operational entity (see Table 19.1). Finally, the statement should conclude with a descriptive overview of how the existing situation is expected to change strategically during the period covered by the proposed organization master plan and the implications and consequences such changes may have on the physical development of the organization (Sawyer, 2013, p. 6).

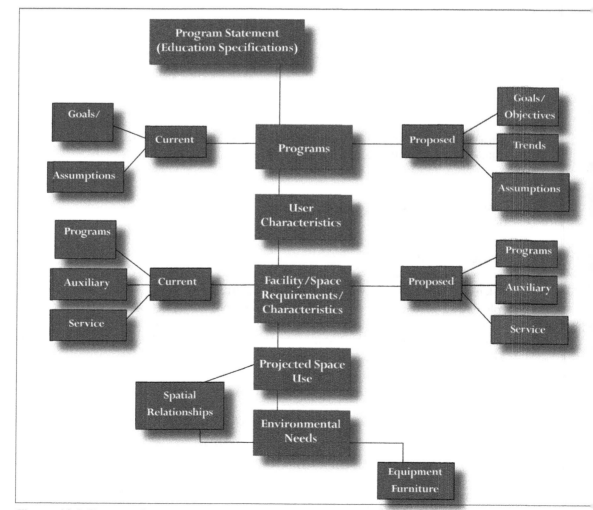

Figure 19.2. Program Statement (*Source:* White & Karabetsos, 1999; Sawyer, 2013)

Table 19.1

Sample Building Program Statement Outline

Part I. Objectives of the Programs
  a. Instructional (professional service)
  b. Recreational sports
  c. Adapted activities
  d. Athletics (interscholastic and intercollegiate)
  e. Club sports
  f. Community/school programs
  g. Others

Part II. Basic Assumptions to be Addressed
  a. Facilities will provide for a broad program of instruction, adapted activities, intramural and other sports
  b. Demographics of the population who will use the facility
  c. Existing facilities will be programmed for use
  d. Basic design considerations. What is most important?
  e. Facility expansion possibilities will be provided for in the planning
  f. Outdoor facilities should be located adjacent to indoor facilities
  g. Consideration will be given to administration and staff needs
  h. Existing problems
  i. Others

Part III. Comparable Facility Analysis
  a. Visit comparable facilities that have been recently constructed
  b. Compare cost, design features, etc.

Part IV. Factors Affecting Planning
  a. Federal and state legislation
  b. Club sports movement
  c. The community education or "Lighted School" program
  d. Surge of new noncompetitive activities being added to the curriculum
  e. Expansion of intramural sports and athletic programs
  f. Sharing certain facilities by boys and men and girls and women (athletic training rooms and equipment rooms)
  g. Coeducational programming
  h. Emphasis on individual exercise programs
  i. Physical fitness movement
  j. Systems approach in design and construction
  k. New products
  l. Others

Part V. Explanation of Current and Proposed Programming
  a. Instructional
  b. Intramural sports
  c. Club sports
  d. Adaptive programs
  e. Community/school
  f. Recreational programs
  g. Priority listing of programs
  h. Others

Part VI. Preliminary Data Relative to the Proposed New Facilities

(*Source:* White & Karabetsos, 1999; Sawyer, 2013)

It is important to compile a 10-year listing of projected capital improvements for the organization. Capital improvement items should include buildings, landscape, circulation (i.e., pedestrian and vehicular traffic), infrastructure (i.e., chilled air, electricity, roadways, sewage, sidewalks, steam, telecommunications, water, etc.), land acquisition, and actions that will change and modify the existing physical plant (e.g., new state highway right-of-way) (Sawyer, 2013, p. 6).

The objective of the survey of existing conditions is to discover and describe elements that, in combination, typically help create, inform, and/or express the organization as a physical place designed and operated as an organization for a specific purpose and located in a setting that has tangible physical characteristics. Certain items should be identified and defined in graphic and narrative formats so as to describe location, function, and physical character of elements. Such items include the following (LaGro, 2007; Russ, 2009):

- land ownership;

- land forms and topography;

- microclimate;

- soils and related subsurface conditions;

- recreational, social, and cultural patterns;

- land use;

- building use;

- buildings rated by physical condition, building entrances, exits, and service points, pedestrian and vehicular circulation systems; and

- public transportation, parking, landscapes, ecological and natural settings, views, vistas, and related design features, major utilities by location, type, and condition, site history and heritage, site and building accessibility, and site and building problems.

Synthesis and Evaluation of Findings

After establishing an ad hoc planning advisory committee, completing briefings and initiating plan studies, and identifying and confirming master plan goals and objectives, it is time to synthesize and evaluate those findings. This effort should begin to clarify issues and opportunities that should be addressed by the organization and should establish and confirm the direction of the master plan. According to LaGro (2007) and Russ (2008), the issues and opportunities that should surface during the synthesis and evaluation effort relate to the following:

- "The organization's image.

- A sense of place for the improvements.

- Existing and new initiatives that may require new building(s) and infrastructure, improvements and revitalization of existing physical resources, and potential demolition.

- Expansion of present facilities should occur only after careful and thorough evaluation of projected needs and capabilities of existing facilities.

- Once needs are established, the following approaches, listed in priority order, are generally considered the most appropriate way to proceed with the program requirements: (Russ, 2008) (1) higher usage of existing space, (2) renovation of existing structures, (3) infill (i.e., adding vertically or horizontally to existing structures), and (4) expansion of facilities into new areas on the organization's site (p. 177)."

According to LaGro (2007) and Russ (2009), during this phase, the master plan needs to take into consideration generally accepted land use guidelines, such as (1) the highest and best use should be made of all land, (2) avoid land-use conflicts (i.e., neighboring residential and commercial areas), (3) areas should complement each other and promote a visual interest and functionally fit the remainder of the organization's site, (4) facilities should be constructed only on sites that best meet programmatic and environmental objectives of the organization, and (5) the organization should develop a no-build policy relating to the preservation of historic sites or open spaces.

Further, the master plan should contain goals and objectives for circulation and transportation on the organization's site. According to Sawyer (2013) these goals and objectives should include, but not be limited to (1) general access to the organization, (2) vehicular circulation, (3) parking, (4) pedestrian and bicycle circulation, and (5) transit (p. 9).

Another extremely important aspect of the master plan will be the utilities and service elements. A consolidated utility system consistent with the projected needs of the organization should be developed. This system should be designed for simplicity of maintenance and future needs for extension or expansion of the utility network (Sawyer, 2013, p. 9).

The master plan should consider the landscape design. The primary landscape goal for the campus should be to present an image with a high degree of continuity and quality. The landscape design should take into consideration the organization's buildings and grounds, accessibility issues, fire, security, energy conservation, and desired development beyond the organization's property line (Sawyer, 2013, p. 9).

The following steps assume an organization planning a new facility from the ground up (Flynn, 1985; Sawyer, 2013).

Regional Analysis

Sufficient data must be gathered about the off-site surroundings to ensure that the project will be compatible with surrounding environments, both manmade and natural. This part of the design process is referred to as the regional analysis. It should include the following (Sawyer, 2013):

- Service area of the facility under construction (i.e., major facilities such as parks, large commercial areas facilities, and minor facilities, such as children's playgrounds, senior citizen centers, local library, etc.).

- User demand (i.e., determining the kind of use desired by clients, activity interests, demographic makeup of residents, local leadership, and calculating the number of users).

- Access routes (i.e., major and secondary routes).

- Governmental functions and boundaries (i.e., contact the local planning agency and local government offices).

- Existing and proposed land uses (i.e., gathering information about abutting land ownership, adjacent land uses, land use along probable access routes, off-site flooding and erosion problems, offsite pollution sources, views [especially of aesthetic and historic interest], and significant local architectural or land use characteristics).

- Regional influences (i.e., check for anything unusual or unique that could either enhance or cause problems to the project) (p. 9).

Site Analysis

The planning committee will need to consider various pieces of information prior to selecting the building site. The considerations for site selection (Flynn, 1985; LaGro, 2007; Miller, 1997; Russ, 2009; Sawyer, 2013) include the following:

- Access to the site (i.e., ingress and egress, surrounding traffic generators, accessibility via public transportation)

- Circulation within the site (e.g., roads—paved and unpaved, bicycle trails, walks and hiking trails)

- Parking

- Water supply

- Sewage disposal

- Electrical service

- Telecommunication service

- Other utilities, including oil/natural gas transmission lines, or cable TV

- Structures to be constructed or renovated

- Environmental concerns and conditions on and off property (e.g., noise, air, water, and visual pollution)

- Easements and other legal issues (e.g., deed restrictions, rights of way, and less-than-fee-simple ownership)

- Zoning requirements (i.e., changing the zoning is usually time consuming and expensive and frequently not possible)

- Historical significance

- Any existing uses (activities) on the site

- Climactic conditions prevalent in the area by season (e.g., temperature, humidity, air movement velocity, duration, and direction, amount of sunshine, precipitation—rain, sleet, snow, sun angles and subsequent shadows, special conditions—ice storms, hurricanes, tornadoes, heavy fog, heavy rainstorm, floods, and persistent cloud cover)

- Nuisance potentials (e.g., children nearby, noise, etc.)

- Natural features (e.g., topography, slope analysis, soil conditions, geology, hydrology, flora and fauna)

- Economic impact of a site (e.g., labor costs, growth trends, population shifts, buying power index, available work force, property taxes, tax Incentives, surrounding competition, utility costs, incentives, area of dominant influence [ADI], designated market area [DMA], and established enterprise zones)

- Natural barriers and visibility

- Supporting demographics (e.g., age, gender, occupation, marital status, number of children, expenditures, education, income, number of earners in the family, ethnic background, etc.) and psychographics (e.g., lifestyle data or lifestyle marketing)

- Security concerns (e.g., proximity of police, fire, emergency medical personnel, hospitals) (pp. 9–10)

The most important aspects of site selection are location, location, and location. If the site is not in the most accessible location with a high profile for people to recognize, it will have a negative effect on the success of the venture.

The following seven steps, according to Flynn (1985) and Sawyer (2013) apply to both new ventures and established organizations planning major overhauls:

Master plan agenda. The master plan agenda is a specific list of issues, opportunities, and projected physical improvements. The plan will include the number and type of structures to be constructed or renovated, the estimated capital costs over a set period of time, approximate locations of new structures and probable priority to be considered in the preparation of the master plan (Sawyer, 2013, p. 10) (see Figure 19.3).

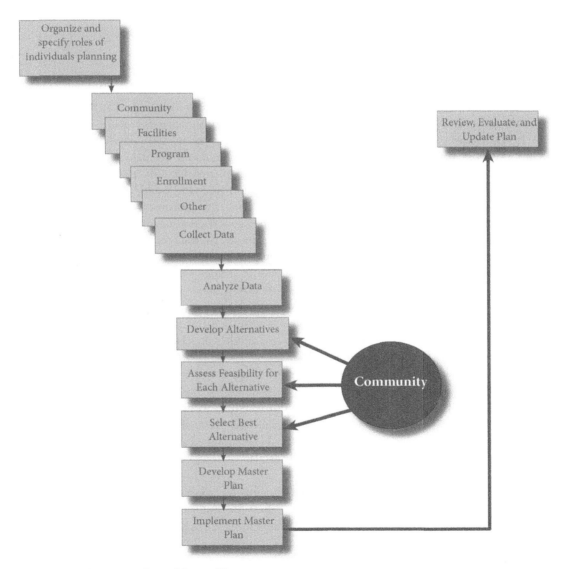

Figure 19.3. Developing a Master Plan (*Source:* White & Karabetsos, 1999; Sawyer, 2013)

Review and discussion. This step offers the organization and its stakeholders the opportunity to review and comment on the work completed on the master plan to date. The planning committee should be present at these open forums to answer questions and understand the issues and concerns raised. The presentations for these open forum meetings should include (Sawyer, 2013):

- a description of the process,
- a summary of the organization's profile,
- a review of the projected capital improvements,
- a summary of the surveys and analysis of existing conditions,
- an accounting of issues and opportunities,
- a list of items on the master plan agenda, and
- a description of the next steps in the planning process (p. 10).

The committee should review and evaluate all reactions and concerns raised at the meeting(s). Then the committee should determine appropriate modifications to the master plan.

Preparation of the draft master plan. The preliminary master plan should be expressed in both general and specific terms. The former is intended to communicate the major features of the campus plan. The latter view enriches the vision by showing in greater detail the character, justification, feasibility, and phasing of selected significant improvements. Flynn (1985) and Sawyer (2013) indicate the following components typically appear in a master plan: (1) new construction; (2) building and site reconstruction, renewal, and demolition; (3) revisions to and extension of the circulation systems; (4) new and improved landscape projects; (5) parking patterns; (6) transportation proposals; (7) infrastructure projects; (8) joint organization and community development; (9) drawings and illustrations; (10) block models; (11) organization design guidelines for buildings and building materials; and (12) landscape guidelines including views, boundary identification, major entrances and exits, service entrances and exits, building sites, vehicular and pedestrian circulation systems, parking, water features, rock formations, gardens, open spaces, and passive or recreational spaces (Sawyer, 2013, p. 10).

Review of preliminary plan. The planning committee will present the preliminary plan to the organization's constituencies, administration, board, and community at large. These groups will review the preliminary plan. After careful review, a combined report will be generated with any suggested modifications and justifications for the modifications (Sawyer, 2013, p. 10).

Revision of the master plan to obtain consensus and approval. After the preliminary plan review has been completed, the master plan should be revised to include any recommended changes from the stakeholders. The revised plan should be published and distributed as a draft master plan for use in the plan-approval process. The master plan remains a dynamic and flexible document even after approval (Sawyer, 2013, p. 10).

Documentation and dissemination of the master plan. The ad hoc planning advisory committee is transformed into a standing planning advisory committee, according to Sawyer (2013), with the following responsibilities: (1) serve as a conduit for the organization's community to present issues and suggestions regarding the master plan; (2) review all capital expenditure projects; (3) confirm conformance to the campus plan; (4) expedite the resolution of nonconformance; (5) review, resolve, and recommend plan amendments; and (6) participate in an annual review of the master plan and cyclical master plan revisions (p. 10).

Master plan amendment process. The master plan will need to be amended periodically to stay current with new trends and developments. The standing planning advisory committee should plan to revise the master plan every five years. The process would be the same as the original process that established the master plan. The standing planning advisory committee will annually review the master plan. If a major new initiative has been approved by the administration and requires modification of the master plan or a major failure of a structure or utility occurs, the committee can request that a modification be made in the master plan. This recommendation would be forwarded to the administration and board for approval (Sawyer, 2013, p. 10).

Implementation of Plan

After the master plan has been approved as a guideline for the organization's future planning, it is important to remember that the master plan is a guide for the entire organization. It is not a specific plan for a particular structure. Once approval and funding have been gained for a specific structure, then the developmental process begins for that structure. The common components that compose a development process for a single structure or complex include research; regional analysis; site analysis; program; functional analysis; combined site, function, land use; refinement and site plan/overall design; construction documents; bidding; construction; and review (Sawyer, 2013, p. 11).

Design Team

The design team (see Figure 19.4) is composed of the project planning committee, architect(s), engineers, facility consultant(s), interior designer(s), construction manager, acoustical consultant(s), and turf management specialist(s). Generally, the architectural firm selected by the organization employs engineers (e.g., civil, electrical, mechanical, and structural), interior designers, acoustical consultants, and turf management specialists. The organization often hires a facility consultant to work with the program committee and architect. However, in some cases, the architectural firm as part of the design team may employ the facility consultant (Sawyer, 2013, pp. 11–12).

A facility consultant can provide numerous services. If the consultant is part of the owner's team rather than the architectural team, this individual should serve as a liaison between the project planning committee and the architect. It is important to understand that the majority of architects employed by an organization have little or no experience in designing these types of facilities. It would be preferable to select an architectural firm familiar with these types of facilities. If this is not possible, then the facility consultant becomes very important to the process (Sawyer, 2013, p. 12).

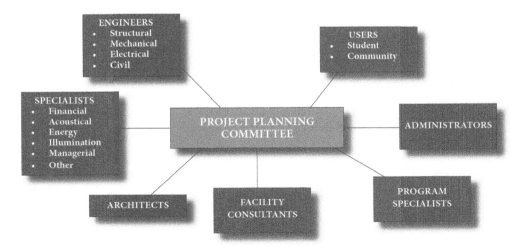

Figure 19.4. Project Planning Committee (*Source:* White & Karabetsos, 1999; Sawyer, 2013)

Selecting an Architectural Firm

The selection of an architectural team should be based solely on the reputation and experience of the company and a formal review process. Once a project is approved then an advertisement (a request for qualifications [RFQ]) should be placed in the news media seeking qualifications of interested architectural firms for the specific project. Later, a letter would be sent to specific firms who qualify, inviting them to submit proposals (Sawyer, 2013, p. 12).

Tips for Drafting the Request for Proposal

The request for proposal, (or RFP), is composed of the following components (Noyes & Skolnicki, 2001; Sawyer, 2013): (1) Prepare an RFP and communicate to a broad list of applicants to ascertain their qualifications and experience for this particular type of project. (2) Draft an evaluation sheet for the selection committee to use to determine who is qualified. (3) Based on responses to the RFQ, select no more than 20 firms to which to send the RFP. (4) Draft a second evaluation sheet to narrow the pool to three to five finalists for the selection committee. (5) Provide the applicants adequate time to prepare a proposal—between three and four weeks, or longer if holidays are involved. (6) Request the firms include in their proposals the following: a list of recently completed projects (last 10 years), the estimated budgeted costs and actual costs for each project, and in-house professionals available to work on the project. (7) The owner needs to provide the applicants with adequate background for the project. (8) The finalists will participate in an interview process (Sawyer, 2013, p. 12).

Prior to the Interview

Prior to interviewing the finalists, the program committee, facility consultant, and administration representatives should travel to at least two facilities built by each firm and review the final result of their efforts. The travelers need to speak with the facility manager and users and ask about the best features of the facility and the worst features. What would they do differently? After completing the tours, draft a number of questions to ask the architect during the interview (Sawyer, 2013, p. 12).

The Interview

After the field of applicants is narrowed to three to five, the firms should be interviewed. Each firm should demonstrate its competence and philosophy in the following areas (modified from the American Institute of Architects [http://www.aia.org] suggestions):

- client's role in the design process,

- number and type of consultants required,

- design or build versus conventional design versus fast-track process,

- extent of engineering services,

- construction supervision,

- number of sets of plans or specifications to be provided,

- construction cost,

- factors that may influence construction,

- time schedule and target dates for completion,

- architectural fee and payment schedule, and

- development of a budget.

Criteria for Selection

The successful firm should be open and flexible with the program committee and facility consultant, experienced with this type of project, and able to demonstrate that they have completed facilities within the budget developed (Noyes & Skolnicki, 2001; Sawyer 2013). The firm should be able to demonstrate awareness, a user-friendly process, past success with other similar projects, and past fees as related to similar projects. Finally, the firm should be willing to provide accessibility to the architects and engineers during the planning and building phases (Sawyer, 2013, p. 13).

Research for Facility Development

In its research, the planning committee should be concerned with (1) knowing and understanding the current and future needs and desires of the people who are involved in and/or affected by the proposed project and (2) knowing everything reasonably possible about the project function and/or activity and the space requirements (Sawyer, 2013, p. 13).

Designers Design for People

At least four groups of people may need to be involved in the research and eventually be satisfied, including clients (board of directors, etc.), users, affected neighbors and/or public, managers and operators, and possibly others. Each of the relevant groups must be identified and its needs, concerns, and desires understood. There will almost certainly be some conflicts between the various groups. Understanding these problems in advance may make it possible to resolve them during the design phase (Sawyer, 2013, p. 13).

Maintenance and Operations

Maintenance and operational needs, small but significant, must be clearly understood. They can make a project successful or doom it to future failure. According to Sawyer (2013), the following are some specific items to consider:

Maintenance

- Will maintenance be conducted by in-house labor or by contract?
- Is special equipment used or needed (e.g., riding lawn mowers, etc.)?
- Does maintenance staff have any requirements for any standard equipment (e.g., motors, lights, shower heads, pumps, etc.) used or preferred by the maintenance staff?
- How capable is staff to maintain sophisticated equipment?
- What are maintenance space requirements, such as equipment clearance around motors and pumps, so routine maintenance can be performed, etc.?
- Are there any special fire protection requirements?
- What special storage requirements are needed for flammables and chemicals?

Operations

- Security—Is it needed? If so, what type (patrol, electronic, entrance only, dogs, by whom)? If patrolled, how—by foot, car, motorcycle, horse, bike, or boat?
- Hours of operation—Is night lighting required?
- Trash pickup—In-house? Contract? Kind of equipment used?
- Deliveries—Food, supplies, etc. When are separate entrances and exits needed?
- Communications system—Speakers, phone, radio, bell system, public address system?

- Safety/first aid—Are special facilities needed? Where? Extent? Emergency vehicle access?

- Peak use—How is it handled? Restrict use or provide overflow capacity?

Special Programs
- Will there be any? If so, what kind (e.g., concerts at noon, employee training, visitor information and/or education, arts and craft shows, special exhibits)?

- Any special space requirements for programs? Lighting? Service areas? Other utilities? (p. 13).

Facilities and Their Requirements

Most facilities have specific site requirements. Technical data must be gathered on all the proposed facilities. At a minimum, the following must be known (Sawyer, 2013):
- Size (actual dimensions plus any buffer spaces or required accessory space)

- Grade requirements (i.e., maximum and minimum heights)

- Any special construction requirements (e.g., aquatic centers, tennis courts, or ice hockey rinks)

- Utility needs (i.e., type and amount) (pp. 13–14).

Predevelopment Review

Along with the master planning process, a thorough review of facility needs should be completed for a proposed new or renovated facility. This review should be completed before an architect or consultant is brought on board. This can save time and money as well as assuring that the structure will fit the proposed program. It is important to develop a checklist at the beginning, not the end, of the planning process. This will help focus and guide the dream and planning process. See the appendixes for examples of specific checklists as a guide in developing your own checklist for the proposed project (Sawyer, 2013, p. 14).

Program

Program, as used here, is the organization of the information needed for planning a project to provide an appropriate facility to meet the needs of the affected people (client, users, neighbors, and staff). (See Sample Facility and Equipment Program Statement in the Appendices available in the student and faculty resource center at www.sagamorepub.com). Program needs should include a list of activities, facility needs for each activity listed, number of participants in each activity during peak periods, size of each facility ranging from minimum to ideal, and a description of the relationship between activities and facilities (i.e., Can certain activities coexist with other activities at the same time in one facility?) (Sawyer, 2013, p. 14).

Functional Analysis

Functional analysis is the process of analyzing and organizing the information provided in programming and relationships by translating that analysis into graphic symbols. It establishes the preferred or ideal physical relationships of all the component parts of a project. The process commonly consists of four parts: space diagrams, relationship charts and/or diagrams, bubble diagrams, and land-use concepts. All of the elements contained in the activity/program must be considered and their desired functional and physical relationships accommodated (Sawyer, 2013, p. 14).

Combined Site, Function, and Land Use

Two issues are keys to land use: people needs and site constraints. At this point, the various constraints and opportunities presented by the site must become integrated with people needs. It is also the time when the reality of the site constraints may require changes in the program. This step combines the site analysis with the functional analysis. If changes are made in the program, the changes must be incorporated throughout the functional analysis phase. This step in the site design process is where analysis of the site data is most completely utilized.

LaGro (2007) and Russ (2009) suggest if the site selected is too small, the following options should be considered:

- Physical modification of the site. This may be the least desirable option, because it is almost always undesirable from an environmental standpoint. It frequently is not aesthetically pleasing, and it is usually expensive.

- Expand the site if adjacent land is available. This is frequently not possible and can be expensive.

- Change to another site. This can be expensive, and alternate sites may not be available.

- Cancel the project. This is not usually desirable or possible.

- Creatively look at new ways of solving the problem.

The location is the most difficult choice. It is always difficult to abandon the proven acceptable way of designing and operating facilities. When successful, however, it can often lead to outstanding, innovative solutions.

Refinement and Site Plan/Overall Design

After the land-use step has been completed, the planning committee needs to refine the focus of the building project before it moves to the site plan/overall design step. After the refinement is complete, then, and only then, should the planners consider site planning and overall design. A site plan shows the entire existing and proposed site features superimposed on a topographic base map at an appropriate scale. It functions as the coordinating plan that ensures that all the project parts fit together. This is the point in the site design process where imagination and creativity are really important. In addition, this plan is almost always the feature part of any presentation to the client and other interested parties. Finally, accompanying the site plan will be a number of drawings, including utilities (e.g., water sources, sewer lines, and electricity/communication lines), grading and drainage, circulation, scale drawings, relationships, and three-dimensional aspects (Sawyer, 2013, p. 14).

Construction Documents

(Source: American Institute of Architects, http://www.aia.org)

Construction documents control the actual constructed results and consist of two separate parts: working drawings and specifications, the written companion to the working drawings. Upon completion of the working drawings and specifications, the project is bid and, if the bids are satisfactory, the contract is awarded.

Working Drawings

All working drawings must be clear, concise, and understandable to the people who are going to construct the building. Only as much detail as is necessary to build the project should be included. More detail might give the client more control but will definitely cost more money for design and will result in higher bids. All pieces must be clearly presented in such a manner that will allow accurate building.

All construction drawings must be accurate, clearly labeled, and dimensioned. If in doubt as to the need for a label or a dimension, include it! Normally, written numbers on the plan take precedence over field-scaled distances.

A useful tool in outlining the numbers and kinds of construction drawings is a plan control list. Each drawing expected to be needed is listed by description. This enables the designer(s) to coordinate work and helps to ensure that all aspects of the project are included.

With the completed list of plans, an estimate of time required to complete the working drawing and the necessary scheduling of work assignments can be carried out. This plan control document will probably be revised during the preparation of drawings. In its final form, it will become the drawing index listing for Sheet 2 of the working drawings package.

The more detailed and elaborate the working drawings, the higher the cost of preparing them, and very frequently, the higher the cost of building the project. A rule of thumb: The smaller the job, the fewer the construction documents. Small contractors do not like excessive control and paperwork. They frequently will not bid on projects with elaborate specifications, and if they do, they bid high. Frequently, too much control will cause bids to be higher, but does not result in an increase in quality.

The construction drawings must be reviewed by the maintenance staff to 1) ensure compatibility of parts with existing facilities, 2) see if the project can be effectively maintained at reasonable cost, and 3) determine if alternative materials or design modifications would reduce the costs and/or simplify maintenance. A detailed cost estimate is almost always necessary at this point in the design process. If costs estimated for the time of construction are too high, then the project may have to be reduced in scope and/or redesigned. Be certain that lifetime operations and maintenance costs are also considered in the estimate.

The construction drawings should include the following: demolition and site preparation, utilities, landscape and site improvements, structural, architectural, mechanical/HVAC, mechanical/plumbing, mechanical/fire protection, and electrical/telecommunications.

Specifications

The written portion of the construction documents comes in three parts: bidding and contract requirements (including the bid documents)—Division 0; general requirements—Division 1; and construction specifications Divisions 2-16.

This part of the design process is often most disliked by designers because of the massive detail required. It is, however, of the utmost importance in ensuring that the design is actually built according to the way it was envisioned.

Specifications should be organized in the 16-division format developed by the Construction Specifications Institute (CSI) as follows:

Division 0:	Bidding requirements, contract forms, and conditions of the contract	Division 9:	Finishes
		Division 10:	Specialties
Division 1:	General requirements/special conditions	Division 11:	Equipment
Division 2:	Site work	Division 12:	Furnishings
Division 3:	Concrete	Division 13:	Special construction
Division 4:	Masonry	Division 14:	Conveying systems
Division 5:	Metals	Division 15A:	Mechanical (HVAC)
Division 6:	Wood and plastic	Division 15B:	Mechanical (plumbing)
Division 7:	Thermal and moisture protection	Division 16:	Electrical
Division 8:	Doors and windows		

General Notes

- Include everything in the specifications that you want to see in the final constructed product.

- Make sure that Division 1 includes the contractor providing "as-built" drawings, catalogue cuts, and, where appropriate, an operation manual and training of operating and maintenance staff.

- Include only information necessary to the specific project—especially if it is a small one. As with plans, small contractors don't like and frequently don't understand long, involved specifications; therefore, they will not bid or may increase their bids accordingly. The heavier, thicker, and more complicated the specifications are, the higher the bid.

- Conversely, the less detail you have in the specifications, the greater the opportunity for mis-understandings between the owner and contractor.

- All phases of specifications are readily adaptable to computerization and/or word processing. Much time can be saved if "canned" specifications are used, thus speeding up this tedious but crucial task. Computerization will probably lead to standardization of details and format. (Sawyer, 2013, p. 15).

Schematic Design Phase

In the schematic design phase, the architect prepares schematic design documents that consist of drawings and other documents illustrating the scale and relationship of project components. These are based on the mutually agreed-upon program with the owner, the schedule, and the construction budget requirements and they are submitted to the owner for approval.

The products from this first phase of the project consist of the following: renderings (architect's conception of the building) and models, floor plans and elevations, narrative (a description of the project with sufficient detail to allow an initial review by the organization), outline specifications (e.g., exterior materials, interior finishes, mechanical and electrical systems, identification of significant discrepancies between the project requirements and the budget), and cost estimates.

The project management issues for this phase consist of cost and budget, program expansion, schedule slippage, design review, quality assurance, use of design and estimating contingencies, code compliance, and building committee(s) (Sawyer, 2013, p. 16).

Design Development Phase

Based on schematic design documents and any adjustments authorized by the owner in the program, schedule, or construction budget, the architect prepares further design development documents for approval by the owner. These consist of drawings and other documents to fix and describe the size and character of the project as to architectural, structural, mechanical, and electrical systems, materials, and other appropriate elements.

The products for this phase include drawings (site and landscape, utilities, structural, architectural, mechanical, electrical, and special equipment), narrative, specifications, and cost estimates.

The project management issues for this phase consist of cost and budget, scope creep (common elements previously eliminated from the project that reappear in design development), design review, technical review (specific reviews initiated by the owner to ensure the organization's guidelines for design and construction are being complied with), and use of design contingencies (Sawyer, 2013, p. 16).

Construction Approaches

Lump-Sum Contract

The traditional approach is commonly known as the lump-sum contract. In this method, a general contractor is selected based on the lowest bid. The general contractor is responsible for selecting all subcontractors and all construction materials. It is not advisable to enter into this type of contractual relationship because the general contractor has too much control of the profit and loss for a job.

Pros. This is a simple, traditional approach with a defined project scope, suitable for small or straightforward projects, and fiduciary architect/engineer (A/E) and nonfiduciary general contractor roles are clear.

Cons. The builder has no input in design; the price is uncertain until bids are received; it is the slowest project delivery; there is no control over subcontractor selection; an adversarial relationship could exist among the A/E, owner, and contractor. It is prone to cost growth through changes and claims; there is a high incidence of litigation (Sawyer, 2013, p. 16).

Construction Manager

Many public projects employ a construction manager to oversee the progress of the construction through all phases. This method allows for multiple bids, such as one for mechanical, another for electrical, and another for general construction of the structure.

Pros. There is builder selection flexibility, pre-construction services, a faster delivery schedule, early budget input and control, and change flexibility. Money is saved with controlled purchasing, optimal trade contractor selection through competitive bidding, and effective minority- and women-owned business enterprises procurement.

Cons. The owner assumes contractual cost and schedule risk, and there is no single point of contract accountability. The owner must manage more contracts, and the price is not guaranteed. Potential additional design costs and potential claims exist (Sawyer, 2013, p. 16).

Design and Build

The next approach is design and build. This method places the responsibility for completing the project on the architect and builder who work for the same company. This option sets a fixed price, encourages interaction, and eliminates additional costs arising from design changes. A variation of design and build is called fast tracking. It is used in large projects in which contracts are let incrementally or sequentially so that the construction time may be reduced. This variation may be not be allowed in public projects due to federal or state mandates.

Pros. There is a single point of responsibility for design and construction; it offers the fastest schedule for delivery and allows for early identification of guaranteed costs.

Cons. There can be loss of owner control, quality, or both and loss of checks and balances. Contractors' profits may be excessive, and competitive bid design and build selection with guaranteed maximum price is problematic (Sawyer, 2013, p. 16).

Design/Build/Finance/Leaseback

Another approach is design/build/finance/leaseback. This approach encompasses all the design associated with the construction project as well as obtaining funding and securing a location for the project. Furthermore, this approach also includes operations and maintenance support after the building is occupied for a specific time frame. The financially challenged owner will find this approach more acceptable. The owner will lease the facility for a specific number of years and will own the facility at the end of the term.

Pros. This approach offers a lease commitment versus a capital expense and an early lease cost determination. There is single-source management of the entire program and risk assumption, lease, financing, and ownership flexibility, and it avoids long-term capital ownership commitment.

Cons. Potential interest rates are a risk. There is diminished owner control and potential for higher operating costs. Future facility control is limited, and residual value is reduced or eliminated.

Building Project Budget Components

It is important to understand what a building project will cost. The following are the common cost components suggested by the American Institute of Architects (AIA):

- land acquisition costs,

- land development costs,

- permitting procurement costs,

- utility tie-in, connection, or impact fees,

- attorney's fees for zoning and permitting,

- regulatory costs,

- consultant fees,

- costs or relocation, staff, and new building simulation drills,

- costs of building commissioning and activation,

- furniture, fixtures, and equipment (FF&E) costs,

- data, security, and telephone infrastructure costs,

- costs of testing and inspection services,

- costs of A/E,

- costs of a construction manager, and

- construction costs.

Construction Document Phase

Based on the approved design development documents and any further adjustments in the scope or quality of the project or in the construction budget authorized by the owner, the architect prepares construction documents for the approval of the owner. These consist of drawings and specifications setting forth in detail the requirements for the construction of the project.

Construction documents (developed by the American Institute of Architects [AIA] and the Associated General Contractors of America [AGCA] consist of the following: invitation to bid, instructions to bidders, information available to bidders, bid forms and attachments, bid security forms, construction agreement, performance bond, payment bond, certificates, contract conditions (i.e., general conditions, and supplementary conditions), specifications (Divisions 1-16), drawings, addendum(s), and contract modifications.

The program management issues for the phase consist of: code compliance, scope creep, schedule slippage, design review, technical review, quality assurance, use of design and estimating contingencies, design contract interpretation and enforcement, bidding and construction strategy (i.e., a lump-sum bid for all components or multiple bids for general contractor, mechanical, electrical, and add-ons or reductions), cost overruns or under runs, design-bid-build (i.e., project designed by an architectural firm and bid out to construction firms to build), design and build and a variation of design and build called fast tracking.

All designers must keep current on the latest product information available in their field of expertise. When the plans and specifications are completed, the project is ready for bid (Sawyer, 2013, p. 17).

Bidding

Bids are opened in front of witnesses, usually the contractors or their representative(s), and an attorney (normally required by a government agency). The bidding process includes (a) bidding and advertising, (b) opening and review of bids, and (c) award of contract. The bid documents include invitation to bid, instructions to bidders, the bid form, other sample bidding and contract forms, and the proposed documents (e.g., drawings and specifications) (Sawyer, 2013, p. 17).

Bidding and Advertising

Bidding is the process of receiving competitive prices for the construction of the project. A bid form should be provided to ensure that all bids are prepared in the same manner for easy comparison. The bids can be received in many ways. The most common are

- lump sum (one overall price),
- lump sum with alternatives (either add-ons or deletions), and
- unit prices.

All bids on large projects should be accompanied by some type of performance bond, ensuring that the contractor will perform the work as designed at the price bid in the time specified. This ensures that bidders are sincere in their prices.

The time and place of the receipt of the sealed bids must be clearly shown on all bid packages. No late bids can be received without compromising the entire bidding process (Sawyer, 2013, p. 17).

Small Projects (Up to $25,000)

A bid of this size can normally be handled informally. The process of calling a selected list of local contractors will usually be sufficient and will probably result in obtaining the best price.

Larger Projects (Over $25,000)

A formal bid process is usually necessary to ensure fairness, accuracy, and a competitive result. The process starts with advertising for bids. Advertising frequently is initiated prior to the completion of the plans with an effective date for picking up the completed plans and specifications. The larger, more complex the project is, the wider the range of advertising necessary. Governmental agencies usually have minimum advertising standards. They advertise in the legal advertisement section of the local paper and papers in larger nearby cities and in professional construction journal(s). In addition, designers or clients frequently have a list of contractors who have successfully built past projects and/or who have indicated an interest in bidding on future projects.

As a minimum, the advertisement should consist of

- a description of the project and kind of work required,
- the date and place plans can be picked up,
- the cost of plans and specifications (usually only sufficient to cover printing costs),
- the bid date and time, and
- client identification.

The approximate value of the project is sometimes included although some designers and clients do not wish to give out this information. With complex projects, it is desirable to schedule a pre-bid conference to explain the design and bidding process to prospective bidders. During the bidding period, one or more prospective bidders frequently raise questions. If the questions require design modifications or clarifications, the questions must be answered in writing in the form of an addendum to all holders of plans (Sawyer, 2013, p. 18).

Opening and Reviewing of Bids

The designers or their representatives are usually present at the bid opening. After the bids are opened and read, it is necessary to analyze them and decide to whom the contract is to be awarded. The technical analysis is usually by the designers who consider whether the bid is complete, the prices are reasonable, and the contractor is able to do the work. A recommendation is then made. The legal analysis by the attorney is conducted concurrently with examining whether bonds are attached, all necessary signatures are included, and all required in formation is provided (Sawyer, 2013, p. 18).

Award of Contract

Assuming favorable analysis by all involved and that the bids are acceptable to the client, the contract will be awarded. Most contracts are awarded to the lowest qualified bidder. Sometimes, however, the low bidder is not large enough or does not have the expertise to do the work required. Occasionally some bids are improperly prepared. In these situations, they may be rejected and the next lowest qualified bidder will be awarded the contract, or the project is rebid. This can lead to problems with the disqualified bids or bidders and is why an attorney should be present (Sawyer, 2013, p. 18).

Payments

Drawdown. Who pays what and when? The key to a successful construction project is timely payments. Normally there is an agreed-upon payment schedule based on the submission of proper invoices for work completed and materials used from the contractor to the owner. This is generally done on a weekly basis.

Progress payments. The owner agrees to make progress payments to the contractor percentage of work completed. The payment requests are submitted based upon the amount of work completed on a line item from a preapproved schedule of values.

Retainage. This is the portion of the construction contract amount that the owner typically holds back until all elements of the work are satisfactorily completed. This amount is established in the beginning of a project and is normally specified in the contract as a percentage (Sawyer, 2013, p. 18).

Construction Phase

The architect should visit the site at least twice monthly at appropriate intervals during the construction stage and make the owner generally familiar with the progress and quality of the work in writing. The architect has other responsibilities, including certifying the payments represented to the owner for payment.

The construction step of a project goes through several phases. The number of phases depends upon the scope of the project and the contracting agency. Two general guidelines govern the construction step: (1) the larger the project, the more steps required, and (2) governmental projects usually have more contractual controls. At least some, and perhaps all, of the following steps will be required during construction (Sawyer, 2013, p. 18).

Pre-Construction Conference

A meeting between the contracting agency and the contractor(s) prior to the commencement of construction to review the contract items and make sure there is an understanding of how the job is to be undertaken (Sawyer, 2013, p. 19).

Construction

The actual construction begins this phase, which could take as much as five years, depending on the scope of the project. However, construction can generally be completed in 18 to 24 months on an average project (Sawyer, 2013, p. 19).

Change Orders

Change orders are defined as official documents requested by either the contractor or the contracting agency that change the approved contract documents. These changes usually include an adjustment of the bid price and a benefit to the contractor. It is better to avoid all change orders. Where this is not possible, be prepared to pay a premium price and to accept delays in contract completion.

The owner (or construction manager) needs to do the following to manage change orders (Sawyer, 2013):

- evaluate the proposed change for impact on the construction budget and schedule,
- determine if the proposed change Is cost effective,
- secure independent estimates of verified change order requests and recommend approval levels,
- challenge the validity of change order pricing by the contractor,
- prepare a proper change order agreement,
- make changes to the project budget and schedule, and
- maintain a log of all change orders approved (p.19).

Pre-Final Inspection and Preparation of Punch List

The initial review of a completed construction project is called a pre-final inspection. This inspection should have all the affected parties' decision makers present including the owner or his or her representative, the architect, the contractor(s), and any subcontractors. At this time, it is also desirable to have the facility operation supervisor present. During this review, a "punch list" is prepared of any work that needs to be completed by the contractor prior to a final inspection. All items that are not completed or are not completed according to specifications should be included on the list. The punch list is then agreed upon and signed by all affected parties. The contractor must then correct and/or finish all the items on the list. When the punch list is completed, it is time to call for a final inspection (Sawyer, 2013, p. 19).

As-Built Drawings and Catalogue Cuts

Defined as the drawings prepared by the contractor showing how the project was actually built. These drawings will be of great value to the operations and maintenance staffs. They must know exactly what facilities were actually built and their locations to be able to maintain the project effectively.

Catalogue cuts are printed information supplied by the manufacturers on materials and equipment used in the project construction. This material is necessary so that the operating staff will be able to learn about the material and equipment. In addition, it is needed for locating necessary replacement parts. It must also be included in working drawings and specifications of future renovations and/or expansion of the project (Sawyer, 2013, p. 19).

Preparation of an Operations Manual

An operations manual contains written instructions on how to operate and maintain special equipment. The minimum data included should be how to start up, how to shut down, inspection(s) time intervals and what should be inspected, schedule of required maintenance, safety precautions, and who to contact for specialized repair assistance (Sawyer, 2013, p. 19).

Training on How to Operate the Project

This contract item is usually included only for larger projects that are unfamiliar to the people who will operate them (Sawyer, 2013, p. 19).

Final Inspection

The final inspection should concentrate on items not found acceptable during any previous inspections. The same review team that made the pre-final inspection should be assembled for the final inspection (Sawyer, 2013, p. 19).

Acceptance of Completed Project

Assuming all the work has been completed as shown on the plans and described in the specifications, the project should be accepted and turned over to the owner or operator. Further, if the contractor has posted a performance bond guaranteeing the work, it should be released by the contracting agency.

If at all possible, avoid partial acceptances. Sometimes it is necessary to take over a part or parts of a project prior to completion of the entire project. If this becomes necessary, the contractor will have the opportunity to blame future problems and/or delays on having to work around the people using the project (Sawyer, 2013, p. 19).

Maintenance Period

When living plants are involved, many contractors have a maintenance period included after the acceptance of the project. This can last anywhere from 30 days or more (for lawns) to 90 days for flowers and, frequently, one full growing season for ground cover, vines, shrubs, and trees (Sawyer, 2013, p. 19).

Bond Period

Most government projects and some larger projects require the contractor to post not only a performance bond, but also a one-year (or some other specified period) warranty on the quality of the work. Usually the bond requires the contractor to replace or repair any defective or damaged items during the time covered by the bond. Typical items would be leaking roofs, infiltration of ground water into sewer lines, puddling of water in parking lots or tennis courts, etc. (Sawyer, 2013, p. 19).

Bond Inspection and Final Acceptance

At the end of the bond period, the original final inspection team holds another inspection. Prior to release of the bond, any problems that have been uncovered during this inspection must be rectified at no cost to the contracting agency. It is important to note that when the bond is released, the contractor no longer has any responsibility to the project (Sawyer, 2013, p. 20).

Review

The project has been completed and turned over to the client. Does the project do what it was designed to from the standpoint of the (a) client, (b) user, (c) affected neighbors and/or public, (d) manager and operator, and (e) design team? There are two basic kinds of information to be gathered: information on people and on physical conditions (Sawyer, 2013, p. 20).

References

Flynn, R. B. (1985). *Planning facilities for athletics, physical education, and recreation.* (8th ed). North Palm Beach, FL and Reston, VA: The Athletic Institute and American Alliance for Health, Physical Education, Recreation, and Dance.

Fried, G. (2009). *Managing sport facilities* (2nd ed.). Champaign, IL: Human Kinetics.

Horine, L., & Stotlar, D. (2013). *Administration of physical education and sport programs* (5th ed). Columbus, OH: McGraw-Hill.

Long J. G. (2012). *Public-private partnerships for Major League sport facilities.* Florence, KY: Routledge/Taylor and Francis Group.

LaGro, J. A. (2007). *Site analysis: A contextual approach to sustainable land planning and site design.* Hoboken, NJ: John Wiley & Sons.

NIRSA. (2009). *Campus recreational sport facilities: Planning, design, and construction guidelines.* Champaign, IL: Human Kinetics.

Puhalla, J., Krans, J. V., & Goatley, M. (2010). *Sports fields: Design, construction, and maintenance.* Hoboken, NJ: John Wiley and Sons, Inc.

Russ, T. (2009). *Site planning and design handbook* (2nd ed.). Columbus, OH: McGraw-Hill.

Sawyer, T. H. (2013). *Facility planning and design for health, fitness, physical activity, recreation, and sport* (13th ed.). Urbana, IL: Sagamore Publishing.

CHAPTER 20

Event Planning Principles

Thomas H. Sawyer
Professor Emeritus, Indiana State University

Tonya L. Gimbert
Indiana State University

Introduction

Event planning and management pose many challenges to the event planner. Capell (2013), Goldblatt (2010), Kilkenny (2011), Lawrence and Wells (2009), Malouf (2012), Raj (2013), and Saget (2012) suggest the following are the common questions that event planners need to ask prior to placing any event:

- What type of event should be held?

- What is the purpose of the event?

- How can the theme and creative aspects enhance the core event?

- Why does this event have potential to be successful?

- Where will the event be held?

- What are the strengths and weaknesses of the event?

- What are the advantages and disadvantages of the event?

- What is the definition of success for the event?

- How will technology to be used internally and externally in the management of the event?

- What is the budget?

- What contracts are important to consider?

- Which marketing strategies are the best fit for the event?

- What role will sponsorship play in the event?

- Is there a need for participant registration?

- Will tickets be sold – how, when, and at what price?

- How will media be leveraged to ensure the event earns as much coverage as possible?

- How will the event manager ensure event is safe and secure?

- What emergency planning is needed?

- What planning documents are needed?

- How will the event be staffed?

- How will staff be motivated to work hard?

- What is needed for the event day operations?

- What equipment is needed?

- How will the event flow?

- What happens when the event is over?

Event Management

Fitness, physical activity, recreation, and sport events encompass a variety of business-related tasks. Event management in these areas is unique because it requires the managers to have a broad base of knowledge in many different areas of these industries. The process of event management, according to Capell (2013), can be divided into three phases: conceptualization, development, and execution. Goldblatt (2011), Lawrence and Wells (2009), and Raj (2013) suggest that event management can be defined as a process by which an event is planned, implemented, and executed. According to Goldblatt (2011), Lawrence and Wells (2009), Malouf (2012), and Raj (2013), event management encompasses the following tasks:

- acquisition;

- allocation;

- analysis of time, finances, people, products, and services;

- assessment;

- control; and

- direction.

According to Goldblatt (2010), Kilkenny (2011), and Malouf (2012), successful event management requires attention to the following management areas:

- alcohol,

- beverage services,

- box office and tickets,

- building maintenance,

- contract negotiations,

- crowd control,

- emergency medical services,

- evaluating event,

- facility rental,

- food services and catering,

- hospitality and VIP protocol,

- marketing, advertising, and public relations,

- merchandise, concessions, and novelty sales,

- parking and traffic,

- permits and licenses,

- recruitment and training of personnel,

- risk and safety, and

- venue logistics.

Right Holders

Saget (2012) indicates right holders are organizations that control and own the rights to an event. The right holders could also be national governing bodies or other governing bodies as well as universities. The rights include name, logo, and/or brand.

Event Sanctions

Kilkenny (2011) notes a sanction is not a punishment, but rather it is the official recognition by the rights holder. Event sanctions are considered an official approval for the event and are granted by the governing body associated with the sport. Malouf (2012) and Saget (2012) indicate the sanctioning process allows the governing body to control the game so that it is played under authorized rules with approved equipment. According to Kilkenny (2011), sanctioning is important for the following reasons:

- "ensure fairness, safety, and consistency among competitions,

- provide for course certifications to ensure consistency across venues,

- require a certain amount of medical personnel to be available, and

- secure the provision of insurance coverage (p. 146)."

Type of Events

There are four categories of events: ancillary, mega, recurring, and traveling. An ancillary event is one that supports the main event, such as a concert and/or fireworks before or after a main event. While a mega event is the main event that takes years to plan, such as the Summer Olympics, Winter Olympics, World Cup Soccer, or the Commonwealth Games. If a mega event happens on a regular schedule, it is considered to be a recurring event. Finally, a traveling event is a recurring event that changes venues, such as the World Series, Super Bowl, and NCAA Men's and Women's Basketball Tournaments.

Event Feasibility

Before event planning begins, the event manager must evaluate the feasibility of the event. Lawrence and Wells (2009), Malouf (2012), Raj (2013), and Saget (2012) suggest the event manager should answer the following questions:

- Are there potential sponsors?

- Are ancillary facilities needed?

- Are permits required?
- Does hosting this event require a bid submission?
- Is lodging required?
- Is an event sanction needed?
- Will a sanction be approved?
- What will a sanction cost?
- Will there be ancillary events couples with main event?
- Where will the primary event be held?
- What competing events are taking place?
- What type of public transportation exists for participants, spectators, officials, and volunteers?
- What are the security needs?
- What are the staffing needs?
- What are the rough costs?

Event Bidding

Often an event bid is required to secure an event, such as NCAA National Division I, II, or III Cross Country event. Bidding on an event involves competing with other potential host sites for the right to host an event. The process could be as simple as completing a one page document to a multi-year, multimillion-dollar endeavor (e.g., Summer Olympic Games). The bid process allows governing bodies to screen sites and organizers to ensure that the parameters set for the event can be met successfully by the host site.

The Organizing Committee

Capell (2013) and Saget (2012) indicate the key to success of any event is the organizing committee. The committee plays a large role in the bidding, obtaining, and hosting of the event(s). These committees are most often local in nature. Many communities have a convention and visitors bureau which assists in attracting various events, tourism, and business to the local area. In some communities, a sport commission exists specifically to attract sporting events to the area and assist in hosting the event. The composition of these communities consist of influential individuals within the community including local and regional politicians, community leaders, members of the media, business leaders, representatives of special interest groups, and prominent sport figures.

The organizing committee, according to Kilkenny (2011) and Malouf (2012), need to consider the following before submitting a bid for an event:

- date and time,
- equipment,
- finance,
- geographic location,
- lodging and transportation,
- media and sponsorships,

- permits,

- staffing,

- security, and

- venues.

Event Budgeting

(See Chapters 10 and 12 for greater details)

Earlier in this book, financial planning, revenue streams, and budgeting were discussed. In this section, budgeting will be covered specific to events. Every budget item presented below is going to vary by event depending on the type and scope of the event.

Event Revenue Streams

The following are the common types of revenues linked to events (Capell, 2013; Goldblatt, 2010; Lawrence & Wells, 2009; Kilkenny, 2011; Malouf, 2012; Raj, 2013; Saget, 2012):

- Ancillary events, such as a concert before or after the event

- Concession sales

- Housing and travel packages are agreements with airlines, care rental companies, and hotels for special rates for participants and revenue for the event. This is often arranged by a travel partner.

- Merchandise sales

  - Per capita spending or per cap is the amount of money spent per person during the event.

  - Flat fee agreements; a flat fee is charged to set up and sell products (e.g., exhibitor fee).

  - Per person fee is an agreement that the event is charged a small amount for each person in attendance.

  - Percentage of gross sales is an agreement where the event pays to the venue or city a percentage of the gross revenue. Commonly, the percentages range from 70% to 80% for the event and 20% to 30% for the revenue or city.

  - Specialty merchandise – is souvenir merchandise to prove that a person has attended an event or "limited edition or collectors' items."

- Processing fee is the amount charged to participants to process their registrations.

- Registration fee is the amount charged to participants to enter a competition or attend a conference or event.

- Sponsorships

- Ticket sales

- Transportation fees, such as buses to and from the event site.

Event Expense Items

Every event has expenses. The event organizers need to be cautious when planning an event not to exceed their budget. The objective is to either break even or make a profit in the end. The following are some examples of common expenses an event has (Capell, 2013; Goldblatt, 2010; Lawrence & Wells, 2009; Kilkenny, 2011; Malouf, 2012; Raj, 2013; and Saget, 2012):

- Awards

- Broadcast coverage—radio and television

- Ceremonies—opening, closing, and award

- Contingency funds include money to cover costs that may arise due to an unexpected event or circumstance.

- Equipment—e.g., communication equipment such as cell phones, phones/landlines, two-way radios

- Exposition is a sponsor and/or vendor display that often ties into a larger event.

- Housing/accommodations

- Marketing

- Meals

- Staffing

- Transportation

- Venue rental

Event Marketing

(See Chapter 13 for greater detail)

The following information is event specific but builds on the marketing chapter earlier in the book. The event manager is responsible for organizing an event marketing plan. The event marketing plan should include advertising, promotional, and publicity campaigns.

The advertising campaign is a plan utilizing all forms of media including direct mail, newspaper, online, outdoor, radio, and television. The advertising budget should not exceed 15% of the projected gross revenue. Further, any time cash is spent on advertising, it is considered to be paid advertising. Finally, most promoters (event managers) seek trade or in-kind advertising with media outlets. Many media outlets (e.g., newspapers, radio and television stations) use event tickets to build deeper relationships with their existing advertisers.

The promotional campaign could consist of special discounts, giveaways, theme nights, and other publicity that are sponsored by a media outlet. It is extremely important the event manager partner with local media outlets for the promotional campaign. It is a key to the events overall success.

The publicity campaign is generally not paid for by the event. It is news coverage for the event that is generated with some type of announcement or interview. Announcements generally come in the form of a press release. Sometimes hiring a local public relations firm makes sense.

Another marketing tactic that is sometimes used is "guerrilla/grassroots marketing." It is an aggressive way to market an event. The event manager can hand out flyers or discount coupons in high traffic areas or display mini posters (22" x 16") for the event in merchants' windows. The event managers need to be careful when handing items out that it is permissible.

Advertising

The event manager needs to ask three key questions when considering where to advertise (Kilkenny, 2011; Lawrence & Wells, 2009; Malouf, 2012):

- What is the best media to use for the particular event?

- How important is creativity to get the message across to the target audience?

- Is there a way to buy space and time that will stretch the advertising budget?

The event manager needs to understand that advertising is an investment in the success or failure of an event. Further, it is important to ascertain as much as possible about how to reach the event's target market.

The event manager must determine four key elements when considering television advertising: cable, cost, production quality, and reach. He/she must also determine the best bang for the buck between radio and television. Further, the event manager must decide what will be the best mix of traditional media outlets between newspaper, radio, and television. Finally, he/she must determine what non-traditional media outlets should be used and the appropriate mix between direct mail, on-line, and outdoor.

Event Sponsorship

(See Chapter 15 for greater detail)

Registration for Events

The key to revenue success for any participant event (e.g., professional meeting or sporting event) is participant registration. Participants do not purchase tickets, spectators do. This section deals with participant registration, not ticket sales.

Online v. Paper Registration

During the technology transition time, there are still events that allow paper registration, which is time consuming (re-entering all the information into the data base). Every year, the number of paper registration events declines dramatically. Yes, it costs to develop an online registration system, but it is a one-time cost for the development not a recurring cost. It is faster and more efficient for the participant as well as organizer. It also allows for electronic payment of fees. Finally, for a nominal fee, there are a number of companies that will handle all of an event's online registration needs.

The Registration Form

The registration form must be simple and clearly and logically organized. Goldblatt (2010), Lawrence and Wells (2009), Raf (2013), and Sargent (2012) suggest the following items be included when developing the registration form:

- Date

- Time

- Location

- Fee(s)

- Rules

- Waiver/release

- Divisions/age groups

- Awards

- What is included in the registration/entry fee

- Spectator information (e.g., cost, parking, and viewing)

- Facility rules (e.g., cameras, external food and beverages, etc.)
- Cancellation policy
- Refund policy
- Required membership information
- On-site registration/check-in/packet pick up times and what they need to bring (e.g., ID, birth certificates, etc.)
- Local hotel/attraction/restaurant information
- Weather policy
- Number of games guaranteed
- Forfeit policy and/or mercy rule
- Tie-breaking policy
- Any deviation form acceptable rules
- Protest policy
- Cooler policy
- Contact information for questions

On-Site Registration/Check-in

Participants expect that on-site registration and check-in will be easy, efficient, and speedy. It is imperative that the event manager ensure that there are not long-lines. This will require adequate amount of staff and a system to channel participants in the right direction to the correct tables. Signage is very important to make this process flow efficiently.

Every participant should complete a waiver. The waiver should be collected and filed (see Chapter 5 for greater detail). Along with the waiver should be a warning document explaining all the inherent risks involved in the activity.

The Box Office and Event Ticketing

(See Chapter 14 for greater detail)

Safety and Security for Events

(See Chapter 6 for greater detail)

References

Capell, L. (2013). *Event planning for dummies.* Hoboken, NJ: John Wiley & Sons.

Goldblatt, J. (2013). *Special events: A new generation and the next frontier* (6th ed.). Hoboken, NJ: John Wiley & Sons.

Kilkenny, S. (2011). *The complete guide to successful event planning* (2nd ed.). Ocala, FL: Atlantic Publishing Group, Inc.

Lawrence, H., & Wells, M. (Eds.). (2009). *Event management: Blueprint.* Dubuque, IA: Kendall Hunt.

Malouf, L. (2012). *Events exposed: Managing and designing special events.* Hoboken, NJ: John Wiley & Sons.

Raj, R. (2013). *Event management:Principles and practice* (2nd ed). Thousand Oaks, CA: SAGE Publications.

Saget, A. (2012). *The event marketing handbook.* Detroit, MI: Dearborn Trade Publishing.

CHAPTER 21

Volunteers
The Key to Successful Event Management

Thomas H. Sawyer
Professor Emeritus, Indiana State University

Tonya L. Gimbert
Indiana State University

Introduction

Prior to 1970, relatively little was known about the scope and size of the volunteer sector. Since then, several major national surveys have provided information useful in drawing a profile of the volunteer corps in America. Table 21.1 outlines several characteristics of volunteers. In youth, interscholastic, and intercollegiate sports, volunteers are very important to the successful operations of these programs. The volunteers are often ticket sellers, ticket takers, ushers, swimming and track and field officials, youth sports coaches, and fund-raisers. If volunteers were not involved in these programs, they would not exist. Nonprofit youth organizations would never be able to employ adequate numbers of paid personnel to operate numerous youth sports programs. This chapter will outline everything the sports manager will need to know about volunteers and how to manage the volunteer corps.

Before beginning to understand what a manager should put into place regarding the management of volunteers, it is important to understand the characteristics of volunteers as outlined in Table 21.1. Further, the manager needs to consider the characteristics below when dealing with volunteers (Connors, 2011; Lotich, 2012):

- The 25% rule = 25% of the volunteers will do nearly all that is asked of them.

- The 20% rule = refers to those individuals who are truly effective, who are the real producers and "result-getters."

- Volunteers have feelings, so make them feel valuable and wanted, treat them with respect, and provide them with special privileges to reward them for their contributions.

- Volunteers have needs and wants. Satisfy them.

- Volunteers have suggestions. Seek their input.

- Volunteers have specific interests. Provide options and alternatives for them.

- Volunteers have specific competencies. Recognize these skills and do not attempt to place square pegs in round holes.

- Volunteers are not paid staff.
- Do not to involve them in staff politics.
- Volunteers desire to be of assistance. Let them know how they are doing (feedback), answer their questions, and provide good two-way communications.
- Volunteers have the potential to be excellent recruiters, especially through networking of other potentially helpful volunteers.
- Volunteers can be educated to assume a variety of roles within the fund-raising process.
- Volunteers are able to grow in professional competency with appropriate and timely training, motivation, and opportunity.
- Volunteers are individuals working with other individuals. Encourage them to work as a team, not as competing individuals.
- Volunteers are not (usually) professionals within the organization or profession. Treat them with a special understanding and empathy.

Role of Volunteers

The role of the volunteer should be examined prior to the development of a volunteer management program. Each volunteer position should have a job description with the minimum qualifications listed. Further, there should be a clear description of what the volunteer will be required to accomplish. After a preliminary survey, appropriate roles for volunteers should be defined. If volunteer roles already exist, some of the following questions may reveal areas for improvement (McCurley & Lynch, 2010; Renz, 2010; Connors, 2011; Lotich, 2012):

- Is there an organizational chart that shows how various components of the program relate to another?
- Are there job descriptions for each position?
- Are the job descriptions updated regularly?
- Are they useful in the guidance and supervision of volunteers?
- Do volunteer jobs provide enough challenge, authority, and responsibility to be rewarding?
- Are volunteers an integral part of the planning, implementing, and evaluating process in all programs?
- Is there a systematic approach to recruiting new volunteers that emphasizes matching the volunteer with the job?
- Are there sufficient opportunities for orientation?
- Are there regular, ongoing opportunities for training?
- What kind of supervision system is there for volunteers?
- Is there a recognition program that goes beyond annual formal recognition dinners?

Recruiting Volunteers

Once organizers have determined the structure of the board, you can begin recruiting and retaining a volunteer base among employees. Many volunteers join organization boards because they enjoy serving others and would like to increase employee morale. Look for people who possess qualities such as honesty, trust, teamwork, leadership, enthusiasm, humor, responsibility, and competence. Board members should also have a business interest, whether it is in marketing, coalition building, training, finance, or technology. A balanced board of directors can assist with the growth of the programs.

Recruiting volunteers to help with organizations seems to become more difficult every year. Most people's time is stretched so thin, there is little time for an employee to volunteer. A lament of managers is that the same group of people (pre-baby boomers and baby boomers) volunteer over and over. The younger employees (Generation Xers who often ask, "What is in it for me?") rarely are seen volunteering for anything. However, the Millenniums seem to what to be involved in community service as evidenced by their experiences while attending institutions of higher education. This will be a needed shot in the arm for nonprofit agencies in the United States.

Ask yourself these questions: Why would I volunteer? How does this appeal to me? How can this be more appealing to me?

The event for which volunteers are needed should be promoted as if it were the event of the year. Emphasize the uniqueness of the challenge, aim to achieve a new goal each time, make it competitive (offer prizes), and throw in a perk or two. It is easy to obtain employee volunteers for high-profile events.

It is difficult to obtain volunteers for a simple fund-raising project. In the latter case, incentives for people to volunteer are needed, such as discounts on tickets to local events or logo merchandise or a banquet and a small gift. Recruiting must be an ongoing process. The volunteer recruiter needs to inform people that volunteering is a great networking opportunity that leads to making new friends and gaining new skills such as communication, organization, planning, time management, budgeting, negotiation, and priority setting. Further, Lotich (2012) and Renz (2010) suggest other methods can be used to recruit volunteers, including (1) making the event or activity fun, (2) finding out what the employees respond to, (3) involving the employee and family, (4) making it easy, attractive, and interesting to volunteer, (5) making the employee responsible for something (6) treating the employee (volunteer) with respect (7) asking for referrals, (8) planning social events for the volunteers, (9) paying for a volunteer's training, and (10) placing volunteers' photographs on bulletin boards, websites, or in e-mail messages.

Successful volunteer recruiting is not an isolated activity. Recruiting actually begins with carefully written job descriptions that delineate the volunteers' responsibilities. It is nearly impossible to recruit someone for a job that is not well defined.

Before recruiting begins, groundwork must be done to ensure a successful recruiting experience. Some of the topics that need to be discussed include the following (Connors, 2011; Lotich, 2012; McCurley & Lynch, 2010; Renz, 2010):

- Recruiters — Who will do the recruiting? Whoever the recruiters are, they should have or be willing to develop the following characteristics: (1) knowledge of the jobs for which they are recruiting, (2) detailed knowledge of the organization and its programs, (3) knowledge of how the programs are administered, (4) understanding of the culture of the prospective volunteer, (5) ability to communicate effectively with a wide range of people, (6) commitment to the purpose and goals of the organization, (7) enjoyment in meeting and talking with people, and (8) commitment to assisting the organization and its programs to grow (p. 27).

- Job descriptions.

- Prospective volunteers—A system for identifying potential volunteers.

- Match people with jobs.

- Obtain approvals—It is wise to obtain approvals from each volunteer's supervisor.

- Annual plans—Determine the volunteer needs on a year-round basis and use an annual calendar to schedule various steps in the volunteer management system. The manager, according to Connors (2011), McCurley and Lynch (2010), and Renz (2010), should take a moment and answer the following planning questions: (1) What times of the year are optimal for recruiting within the organization? (2) When do terms of office in clubs and associations expire?

(3) What documents need to be in place before recruiting begins? (4) What methods will be used to recruit? (5) Who will serve as recruiters? (6) What training will be provided for the recruiters? (7) What orientation and training will be provided for the new volunteers? (8) What recognition events will be planned?

- Recruiting techniques—The following, according to McCurley and Lynch (2010) and Renz (2011), are some useful recruiting techniques: (1) grow your own, (2) appointment by management from within, (3) management for referrals, (4) friendship groups, (5) family involvement, (6) benefits packages, (7) peripheral groups, and (8) use of media to communicate volunteer opportunities.

Job Descriptions for Volunteers

Written job descriptions delineate volunteers' responsibilities and are a key part of a risk management plan for the organization. Although liability rules vary from state to state, it is not likely that the organization is immune from liability merely because an employee is acting as a volunteer. The simple fact of whether a person is paid or unpaid has very little bearing on the case before the bar. In the eyes of the court, if the person works for the organization, he or she is representing the organization. Therefore, the manager must develop specific job descriptions for all positions whether or not the people holding the positions are paid.

Many human resources management professionals have indicated that the benefits of having a job description include a foundation for recruiting, comfort and security, performance, continuity, communication and teamwork, it supports a risk management plan. Table 21.1 describes the common steps in developing a job description.

Table 21.1
Common Steps in Developing Volunteer Job Descriptions

There are five common steps in human resources management, according to McCurley (2010) and Renz (2011), that should be followed in developing a job description:
- Explain the concept to the chief executive officer and board and outline its benefits to them.
- Form a committee to develop the job description and have the committee answer the following questions: Does the organization need individual position and committee leadership job descriptions? What job descriptions are needed? What will be the outline for the job description? What will be the procedure for the annual review of job descriptions so they can be updated and improved over time? Who will be responsible for writing the job descriptions? Who will review the job descriptions before they are finalized?
- Establish job clusters such as committee chairs, club or league president, trip coordinators, and project leaders.
- Evaluate job system.
- Format job description: title, function statement, reports to, staff liaison, task to be performed, time commitment, training, evaluation, benefits received, and qualifications.

Motivating Volunteers

Everyone who has time to volunteer should understand there are many reasons why they should volunteer, including involvement, reward or recognition, networking, companionship, fulfillment, "the next best thing to being there," "nothing else to do," and "it is just plain fun." See Table 21.2 for questions a sports manager needs to ask before developing the motivation plan.

Table 21.2
Questions for the Sports Manager to Ask About Volunteers before Establishing the Motivation Plan

Before recruiting volunteers, the sports manager should ask the following questions:
- Do you have enough time to volunteer?
- How can you help the organization?
- Will you be able to learn from the experience?
- Will you like what you will be doing for the organization?
- What are the rewards and benefits you are seeking?
- Will your time be well spent?
- Most importantly, will you have fun?

Retaining Volunteers

After recruiting volunteers, according to McCurley and Lynch (2010), the next trick is to keep them as volunteers in the future. McCurley and Lynch suggest this can be accomplished by making "(1) the event or activity attractive to belong to; (2) certain the event is well organized; (3) people feel needed and appreciated; (4) sure there is a friendly atmosphere; (5) certain volunteers understand what their responsibilities will entail, including time commitments and workload; (6) a special effort to call volunteers by their first names and know something about them or the work they do; (7) sure to encourage volunteers' input; (8) a special effort to recognize or reward their volunteer efforts for the organization; (9) the event or activity fun; and (10) certain that everyone receives an appropriate thank you (e.g., free lunch or dinner and a framed certificate) (p.137)."

Educating Volunteers

A volunteer is no different (except that he or she receives no monetary remuneration) than any other employee on the staff. It is important to provide training to the volunteers. The training can be simple or elaborate. The key point to consider is that the volunteer should be clearly informed about goals, procedures, schedules, expectations, responsibilities, emergency procedures, and staff rosters.

Information should be provided orally with a backup hard copy for each volunteer. This material should be placed in a neat folder with the volunteer's name imprinted on it. Personalizing the material gives the volunteer a feeling of self-worth and importance and, in turn, will motivate the volunteer to be a more valuable resource.

Orientation and Training for Volunteers

Once the volunteers are on board, it is important to provide them with a sound orientation and a continuous education program. Without good orientation and training, volunteers may not be able to do their assigned jobs well or receive the intrinsic rewards they expected. The purpose of orienting and training volunteers is to ensure the highest possible degree of satisfaction with and contribution to the portion of the program that they are to implement.

- Orientation helps volunteers become acquainted with one another and the staff, learn the organization's culture, and learn about their own volunteer role in relation to the entire organization. Orientation differs from in-service training, with orientation usually occurring at the beginning of a volunteer's commitment and in-service training at various times during a volunteer's commitment with the organization.

- Training, on the other hand, introduces new skills, knowledge, and abilities or reinforces existing ones, can be used to plan and manage program changes; and provides opportunities for self-renewal and growth.

The orientation program. The orientation program should be conducted by the head of the volunteer management system and key volunteers. The orientation program should be conducted more frequently than once a year if the organization is bringing in new volunteers on a monthly or weekly basis. Many organizations establish cohorts of volunteers who go through the orientation together. It is not uncommon to see an organization scheduling quarterly orientations.

Orientation can be scheduled as

- large group sessions;

- small group sessions;

- personal, one-on-one orientation sessions; or

- personal, one-on-one mentoring systems.

The agenda for an orientation session may include

- a philosophical and conceptual framework of the organization,

- content of the various programs,

- organization of the various programs,

- governance of the organization,

- history of the organization,

- policies and procedures of the organization,

- bylaws and the proper conduct of business,

- ethics issues,

- benefits of volunteering and special privileges,

- identification of key people in the organization,

- telephone numbers of key people, and

- realistic job previews.

Orientation and training checklist. The following set of questions, according to McCurley and Lynch (2010) and Renz (2010), should be used in guiding the final plans for an orientation or training session:

- Does every new volunteer have an opportunity to be oriented to his or her role either in a one-on-one conference, a small group, or a large group meeting?

- Are there orientation materials prepared for volunteers: job descriptions, volunteers' handbooks, policies, etc.?

- Are orientation and training meetings planned with plenty of volunteer input and participation?

- Are volunteers offered leadership roles in orientation and training of other volunteers?

- Does the organization provide books, films, tapes, trips, or other educational materials for volunteers?

- Does the organization pay for volunteers to attend appropriate training events or take courses at other institutions?

- Are all orientation and training programs evaluated?

The Volunteer Personnel Management System

The sports manager should ask a series of questions after he or she understands the environment that the volunteers will be asked to work in. I think Rudyard Kipling put it best when he said, "He kept six honest serving men (They taught me all I knew). Their names are What, Why, When, How, Where, and Who." If you keep this in mind at all times, whether it be managing volunteer personnel or the budget, you will be successful in most of your efforts.

One of the most notable trends in volunteerism has been professionalization. In most organizations using the services of volunteers, there has been a gradual realization that volunteers should be recognized as the valuable staff members they are. As a result, the management of volunteers has taken on many of the characteristics of the management of paid staff. Managers in voluntary organizations perform many of the same personnel functions for volunteers as for paid staff: they design and define volunteer jobs and write job descriptions, recruit and interview volunteers aggressively, orient, train, supervise, evaluate, and reward. See Table 21.3 for reasons why to professionalize volunteer management.

Table 21.3
Reasons for Professionalizing Volunteer Management

Many experts (McCurley, 2010; Renz, 2010; Connors, 2011; Lotich, 2012) indicate there are several reasons for this professionalization of volunteer management, including the following:

- Many voluntary organizations and volunteer programs are quite large (e.g., Girl Scouts, Boy Scouts, American Red Cross, Salvation Army, United Way, and others).

- Increasing concern about liability has forced organizations to improve control of programs conducted by volunteers.

- Volunteers have become more sophisticated and discerning about the organizations to which they donate their time and energy.

- Management positions in voluntary organizations have become more professionalized.

- Managing volunteers is, in many ways, more difficult than managing paid employees. Since volunteers are, by definition, not paid, the incentive structure is intrinsic rather than extrinsic.

Supervision of Volunteers

Supervision is a managerial function that helps to ensure the satisfactory completion of program objectives. The effective volunteer manager maximizes volunteers' expectations by providing support and resources. Further, the manager ensures that the volunteers possess the skills and abilities to get the job done. Finally, the supervisor must discuss problems as well as successes with volunteers and suggest constructive ways to improve.

As a process, supervision involves three elements:

- Establishing criteria of success, standards of performance, and program objectives such as the job description and annual plan of work.

- Measuring actual volunteer performance with respect to these stated criteria of success through observation, conferences, and evaluation.

- Making corrections, as needed, through managerial action.

Working With Difficult Volunteers

Working with volunteers generally is enjoyable. They want to be involved and are not motivated by compensation. However, there are volunteers who create problems and cause difficult supervisory problems. See Table 21.4 for suggestions for working with difficult volunteers.

Table 21.4
Dealing with Difficult Volunteers

When conflict arises, experts (Connors, 2011; Lotich, 2012; McCurley, 2010; Renz, 2010) suggest it can usually be traced to one or a combination of the following factors:

- Lack of agreement about the program's goals and components.

- Ill-defined and unmeasurable objectives.

- Absence of a preconceived plan.

- Exclusion from the planning process of those who will be responsible for carrying out the plan.

- Inaccessibility of leaders.

- Distortion of information accidentally or deliberately.

- Lack of trust, which induces people to withhold opinions that are negative or critical. People will play it safe rather than risk the wrath of someone else.

- Hidden agendas and other manipulations that reduce trust in the long run.

- Ineffective listening, which often represents a desire to dominate and an unwillingness to tolerate others' views.

- A belief in absolutes, which leads to a tendency to cast blame.

- A belief that only two sides of an issue exist and that one must be "right" and the other "wrong." This belief precludes compromise.

- Individual differences in race, age, culture, or status. Sometimes, it is difficult to appreciate others' points of view.

- Misunderstandings about territory, policy, authority, and role expectations.

Recognition of Volunteers

Recognizing volunteers for their work is widely accepted as an important aspect of successful management. There is no single recognition event that will make everyone happy. Understanding that different volunteers are satisfied by different rewards is essential to the success of a recognition program.

Recognition is not just a way of saying thank you; it is also a response to individual interests and reasons for being involved in the program.

The common types of awards include the following (Connors, 2011):

- "Group recognition

- Individual recognition

- Informal recognition (e.g., get well cards, birthday cards, flowers, thank-you notes, have a happy vacation note, photographs, lunch, or coffee)

- Public and media recognition

- Formal recognition (p.84)."

The planning for a recognition, in many cases, is as important as the recognition itself. The first step is to appoint a recognition planning committee. According to Connors (2011), Lotich (2012), and McCurley (2010), the functions of the planning committee would include the following:

- Planning and conducting recognition event(s)

- Evaluating recognition event(s)

- Determining whether or not to establish formal awards program(s)

- Researching the reasons why people have volunteered to work with the organization so that future recognition can be planned to meet their needs

- Maintaining a record-keeping system that will provide data on volunteers' contributions to the organization

The recognition planning committee needs to address a number of questions as it develops the format for volunteer recognition. Connors (2011) and Lotich (2012) suggest these questions include the following:

- Does the organization see recognition as an event rather than a process?

- Has the organization fallen into a rut with traditional recognition events?

- Are there parts of the awards program that no one understands because the meaning is lost in the past?

- Is the awards program really fair to everyone?

- How many people are recognized as individuals?

If the recognition planning committee decides it is important to have a formal awards program, a number of items need to be considered. These items include, but are not limited to, the following (Connors, 2012; Lotich, 2012):

- Each award has a name that distinguishes it from other awards.

- Awards are incremental, with some reserved for people with long tenure and distinguished service, including retirees, and others for short-term or one-time service.

- Each award has written criteria that must be met.

- Awards criteria and nominating forms are distributed to all volunteers.

- Favoritism in nomination and selection is scrupulously avoided.

- Volunteers are involved in the decision-making process.

- Award nominations are handled confidentially.

- There is an official time when formal awards are presented to recipients.

- A permanent record of award recipients is maintained, preferably on a large plaque visible to all in a prominent location.

- The formal recognition system is regularly reviewed.

- Name something after an outstanding volunteer (Be cautious—this idea has long-term implications).

- Design a formal award program.

- Make a monetary gift in a volunteer's name to his or her favorite volunteer agency.

- Hold a banquet, brunch, luncheon, or party at a unique location.

References

Connors, T. D. (2011). *The volunteer management handbook* (2nd ed.). Hoboken, NJ: John Wiley and Sons.

Lotich, P. S. (2012). *Smart volunteer management.* Phoenix, AZ: CreateSpace Independent Publishing Platform.

McCurley, S., & Lynch, R. (2010). Volunteer management (3rd ed.) InterPub: http://www.interpubgroup.com

Renz, D. O. (2010). *The Jossey-Bass handbook of nonprofit leadership and management.* San Francisco, CA: Jossey-Bass.

CHAPTER 22

Facility Operations and Maintenance

Thomas Rosandich
United States Sports Academy

Most maintenance managers will agree that maintenance requirements are almost never given adequate consideration when facilities are designed. Even when some consideration is given to maintenance during the design phase, changes in design during construction often nullify the original plans. The construction contractor is most usually concerned with completing the building in the manner that will generate the most profit, and as such, is not usually concerned with maintenance and repair requirements once the warranties expire. Further, there is a natural tendency on the part of architects to focus on the visual aesthetics of the design, often at the expense of more utilitarian concerns such as cost efficiency in operations (Sawyer, 2013).

Given that the largest cost of a sports facility is borne through the many years of operation following construction and commissioning, maintenance professionals (typically the designated facility maintenance manager) need to participate in the design process. These maintenance professionals should remain involved until the project is completed. So while there should be no question at this point that the maintenance manager can have a lot to offer in terms of the planning of the facility, further discussions are in order as to the practical considerations for operations and maintenance (O&M) in the project planning. This chapter looks at some of the design requirements for the sports facility from the perspective of the maintenance manager. The first part relates specifically to maintenance and support areas and the second to general "generic" maintenance concerns for the facility as a whole.

Written Plans and Procedures

According to OSHA guidelines, employers must have a written plan that details the workplace's general safety and health program elements (Means, 2012). In the plan, you should specifically describe the training employers need to undergo and assign responsibility to implement the plan to some person or panel in the company.

Means (2012) and Standiford (2012) suggest in order to write the plan, an employer must evaluate his workplace and determine what kinds of health and safety issues might arise. Some conditions include hearing loss (if workers are around loud machines or noise) or injury from falling (if workers must use scaffolding or work above ground). Each workplace must be assessed separately. An employer must use his reasonable judgment to assess the dangers and write a plan that encompasses those hazards.

Employers must implement a way for employees to voice their complaints about the safety and health guidelines in the company. Employers should include this procedure in their plan and train their employees on how to use the process.

General Work Environment Issues

Employers must implement a housekeeping procedure to clean and sanitize bathrooms and cafeterias. In addition, all work areas must be clean and sanitary and free from debris. The floors must be kept dry where possible, and walkways must be clear. All stairs with four or more steps must have handrails, and each step must be the same height and distance as the other steps.

Emergency and Evacuation Procedures

All emergency exits must be marked and kept unlocked. An illuminated sign must be above the exit indicating the door is an exit. All exits must be free of clutter and debris so that employees can quickly exit in an emergency. First aid kits should be readily available. The kits should have enough supplies to treat common injuries (minor cuts, scrapes and swelling) at the workplace. The employees must be trained on what to do in an emergency and where the emergency supplies are located.

Disclaimer

Means (2012) suggest that OSHA standards are vast and encompassing. Each workplace requires special attention to the unique potential areas for concern. With that in mind, this article covers a basic checklist. It is by no means a comprehensive checklist of OSHA standards. Essentially, OSHA is a set of rules governed by common sense. An employer must use his reasonable judgment to assess his workplace and determine the potential problems in order to flesh out this checklist.

Safety Concerns and Inspections

A facility safety inspection is a means of self-checking to identify potential hazards, seek out any failures and conform to safety measures. It is also a way to prevent accidents. Means (2012) and Standiford (2010) suggest every facility should have a well-trained team of internal safety inspectors who maintain safety levels through regular inspections, following Occupational Safety and Health Administration (OSHA) standard checklists. If the team finds any violations, it should address and correct them immediately, bringing the facility up to proper safety levels.

Safe Operation

Safety inspectors confirm that all work areas are orderly and clean, free from tripping hazards, wet spots, greases and oils, protruding objects and miscellaneous debris. Holes, openings, ditches, and the like require appropriate covers, grates, or guardrail protection. Elevated platforms and work spaces also require guardrail protection, in addition to toe boards. Any aisles or passageways used for forklift use must be properly marked. Inspectors check that all areas are sufficiently illuminated and ventilated, maintaining a noise level conducive to normal and safe working communication.

Work areas should have proper noise insulation, especially manufacturing facilities that employ heavy and noisy machinery. Hearing protection should be available for employees in such work areas.

Warning signposts should be clearly displayed in hazardous areas such as chemical storage units. If the nature of the work requires employees to wear personal protective equipment such as safety shoes or helmets, such equipment should be reliable and standard-compliant. In cases where heavy machinery is used, only trained personnel should operate such machinery. Employee facilities such as bathrooms and cafeterias should be clean and hygienic. In case of manufacturing plants, the cafeteria should be away from toxic-material storage units.

Emergency Facilities

There should be a proper emergency-response system in place, and employees should be trained in such systems. Regular emergency-response drills are necessary. Check for adequate emergency exits to allow for immediate escape and make sure that these exits are easily accessible. Exit routes and entrances should be visibly marked and have adequate lighting. Check for the presence of fire extinguishers: Fire extinguisher areas should be prominently marked, and equipment should be in good working condition and within easy reach. A first-aid kit with physician-certified supplies should be accessible. Medical supplies should be regularly replenished, and employees should be trained in first-aid techniques.

Preventative Measures

Preventative building maintenance is the collection of tasks that maintenance workers—or home-owners—perform in order to prevent problems from occurring in the buildings where they work or live. The most effective way to carry out this responsibility is to create a checklist of all the chores that must be done for appearance, safety, energy savings, and to ensure that equipment runs properly and does not wear out prematurely. Rely on the checklist to help you plan ahead for the necessary chores, ensure that your efforts are structured and effective, and prevent the possibility of a task being overlooked.

Building Components

To create a checklist, develop a list of all the building components. That means taking inventory of the different parts, or structures, of the building. Stairwells, staircases, rails, verandas, hallways, doors, windows, walls, and roofs are all examples of building components. So, too, are HVAC systems, fire and equipment, elevators, and electrical systems. It is important for you—and perhaps, your manager—to have a thorough understanding of all the different parts of the building so that nothing gets overlooked.

Conditions

A list of all the building components is important. However, it is equally important to have a detailed description of the condition of those components. A list of building components and their conditions will have items that need fixing such as loosened railings, cracked windows, damaged walls, exposed wires, leaking roof areas, and damaged fixtures. However, this detailed assessment should also contain items that are in perfect working condition but still require periodic preventative maintenance, such as HVAC systems or fire extinguishers. A comprehensive checklist will give you a tool to track the health of your building components: what items are likely to get damaged or wear out; what you can do to prevent or fix any damage or extend the life of a component; and when to schedule all the tasks involved in upkeep.

Priorities

A detailed list of building components and conditions will help you prioritize your preventative maintenance chores. That creates your plan of action. For example, if you work in an apartment complex, the problems that affect tenants, such as leaking roofs or sinks should be taken care of quickly. Any problem that could present danger, such as a loose railing, must be dealt with immediately. But your workweek will also include preventative maintenance tasks designed to eliminate these types of problems from occurring. If you perform a regular roof inspection, the chances of a leak happening, which would require immediate attention, is minimized. With your checklist, you will be able to develop a year-round schedule of all the tasks you will need to accomplish to ensure that appearances are maintained, equipment functions properly and problems are avoided.

Fire Safety

Prior to routine inspections by the local fire marshal, a facility's in-house safety inspectors confirm that all fire extinguishers are clearly marked, accessible, in good repair and properly mounted. The number of fire extinguishers must be adequate and appropriately distributed for the size of the facility. Each fire extinguisher requires its own inspection tag, to be initialed and dated upon inspection. Fire safety includes fire sprinklers in proper repair, which require 18 inches of clearance directly beneath each sprinkler head, per OSHA guidelines.

Building Safety

Means (2012) indicates commercial building maintenance inspection reveals discrepancies in structural aspects of the property, as well as any violations against safety standards. Potential problems that could result in expensive renovation or make the property unsuitable for occupation also surface during an inspection. Maintenance inspection checklists describe the elements that should be covered in an inspection so that maximum information is offered to clients.

Building Exteriors

The property address should be visible and clear to locate. There should be an unobstructed access road to the building. Building exits to the street should be conspicuous. Trees and shrubs on the premises should be pruned. The exterior walls should not have any signs of cracks or other impairments. Windows should be intact without any cracks or damaged window panes. Entrance doors should close slowly to prevent injury to fingers. Check parking facilities and the numbers of spaces allotted for the property.

Building Interiors

Check if staircases and door openings have standard railing support. There should be enough ventilation, and the ventilation equipment should be functional. Work areas should be clean and organized, with spaces for employee belongings. Work surfaces should be safe even when wet; this is particularly significant in manufacturing facilities. Floors should be safe, free of protruding nails, holes, or loose boards. Appropriate resources to handle extremely cold and hot conditions should be in place: Employees should be able to recognize symptoms of heatstroke, heat cramps and other conditions resulting from high exposure to such elements.

Electrical Safety

Electrical safety is imperative to facility and employee safety. In-house inspectors must review all extension cords in use, assuring they are equipped with proper plugs on three-conductor cables. Extension cords must not be used in place of permanent wiring, not run through walls, ceilings, or doors, not taped or damaged and not daisy-chained to one another. Power cords within the facility are to be in good repair with no signs of fraying and with ground pins in place. Thirty-six inches minimum clearance must be provided around all electrical panels and they must be completely free from obstruction, per OSHA guidelines. Facility safety inspectors are responsible for testing ground-fault circuit interrupters (GFCIs) and maintaining clearance around all electrical outlets. They also confirm that proper protective covers are in place over electrical boxes, raceways and fittings.

Means (2012) and Standiford (2010) suggest the following electrical safety tips:

- All electrical machines should be properly grounded.

- Junction boxes should be closed.

- In case the nature of the work requires usage of portable hand tools, such tools should be grounded and double-insulated.

- There should be adequate lighting in work areas for comfortable work performance.

- Lighting should not reflect and produce glare on work surfaces, computer screens and keyboards, as this can strain the eyes.

- The emergency lighting system should be adequate and functional and tested regularly.

Chemical Storage Safety

In-house inspection includes chemical and flammable substance storage safety. Cabinets, bottles, cans, vials, flasks and containers must be properly labeled. Rags, glass, and trash in this area require their own, separate disposal receptacles. Inspectors review spill-containment materials on hand and confirm Material Safety Data Sheets (MSDS) are readily available for each hazardous substance present.

Design Considerations for Operations and Maintenance

Physical education, athletic, and recreational facilities should be maintained in a sanitary and hygienic condition. The very nature of many of the activities conducted within these facilities and the many uses of water within them magnifies the need for consistent, superior custodial care. Unless custodians are provided with adequate and convenient facilities and equipment, the prospects of achieving the desired level of sanitation are significantly diminished.

Among the facilities required by the maintenance and custodian staff for the care and operation of sports facilities include workshops; storage for tools, spare parts, and supplies; janitorial closets; laundry facilities; office and administrative space; and staff break rooms with locker facilities.

Central Custodial Complex

The size and configuration of the custodial complex in any sports facility is contingent upon a number of factors, the first of which is the size of the building and the nature of the programs being conducted. The needs of a small, privately held health club, for example, will vary markedly in both size and scope from those of a multipurpose municipal facility or a university sports complex.

But even between facilities of comparable size, the nature of the organization that owns them will have a significant impact on the size and composition of the custodial complex and the way that it is managed. For example, the physical education, intercollegiate sports, and recreational facilities of a major university can be very similar in size to that of a national sports complex or a municipal stadium. However, in the university situation, there will typically be less space given over to operations and maintenance (O&M) within the sports facility itself, because it is likely that elsewhere on campus will be a centralized buildings and grounds operation that will be responsible for the heavy maintenance activities of the entire university. Thus, within the sports facility there may, at most, be a small work space with a storage area for tools and spare parts, which would be totally insufficient for a free-standing, independent operation of comparable size.

Free-standing sport facilities, such as a municipal civic center or a national sports complex, will typically have a self-contained operation for O&M activities. Instead of a small work area for on-site repairs, a free-standing sports facility will need expansive work spaces with a much larger variety of tools and storage for spare parts. Nevertheless, O&M facilities of all types do have a number of elements in common.

In large facilities, a central custodian headquarters should be planned to include a toilet, shower, lavatory, and dressing area with individual lockers. This unit should also have a separate break and meal area equipped with a sink, hot-and-cold water supply, microwave oven, and a small refrigerator. Additionally, a small, apartment-sized breakfast table and chairs should be provided.

While there is no question that a properly furnished break area and locker room facilities for the O&M staff are appropriate, there is a definite need for a separate O&M office. The area for the administrative office in a typical collegiate facility should be about seven square meters. It is important to note, however, that this space allocation for the administrative office is a minimum, and that the size of the space allocated will grow as the complexity and size of the O&M operation grows. The administrative area should have enough office space to accommodate a desk, filing cabinets, and communications equipment. With today's communication technology capabilities, the administrative office must have a networked computer (either a networked personal computer or a terminal in the case of a mainframe operation) with a printer. Traditionally, the office of the O&M supervisor has been physically located in the workshop or storeroom area. However, because of advances in the application of communications equipment and powerful management tools, such as networked micro-computers, the physical presence of the supervisor in the workshop area is no longer a necessity (Means, 2012; Sawyer, 2013; Standiford, 2010).

A further case can be made that, because of the coordination required between the different administrators who manage the sports facility, the office of the maintenance supervisor should be located in the same area as other administrators. Regardless, however, of where the office of the maintenance manager is physically located, the office (and those of the other facility administrators) should be hard-wired for communications and micro-computer networking.

There is little point in having the maintenance manager's office hard-wired for data and communications if the work areas of the operatives are not. Thus, each of the main components of the O&M complex, such as the workshop area, storage for spare parts and supplies, and the administrative office, should similarly be hard-wired for data and communications and should have a desk area that can accommodate microcomputer and communications equipment.

With the exception of the manager's office as outlined above, ideally the rest of the maintenance offices and workshops will be grouped together in one of the service areas of the building. General characteristics of the O&M area include direct or easy access to the exterior of the building, preferably with a loading dock to facilitate the handling of deliveries, which will often arrive by truck. The landing area at the loading dock should be spacious enough to allow the easy movement of cargo pallets and bulky containers and to allow sorting and organization of materials being received before they are moved into storage.

The storerooms and workshop areas should be located close to each other. This will reduce work hours wasted in retrieving parts and supplies before they are used. In addition to easy access to the exterior of the building, the custodial complex should be easily accessed via wide and level (i.e., without impediments) corridors. Wherever feasible, the doors between service and storage areas should "line-up," so custodial operatives do not have to turn corners with cumbersome loads.

Access to the central custodial complex and its various work and storage areas should be through double doors. If some material other than steel is used for these doors (for aesthetic reasons, for example), they should be equipped with kick plates and bumper guards. The service or freight elevator, in the case of a multi-story building, should also be situated in close proximity to facilitate logistic operations. Such elevators should have a ceiling, if possible, of 10 feet and should be as wide as possible. Quite simply, such elevators are going to have to handle the largest pieces of equipment being moved between floors of a multi-story sports facility and should be planned accordingly. Such appropriate logistical considerations will typically yield dividends in the cost-efficient use of personnel and are discussed further below.

However, while easy access to the custodial complex is desirable, the area must still be secured against unauthorized entry. Bear in mind that the typical sports facility will have large numbers of participants and spectators passing through the building and to have them enter service areas, either intentionally or otherwise, are undesirable.

General guidelines offered by Lewis and Payant (2007), Means (2012), Sawyer (2013), and Standiford (2010) for O&M facilities within the building are outlined below for each individual area.

Maintenance workshops. Among the most obvious concerns of the maintenance manager during the design phase of the sports facility are the work and support areas that will be utilized by the maintenance crews. The size and location of their work areas will have a significant impact on how well O&M workers can do their jobs. The argument could be made that perhaps the most important of all of the facilities in the custodial complex is the workshop area.

The workshop itself should be situated against an outside wall of the building in the service area, which will allow an exhaust fan to vent outdoors the hazardous fumes and odors generated by activities conducted within. Preferably it should also be situated immediately adjacent to the loading dock entrance and service reception area and have access to the core of the building.

The floor should be of hardened concrete and have a noncorrosive drain. There should also be sufficient open floor space between such permanent fixtures as the storage bins and shelving, work bench, and slop sink to allow free movement around large pieces of equipment that may be brought to the workshop for servicing. The door into the workshop area itself should be a lockable sheet-metal type without a floor sill or threshold. Because of the level of noise generated in the workshop area with power tools, the walls should be of sufficient thickness to inhibit the transmission of sound to surrounding spaces. The walls should also be finished with a stain-resistant and easy-to-clean surface.

As stated earlier, the actual size of the workshop area will depend on whether it is a self-contained operation and how much activity it will be required to handle. Regardless of the size, however, some common characteristics should be considered. The first is a spacious workbench equipped with vises, small mounted power tools such as grinders, and a non-skid surface. The workbench area should be well lit by fluorescent lighting in the 100-lumen range that is mounted directly overhead. There should be sufficient electrical outlets around the room, particularly in the workbench wall near the vises and bench-mounted power tools. Also depending on the type of operation, sufficient floor space may be needed to mount free-standing equipment such as pipe-threaders and certain types of woodworking tools.

The maintenance workshop area should be both air conditioned and well ventilated. Because maintenance personnel use highly toxic and volatile substances such as paint, solvents, and cleaners, the workshop areas and central storage areas have exhaust fans that operate automatically and are vented to the outside.

Another area that needs to be considered is the tool room (also known as a tool crib). While maintenance workers frequently have a set of commonly used tools assigned to them, such as those contained in a lockable tool box, many specialized or very expensive tools and equipment are not assigned to individual craftsmen on a permanent basis. Examples of the specialized tools required for building maintenance may include welding equipment, a variety of metering devices (such as volt meters), and certain power tools. Because these types of tools and equipment are typically high-value items, access needs to be controlled and sign-out procedures employed as with any other inventory item. It is therefore cost effective from a labor standpoint to have the tool room physically located near the workshop area and/or combined with other stockroom activities such as the spare parts store room.

Storage. Storage falls into a gray area between strictly O&M concerns and sports activity and program concerns. On the one hand, storage space is needed for tools, spare parts, and consumables, such as cleaning supplies and dispenser items (toilet paper, paper towels, and hand soap) to support O&M activities. On the other hand, sufficient storage space is needed to support program activities in the building, such as that required for sports equipment, uniforms, and ancillary activities.

Experienced administrators of the various activity programs and experienced supervisors of storage and distribution rooms agree that the most prevalent fault in the planning of these facilities is the failure to allocate sufficient space. As a result, programs suffer in one way or another, and students do not enjoy all of the benefits they should receive. Operations costs increase disproportionately. Thus, it is useful to consider all the storage requirements for a sports facility for both O&M and sports and activity programs concurrently.

Storage for O&M operations. A wide variety of spare parts and consumable supplies is required to keep any building functioning properly. Examples of spare parts required for a typical sports complex can range from lightbulbs, ballasts, filters, and fan belts for air-handling units to replacement modules for scoreboards. Consumables similarly include a wide variety of materials, ranging from equipment lubricants, chemicals such as chlorine for the pool, cleaning supplies required for custodial work, and dispenser items required for the restrooms and locker rooms. Secure tool storage and space for storing bulky maintenance equipment, such as scaffolding and/or hydraulic lifts, are also needed.

There are a number of considerations in determining the size and location of storage and supply rooms to support O&M operation. Obviously, whether the O&M operation is self-contained is one of them. Another is whether the supply room is run on an open-stock or closed-inventory basis and how much inventory is dispersed to other storage locations around the facility, such as in janitorial closets.

If the nature of the organization is such that the sports facilities are a self-contained operation, then the space required for the storage of O&M-related equipment and supplies will obviously be greater. More space must be set aside for larger quantities of tools and supplies and for bulky equipment such as scaffolding. If the sport facilities are, for example, part of a centralized O&M operation on a university campus, it is likely that the high-value tools and equipment, such as lifts and scaffolding, will be kept elsewhere at a central location.

Whether the supplies are run on an open-stock or closed-inventory basis is another consideration. Low-value, high-usage standard stock items such as nails, nuts and blocks, paints, and lubricants are frequently designated open-stock items. Maintenance personnel can obtain them directly from bins without a requisition form, and there is no control over who takes them or what job they are used on. Such items can be stored right in the workshop area, for example, which will further enhance efficiency of the O&M operation. While such an arrangement reduces the need for separate storage space and an inventory clerk, it also invites increased pilferage by employees.

Perhaps the best use of an open-stock situation is in operations where maintenance is centralized, such as on a large university campus. As explained earlier, it is likely that a central O&M complex will serve the whole campus with sufficient volume and value of materials to require a closed-inventory system within the central maintenance complex. Thus, the sports facility, which is at best a peripheral operation, will likely have a smaller workshop area and tool crib with an open stock of standard-issue items.

A self-contained sports facility, such as a municipal stadium or national sports complex, on the other hand, will likely have a closed-inventory system or a combined open-stock, closed-inventory system. Because high-value tools and spare parts required for O&M operation must be retained on the premises, there is a need for access control and accountability and thus for an established inventory system and issue clerk. However, in terms of operational efficiency, it still makes sense in this type of an operation to place some items such as standard issue nuts and bolts in workshop areas and to disperse restroom cleaning supplies and equipment to the janitorial closets. The point is, however, that the space given over to this storage will be markedly greater.

In terms of the physical characteristics of storage areas and supply rooms, these should be situated in close proximity to the areas that they service. For example, tool and spare parts issue should be close to the workshop area, with the space required determined by the criteria discussed above.

The storerooms require temperature and humidity control, as inventory items frequently have specific requirements for storage. The floors should be of hardened concrete with a nonslip surface that is easy to clean. The room should be brightly lit with luminaries located between rows of shelving to ease identification of inventory, which is frequently described on small punch cards or tags affixed to the shelving.

For limited-access storage, there should be a distribution window that can be easily secured when the inventory clerk steps away from the service area to retrieve an item. Near the distribution window should be space enough for a desk and filing cabinet, which should be hard-wired for communications and networked computer equipment (Sawyer, 2013). The distribution window should have a counter upon which any transactions can be completed.

Doorway access to the stockroom should be planned to accommodate the largest pieces of equipment or machinery that will enter the area. Unless otherwise indicated, a doorway that is at least 60 inches wide and 84 inches high is recommended, with thresholds that are flush with the floor (Means, 2012). The doors will also require good-quality, tamper-proof locks and should be of fire-resistant sheet metal.

Shelving is an obvious requirement for the storage of supplies and inventory. These requirements include adjustable steel shelving with a depth of between 18 to 24 inches and a width of 36 to 48 inches (Lewis, 2007; Means, 2012). The first shelf should be at least six inches off the floor and the top shelf no less than 12 inches from the ceiling (Means, 2012). So far as possible, shelves should be adjustable and standard sizes used.

Sports equipment storage and repair. In most sports facilities, storage and work areas for sports activity and team equipment is separate from that used for general facility O&M. Regardless, many of the physical descriptions of the space required and fixtures contained in the storage rooms used for spare parts and supplies in the O&M operations are also applicable to storage areas for the sports and activity program. It should be noted that virtually all professional teams and most collegiate programs have professional equipment managers whose responsibility includes inventory control and servicing of team clothing and equipment. Just as a maintenance professional should be included in the design process to review the facilities program from an O&M perspective, so, too, should the equipment manager be consulted with respect to sport equipment storage and repair areas.

Lewis (2007), Means (2012), and Standiford (2010) recommend that the space given over to the storage of sports equipment include a small area to facilitate the repair of program-related equipment. A well-equipped work area can result in considerable savings over an extended period of time, and sports operations tend to work at a higher level of efficiency with this capability.

Examples of equipment that should be housed in a workshop of this type include a small workbench similarly equipped to that in the main facility workshop area described above. Some of the equipment will vary, because the nature of the work to be done is quite different. Examples of equipment that should be included in this work area are racquet-stringing machines and sewing machines for uniforms. Additionally, the laundry facility will typically be located in or near the equipment manager's facility.

As custodial workers are frequently asked to set up and remove equipment used in various sports activities, of particular interest to the maintenance manager are the location and characteristics of equipment storage rooms situated about the building. Generally, an equipment storage facility should be located adjacent to each major activity area in the building. Each of these auxiliary storage units should be designed to accommodate equipment anticipated to be used in that particular area, such as hydraulic basketball and other game standards in the main gymnasium, racing lanes and recall lines in the swimming pool area, and gymnastics equipment and mats in their specific area. In all cases, design considerations include doors of sufficient size to accommodate bulky equipment (preferably "lined up" to reduce the number of corners to be negotiated when moving equipment), no door sills or thresholds, and appropriate shelving needs.

Janitorial closets. The janitorial closet is the staging area for all custodial or housekeeping work. If the custodian works out of a room that is disorganized and dirty, it is likely that the cleaning effort will suffer accordingly. Also, much of the damage to custodial equipment occurs in the janitorial closet. An example of this is how mop buckets are frequently wheeled into the closet and not emptied, or floor scrubbing equipment is not cleaned after use. Thus, every effort should be made to design janitorial closets that will facilitate the custodial work. Lewis (2007), Means (2012), Sawyer (2009; 2013), and Standiford (2010) recommend when determining the number of janitorial closets, a number of variables need to be considered, such as

- the number of floors within the facility,
- the type of floor finishes to be maintained,
- the proposed use of the areas, and
- the number of restrooms in the facility.

There should be at least one six-square-meter custodial room for each 930 square meters of floor space, and at least one such room on each floor of the facility. The room should be designed with a large enough open area where equipment can be assembled and checked and janitorial carts properly stocked prior to starting a job (Sawyer, 2013). Each janitorial closet should have a service sink with a pop-up drain and a temperature-mixing type of faucet; floor sinks are preferable to large wall sinks for this purpose. Shelves and hanging boards should be constructed in each janitorial closet to facilitate the storage of supplies and tools (Lewis, 2007; Sawyer, 2013). Hanging boards, however, should be designed so that wet mops do not rest flush against the wall. Lastly, the janitorial closet should have a good level of illumination (at least 50 lumens) so that equipment can be properly cleaned after the job and before being stowed, and the fine print on chemical containers can be read (Lewis, 2007; Means, 2012).

While the foregoing is a general guide to the dimensions required for janitorial closets, the general rule of thumb is that the closet should have sufficient space both relative and particular to the area that is being served. High-volume activity areas with greater traffic flow have greater requirements and will need a larger space to accommodate the supplies and equipment needed to properly service them. Additionally, areas serviced on a seven-day cleaning schedule will require 35% to 40% more supplies than those cleaned on a five-day schedule, which would suggest a larger space allocation (Means, 2012; Standiford, 2010).

As an example of how the size of a janitorial closet should be determined in part by the area being serviced, consider the open floor space required to store floor maintenance equipment. A closet located in a corridor that features tile flooring would require an area large enough for power scrubbing equipment, whereas one in the vicinity of a carpeted office complex could get by with the smaller area required for a commercial-grade vacuum cleaner. Janitorial closets should also be located in or next to restroom and locker room complexes for a number of reasons. First, this location provides a water and sewage source for the mop sink and thus is cost effective from a design and construction standpoint. The second reason is that locker rooms and restrooms typically must be cleaned more often, and work hours are saved if the supplies and equipment are positioned near these areas. And finally, such a location facilitates storage of restroom cleaners, maintenance supplies, and dispenser stock.

As another example of the need to service high-volume traffic areas, a small room should be located near each entrance of the building to store maintenance supplies and tools (Sawyer, 2013).

Quite simply, everyone who enters or leaves the building will do so through one or more designated entries, which leads to excessive wear in these areas. The first 12 feet on the inside of an entry doorway is called "the walk-off area" and functions exactly as the name implies: it is within this radius that dust, dirt, oil from the parking lot, and water from rain and melting snow are deposited. Thus, a well-conceived maintenance plan will call for the regular policing of this area to prevent soiling materials from spreading beyond the walk-off area. To facilitate this frequent cleaning, a small custodial storage area should be situated nearby.

The failure to provide janitorial closets in the proper location and of the proper size can be illustrated by the following example. A building was constructed in which the janitorial closets were only 1.5 square meters in size, most of which was taken up by the mop sink. As a result, most of the supplies and power cleaning equipment had to be stored in the basement of the building, and carting supplies and equipment to the place where they were needed each night amounted to 30 hours of labor per five-night workweek. This amounted to an additional three-fourths of a worker-year labor expense, which would have been unnecessary if the facility were properly planned. Additionally, pilferage of supplies and theft of equipment increased, leading to the additional requirements of building a lock-up room in the basement of the building and the administrative controls (and expense) to run it.

Laundry room. In most physical education, sport, and recreational facilities, it is now more cost effective to establish in-house laundry facilities than to contract out for cleaning uniforms and towel services. As the operation of the laundry most frequently falls to the custodial staff, and the laundry facility itself is most likely to be situated within the maintenance support areas of the building, it is appropriate to consider planning guidelines for the laundry operation along with the rest of the O&M facilities.

So far as possible, the laundry facility should be physically located on the ground level of the building against an outside wall to facilitate venting of the dryer. Nonskid concrete floors are recommended, since the floors in the laundry should be hardened and impervious to water. Floors should be sloped to a drain trough that leads to noncorrosive drains. The slope should be 1/8 inch per linear foot (Means, 2012). The planarity of the floor is important, since puddles can be dangerous. Floor materials should extend up the walls at least 12 inches, with corners rounded or covered (Means, 2012). The thickness of the floor should comply with the equipment manufacturer's recommendations, but in any case, the floor should be able to withstand heavy, vibrating equipment.

As with other maintenance and service areas, the laundry facility should have double-hinged, double-doors without a threshold or a sill to facilitate the installation of laundry equipment during construction and the subsequent movement of laundry carts and supplies in and out of the premises. As a laundry is a noisy place, the walls and ceilings should have good sound absorption or non-transmission properties and yet be impervious to water. The wall finish should also be easy to clean and stain resistant.

While the floor space required for the laundry is contingent upon the size of the machines and the projected work load, sufficient space should be included in the plan for the storage of supplies and sorting/folding tables. Lewis (2007), Means (2012), Sawyer (2009; 2013), Standiford (2010), and others provide guidelines by noting that the size of the laundry facility is determined by the size of the workload. The capacity of laundry equipment is determined by weight (pound). To calculate the number and the size of the machines that will be required compare the anticipated daily quantities of articles to be cleaned multiplied by their respective weights with the poundage capacity of the machines under consideration, which will give the number of loads they can handle per day. Most process formulas will handle two loads per hour. Facilities with multiple goods classifications (i.e., nylon game uniforms and cotton-blend towels) should opt for two or more machines. Drying equipment needs to be matched up with the washers/extractors and typically has a larger capacity. For example, a 50-pound dryer is a good match with a 35-pound washer.

Once the number and types of machines have been determined, it is a relatively simple matter to size them, as the dimensions of the units can be easily obtained from prospective vendors. The machines should be mounted a minimum of two feet away from the walls and with a minimum of 18 inches between machines (Means, 2012). Generally, however, sufficient space should be left around them for circulation and work and for equipment servicing as may be required. Combine this with the space required for processing the work and storage to determine the net usable footage required for the laundry.

As with all equipment, access to utilities needs to be considered in the plan. While hot and cold water, sewage, and electricity are obvious, gas driers are the most cost efficient to use, so an appropriate hook-up is in order. The room should also have good ventilation and air circulation in addition to outdoor vents for exhaust generated by the equipment.

In terms of the equipment itself, programmable microprocessor controls on the laundry equipment are highly recommended. Also recommended are liquid detergent supply systems that can provide pre-set, automatic injections of chemicals, as such devices may serve to remove judgment calls by operators, especially if the operators are part-time helpers (such as students) (Sawyer, 2013).

Generic Concerns for Building Maintenance

While the foregoing discussion focused on the design parameters of the facilities specifically required for the O&M effort, aspects of sports facility design as a whole should be considered from the maintenance standpoint. These are really non-specific issues that can nonetheless produce significant operating costs. Many of these considerations are quite simple, yet because of their very simplicity, they are easily overlooked as more obvious design considerations hold the attention of the architect and design committee.

Building logistics is a key when discussing the custodial complex, yet so much staff time is spent moving equipment around the typical sports facility that further, more specific attention is warranted. Simple accessibility to equipment and fixtures requiring maintenance tends to get short-shift in the design process, with potentially disastrous consequences.

Standardizing Building Fixtures and Equipment

By now it should be clear that the variety of building finishes, fixtures, and equipment in a multipurpose sports facility can be staggering. Similarly, the need to inventory and control spare parts and consumable supplies for the maintenance effort can be a very large undertaking. However, by making a conscious effort to standardize building fixtures and equipment during the design phase, the costs of acquiring and carrying building spares can be significantly reduced.

Such reductions are accomplished in two ways. The first is the direct savings realized through a reduction in stocking spare parts. Standardization of finishes and fixtures allows the maintenance manager to reduce the number of items carried in the spare part inventory, which means a smaller financial burden in carrying costs. As a simple example, consider the effect of standardizing light fixtures. If all the fluorescent light fixtures in the building are the same, the number and variety of ballasts and lighting tubes that must be kept on hand can be considerably smaller than if there were a variety of different fixtures scattered throughout the building. Standardization also prevents the cost of wasted labor that results from bringing the wrong replacement tube to the fixture; the chances of this increase with a wide disparity in fixtures.

The second reduction is more indirect, but significant nonetheless. A smaller inventory requires less room for storage. Additionally, a smaller inventory is easier to administer and control, reducing administrative costs and loss through mishandling and pilferage. Concerted efforts can be made in many areas in standardizing building fixtures, including light fixtures and switches, breaker switches and boxes, bathroom fixtures and dispensers, locker room equipment, door hardware, locks and keys, and moveable equipment.

Logistical Concerns

Operating costs can also be realized by taking into account the needs of the maintenance staff in logistical operations. A logistical operation pertains to the handling of furnishings, equipment, and materials within the facility.

One area that tends to distinguish sports facilities from other types of buildings is the nature of the equipment contained within. A multi-station weight machine is, by its very nature, a very heavy and bulky piece of equipment to move around, particularly without disassembly. Gymnastics apparatus and mats, wrestling mats, and portable basketball goals are other examples of heavy, unusually configured equipment that is frequently moved around the building. An awareness of these characteristics is important during the design phase of the facility. For example (and as stated on several occasions already), the doors between spaces should line up to reduce cornering, and the doors from the loading dock (or main access from the exterior of the building), and equipment storage rooms should be double doors with flush sills and sufficient height to facilitate equipment movement.

Other design considerations from a purely operational point of view include using ramps between levels in the sports hall, provided the change in level is not too significant. Another approach is to ensure that freight or building service elevators are of sufficient size (including height) to facilitate the movement of equipment between floors. Similarly, making stairwells and landings large enough to handle bulky items, such as boxes of supplies or furniture, will help with logistical concerns.

Lastly, the design phase must recognize all the activities that will take place within the facility. For example, food service or concessions within the building will require the movement of groceries into and garbage out of the building, preferably through service passages.

One sports facility in southwest Asia was built at a cost in excess of $80 million, in which virtually all of these concerns were ignored in the preliminary plan. Fortunately, once construction was underway, a design review was able to rectify the worst of the errors, but only at considerable additional expense. Had the design errors not been caught, the only access to a second-floor food-service facility would have been via the VIP elevator. A worker seeking to get on board with a bag of garbage when the elevator was already occupied by a member of the Royal Family would have been problematic at best. Similarly, the design included three steps between each wing of the building and no way to move equipment between them. It was a situation rectified by the addition of a ramp after the fact.

Access of Building Operating Equipment

As unfortunate as the logistical situation was in this facility, service access to building operating systems was even worse. There was no way to access light and sound fixtures over the pool or the gymnasium floor because of a novel roof design.

The roof in the facility was a translucent, Teflon-coated fiberglass structure designed as an Arabian tent. But the design did not include access by service passages or catwalks to the fixtures suspended from the ceiling. Lights were changed, for example, by erecting scaffolding or using a personal hydraulic lift, both of which were expensive and time consuming. Unfortunately, the hydraulic lift could not be utilized in the pool area, which necessitated the erection of scaffolding in the swimming pool. Thus, the only way to change the lights was to drain the pool. This is a classic case of the architect's placing aesthetics before the more pragmatic and mundane concerns of operating the building, with quite costly consequences.

The point of this discussion is that maintenance requirements of building operating systems must be considered during the design of a facility. By taking into account such operational requirements as easy access to equipment, particularly control panels and lubrication ports, which require frequent attention, accompanying labor costs can be substantially reduced.

Utilities

In addition to access to control panels and operating systems for routine maintenance, the astute placement of electrical outlets for cleaning equipment and water spigots for hoses can effectively reduce labor hours in the maintenance effort.

Most floor-care equipment requires electrical outlets, whether they are power scrubbers or vacuum cleaners. Therefore, the placement of electrical outlets needs consideration, particularly in corridors, lobbies, and activity areas. Inappropriately situated outlets can cause considerable additional operating expense, both for labor (the need to continually move power cords) and for supplies (the need to purchase excessive numbers of extension cords). Additionally, the need for exterior outlets on the building should not be overlooked. For example, certain types of window-washing equipment require access to power, as do many other types of maintenance and custodial equipment, such as blowers for grass clippings.

Water spigots on the exterior of the building should be treated similarly to electrical outlets on the interior of the building. Water hoses are commonly used for washing down sidewalks and exterior windows, particularly those located near the ground. Thus, careful consideration to the number and placement of spigots similarly warrants close attention in the design phase.

Windows

The whole topic of windows deserves special mention. The arrangement and proportioning of windows is called fenestration. Consideration of the relationships of lighting, color, use of materials, acoustics, and climate control cannot ignore the importance of fenestration. The size and placement of windows cannot be left to chance, personal whims, or merely traditional use.

The generous use of windows has been in vogue in the past few decades, at least in part because of the pleasing visual effects obtained by the architect. But the excessive use of glass in a sports facility may give rise to a host of problems, including high operating costs from heat gain and loss and inordinate cleaning costs.

Glass is a poor insulator. It causes significant heat gain during summer months through the greenhouse effect and a corresponding increase in air-conditioning costs. During the winter, the process is reversed, and large glass areas cause significant heat loss with a similar increase in operating costs. Similarly, large amounts of glass tend to increase maintenance costs as dirt is more visible. Any person who has glass patio doors, for example, can attest to how much attention they require when weather conditions make handprints and streaks more visible. In commercial buildings such as sports facilities, the amount of cleaning required depends on many variables, such as the local environment (rainfall, dust, and pollution) and the extent of the maintenance effort (or, how dirty you are willing to let the glass get?).

Two basic methods are usually used for window cleaning: "over the roof" or "up from the ground." In both cases, special equipment is required for any structure in excess of one story. The cost for these systems can vary from as little as $15 for a garden hose and squeegee with a six-foot handle to as much as $50,000 for a scaffold for "over the roof" work (Means, 2012). Regardless of the system used, plans for water and electrical power sources for window-washing equipment should be included in the design phase.

It should be noted that in sports facilities, if windows are to be incorporated in the design, they should be at least 1/16th of the floor area (Means, 2012). Additionally, it is recommended that windows be placed nearer the ceiling than the floor. For a multipurpose gymnasium designed to accommodate both international-level volleyball and team handball, the minimum total area of glass windows would be approximately 66 square meters (over 700 square feet) located some 7 to 12 meters (22 to 40 feet) off the ground (Standiford, 2010). Under these circumstances, accessibility and labor costs related to maintaining an appropriate appearance must be considered during the design phase.

Returning to the sports facility in southwest Asia cited earlier, the architect achieved a stunning visual effect with a bank of blue-tinted windows two meters wide and 50 meters long extending the length of the sports hall wall some 15 meters from the ground and cantilevered at an angle of approximately 140 degrees to the roof line (Standiford, 2010; Means, 2012). However, the design made accessing the windows extremely difficult, and in the six years that the author observed the building, the windows were never washed. The result was an originally unique visual effect that was severely degraded because the design did not take maintenance into consideration.

Reference

Lewis, B., & Payant, R. (2007). *Facility manager's maintenance handbook* (2nd ed.). New York: McGraw-Hill.

Means, R. S. (2012). *Facilities maintenance and repair.* New York: RS Means.

Sawyer, T. H. (2013). *Facility planning and design for health, physical activity, recreation, and sport* (13th ed.). Urbana, IL: Sagamore Publishing.

Standiford, K. (2010). *RCS: facilities maintenance* (20th ed) Clifton Park, NY: Delmar Cengage Learning.

Index

SAGAMORE PUBLISHING

RELATED PRODUCTS

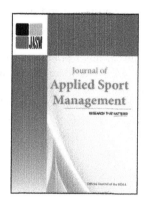

COMING SOON FALL 2015